THE PEACE TACTICS OF
NAPOLEON
1806–1808

THE PEACE TACTICS OF
NAPOLEON
1806–1808

By

H. BUTTERFIELD, M.A.

Fellow of Peterhouse

1972

OCTAGON BOOKS

New York

First published in 1929

Reprinted 1972

by permission of the Cambridge University Press

OCTAGON BOOKS

A DIVISION OF FARRAR, STRAUS & GIROUX, INC.

19 Union Square West

New York, N. Y. 10003

Library of Congress Cataloging in Publication Data

Butterfield, Sir Herbert, 1900-

The peace tactics of Napoleon, 1806-1808.

Reprint of the 1929 ed.

1. Tilsit, Treaty of, 1807.   2. Napoleon I, Emperor of the French, 1769-1821—Empire, 1804-1814.   3. France—Foreign relations—1789-1815.   4. Europe—Politics—1789-1815. I. Title.

DC230.T5B8   1972   327.44   70-159170

ISBN 0-374-91130-4

Manufactured by Braun-Brumfield, Inc.
Ann Arbor, Michigan

Printed in the United States of America

CONTENTS

Book III

TILSIT

Book IV

ENGLAND AND THE SYSTEM OF TILSIT

APPENDIXES

PREFACE TO THE OCTAGON EDITION

Behind the tangle of diplomacy, the subtle moves of statesmen and the routine of foreign offices one can sometimes see the shape of great and dramatic themes. Diplomatic history needs to be studied in detail and followed day by day if one is to catch the real flavour of it, or the cleverness of its agents; but, besides dealing with the critical stage in Napoleon's transition to "Grand Empire"—the most crucial period in his imperial diplomacy—the present book seeks to describe and elucidate two of these large-scale themes, which bring the whole story to a climax.

At the beginning there is not merely a great extension of empire but the passage to a new theory and plan of empire, after the thoroughness of the Prussian defeat at Jena. We see Napoleon hovering for a time between alternative policies—between reconciliation with Prussia and a determination to treat her worse than he had ever before treated an enemy. We can discern both the pattern of the thinking and the operations of the will that lie behind one of Napoleon's big strategic decisions.

The story culminates in the treaty of Tilsit—a further development of the new type of continental empire. From the scraps of evidence that remain, it is clear that Prussia (which was doomed to suffer most from it) was the very initiator of the essential plan and policy of Tilsit, the original inventor of the conjuring-trick that was involved. It was her ministers who, in their desperation after the defeat at Friedland, thought they might save themselves if the Czar would steal a march upon Napoleon by offering him his alliance. It was the Prussians and Russians who set out to hoax Napoleon at Tilsit, having it particularly in mind that they would enchant him with the idea of the partition of Turkey. But the tables were turned on them; the would-be magician was the one who was bewitched—caught by the very spell he himself was trying to cast on Napoleon.

Between these two points it is a question of diplomacy in time of war. Peace-negotiations and offers of peace may themselves be a *ruse de guerre* in any age of history. Such diplomacy needs to be seen in close relationship with the military events themselves, and with all the circumstances that affect the mood of courts and the disposition of statesmen. An attempt has been made to reproduce the diplomatic history not merely in its dry lines but in its full narrative context; and to show diplomacy as the medium through which states manufacture policy and a Napoleon does a great deal of his thinking.

In the period covered by this book the ambition of Napoleon comes to its greatest imaginative sweep.

The passage of time since its publication has not altered my judgment on these matters.

H.B.

18 January 1967

PREFACE

The following work deals with the overtures and parleys and negotiations for peace which come in an unbroken series during the war of the fourth coalition. It is therefore a study of diplomacy in time of war; of negotiations that form the running line of accompaniment and commentary to the military story; of peace overtures that are often mere subterfuges in the game of fighting—strategic moves, or pieces of propaganda, or means of sowing dissension between allies, or tricks to gain time. It is also a study of the postures and moods of the various powers of Europe, as these were altered by military events and registered in the demands of diplomats; and in this way it seeks to give the inner history of the war, the essential story of the ups and downs of the struggle. It is in particular a study of the diplomacy of Napoleon—the objects for which he was fighting and the methods he used to gain his ends—in the period when it might be claimed that his genius was at its finest and his power was at its height. The story has been told with special reference to the personalities engaged in the work of diplomacy, so that it might become apparent how much in these Napoleonic times the course of events could be deflected by the characters and the idiosyncrasies of ambassadors and ministers who were far from home. It is intended that the result should be at least a sample picture of the Napoleonic era, and should illustrate the strange tangle, the hidden undercurrents and the clash of personalities, that lay behind a Napoleonic war.

The problem is set during the course of the Prussian negotiations for peace, which began immediately after the battle of Jena and finally led Napoleon to an important declaration of policy at a time when he had to face a revived coalition. In tracing out the consequences of this new statement of policy, and in following the various overtures and discussions that ensued, the narrative describes the attitude and conduct of the powers of Europe in the six months before the battle of Fried-land. Tilsit comes in the centre of the story and an attempt has been made to interpret the diplomacy that surrounds the meeting of the two emperors on the raft in the river Niemen. This interpretation has been supported on one or two contro-versial points by special treatment in Appendixes. Finally the book shows the "system of Tilsit" in operation and traces its effects upon the problem of maritime peace, breaking off at the moment when the last thread is cut and the isolation of England is secured—at the moment when new problems in Spain open a fresh period in the history of Napoleon.

Manuscript materials from the British Museum and the Records Office in London, the Archives of the Ministry of Foreign Affairs in Paris, and the Court and State Archives in Vienna have been used, and have been collated with published records and printed correspondence, e.g. the collections from the Prussian and the Russian Archives.

Any virtue that this study may possess owes so much to the kindness of Dr Temperley that the opportunity of a Preface must be taken to say an inadequate word of thanks.

H. BUTTERFIELD

November 1929

INTRODUCTION

CHAPTER I

PRUSSIA'S ATTEMPT TO MAKE SEPARATE PEACE WITH NAPOLEON AFTER JENA

THE fine show of armies arrayed and kings in proud posture had collapsed into medley and muddle in the twin battles of Jena and Auerstädt. It littered the countryside and strove painfully to sort itself out afresh, as the din subsided and the smoke cleared away. Napoleon, sprawling upon the ground to study his maps, fell into an undignified sleep, and his guard took silent stand around him. Murat, writing to his master, apologised: "Your Majesty will pardon my scribble, but I am alone and dropping from fatigue",[1] and he who was no weakling blundered the strokes of his pen, as if he had been drunk. The release from the tension of battle liberated the worst elements in an army. The forces of the very victors seemed endangered by indiscipline.

"The footsteps of the corps d'armée", wrote Soult a few days later, "are marked by fire, devastation, and crimes atrocious beyond belief. The orders of the leaders are despised, the lives of officers are endangered, and as a crowning evil the resources and food afforded by the country are destroyed as French troops come upon the scene."

A stray English traveller who came by soon after the battle found a devastating sight, the ground littered with papers, letters, account books, pamphlets and miscellaneous unwanted goods, while the French rummaged baggage waggons, tossed part of the booty to the country people clamouring around, and with the recklessness of light-hearted soldiery invited all passers-by to stop and share their luck.[2] All was in disarray and men went off to shoot game or to steal poultry, to ransack houses or to pilfer from farms. "Never was pillage carried further than in this campaign and disorder extended even to insubordination."

[1] *Lettres et documents pour servir à l'histoire de Joachim Murat*, IV (1910), 391.
[2] *Private and confidential...narrative of the circumstances which led to an interview between the Emperor Napoleon and G. Sinclair*, by Sir George Sinclair (1826).

The Prussians, in still worse condition, had all their evils complicated by panic. In the morning they had lightened their burdens by throwing away their food, and the end of the battle found them scattering through the villages to satisfy hunger and thirst, digging up potatoes and turnips in the fields, and rushing blindly, officers and men alike, ignorant of the true direction for retreat. An English minister, Lord Morpeth, took to his heels, abandoned his mission before it had really begun, and found a speedy vessel for England. Haugwitz, who had the direction of Prussian policy, made hurried escape to Magdeburg. The king himself had great difficulty in evading capture, and only after many miles of riding hither and thither, many hours in the saddle without food of any sort, did he find his way in the face of the French watch fires and through the midst of his own straggling forces, to a brief day of rest at Sömmerda. On his way he saw the two streams of fugitives from Jena and Auerstädt meet and cross in confusion; and everywhere were tumults and alarms, fugitives and panic-stricken herds, disorders and wild rumours, and an infectious atmosphere of despair. The queen had left her husband on the eve of the disaster and was making her way to Berlin. Stories of battle followed her, reports began to be spread concerning a great defeat of Napoleon, it was even whispered that Murat was dead; but when she was but a few hours' journey from Berlin the truth overtook her and a little later she received a sorry letter from the king. She found Berlin in a fever; her children had already been sent to Stettin and it soon became apparent that she must continue her journey, merging it now into a flight for existence. She wrote to the king: "Everywhere there is the hope that all is not yet lost and that God will help us. You still have troops and the people adore you and are ready to do anything". But the king, Frederick William, had never had any heart in this conflict, and it was noticed that he now showed a sort of bitter satisfaction at having found his own premonitions come true. Even before the battle there had been a heart-breaking series of war councils at Erfurt, there had been distraction and delay; and now that the battle was over it was easy for the military men who were at hand—men like General

Zastrow and General Köckritz—to whisper the right word in his ear and induce him to ask for an armistice.

The war had lasted only a little over a week. The Prussians had gone into it with flags flying. All the wild enthusiasms, the bragging pride, the rattling swords, had sounded the din of a confident untried nation newly entering upon war; and the memory of Frederick the Great had lured these people on. It was on the 5th of October 1806 that the Prussian minister at the court of the Emperor Napoleon had handed an ultimatum to the foreign minister Talleyrand, and the ultimatum had expired on the 8th. On the 12th, after hostilities had commenced, Napoleon had made a final appeal for peace and had asked the Prussians to prevent the great battle that seemed impending; but the Prussian king claimed that the letter did not reach him in time, and Jena was fought on the 14th. Frederick William's demand for a suspension of arms came as his answer to this final overture from Napoleon. With it was coupled a regret that the pacific proposal had arrived too late to prevent the carnage. In this way, at one touch from Napoleon, Prussia crumpled, and cringed, and came whining back to the side of France.

Napoleon refused to grant an armistice. His reply to the request betrays his preoccupations in this October of 1806.

Any suspension of arms which would give time for the Russian armies, whom you seem to have appealed to in the winter, to arrive, would be too inimical to my interests for me to be able to subscribe to it....I do not fear the Russian forces....I met them in the last campaign. But Your Majesty will have more to complain of than I. Half of your States will be the theatre of war....The other part will be ravaged by your allies and will suffer still more. It will be an eternal subject of regret to me that two nations which for so many reasons were meant to be friends, have been drawn into a conflict so purposeless....Still I must repeat to Your Majesty that I shall be glad to see a way, if it is possible, of re-establishing the ancient confidence which reigned between us, and of reconciling the sentiments that I bear towards you with my duty and with the security of my people, compromised once again by this, the fourth coalition in fifteen years.[1]

[1] *Correspondance de Napoléon Ier*, t. XIII, No. 11,031.

Napoleon had been fighting this Prussian war, in fact, with his eyes fixed upon a corollary, and that corollary was the entry of the Russians into Poland. It was a contingency he had merely divined, but if it should occur at all, he would owe Prussia a grudge for it. So in his reply to their demand for an armistice he turned even the approach of Russian friends into an added terror for these Prussians, that they might fear it more than he himself did, and so end by trying to prevent it. Frederick William misread the conclusion of this letter, thinking that he saw in it a promise of kind treatment and quick forgiveness. In reality it was a pointed and deliberate and ominous expression of a doubt. Napoleon was not sure whether policy and events would leave room for the good sentiments that he still affected to have for the Prussian king. He was not sure that he could afford to be friendly to the court of Berlin at all if the Russians brought war into Poland.

At Magdeburg the king of Prussia met Haugwitz who had charge of foreign policy and had led the country into war; also Lucchesini who had been ambassador at Paris, and the secret-cabinet councillor Beyme. They were depressed to hear of the refusal of the armistice and they discussed the course that Prussia ought now to pursue. They all agreed that it was necessary to appeal for peace. Beyme wrote an alarming letter to his wife in Berlin, in which he declared that "the situation was such that one must not bid but beg for peace; it would be presumption to make a proposition; one must surrender completely".[1] The words were spread abroad; it was no secret that negotiations were being entered upon; and everywhere arose an expectation of early peace, a certainty that the treaty would be an ignoble one for Prussia, a feeling that it was useless to go on fighting while the king and his ministers were surrendering everything in abject negotiation. One can understand why, in such an atmosphere, Prussia offered little resistance to the French.

Lucchesini was chosen to conduct the discussions with

[1] L. von Ranke, *Denkwürdigkeiten des Staatskanzlers Fürsten von Hardenberg*, III (1877), 211; 16.

Napoleon, and he received full powers to conclude a treaty. He was instructed to consent to the cession of Prussia's Westphalian provinces up to the Weser, to agree to the sacrifice of Bayreuth, but to use every effort for the securing of an armistice. He was not anxious for the odious mission, and wrote:

> On the morning of the 18th [of October] the king and Count Haugwitz forced upon me the wretched commission of going to ask the French Emperor for peace. I could not get out of this thankless and mournful task. I was charged to draw up my own instructions and to write the letters to the Emperor myself. The king approved and signed them and then left for Cüstrin. I left Magdeburg at noon on the 18th.[1]

On the 20th he reached the French armies and despatched the king's letter to Napoleon, but was himself detained at the outposts. "I have sent Duroc to see what he wants", Napoleon wrote soon afterwards, "and I am waiting for his return. The Prussian king seems quite decided ɩo come to terms. I will do this, but I shall not let it prevent me from entering Berlin."[2] He appointed Duroc to treat with Lucchesini and at midnight on the 21st of October the negotiation for peace began.

The Prussians were not wise in their choice of a negotiator. Lucchesini, when ambassador in Paris, had more than once proved an obstacle to the smooth working of the Franco-Prussian alliance, and long before the emergence of the controversies which had led to war, Napoleon, who disliked and distrusted him, had talked of having him recalled. He had been responsible not for creating but for exaggerating the fears and distresses that had precipitated the recent struggle, for he had not only transmitted some wild rumours to Berlin, he had advised his king to take carriage and fly direct to St Petersburg; and Napoleon had been to this extent correct in charging him with keeping bad company, listening to wild talk, taking his information from speculators, and writing despatches that made trouble. From that moment Napoleon had abused his character, and had

---

[1] Lucchesini's account of his mission in Bailleu, *Preussen und Frankreich, 1795, bis 1807*, II (*Publikationen aus den K. Preussischen Staatsarchiven*, Bd. xxix), 631–4.

[2] *Corresp. de Nap. Ier*, t. xiii. No. 11,045.

complained to Berlin of his unfitness, until the man had been glad to be recalled. It was not tactful of the Prussians, when they were seeking the best escape possible from the predicament into which the war had brought them, to send for the purpose the very man whom Napoleon had seized upon as the prime mover of the quarrel, the cause of all the trouble.

Napoleon was more careful in his choice of a negotiator, and the appointment of Duroc was significant. It was necessary to prevent Talleyrand from having a hand in the discussions; he might juggle with the negotiation and insinuate his own ideas into the affair, or try by devious processes to smooth down the severities of his master. No diplomat, but a tool, a cat's-paw, the secretary of Napoleon, was chosen to treat with Lucchesini. He was still to be mere secretary, nothing more than a scribe, the unprotesting servant of his master's whims. Napoleon loved Duroc for his faithfulness in this kind of service. "His cold and unexcursive mind", wrote Bourrienne, "suited Napoleon, whose confidence he enjoyed until his death." General Rapp has summed up those qualities in him which made him particularly useful to his master in the negotiation of the peace with Prussia:

> Duroc was a man whose services were almost indispensable to the Emperor. He always enjoyed the highest favour and the greatest confidence, which he in every respect deserved. Few men were so distinguished for tact, spirit of business, and skill, as Duroc; and at the same time few were so remarkable for modesty. His devotion to the Emperor was without bounds. He had a good heart and was an honest man; his only fault was his fear of displeasing and his excessive timidity.[1]

Napoleon in appointing this man to treat with the Prussians really kept the whole negotiation entirely in his own hands.

At midnight on the 21st of October Duroc and Lucchesini began a conference that lasted for a few hours and discussed the terms of the proposed peace treaty. The Prussian plenipotentiary spent the rest of the night in thinking out a reply to the proposals that had been put before him, ready for the second interview that took place on the 22nd: he was kept moving about from

---

[1] Rapp, *Mémoires écrits par lui-même* (1823), p. 118.

place to place as the French armies advanced, but Napoleon refused to see him personally. On the 23rd, at Wittenberg, a more official conference was held, and on the following day Lucchesini was informed of what Napoleon's intentions were. He was given the basis of the proposed treaty of peace. On the morrow again he was in Potsdam and wrote to his master. The terms that had been offered him were so exacting and costly that he would not take it upon himself to sign them.

Napoleon's conduct in the meantime had given the Prussians little reason to expect an easy conclusion of peace. The French armies were sweeping across the country and into the four corners of Germany to hunt out the remnants of Prussian military strength. The battle of Jena had been made the starting-point for the complete subjugation of the defeated state under a system of military occupation and financial exaction. Napoleon entered Berlin in triumph. He seems to have been intoxicated by the very act of fighting, and the exhilaration of conquering so easily. One would have inferred that he had no motive left for ever desiring the Prussians as his friends, no political object in view to make him wish to soften their humiliation. He seemed like a man with a great resentment, as though this war, for all its laurels and victories, had cut across his path and had intervened to spoil his plans.

So while Lucchesini had been engaged in flying conferences, negotiating peace with Duroc but at the same time moving from town to town to keep pace with the advance of the French armies, crowds of fugitive Prussians, a little ahead of the invaders, were being driven into exile and were flying to escape capture. From Berlin the wealthy, the noble, the official classes had taken to flight on hearing of the battle of Jena. All who had the means had hastened away; all the booksellers, it was noticed, seemed to remember Palm; and it was said that on the afternoon of the 17th of October not a vehicle was left in the city, not a horse, not even a donkey. The military governor of Berlin was amongst the refugees; the government was dispersed, the king and queen were known to be in flight somewhere, and were trying to meet one another. The journeys of these Prussians were suffered under the most nerve-racking conditions. A description exists of how from Berlin the travelling carriages were pursued by the hootings of scoundrels and the menaces of the dregs of the populace who did not like to see themselves so deserted, and hastened back to scrape at the heels of the French. Sometimes the road would be blocked with fugitives; fear drove them on, bad news followed them round; mishaps did not fail to occur on journeys so taken under pressure. Horses would be driven to the last stages of exhaustion and fatigue; the breaking of a carriage wheel would come to overwrought minds as a nerve-racking catastrophe and would hold up a procession of miserable refugees; and all the attendant circumstances were calculated to induce dejection. If a pause were made, and if at last there were some feeling that the flight might be at an end, still the sound of cannon, or the rumour that troops had been seen across the river, would start the race again. It was in such an atmosphere as this, and not in cool council chambers, that the king had to decide important questions of policy. The court was in full flight. The ministers were dispersed and overtaken with panic. Conferences would be driven from town to town, held so to speak under the cannon's mouth. It was natural that these people should judge the situation of Prussia from their own immediate circumstances. It was difficult for them to meet their political problem with a mighty exercise of will, when every petty detail of their daily life was conspiring to keep them in dejection. It is easy to understand why they looked to Lucchesini, and put their hope in the clemency of Napoleon, and set their hearts on the conclusion of peace.

Frederick William himself, waiting for news from his minister Lucchesini, was in one of those moods when a queer psychoanalytical apathy fell upon his repressed mind, and he would busy himself with odds and ends of futile occupations and interests, like a harassed man who picks at a piece of string. He, who was "rather the conscientious drudge of state than its first servant", could not bear the awfulness of responsibility and shrank from taking a decision in matters he knew to be so momentous. From his way of walking around, from his habit of toying with trifles, people said he was indifferent—that he might have had ten kingdoms to lose. Blindly he clung to his old ministers, Haugwitz, Zastrow and Beyme, keeping the more vigorous Hardenberg out of his counsels, lest he should hinder the conclusion of peace. The queen herself was aware that it was her own policy of war with France that had come into discredit: she might be anxious to continue the struggle but she would not interfere in politics any more. On the 20th of October she joined the king at Cüstrin, where the inhabitants of the surrounding country were already rushing within the fortified walls, dragging everything they could carry. All the hope of the ministers was centred in the negotiation that Lucchesini was conducting; but there was a certain nervousness, since Lucchesini had been keeping silent for a time. Frederick William wrote a pitiable letter to Napoleon, expressing his anxiety and complaining of the delay; and this letter seems to have crossed with Lucchesini's despatch announcing the terms which Napoleon had dictated.[1]

Lucchesini's report now reached the Prussian king, and the Prussians were at last able to know the kind of treatment Napoleon intended giving them. The peace terms that were now presented were the ones that Lucchesini had not dared to undertake the responsibility of accepting, and they showed Napoleon more severe than the Prussians had contemplated. Prussia, according to these terms, was to renounce the provinces she had hitherto possessed between the Rhine and the Elbe and to abandon her former relations with Germany. She was to engage not to interfere in the affairs of Germany but to promise that she would recognise the drastic changes that Napoleon contemplated there, particularly the great extension of his Confederation of the Rhine. She was allowed to retain the Duchy of Magdeburg and the old Mark of Brandenburg, so that as a result of the territorial rearrangements her centre of gravity was to be shifted eastwards; in future she was not to allow preoccupation with

---

[1] The letter is quoted from the French Archives by Driault, *Tilsit* (1917), p. 41, and (rather differently) by Lefèbvre, *Histoire des Cabinets de l'Europe*... (1866), ii, 399–400; so presumably it was despatched; but cf. Ranke, *Hardenberg*, iii, 219 (note).

German affairs to obscure what Napoleon regarded as her true
function in Europe—she was to concentrate upon her rôle of
buttress against the powers of eastern Europe, and cease to be
the competitor of Napoleon in Germany. She was given a geography that would itself set the conditions of her future policy
and turn her attention eastwards. This treaty was Napoleon's
answer to the challenge that the court of Berlin had given to him
in the year 1806. He had wanted to keep Prussia as an ally, as
a client state; she had been useful to him because she could
check or frighten Russia; but she had chosen to adopt rather
the rôle of a German power, she had entered into competition
with him for that hegemony of Germany which Austria had
allowed to slip from her hands, she had been willing to leave him
his influence in south Germany, his Confederation of the Rhine,
but she had come to issue with him over the question of the
leadership of the north. This being the nature of the struggle,
and Napoleon having won in any case at Jena what he might
consider as a special title to the overlordship of Germany, it was
natural that the guiding principle of the peace treaty should be
the final settlement of the problem of Prussia's place on the map—
that is to say, the exclusion of Prussia from the Germanic system.[1]

On these terms a Prussia greatly weakened, and so unable to
imagine herself a possible rival to France, was to pay a huge
indemnity for the war she had brought about, and was to return
to her place in the French system of politics; she was to co-
operate with Napoleon in the war against England by closing
her ports to British vessels, and she was to guarantee the integrity
of the Ottoman Porte, agreeing to join France in its defence if
the Russians should attack it. This last clause reveals the
context of the whole treaty and gives at least a clue to the situation from which it proceeds. There was no mention of what
Prussia must do if the Czar turned his forces into Poland. That
contingency was not contemplated for the moment; in truth it
had never been more than a wild surmise of Napoleon's, and he
was now beginning to doubt it and to change his ground a little.
One of the bulletins of the French army at the time when these

[1] For this treaty see Bailleu, *Preussen und Frankreich*, ii, 577.

terms of peace were communicated to Lucchesini, stated: "We have not yet received news of the conclusion of a treaty between Prussia and Russia, and it is certain that no Russian troops have appeared to this day on Prussian soil". Later, on the 13th of November, when it had become known that the Russians were indeed advancing, Napoleon wrote to one of his ministers, "All my intelligence told me that the Russians retreated when they learned what had happened to Prussia". It is to be noticed that when he became certain that the Russians were coming to meet him he considered this whole treaty as inadmissible and immediately cancelled all its arrangements.

The king of Prussia found these terms much more exacting than he had anticipated. He had thought of a speedy forgiveness and then reconciliation, and a return to the fold. On the 26th of October he sent Count Zastrow to Charlottenburg to join Lucchesini in pursuing the negotiation and to make a strong attempt to secure better terms of peace. He "could not disguise" from the Emperor that the severity of his stipulations had distressed him all the more in that the letter he had received after Jena had given him hopes of a reconciliation on more easy terms. He talked again of his "sincere desire to re-establish the old relations with France".[1]

Napoleon gave Zastrow a friendly interview, and spoke kindly of Haugwitz. On the 28th of October the two Prussian negotiators recommenced the discussions with Duroc. Two days later, in a note to that minister, they accepted the bases which Napoleon dictated for a peace—bases in some ways modified from those given at Wittenberg a week before.[2] The French demands had not become more merciful or kind; Napoleon gave it to be understood that he would require Frederick William to forbid the entry of Russian troops into his territory and to engage to fight at the side of France in the event of a war with Russia; the Prussian king felt the conditions grievously hard and was very unwilling to accept them. On the 6th of November a conference was held at Graudenz to discuss the advisability of submitting;

[1] Letter of Frederick William to Napoleon, 26 Oct. 1806, in Ranke, *Hardenberg*, III, 219–20. [2] *Ibid.* III, 221.

the whole assembly was of the opinion that it was out of the question to think of renewing the war, and Haugwitz put forward the idea that the slightest hesitation or delay would provide Napoleon with an excuse for raising his demands.[1] Everything was done to prevent or to evade the necessity of having to fight Russia, whose armies were by this time unmistakably advancing into Poland. It was decided to attempt to persuade the Czar to avoid hostilities, and a messenger was sent to St Petersburg to make the treaty palatable to the Russians. On the 7th of November Frederick William wrote a letter to Napoleon:

> In spite of the dreadful sacrifices which you, Sire, have just imposed upon me, I do not desire any less sincerely that this peace, already assured by my acceptance of its bases, shall enable me soon to re-establish with Your Majesty the friendly relations which a moment of warfare has suspended.... I have not even waited for the signature of the treaty before stopping the advance of the Russian troops.[2]

These Prussians, it seems, were anxiously holding their breath, lest Napoleon should change his mind again and revoke the agreement he had offered. Haugwitz, grovelling to the victor, still wrote to Lucchesini to induce him to seek an amelioration in the terms of the treaty; Prussia must not be made too weak to act as a check against Russia, he said; Prussia was only too anxious to be at the service of France; and he pressed the idea and fawned like a servile courtier, engaging his word "as a man of honour, who for twelve years has consistently worked to cement the relations between France and Prussia". If only Talleyrand would appear, thought Haugwitz—he at least could work on lines less wild and impolitic "than that terrible principle of the destruction of Prussia to guarantee the future repose of France".[3] Talleyrand distrusted some of the drastic measures

[1] Ranke, *Hardenberg*, v, 396, Protokoll der Konferenz abgehalten in Graudenz am 6 Nov. 1806.

[2] E. von Höpfner, *Der Krieg von 1806 und 1807* (1855), Part i, vol. ii, p. 389; A. Lefèbvre, *Histoire des Cabinets de l'Europe 1800–1815*, ii (1866), 402–3.

[3] Haugwitz to Lucchesini, 7 Nov. 1806, in Bailleu, *Preussen und Frankreich*, ii, 578–9; cf. Hauterive to Talleyrand, 19 Oct. 1806, *ibid*. ii, 612–13: "Je vois, mon cher ami, que vous n'êtes pas persuadé encore que la Prusse est une puissance vile".

of his master, and loved to tone them down, and regarded the victory of Jena in the moral effect it had upon Napoleon as tantamount to a disaster for France. Lucchesini also thought that in him lay the one hope of Prussia. Prince Ferdinand, great-uncle of Frederick William, sought an interview with the conqueror, wrote "as the brother of Frederick the Great, as the oldest member of the family, and as the oldest soldier in Prussia ", in order to beg for pity—wrote also to Murat to ask for the amelioration of the peace terms; but his efforts were ignored. There was some talk even of Frederick William himself going to make personal appeal to Napoleon. It was in vain to try to bend or soften that rough imperious will—nothing was to be done save to reconcile oneself to the great sacrifices demanded and hope that now Napoleon would at least not change his mind and harden his heart anew—would not retract his offers and hurl the whole question into the melting-pot once more.

Having agreed to the treaty the Prussians still trembled, and for some time they were kept in suspense. The actions of Napoleon became strange and inconsistent; the shadow of the man loomed threateningly again; and every sign in the sky seemed malevolent. The negotiators at Charlottenburg were left to themselves. Their note of the 30th of October, accepting the terms of the French treaty, dropped into an awful void and never had an answer. The Prussians found themselves helpless and bewildered before one of those long inauspicious silences of Napoleon—silences of a man who was brooding new terrors for the world. The Emperor had decided to change his plans.

* * * *

The whole history of the year 1806 proves that the real antagonism in Europe at this time had been between France and Russia. Throughout the year both powers had turned their attention to the Adriatic and the Near East and had seen there the next, the most immediate, conflict of their interests. The Czar had watched anxiously the eastward extension of Napoleon's power in the Mediterranean and was jealous of the growing influence and supervision of France over the politics of Constantinople; Napoleon could hope, in fact, that he would declare war against the Turks in order to destroy the French predominance there. For some time Napoleon, when he had concluded treaties with various powers, had made a cardinal point of securing a clause, apparently innocent but really directed against Russia, guaranteeing the "independence and integrity" of the Ottoman Porte; that is to say, he envisaged a war with the Russians that should be fought ostensibly on behalf of Turkey. So long as there was a power like Prussia, even half-unwillingly and merely ostensibly allied to France, but acting as a barrier on the Polish frontier of Russia, the government of St Petersburg would find in it one reason for carrying on the conflict with France not in that region but in the Turkish Empire. Prussia indeed by being a buttress in the east had had her place in the Napoleonic system in Europe and had formed part of that disposing of forces which Napoleon had hoped to maintain. That was why he had considered war with her as a "civil war" and could not forgive her for forcing it upon him.

From the moment when the problem of Prussia had become serious, the Russians had never ceased to occupy Napoleon's attention. They had denounced a peace treaty signed by their plenipotentiary in July, and it was plain that they would find in the new crisis their own opportunity. Over and over again Napoleon had betrayed his apprehensions. He seems to have been very anxious that the Russians should not come to meet him in Poland. It would give him war in the wrong quarter: "My concern with Russia is in connection with the Porte",[1] he had written to Talleyrand in July. Moreover, it meant a winter campaign in a region which by its climate and geography made warfare difficult for Frenchmen and victory only less miserable than defeat. Circumstances were particularly unfavourable for such a struggle if France had to fight without the intended assistance of Prussia. Perhaps, finally, it is not fanciful to say that Napoleon saw himself deprived of what he had conceived to be a chance of gaining a foothold in the Ottoman Empire. In any case he made it clear to the Prussians that their fate was to depend upon the conduct of the Czar.

[1] *Corresp. de Nap. Ier*, t. xii, No. 10,448.

A proclamation issued to the French army on the 26th of October contained these words: "The Russians boast that they are coming upon us; we will march to meet them; we will spare them half the journey. They will find Austerlitz this time in the middle of Prussia". On the 31st of October the advent of this new enemy is still rather doubtful. "We do not hear any more talk of the Russians", the bulletin runs; but its challenging tone shows that there exists an idea that they will come into Poland. "We are longing for a hundred thousand of them to come. But the rumour of their advance is mere nonsense. They will not dare to come to meet us". Four days later, however, the question is decided: "The Russians are a long way off; but it is possible that we shall meet them and be at grips with them in a month's time". This is the moment that finds Napoleon breathless, and the whole man flashes to life. On this day, the 3rd of November, he writes urgently to Paris for reinforcements. He sends for Kosciusko, the Polish rebel, to incite his fellow-countrymen against the Russians and henceforward his correspondence is full of the idea of an insurrection in Poland. At this time Talleyrand whips round to the court of Vienna, where armaments have been made to guard the territory and enforce the neutrality of Austria. These armaments have suddenly taken on an appearance of menace, so Talleyrand writes to the French minister there, writes directly to the Austrian chancellor himself,[1] to demand their instant cessation. Altogether these first days of November are a pivot. Once more Napoleon shows himself alert, breaks out with unbaffled energy, and nerves himself for a crisis. A certain situation has arisen and all the schemes and expedients that were to have been contingent upon it are now given release. Here is something that makes the peace-terms of November inadequate. There is to be a war with Russia in Poland after all—and this war produces a new situation in Europe and leads to a drastic reconsideration of many of Napoleon's plans.

On the 25th of October the French entered the Prussian

---

[1] Talleyrand to Stadion, 2 Nov. 1806, A[rchives du ministère des] A[ffaires] É[trangères], Autriche, t. 379.

capital, and at this time they in Berlin and Napoleon in Charlottenburg discovered documents and correspondence which revealed the solidarity of the Prussian connection with Russia and linked up the two nations more closely than Napoleon had even suspected, and entirely dissipated what doubt there had been concerning the existence of an understanding between the two courts. "Napoleon has found a letter in Charlottenburg", wrote the Countess Voss, "left by the Queen, or, as they say, slipped behind a sofa cushion where it had remained unnoticed, and this letter has made him quite furious." These compromising documents convinced him more than ever of the treachery as well as the unwisdom of the conduct of the court of Berlin in the summer of 1806. In his bulletin of the 26th of October he begins to put his finger upon the connection between the Czar Alexander and the Prussian court as the cause of the war policy of Prussia and he no longer repeats former statements about an unwilling king being rushed into hostilities by a war party in his cabinet. From this moment he bursts out in bitterness against the queen of Prussia and advertises her friendship for the Czar and attacks her with gratuitous insults in his proclamations. If it had before seemed a serious matter to fight the Russians in Poland with a defeated and embittered Prussia sulking in the rear, the objections to this course were redoubled now that it had come to light that Prussia had for a long time been pursuing a dual foreign policy, balancing her alliance with France by a more secret and intimate connection with the Czar.

The prospect of a campaign in Poland had raised a further issue that was likely to make Napoleon withdraw the offer of peace that had been made to Prussia. The whole problem of "the barrier of the east", the buttress against Russia, had been in Napoleon's mind ever since he had come to issue with the court of Berlin, and the approach of the Russian armies in November brought the question to a further stage, since it put Poland more directly under the eye of Napoleon and gave him a more immediate interest in the idea of reviving the kingdom. The national feeling of the Polish people would be at his service in a war against Prussia and Russia, if he could convince them that in return for their assistance he would undo the work of the partition treaties and restore their state to its former independence. It would be the revival of the old connection between France and Poland, and much that was sentimental in the relations between the two nations tended to make such a policy attractive. France had been helpless to prevent the destruction of Poland, but now that Napoleon was striding Europe as an arbiter, remodelling the continent and doing feverish map-making, it was natural that there should be a certain expectancy in the air, and a feeling that France would do her part at last.[1] Opportunist as he was, Napoleon certainly encouraged the Poles to hope for salvation in this way; he dangled the scheme for the restoration of Poland before their eyes; it suited him to take the point of view that "France has never recognised the different partitions of Poland"; and, without promising anything, he hoped at least to secure Polish assistance in the forthcoming campaign against Russia, by merely keeping alive the vague expectations. Further than this he seriously considered the possibility of actually adopting the policy that the Poles desired and reviving the Kingdom of Poland. He saw that this revived kingdom might be made a client state of France as in the eighteenth century, and thus might be used as a substitute for the Prussian barrier in the east. The idea was one which would demand a readjustment of the peace terms he had already offered to Prussia; but, further, it was a course which in any case rendered the future alliance of Prussia less important to him, and made immediate peace impossible. The emergence of the Polish question necessarily threw the fate of Prussia into the melting-pot again. It was a further reason for cancelling the arrangements already made.

The restoration of Poland, then, became an open question, but Napoleon did not definitely commit himself to any scheme as yet;[2] the subject was one upon which his own entourage seem to have had no unanimous opinion. The prolific writer Mont-gaillard presented on the 5th of November a project which com-

---

[1] *Corresp. de Nap. Ier*, t. xiii, No. 11,279.
[2] *Ibid.* t. xiii, Nos. 11,258, 11,279; t. xv, No. 12,603.

prised the re-establishment of Poland, "if it is no longer allowed to be hoped that the cabinet of Berlin will oppose a serious resistance to Russia". Montgaillard thought that after all the humiliations it had suffered the Prussian royal family would never be reconciled to imperial France.[1] Jomini, however, a few days later was urging the merits of an alliance with Prussia, and showing what might be won from the gratitude and friendship of Frederick William if the Prussian lands could be increased by as much of Polish territory as could be scraped together for them.[2] Napoleon at St Helena made claim to have considered such a scheme, declaring that he had desired Hanover, the Prussian provinces of Saxony, Westphalia, and Franconia, and Magdeburg, for himself; but asserting that he would have made Frederick William the ruler of a restored Poland, and would have given part of the Illyrian provinces to Austria in return for the cession of Galicia.[3] It is more than likely that he played with such schemes for the future of Prussia—halting at them, perhaps, for a moment, as his mind went through the kaleidoscope of the possibilities before him, and then idealising them in his memory during exile. But what seems irresistible as the solution of the Polish problem in the later months of 1806 is that Napoleon still held everything fluid, and preserved the mobility and uncommitted freedom of his mind, and was prepared to do anything as he might be called upon to adjust his policy to the exigencies of a growing situation.

At any rate he would have nothing more to do with the peace treaty he had offered to the Prussians. All that had happened

[1] Clément de Lacroix, *Mémoires diplomatiques de Montgaillard 1805–19* (1896), pp. 307–21.

[2] F. Lecomte, *Le Général Jomini; sa vie et ses écrits* (1860), pp. 51–4. Jomini, *Vie politique et militaire de Napoléon racontée par lui-même*, ii (1827), 328–9. See also proposals of Hauterive in Bailleu, *Preussen und Frankreich*, ii, 581–2 (footnote); ii, 612–13; Driault, *Tilsit*, pp. 68–9. On the whole subject of Poland see Handelsman, *Napoléon et la Pologne 1806–7*, pp. 1–22 and 167–76.

[3] *Corresp. de Nap. Ier*, t. xxxii, p. 443 in the quarto edition (p. 358, octavo): "Extraits des récits de la Captivité; Tentatives pour le rétablissement de la Pologne", 20 Aug. 1820; cf. however, "Entwurf einer Proklamation Napoleon's über die Absetzung des Hauses Brandenburg (Ende 1806)", Bailleu, *Preussen und Frankreich*, ii, 581–3.

since he had proposed the terms of it, all that he had learned of the duplicity of the court of Berlin, impelled him to make a different and a more drastic use of his recent victories. This is where the astonishing efficiency of his subjugation of Prussia came into use. After Jena he had remorselessly pursued the remnants of the Prussian armies and had captured the Prussian strongholds. Many victories had been given to him by the shameful conduct, both the cowardice and the treachery, of his enemies. Towards the end of October and in the first days of November news of the capture of Hohenlohe's army, of the capture of Stettin and Cüstrin, and of the fall of Magdeburg and Lübeck reached Napoleon, so that on the 16th of November he could announce: "the campaign against Prussia is entirely finished". Duroc stated that if only the news of the fall of Magdeburg had not come through at an inauspicious moment peace might have been concluded. But Napoleon, having astonished himself by the ease and the completeness of his victory, determined to exploit his success and make more effective use of his advantage than the terms he had already granted would allow. The arrival of the Russians in Poland and the amazing facility of his recent conquests had produced a great extension of the scope of his plans.

On the 9th of November Napoleon decided to recommence the negotiation that had been suspended, and ordered Duroc to meet Lucchesini and Zastrow at Charlottenburg once more in order to tell them

that I consider the battle of Jena as terminated, now that the corps which had been cut off at Lübeck have surrendered, and that in this state of things I do not see anything to prevent us negotiating seriously for the conclusion of peace. The necessary preliminary seems to be an armistice such as they have requested from M. Talleyrand.[1]

The former negotiations and preliminaries and outlines of peace now counted for nothing and were swept away as an outworn pastime; henceforward the two powers were to settle down to "negotiating seriously".

[1] Instruction for Duroc, 9 Nov. 1806, in Bailleu, *Preussen und Frankreich*, II, 579–80.

On the 16th of November the Prussian plenipotentiaries, Zastrow and Lucchesini, signed an armistice which handed over to Napoleon all that his armies had hitherto failed to secure. The Prussians engaged to withdraw their troops to Royal Prussia and the region around Königsberg, and to surrender part of the province of Silesia together with a large number of fortresses that the French had still failed to capture. It was also stipulated that parts of East Prussia should be occupied by neither Prussian nor French troops. A clause of the convention announced the continuance of negotiations for peace at Charlottenburg, and provided that, in case of the failure of these, hostilities should not be resumed by either party without a warning of ten days being given. In addition to these things the king of Prussia was to expel any Russian troops that had entered his territory and to engage not to receive them on Prussian soil during the armistice; that is to say, he was to commit hostilities against the very ally he had called to his aid.[1]

Napoleon described the suspension of arms as "only a military measure, which serves to arrange the question of winter in a season so advanced". At the same time he ordered his marshals, Davout and Lannes, to make no announcement of its signature until the fortresses were actually given up to the French.[2] He was anxious concerning the Poles whose aid he was invoking against the Prussians and Russians; he knew they were jealous of his negotiations with Zastrow and Lucchesini. They were afraid lest, having compromised them, he should desert them and make peace with their oppressors. If he could delay informing them of the armistice until the actual execution of the terms, then, he said, "it will be easy to make the Poles see that by the suspension of arms, their existence is partly recognised. ...In the long run everything is favourable to their cause". Talleyrand wrote:

> The conditions (of the armistice) are such that Poland, if there is a Poland, will recover the liberty of having and expressing an opinion. Our troops will not withdraw from the part of Polish Prussia that we

---

[1] *Corresp. de Nap. Ier*, t. XIII, No. 11,277.
[2] Handelsman, *Napoléon et la Pologne 1806–7*, p. 21.

already occupy; and it is agreed that there will be neither French nor Prussian troops in the other parts of Polish Prussia that we do not hold. So you have Polish Prussia considered as a separate thing from Prussia; and, moreover, you have a Poland that can show itself, if it has the means...a Poland which menaces Russia, and by this can lead her to the peace we desire, that is to say a peace that preserves the Ottoman Porte.[1]

From all this it appears that Napoleon has by no means committed himself to a restoration of Prussia in any future settlement of Europe. If he has not committed himself to the Poles, either, he still leaves himself room to play with them, and opportunity for stirring their hopes. He has merely reaffirmed his desire to have, on the frontiers of Russia, a power that will preserve and uphold his interests in the Ottoman Porte. One wonders what he could have expected the Prussians to see in the armistice to make them welcome it as safety and reassurance and hope. One wonders why the negotiators dared to sign such a document at all. Lucchesini defends himself by saying that they were held like prisoners at Charlottenburg, that their correspondence with the Prussian court was uncertain, that they could not obtain correct information of the true situation of things. They thought the Russians were still far away, and, in that case, they knew that the king could ratify the armistice, and when the Russians arrived find an early pretext for breaking it; but even if the Russians were approaching they felt that the king could refuse to confirm their work. They were afraid of an insurrection of the Poles, and they counted that a suspension of arms would discourage this. They were distressed that the estates of the Prussians seemed condemned to be the theatre of the new war. The Czar Alexander, it was thought, would be ready for peace if Napoleon decided not to attempt the restoration of Poland. Talleyrand begged the Prussian negotiators to make the Czar see the dangers that would fall upon Prussia, if Russia persisted in the war—the danger there would be of Russia herself being thrown beyond the Dwina if the risen Poland and the provinces

---

[1] Handelsman, *Napoléon et la Pologne* 1806–7, pp. 20–1. See also Talleyrand to Andréossy, 18 Nov. 1807, printed *ibid.* p. 215.

conquered by France should receive a chief who would be a mere vassal of France. It was further insinuated to Zastrow and Lucchesini that it was very important for the restoration of Prussia to make Napoleon commit himself to something by the signature of a document such as this. Under such arguments and apprehensions the Prussian negotiators signed the armistice; and, wrapped up in the same insinuations and insidious suggestions, the document came to the king of Prussia, inviting acceptance and ratification.[1]

In a note which came as an appendix to the armistice the real schemes and intentions of Napoleon were made apparent; and it was revealed that the armistice itself was only incidental to the new development of Napoleonic policy. Lucchesini afterwards related that he knew nothing of this note until the suspension of arms was settled and signed; otherwise, he maintained, he would never have put signature to the agreement. Duroc, it seems, received the note suddenly by messenger from Talleyrand, and handed it to Zastrow, who read it and seemed pleased with it, evincing what many contemporaries would have thought a typically Prussian reaction to its contents. "So much the better," he said, "this gives us some more means of forcing the Russians to enter into negotiations with France. Anyhow the treaty is signed." The note recalled the generous conduct Napoleon had pursued in giving up conquests he had made after the collapse of three successive coalitions against him. "But in the course of wars perpetually renewed, France, Spain and Holland have lost their colonies. It is natural, it is just, that the countries which the right of conquest has put into the hands of the Emperor, should serve as compensations for the Colonies." In a similar way "His Majesty cannot give up any of the conquests which the chances of war have put into his power before the

---

[1] A précis of the apology which Lucchesini made for the signing of the armistice can be found in Ranke, *Hardenberg*, v, 421. See also F. v. Ompteda, *Nachlass* (1869), p. 248 (No. 152): "Notatum des Gesandten Ompteda über eine vertrauliche Unterredung mit dem Marquis Lucchesini (Wien) Ende Jan. 1807". It will be noticed that Lucchesini had found his way to Vienna, where, according to Razoumovski, his conversation was hostile to Russia. A. Wassiltchikow, *Les Razoumovski*, t. II, 3me partie (1894), ch. III, pp. 81–2.

Ottoman Porte is completely restored to all its rights over Moldavia and Wallachia, and before its absolute independence is recognised and guaranteed ". In other words, Napoleon refused to conclude separate peace with Prussia.

In his message to the Senate a few days later he outlined the same policy with similar logic—talked again of his extreme moderation in previous wars, and remarked that "a large number of the Cabinets of Europe are sooner or later influenced by England, and without a solid peace with this power our people will not be able to enjoy the blessings which are the first aim of our labours ". He stated that he would not evacuate Poland and Berlin " before a general peace was concluded, the conquered colonies restored and the independence of Turkey guaranteed ", and he made it clear that he was ready to treat for peace with England, Russia and Prussia "but only on bases such as do not permit anybody to arrogate to himself any rights of superiority over us, and such as give back the colonies to their Mother-Countries, and guarantee our commerce and industry the prosperity they have a right to ". This same message to the Senate announced also the creation of "the continental system", which was intended to place Great Britain in a state of blockade and to put her under the ban of Europe.

Napoleon then acknowledged that England, out of reach of the French armies, could be a perpetual foe of France and the source of repeated wars in Europe; but he met the problem by the establishment of a new and sweeping principle of policy. The idea rested on the carrying out of a series of thorough but conditional and temporary conquests in Europe, which were to be the pledge of a general peace. Napoleon would not subdue Prussia for ever or annex the state finally into his Empire, but he would occupy the territory until his enemies should find it to their own advantage to redeem it. To end the French occupation the Prussians would set everything in motion for the cessation of the war. The Czar had been willing to come forward to fight for the salvation of Prussia; now he would be called upon to make peace for the identical object. The continent would find the sufferings of the war so heavy that Europe would range itself against England on behalf of tranquillity. To restore the Prussian monarchy, raise up a barrier against France and bring relief to Europe, the Russians would abandon their thoughts of interference in Turkey, and the British would surrender their colonial conquests. Everything was comprehended in one trenchant principle of policy, for Napoleon had a way of fusing his problems together and resolving them at a stroke, covering the whole political situation by an imaginative leap, a bold synthesis.

It was all a new mapping out of the European situation, a fresh disposing of the forces at play, a great European design that fits in with the other "continental system" which was decreed a few days later at Berlin. Napoleon's attempt to boycott English trade and shipping represented the same kind of conspiracy to range the continental powers against England. Europe was to suffer for England's persistence in the war, and was to be the accomplice of France in bringing the British government to heel. Such plans resulted in a heavy increase of Napoleon's obligations and burdens in Europe; for they demanded that a large extent of territory or coastline should be under the occupation or control of France. They had in fact to be extended before they could come into effective operation against England; and until the alliance of Russia was secured their working was not sufficiently drastic. But there is a sense in which these plans of November 1806 are a half-way house on the way to Tilsit. They represent a stage in the development of the Napoleonic design of beating England through a control of the continent.

In this new organisation of policy the Mediterranean does not occupy the same prominent place as before; the ambitions that centred in Turkey and the east are not in the forefront for the moment; Napoleon has had to change his plans. He no longer holds the picture of a Russia deterred on the side of Poland by the presence of a Prussian barrier and coming to grips with France in the south of Europe. He has a different map in his mind. He accepts the war in Poland, accepts the defection of Prussia—will not even allow this power to return to his system. But he changes his old difficulty into a source of power, for Prussia in the ranks of the coalition is still to serve his purposes and promote his views, and will do so more effectively than if he permitted her once again to become an embittered insincere ally. Prussia is to be a weakness and a burden to her new friends, a complaining partner in the war and a dejected advocate of peace. She is to be this because he has given her the motive and has provided her with just the appropriate cue. Once he has made it known that the Prussian king shall not return to Berlin until Russia and England have come to terms, he can leave the situation to work itself out. The rest is automatic.

Napoleon, having achieved the conquest of this state, had no intention of retaining the country as a permanent part of his acquisitions. He had been at a loss at first as to the use he might make of his good fortune—had even talked of deposing the house of Brandenburg and enthroning another reigning family in its stead. For the future, however, he determined to make a military advantage out of his occupation of the territory; he needed it in his forthcoming campaign in Poland. Further than this, he had found a way of using the conquest as a diplomatic weapon, as a thing of negotiable value, in his dealings with the powers. So Prussia was not allowed to make peace, was not allowed even to accept defeat; she was thrown back into the coalition which she was seeking to escape.

This statement of policy came as an appendix to the armistice that Zastrow and Lucchesini signed on the 16th of November 1806. That armistice had still to be ratified by the Prussian king. According to its sixth article the ratifications were to be exchanged by the 21st of November. Duroc himself was sent to the Prussian king to secure the acceptance of the arrangements. His instructions were peremptory; if the slightest objection were made to the terms he had to propose he was instantly to return. On the 21st of November the whole question of the armistice was discussed by the Prussians in a conference held at Osterode. The military men present expressed the opinion that the stipulated surrender of the fortresses would not be a serious blow to Prussia, as such a loss would be inevitable in the chances of continued war; while the suspension of arms would give the king an opportunity to raise troops. Stein, however, who had been in communication with Hardenberg, pointed out the discrepancy that existed between the terms of the armistice and the general policy of peace that was expounded in Talleyrand's note of the 16th; he showed that if the future of Prussia depended upon the willingness of England and Russia to make sacrifices for her, it could not depend on the conclusion of an armistice that would only alienate these powers from the Prussian cause. The armistice and the note that came as an appendix to the armistice were not complementary but contradictory statements. This was the most disastrous side of the convention which Zastrow and Lucchesini had signed. At the very moment when Napoleon finally and decisively set down Prussia as belonging to the coalition, making her a factor in the system of compensations that England and Russia were to accept at a future peace and so binding up her fate irrevocably with theirs, he asked the Prussian king to engage to commit hostilities in favour of France. The armistice that was offered as a promise of peace contained really a new commitment to war. It was all part of Napoleon's way of giving with one hand and taking away with the other. Stein riddled this fallacy of the armistice. He laid bare another piece of Napoleonic trickery, showing that it was not in the power of Prussia to fulfil the terms of the convention and expel the Russian troops, and that if the armistice were signed Napoleon would soon discover this and denounce the agreement; by which time the fortresses would have been handed over to him and so lost beyond recall. To this reasoning the cabinet councillor Beyme contributed further by showing how the engagement that no troops of either power should remain in East Prussia was one which also told in favour of France, since that region would be affected by the Polish insurrection and so would be lost to Prussia by the armistice. These arguments eventually carried the day.[1] The armistice was rejected. The king placed his fate and future in the hands of Russia. He did not risk much by this, "for the armistice would have robbed him of nearly everything".

---

[1] Ranke, *Hardenberg*, v, 398. See also *F.O.* 64/71, George Jackson's reports Nos. 10 and 11, 21 and 23 Nov. 1806. G. Jackson was the semi-official British agent with the Prussian court, England being at that time still technically in a state of war with Prussia. His correspondence (*F.O.* 64/71) and his diaries (ii, 29–54) throw some light on this period.

Within a few days Duroc brought to Napoleon the news that Prussia, finding the Russian troops already within the borders, had had no choice but to reject an armistice, the terms of which she could not hope to carry out; and a little later Zastrow and Lucchesini received the orders of their court. Lucchesini was commanded to remain with the French and to continue the negotiation for peace in any locality that might be agreeable to the French government. For when Prussia rejected the armistice she did not intend by this to imply that she plunged wholeheartedly into the war against France. She took the step because she had decided that if she had to fight it must not be against Russia. She refused to ratify not because she repudiated or abandoned the idea of ending the war but because she discovered the trickery of the armistice and found that it was not a step towards her object. The two Prussian plenipotentiaries were directed by Talleyrand[1] to Posen, where the Emperor had just arrived. On the 6th of December they had their interview with him.[2] Napoleon declared to them that since the Prussian king had rejected the armistice which they had signed and had disavowed their work it was obvious that they had not the confidence of their court, so he would negotiate with them no longer. He stated that if his armies met the Russian forces in Poland military reasons would not allow him to restore any part of the dominions of the king of Prussia. There could be no negotiation with the Prussians; for, desiring the recovery of their territories, they had nothing with which to negotiate for them. The only reason which could induce France to listen to their overtures would be the hope that they might draw into the transaction other powers like Russia and England with whom there might be made some bargain or exchange. More clearly and decisively than on the 16th of November it was shown to the Prussian plenipotentiaries what Napoleon's new policy implied for their government. The future of their nation was to

[1] Talleyrand describes his interview with the Prussian negotiators on the 29th of November in P. Bertrand, *Lettres inédites de Talleyrand à Napoléon* (1889), No. ccxvii.

[2] For this interview see G. Jackson to Howick, No. 17, 16 Dec. 1806, *F.O.* 64/71; cf. *Corresp. de Nap. Ier*, t. xiv, No. 11,394.

depend on the success of their persuasions with other courts on behalf of a general peace.

Thus, in the beginning of December, Prussia is a member of the coalition against her will, and finds herself at war with Napoleon in spite of herself. Events have reached their full cycle and she has discovered that her action in declaring war against France has produced a situation which prevents her from turning back when she desires. The very coalition which she has called to her aid and for which her conduct is at any rate the signal and the opportunity, has become—as Napoleon foresaw—the very thing which forbids her resumption of former relations with France; and she finds herself more closely and irrevocably bound up with its fortunes than she had ever dreamed of becoming. For a long time she had refused Napoleon's offers of separate arrangement with her, she had insisted on having her war, until there had come a time when Napoleon, face to face with Russia, could not safely admit of a separate treaty with her. It was not merely that he was proud and angry and intoxicated by easy victories—though these things perhaps encouraged him to plans that were too large and to enterprises that were to be too great a burden to France; and such personal factors have weight in history as much as the logic of policy. But Prussia had produced a fresh situation and a fresh problem for Napoleon. For it was not a case of simple arithmetic, of plus and minus, of a coalition of three turned into a coalition of four; the entry of Prussia into the ranks of Napoleon's enemies had reversed a system and smashed a synthesis, and upset the chart of forces that Napoleon had mapped out for Europe. And the new peace policy outlined by Talleyrand on the 16th of November, coming almost simultaneously with Napoleon's real decision to isolate England by measures such as he had toyed with and had revolved in his mind and had even effected in an experimental way before he plunged into them with the decree of Berlin, was really a new synthesis, a fresh way of envisaging the problem and of mapping out the relations of Europe, that Napoleon worked out for the changed circumstances.

It was observed at Osterode when the king rejected the

armistice that he did it "with regret, not with indignation". Prussia had begun the war of the fourth coalition; Napoleon was compelling her to see it through. But she was an unwilling member of the coalition, scarcely more than a mere passenger in it. That was her disposition when December came in, and the campaign in Poland began.

CHAPTER II

THE REVIVAL OF THE COALITION

Pʀᴜssɪᴀ had little to do with the making of the coalition
that faced Napoleon at the close of the year 1806. She would
indeed have found it useful to prevent this renewal of European
warfare and she certainly had not reached the state of mind that
was needed for any "concert of Europe". But there are secret
sympathies and latent accords between the events of history;
a kind of magnet seems at times to draw matters to an issue and
collect a number of affairs to one point, creating some "attrac-
tion" that is more subtle than the direct relationship of cause
and effect. The renewal of war after the lapse of almost a year,
the breakdown of negotiations that had been pursued since the
beginning of 1806, did not come merely as a coincidence at this
period. The Prussian war gave a signal to other powers, and
provided them with an opportunity, and hurried affairs to a
head. It galvanised transactions that had been allowed to drag
themselves to weariness. It awakened old sympathies and
forgotten indignations.

Prussia, true to the self-regarding policy that she had followed
throughout these Napoleonic wars, had met France single-handed
and had not even waited for an ally. Once she had been beaten
at Jena she wished for nothing better than to return to the side
of Napoleon. She liked to regard her friendship with France as
having been merely suspended for the moment by a private
quarrel, an unfortunate interlude of war. The larger European
implications of her conduct were inconvenient to her. The fact
that an ally was coming to join her was the very thing which
spoiled her plans. Napoleon's latest policy of deliberately binding
up her fate with that of a coalition seemed an injustice, and she
resented it.[1] The other enemies of France, for their own parts,
did not return to the struggle out of consideration for Prussia,
but showed themselves disposed to continue the fighting even

[1] See e.g. below, p. 71.

at the expense of this power and against its wishes. Each, in fact, made its diagnosis of the whole European situation and came back into war by its own separate path.

In the summer of 1806 Budberg became chancellor of Russia. After Czartoryski, who "never assembled the diplomatic corps", who only gave a dinner on rare occasions, who avoided interviews and never replied to letters, and whose coldness in speaking made him "unable to kindle men or please them", the new minister, himself a former ambassador, was welcomed by the foreign representatives at St Petersburg, for he was an old-world man, full of the courtly ways of former times—"who affected to Catherinise everything"; and he punctiliously gave his dinner every Thursday, was glad to talk on every occasion, and was extremely polite at listening; while he replied "to the least of our notes with an exactitude that (was) infinitely agreeable to us".[1] He was one of the tribe of "German" statesmen who so often reached the highest office in the service of the Russian state, and although it was feared at first that his call to power was the sign of a more pacific policy which the Czar Alexander seemed now to have at heart, it soon became apparent that Budberg was more warlike than his predecessor, his pro-German prejudices making him specially ready to promote a war for the sake of Prussia. Soon after he assumed office he was faced with a peace treaty which a Russian plenipotentiary, Oubril, had signed in a panic in Paris, and instead of ratifying the document he tore it up with such *éclat*, and made so much noise about the transaction for the sake of impressing the British government, that the whole incident seemed like a deliberate challenge to further war. Nothing was done to save the pride of Napoleon— nothing to temper for him the humiliation of having a solemn treaty thrown in his face. The British minister related that Budberg "assured me he had disapproved of the whole mission entrusted to M. d'Oubril, who had been sent to Paris in a moment of complaisance which he flatters himself will not again occur during his continuance in place".

[1] J. De Maistre, *Mémoires et Correspondance* (1858), p. 268.

The chancellor sent a letter to Talleyrand, giving an outline of the conditions from which he would not depart in any negotiation. Napoleon, according to his terms, was to evacuate Dalmatia and Albania; the Sardinian king was to have an indemnity for recent losses of territory; Sicily was to be left in the hands of its legitimate monarch, and perhaps Naples itself restored to him. Even on these conditions there was to be no treaty until the state of war between England and France had been brought to an end.[1] From this communication it was inferred in London and in Paris that Russia meant still to go on with the peace discussions. An English plenipotentiary, Lauderdale, who remained in negotiation with Napoleon, was actually instructed by his government to treat on behalf of the Czar, working upon the basis of the "four points" which Budberg had put forward.[2] It caused great surprise, therefore, and even some incredulity at first, when there was news of a warlike mood and a plunge into armaments and a rush of inflammatory conversation at St Petersburg. It was not known that the Czar had been coming to a secret understanding with Prussia and that this had reached its head upon Budberg's entry into office. It was not yet realised how much Budberg was out of sympathy with the peace party. Men wondered why the Russians were so bellicose.

Before the end of September the English minister announced that the Russians "consider the negotiations on all sides to be now broken off".[3] Soon afterwards we find him writing:

Budberg is wound up to a pitch of fury against Bonaparte, which His Imperial Majesty's gentle disposition in vain endeavours to curb. I never see him that he does not tell me l'Empereur me chassera plutôt que faire telle ou telle chose, etc. etc.[4]

The same minister found himself roughly handled when it was learned that the English were still hankering after peace,

[1] *Sbornik* (Imperial Russian Historical Society), LXXXII, 459–61.
[2] See below, pp. 39–40.
[3] Stuart to F.O. No. 31, "31 Sept." 1806, *F.O. Russia* 65/64.
[4] Charles Stuart to Lord G. Leveson-Gower, 12 Oct. 1806, in *Private Correspondence of Lord G. Leveson-Gower*, II, 227–8.

playing with new proposals and presuming even to treat on behalf of Russia.

General Budberg exclaimed with great warmth that in the present state of affairs both parties would be degraded by...such conditions, that if His Imperial Majesty thought proper to consent to stipulations so little calculated to restore tranquillity to Europe, he would not be the minister through whom the negotiation should be conducted.

It little mattered that Stuart tried to explain to the Russian government how the new instructions to Lauderdale were an attempt to carry out Budberg's own policy as expressed in his note to Talleyrand. Budberg declared

that the expressions of the letter were misunderstood if they were interpreted to be a fresh overture on the part of Russia, when on the contrary intended to be a mere recapitulation of terms which had been already offered by the French Government to the British Negotiators, and from which at the time he had not formed the slightest hope of success, and that it had not ever been the intention of this Court to send another Minister to Paris, because the first overture would now be expected from France.[1]

And to show that the French government were not anxious for peace, Budberg added that

M. Talleyrand after receiving his letter had merely sent for the members of the Russian Chancery who had been left at Paris...and delivered their passports without the smallest intimation of any wish to recommence the negotiation which had been thus broken off.

Then the chancellor, before closing this interview with the British minister, enlarged upon the attitude of Russia to the whole question of peace in Europe, and explained the motives which induced him to wish for a continuance of the war. He

expressed his firm conviction that while Holland remained in the possession of France it was impossible to make any peace consistent with the security of Europe, because from that frontier or from Italy the French territory flanks every state able to oppose the smallest resistance to her views.

---

[1] Stuart to F.O. No. 35, 11 Oct. 1806, *F.O. Russia* 65/64. Also No. 34, 7 Oct. 1806, "Baron Budberg utterly rejects all idea of the renewal of the negotiation...", *F.O. Russia* 65/64.

He was of opinion that "the present state of affairs offers a more advantageous prospect on the side of Naples". Russia rides a high horse, it seems. This is an astonishing rise in her anticipations. But she has not heard, as yet, of the battle of Jena. She is still burning with indignation against the tenour of Oubril's treaty. She can dare to be warlike, even to the point of making the British minister feel uncomfortable.

[Budberg] deprecated the possibility of peace oń the part of Great Britain with unusual warmth and expressed the determination of this Court to continue the war at all hazards, in terms so exactly corresponding with the opinions I had felt myself compelled to bring forward when it was my duty to expose the disadvantages of M. d'Oubril's treaty, that I could not consistently reply to the various arguments urged in the conversation.[1]

What Budberg was turning into the jargon of a diplomat, and translating into terms of political prospect and foreign office calculation, was an emotional thrill that was sweeping like a whirlwind over Russia. War horses rampant, fever psychology working to pressure with terrific generation of heat, "a kind of patriot explosion" as the French consul at St Petersburg reported[2]—it is impossible to mistake that fierce exultation in crisis which the war of 1914 has helped us to understand. There is an electrified atmosphere, a release of the elemental things in human nature, an infectiousness and facile unanimity of mood— all turned into an exalted religious ardour and felt to be highest idealism. Budberg was not pushing a purely personal policy. Alexander had caught the fever. The British minister announced that "this Government is certainly wound up to a pitch of resentment against France beyond what I have witnessed upon any former occasion". Decree after decree gathered up the military resources of the Empire. Towns and trading corporations and rich seigneurs vied with one another in making voluntary sacrifices for the war. Alexander issued a manifesto to arouse the nation against France; the Holy Synod pronounced "the excommunication of Napoleon", declared that the war was a

---

[1] Stuart to F.O. No. 35, 11 Oct. 1806, *F.O. Russia* 65/64.
[2] P. Bertrand, *Lettres inédites de Talleyrand à Napoléon*, No. ccxxvi.

defence of the altar as well as the throne, and mobilised religious fervour. All French agents were ordered to leave the country, and if French subjects refused to submit to conditions imposed by the government their expulsion was pronounced. With flourishes and beating of drums the Russians hurled themselves into this war, from which they were to make so quiet an exit at Tilsit.

For the breakdown of the negotiation that he had been conducting with England throughout the summer of 1806 Napoleon with some insincerity blamed the death of Charles James Fox. He took pains publicly to deplore the calamity that had robbed the world of so reasonable a statesman and cheated Europe of its chances of peace. Certain suspicious happenings in Paris had caused the British government at the beginning of August to supersede the man originally in charge of the negotiation and to send out a more trusted minister specially instructed to meet Napoleon with firmness. This man, an eccentric Scottish peer called Lauderdale, had a notorious lack of humour and knew none of the supple arts. A certain stiffness that he introduced into the transactions in Paris made it easy to believe that he was not passionate for the cause of peace. Frenchmen were able to argue that this change of ministers was due to the illness and declining influence of Fox—that behind the stubbornness of Lauderdale was the obstinacy of the prime minister Grenville. The truth was that in negotiations which had lasted for months Napoleon had merely played with England, had feinted and dipped and twisted, mocking the earnest efforts of Fox with his own insincerity and evasiveness and repeated sharp practices, till distracted English ministers in Paris and a distracted government at home had come to feel baffled at every point. Fox, as foreign secretary, instead of differing from his prime minister, had steadily refused to be a dupe, had led the way in resisting the aggressions of France,[1] and had approved of

---

[1] See *Dropmore Papers*, VIII, 85, 105, 195, 217–18. Lord John Russell, *Memorials and Correspondence of C. J. Fox*, IV, 136 (Fox to Bedford, 26 Ap. 1806: "You will be happy to hear that it occasioned no difference or even a shade of difference in the Cabinet").

the whole turn that the negotiation had taken as a result of the
sending of Lauderdale. Before his death in the latter part of
September he declared the impossibility of treating with a man
like Napoleon.[1] Lauderdale, far from being an enemy to peace,
had ever been one of the most bitter of the opponents of Pitt,
had stormed violently against the policy of war with France,
and, if we are to believe Lord Holland, had been ready to go
further than Fox himself in pursuing every opportunity that
might lead to an arrangement with France.[2] During August,
when a settlement seemed further away than ever, when also it
was feared that a depressed Czar would ratify the treaty that
his plenipotentiary had signed, and when, to crown the misfortunes, it became apparent that Fox himself could not live
very long, the English ministry, faced with renewed war and the
loss of an ally and the death of its most brilliant leader, carried
on its labours in a gloomy and over-anxious mood, guided by
an uninspiring Grenville who, far from being warlike and arrogant and proud, was only too morbidly conscious of the
responsibilities of his position.

The death of Pitt at the beginning of the year had brought
into power in England a coalition of his political opponents.
A "ministry of All the Talents" had hazardously dovetailed
itself together and stepped into the government of the country,
led gloomily by Grenville. After long sighing the unruly whigs
had come into their share of office, only to curse the evils of these
strange days that had at last tormented them by giving them
their hearts' desire. Fox had been the chief light of this whig
party, had led his followers carelessly, irresponsibly, defiantly
at times, and for years had shown them how to torment Pitt
and storm against the policy of war with France. When Fox
became foreign secretary in the "ministry of All the Talents" it
seemed that the whig peace policy was enthroned at the foreign
office itself, and it was believed that now, at least, the chances
of peace would be explored to the uttermost, perhaps even to the

---

[1] Lord Holland, *Memoirs of the Whig Party during my time*, II (1854),
77 *et seq.*
[2] *Ibid.*

great peril of England. But Napoleon did not understand the
mental reservations with which one must take the extravagances
and vagaries of English party politics; he could not read between
the lines of parliamentary debates or see the difference between
a Fox in opposition and a Fox in the seat of government;
particularly in matters of foreign policy he failed to appreciate
the continuity that governmental action can show even under
the most violent changes of cabinet. He could have wished for
nothing better than to have a whig and a former profligate at
the foreign office in London, and Fox in particular he had met
and talked to, had even embarrassed with extravagant compliments. He thought that this therefore was a moment to be
exploited. He imagined that here was a man whom he could use.
Charles James Fox lived long enough to show that this was but
another of those miscalculations into which Napoleon's defective
sympathies so often led him.

The situation became more hopeful for the cabinet of London
when it was learned that Russia refused to be separated from
England or to be bound by the treaty of Oubril; and as the
arrival of this news coincided with the serious development of
the French quarrel with Prussia, Grenville imagined for a moment
that Napoleon might be cornered into negotiating conjointly
with the courts of London, Berlin and St Petersburg, for a
general pacification of Europe.[1] He pressed the Russians to send
some responsible person to Paris "to treat in the Emperor's
name, but in strict confidence and constant communication with
His Majesty's Government"; failing this he asked that the
Russian ambassador in London should be given the requisite
powers; and, in anticipation, he instructed the minister Lauderdale in Paris to negotiate on behalf of Russia as well as England.[2]

Other powers, however, did not show the disposition to pursue
the possibilities of peace with so much research.[3] Napoleon, true
to his former practices, did everything to amuse and cajole the

[1] *Dropmore Papers*, VIII, 352. Instruction to Lord Morpeth (the minister
despatched to negotiate peace with the court of Berlin), 29 Sept. 1806,
F.O. Prussia, 64/73.
[2] *Dropmore Papers*, VIII, 321–4. Windham to Lauderdale, No. 6, 10 Sept.
1806, *F.O. France*, 27/74.   [3] See above, pp. 34–36.

unimaginative Scotsman with whom he had to treat; he showed
every anxiety for peace with England—and declared that a
speedy settlement would avert the impending war with Prussia[1]
—but he had in view a separate negotiation, an isolated treaty,
with England, and this was what the British government was
determined never to concede. Lauderdale took his stand upon
the ground that a French peace with Russia was a *sine qua non*
of peace with England, that England would not come to terms
unless Russia had been able to do so, and that therefore the
subjects that interested Russia should come up for discussion
first;[2] but Napoleon who was merely playing for time parried
and twisted still, and when finally he allowed the pertinacious
Lauderdale to have his way in the matter, he showed no disposition to grant any of the demands that the Russians had put
forward or to make any appreciable alteration in the treaty that
had been signed by Oubril and rejected by the Czar.[3] The
Russian government, for its own part, was determined to make
no further attempts to renew the negotiation. The Prussians in
the meantime were hurrying into war. It is evident that the
peace discussions in Paris had developed into a game that was
not taken seriously by either party.

Throughout the month of September England showed herself
more and more warlike, more exacting in her demands. If the
discussions were not abandoned until Napoleon had actually left
Paris for the opening of the Prussian campaign, this was because
Lauderdale had determined to throw upon Napoleon all the
blame for the failure of the negotiation. Even after he had
declared his mission at an end he was invited to resume the
conferences, and still replied "that he had no choice in immediately applying for his passports but that so long as he remained

[1] Lauderdale to Earl Spencer, No. 15, 26 Sept. 1806, *F.O. France* 27/74:
Champagny "said he was charged by the Emperor to say that if I would
arrange a peace within a week the war with Prussia that was likely to break
out would be prevented and that measures for a pacific arrangement with
that power should immediately be taken".

[2] Lauderdale to Earl Spencer, No. 16, 26 Sept. 1806, *F.O. France* 27/74,
printed incompletely in *Parliamentary Debates*, VIII, cols. 193–5.

[3] Lauderdale to Earl Spencer, No. 16, 26 Sept. 1806, *F.O. France* 27/74,
in *Parliamentary Debates*, VIII, cols. 197–8.

in France he never would refuse to see the French negotiator".[1]
The British cabinet sent out to him successive instructions
between the 10th of September and the 1st of October, raising
the British demands as the turn of events gave England the
advantage in negotiation, but he did not think it necessary to
make use of these since the conversations were breaking down
already upon questions that concerned Russia. "I have given
the negotiations as much as possible the appearance of going off
on Russian objects," he wrote, "for the purpose...of binding
Russia more closely."[2] The English people were anxious for his
return and looked for it daily. When late in August the news
had come to them that an expedition under Sir Home Popham
had captured Buenos Ayres by a free-lance effort, and a manifesto addressed by that general to the trading corporations of
the country had kindled excitement and sent a fever of speculation running through the land, till even at the foreign office
the hope had gained ground that very soon the whole of the
Spanish colonies in that part of the world might be captured for
England, not only did the government become more exacting
but the people feared lest a peace even on revised terms should
be concluded and the hope was everywhere expressed that
Lauderdale would soon return from Paris.[3] In January 1807
the subject of the whole negotiation came up in parliamentary
debate but the whig ministry had no fear of meeting opposition
on the question of the final rupture. It was rather open to censure
on the ground that it had allowed the protracted discussions for

[1] Lauderdale to Earl Spencer, No. 16, 26 Sept. 1806, *ibid*.

[2] Lauderdale to Grenville (Private), 26 Sept. 1806, in *Dropmore Papers*,
VIII, 358.

[3] Lord Grenville to Lord Lauderdale (Private), 22 Sept. 1806, in *Dropmore
Papers*, VIII, 352: "The capture of Buenos Ayres trumpeted up as it has
been by Popham and his agents, has already produced such an impression
here as will make the surrender of that conquest most extremely difficult,
unless one could get much more for it in the way of security in Europe than
I know how to shape or expect. At all events we are clearly entitled to
include it in our *uti possidetis*, or to ask its full value for it". Lord Grenville
to Howick (Secret), 29 Sept. 1806, *ibid*. VIII, 366–7: "It is impossible not
to believe that rather than see all Spanish America fall into our hands, as
it must now do in twelve months more of war, France would willingly give
up Naples".

peace to obscure the urgency for effective military preparations. "As to the necessity of continuing the war and the propriety of breaking off all negotiation" there was "but one voice."

The Swedish king had his opportunity at this period of showing loyalty to his allies and persistence in hostility to Napoleon, though in his case the decision was not in any sense backed by the suffrages of a nation. He had been an erratic ally to be yoked with. In October 1806 the British government was threatening him with the withdrawal of his subsidies. At the end of the same month the English ambassador at his court reported the unpopularity of his headstrong policy and the unrest that prevailed in Sweden not merely in the lower orders but even among the nobility of the land, and especially in the mercantile classes whose interests were injured by the war. The enmity that Gustavus bore towards France was not based upon the calculation of political interests, but was a personal thing, a romantic hatred for the Corsican, the "Mister Bonaparte", and he counted his kingdom as an instrument, a resource, for the carrying out of his private, personal aims. Misdirected passion, feverish obsessions, morbid mysticism and the play of twisted impulse set Gustavus IV awry, in whatever he undertook. Beneath his sullen, morose exterior he had something volcanic that made him terrible. Proud of his resemblance to Charles XII he hoped to repeat the exploits of his hero. A kind of religious fanaticism cast a shadow over his mind and he loved to brood over the prophecies of Daniel, to discover contemporary history in the Book of Revelation, to gloat over the idea that Napoleon was "the Beast", and to reinforce his crazy politics with the cryptic messages of Scripture. When Napoleon for a time ignored his insults, as though disdaining to punish the Swedes for the ravings of their monarch, Gustavus was said to have purchased busts and pictures of the man, and took melancholy pleasure in wreaking vengeance upon these, as though it eased his passion to kill his foe vicariously. And when he became a poor uncrowned wanderer, with no Napoleon to fight, he turned his unpleasantness upon his queen and diverted his cruelty to her. In 1803 he left his kingdom and was not seen in it for three years; he had taken it into his head to go through Germany calling the courts to follow him in a royalist crusade against France. It is said that some wag posted a placard near the palace gate at Stockholm, offering a reward to the person who could tell the Swedish nation where they might find their king. Equally irresponsible he proved in his relations with his allies, and if they did not please him he would sulk or try to cheat them, and carry on toy wars of his own. It seems to have been his habit to remain inert during a campaign and plunge into action at the very moment his allies had to surrender. Hence he became an incalculable factor, bringing into affairs a fine element of surprise.

At the moment when Napoleon, master of Prussia, resolved to reject any separate peace with Frederick William, and was preparing to push forward to meet the Russians in Poland, he decided to take steps to get rid of this unnecessary enemy in his rear and to induce the Swedish king to abandon his allies; and in the middle of November his minister at Hamburg, Bourrienne, drew the new Swedish chargé d'affaires at that town, M. Netzel, into a discussion that was directed ostensibly to the purpose of ameliorating the lot of Swedish prisoners but in reality to the object of putting forward an overture for peace. The reason for the overture is apparent from the declaration of Bourrienne to Netzel that it was not to be expected, after Napoleon had gained possession of all the Prussian fortresses, "that he should leave Stralsund in his rear". Therefore, "if the king of Sweden would only consent to remain neutral, peace might be concluded". Bourrienne observed to the Swedish minister

that Bonaparte had long remarked the loyalty and noble spirit of the King of Sweden, and that he desired nothing so much as to be at peace with him. That Bonaparte had acted with injustice towards the King of Sweden, but that the Swedish King on his part had to reproach himself on the same score....That no attack had hitherto been made against Pomerania but that His Swedish Majesty was on the point of losing one of his finest provinces; that if he would make peace, the possession of that province should be guaranteed to him with an augmentation of territory to secure its frontier; and that he might consider Napoleon as his friend.

Also, the king must consider that his present allies "in paying him their money only meant to abandon him to his fate".

These arguments might have been convincing to many Swedish people. M. Netzel fell in with them completely. Bourrienne wrote:

> I had good reason to be satisfied with the manner in which M. Netzel received my first overtures. I said nothing to him of the justice of which he was not previously convinced. I saw he understood that his sovereign would have everything to gain by a reconciliation with France, and he told me that all Sweden wanted was peace. Thus encouraged I told him that I was instructed to treat with him....He added...that he would write the same evening to his sovereign.[1]

The Swedish king was asked to recognise the necessity of a prompt decision and a quick reply to this overture. In the meantime the French minister promised to do his utmost to prevent any act of hostility from being committed against the Swedish possessions.

Then, when the news came to Stockholm, more storms and violent outbursts from the volcanic king. Within an hour of the arrival of the overture Gustavus had revealed the whole affair to the English ambassador, and his reply was on the point of departure. M. Netzel had dared to consult what he thought the interests of Sweden, rather than to conduct all things in accordance with the whims of the monarch. He was condemned for his whole course of action. What did he want with talking to this M. Bourrienne at all—about Swedish prisoners or any other matter? The king was amazed that his minister should "so far depart from the positive instructions he had received as to hold any intercourse with the French mission, since the slightest knowledge of his master's sentiments must have suggested to him the impossibility of his approving such a measure".[2] M. Netzel was immediately recalled, and was ordered to make public the reason for his disgrace. A Swedish officer at this time had a skirmish with some of Napoleon's men, and afterwards was told by the French that the affair had been a mistake, since orders had been given for no act of hostility to be allowed against

---

[1] *Mémoires de M. de Bourrienne*, t. VII (1829), p. 225.
[2] Pierrepoint to Howick, No. 97, 18 Nov. 1806, *F.O. Sweden* 73/36.

the Swedes. He was put under arrest for taking notice of the French declaration.[1] The Swedish king's hostility to France was a personal unreasoning hatred of Napoleon; it was not the sort of controversy that could ever be brought to a compromise, or cancelled or smoothed over by any adjustment of interests.

Each of these three allied powers therefore had remained steadfast on the subject of a separate peace with France and in the closing months of the year 1806 had given an example of its determination and good faith. The king of Prussia, however—the monarch who had the most need to give proof of his fidelity— had given fresh cause for uneasiness and doubt to his allies by his persistent and avowed efforts to desert the coalition and come to an arrangement with France after Jena.

The cabinet of St Petersburg had throughout the year complained of the influence of men like Haugwitz and Beyme at the court of Berlin, and had united with the government of England and even that of Austria in an attempt that was seconded by the patriots—men like Stein—in Prussia, to induce the Prussian king to dismiss such ministers. Frederick William had refused to give this guarantee of his intentions. Before the defeat of Jena had made the Prussians forget their allies and think only of saving their country, the Czar had not been entirely confident of his friend; and when he sent Count Tolstoy as his military representative to the Prussian army headquarters, he gave him secret instructions to be on his guard against any treachery. All that had taken place between the two courts, he wrote, "would not suffice to do away with the reasonable distrust which the present composition of the Prussian Cabinet must inspire and which its conduct on occasions still recent has only justified too well".[2]

After the battle of Jena the Russians despaired of the policy of their ally. The Czar was "dismayed" to hear that Lucchesini had been sent to Napoleon on any errand of peace whatsoever. He prophesied the result:

I fear that Napoleon will shew himself moderate and accommodating at first, in order to put himself in a position later to make the

---

[1] Pierrepoint to Howick, No. 98, 23 Nov. 1806, *F.O. Sweden* 73/36.
[2] Alexander to Tolstoy, 27 Sept. 1806 (v.s.) in *Sbornik*, LXXXIX, p. lxxv.

King feel the burden of his oppressive and dangerous friendship. He will certainly not confine himself to demanding provinces from him; he will make a point of drawing him into his system, he will insist on the re-establishment of the Treaty of the 15th of February which in stipulating and guaranteeing the independence of the Ottoman Porte will provide pretexts in advance for a future war with Russia.

If peace were concluded Alexander would attribute it to "enemies of the public cause, playing the game of France in the bosom of the Prussian monarchy". The Prussian ambassador suggested to him that tentative overtures by Lucchesini might lead eventually to a general negotiation for peace in which Russia herself might join; but he brushed the idea aside as he had done when England suggested it in September.

"His Imperial Majesty combatted the idea with warmth" and declared "that he had no confidence in such a negotiation; that besides this he had no motive for subscribing to such a proposition; that France had incited the Ottoman Porte to war against Russia, and that this moment, of all moments, was the least proper for giving a thought to any sort of accommodation."[1]

When the hints of a disposition for a general pacification thrown out in Talleyrand's note of the 16th of November were communicated to St Petersburg the Russian cabinet refused to listen to them.[2] When there was a fear that the Prussians would come to a separate arrangement with France the Czar more than once expressed "the determination not to embarrass the movements of the army by respect for their neutrality". On the 10th of December the British ambassador wrote to his government that "this Court has without hesitation rejected every insinuation brought forward by the Prussian Government urging the expediency of a general negotiation for peace". And at the very end of the year, when things were becoming more desperate, he reported: "The Russian Ministers in the present critical state of affairs fully retain the determination to maintain the contest to the utmost extremity".[3]

[1] Despatch of Goltz, Prussian minister at St Petersburg, 6 Nov. 1806, in Ranke, *Hardenberg*, III, 224–8.

[2] Stuart to Howick, No. 68, 10 Dec. 1806, *F.O. Russia* 65/65.

[3] Stuart to Howick, e.g. No. 57, 28 Nov. 1806, No. 68, 10 Dec. 1806 and No. 76, 29 Dec. 1806, *F.O. Russia* 65/65.

Out of these facts four powers arise, like four shapes looming through a mist. Each has its peculiar countenance as it sets itself to meet France, for each is a personality. So everything is ready for the next scene in this problem of peace, and we have all the elements of what the novelist would call a "situation". Napoleon's overtures for a general negotiation—or rather the hints he gave in that direction—to General Zastrow, in the final interview at Posen on the 6th of December, set the machinery in motion to plot out the next developments. The Prussia described above is the power through which the overture is to be communicated to the coalition, the power whose persuasions are to give it weight, the power for whose interests the whole scheme is to be set working. When it is remembered what place Prussia occupied in the thoughts of her allies, it will be easy to hazard a guess as to the weight that her persuasions will have with them and the solicitude that her interests will awaken in them. When it is remembered, too, that the Russia whose attitude and temper are described above was the closest of all the friends of Prussia, bound to her by the personal friendship of her sovereign as well as by reasons of state, and having every motive for judging her most leniently—and that even she was suspicious and impatient—it will be tempting to prophesy what complexion a fresh overture for general peace will have, coming from Prussia, and what answer the Czar, who refused to listen to Talleyrand's proposal of the 16th of November, will give to the restatement of the overture on the 6th of December. But history defies prophecy and refuses to be worked by mathematics, and, like nature, is full of surprises and incalculable chances; and the fate and adventures of the peace proposal of the 6th of December make a longer story than could have been foreseen.

The story can be tracked down amid the mass of events and issues that make the history of the first six months of 1807; but when this is done, it must be accompanied by a mental reservation, for one can never afford to lose sight of the fact that this is but one tale disentangled from a network of intertwined plots and stories—one thread pulled out of the tapestry of history and put under the microscope. Diplomatic events and developments themselves are an abstraction from universal history, and this question under discussion is but an isolated strand even out of the diplomatic issues of the time. Napoleon was not by any means entirely preoccupied with the question of peace in Europe. He was a military leader and we see him organising armies, calling up recruits, disposing his forces, ordering shoes for his soldiers, arranging the construction of bakeries, busying himself with all the paraphernalia of war. He was a human mortal, and we hear of him enjoying the balls and the brilliant life of Warsaw, adoring the beauty of the Polish ladies, laying siege to the heart of the Countess Walewska, and writing to the Empress to reassure her about his health, or to calm her jealousies or to prevent her from appearing inconveniently in Poland. He was the Emperor, ruling France from the distance, organising propaganda, directing theatres and newspapers, rebuking his chief of police, aiding necessitous manufactures in France, and writing "M. de Champagny, literature ought to be encouraged". Now he looked to the exploitation of Prussia; now he was luring the Poles with vain promises and inciting them to rise against the Russians. Even in diplomacy his hands held the threads of many schemes and purposes. He was arranging a treaty with Turkey, or winning the alliance of Persia, still fingering the idea of the ultimate conquest of India; and constantly he was turning to Austria with bribe or persuasion or menace, trying to win her alliance or to fasten her doubtful neutrality. Only at times— after the battle of Eylau, for example—would he turn aside to write a letter to the king of Prussia, or an instruction to a minister —just as he would turn aside to send a hurried line to the Empress—and in this way would move the problem of peace a step further, and bring a new turn to the negotiations with the coalition.

In the eyes of contemporaries this diplomatic story did not seem to hold the centre of the stage. Few people were in the secret. Napoleon would carry on a correspondence that was kept even from Talleyrand. At one period we find the British cabinet is left wondering, and British ministers abroad merely scent suspicious peace moves. Public opinion in England would catch occasional rumours and indulge in some wild guess-work. The cry would go up that Prussia was betraying the cause and angling for a separate peace. Men would wonder what the Austrians were about. But the subjects of conversation would be the Russian general who was supposed to have sold himself to the French, the latest Russian "victory" that was so unaccountably followed by retreat, the failure of the British fleet to reduce the Turks at Constantinople, the taking of Danzig by the French. The abolition of the slave-trade and the question of Catholic Emancipation and the fall of the "ministry of All the Talents" in March were the great events in English politics. And when the situation was tightest and the fate of Europe was about to be decided, an English correspondent would be writing: "There is no earthly thing talked of but duels and the Yorkshire election".

And away in the east of Europe the French army had crossed the Vistula, and the soldiers did not like it. Were they never to stop until they had reached China? they asked. In Poland they found a flat region of marsh and heath, bog, forest and lake, and rough intractable land; and Napoleon "discovered a new element —mud". In an unhospitable climate and amid hostile inhabitants Napoleon's troops found themselves short of shoes, clothing and food. The thaw was worse than the frost; scarcely anything that could be called a road existed; often the forests made it difficult to deploy large numbers of troops. Communication was difficult, information was hard to get, the guns sank into the mud; "one marched all day to cover three or four leagues"; couriers lost their way—and all this was very far from France. "The dampness of the country...and the frequency of marshes and sluggish streams, choked with the decaying *débris* of the forests" made the land unhealthy and malarious. The French hospitals were filled with fever-stricken soldiers. In front were the Russians, a new kind of enemy. Napoleon, when he mentioned them, would use words like "savage", "barbarian". They were not like other people. To Europe, still, Russia was a legend, a bear; it loomed from the deep darkness of Asia; it spelled hidden, untapped power. The eye lost itself in the mists and snows of the endlessly retreating, uninviting North; a victory that drew the conquerors further into the recesses of that unknown, unexplored desert seemed a grim, unhopeful thing to the French. What did Napoleon want with crossing the Vistula, they asked. Henceforward they were to find that a second Austerlitz was no simple matter. They were to see bitter fighting under conditions that favoured the enemy. They were to be harassed by Cossacks, who seemed something more, and at the same time something less, than human. It appeared that they were to be satisfied with indecisive fights, or half-victories that resulted in retreat. Misery attended them. And in their rear the Austrian armaments loomed, sinister; here was another foe waiting to fall upon Napoleon if he stumbled into disaster.

And yet the rationale of all this, the logic of this muddle and misery, lay in the diplomacy that gave meaning to the fighting and explained what each power was fighting for and determined how long men should go on with the fighting. It is in the diplomatic story which is to be unravelled that the war in Poland can be translated into terms of reason and purpose. What each side sought to win, out of the clash of battle, was, in the last resort, a diplomatic advantage, a "pull" in negotiations. And, since in the year 1807 the outbreak of hostilities did not destroy the thread of negotiation, but kept it moving in unbroken sequence, the diplomatic story is the true index of the fluctuation of fortunes, the real barometer of the war; in a way it is the essential history of the European struggle against Napoleon.

BOOK ONE

THE WINTER CAMPAIGN

CHAPTER I

THE PRUSSIAN PEACE MOVE

FREDERICK WILLIAM OF PRUSSIA, rejecting the armistice of November 1806, threw himself into the arms of the Czar and wrote:

Receive, Sire, my solemn promise that henceforward I will stand unshakable in the resolution I am taking; I shall not sheathe the sword...until your interests, now bound up with mine more indissolubly than ever, induce you yourself to desire it. This is my firm determination.[1]

Haugwitz under these circumstances became an impossible minister. Indeed all the world seemed tired of him, for he had kept the peace at the wrong moments and he had gone to war out of due time. He had advised his master to turn against Russia, all the powers of the coalition were crying out that he should be got rid of, and the Austrians were repeating that his continuance in office was the obstacle to their entry into the war.[2] To the patriots of Prussia and to the allies of Frederick William he had become the symbol of the weakness if not the treachery of the court of Berlin, just as Hardenberg had become the symbol of the vigorous anti-French policy which was desired. So Haugwitz passes out of history.

Stein was offered the vacant post, but he was more intractable than Haugwitz. He saw that the king was unwilling to correct obnoxious principles of government, or destroy the "inordinate secret influence" of men like Beyme; also he looked up to Hardenberg as the man to conduct Prussia through the war. So he made excuses, and pleaded his lack of experience in the conduct of foreign affairs. It did not improve matters that the partisans

---

[1] Frederick William III to Alexander I, 23 Nov. 1806, in P. Bailleu, *Briefwechsel König Friedrich Wilhelm's III und der Königen Luise mit Kaiser Alexander I*, vol. LXXV of the *Publicationen aus den K. Preussischen Staatsarchiven*.

[2] See especially Alexander I to Frederick William III, 18/30 Nov. 1806, in Bailleu, *Briefwechsel*, p. 132.

of reform in Prussia thought to force the king's hand, and procure
the promotion of Stein and Hardenberg. The king, precisely
because he felt so small and was conscious of his weakness and
was sensitive on the subject, resented those who reminded him
of this matter, or attempted to dictate to him; he disliked any
scheme that seemed derogatory to his own royal power. So
Hardenberg was left to sulk and the king allowed Stein to depart,
calling him a "refractory, insolent, obstinate and disobedient
official, who, proud of his genius and talents, far from regarding
the good of the State, guided purely by caprice, acts from passion and from personal hatred and rancour".[1] A Haugwitz was
better than such men; the king fell back upon the old school.
Two military men, Generals Zastrow and Köckeritz, had for years
been his intimate advisers, had been the despair of the coalition
ministers, and had become as hated and feared as Haugwitz.
Zastrow, an old servant of Frederick the Great, succeeded to the
control of foreign affairs, though much against his will. He had
been the recipient of Napoleon's latest intentions on the subject
of peace; he had come from Charlottenburg full of views about
what Napoleon desired from Prussia, and his appointment was
symbolical of the policy his government was about to adopt.
The semi-official British representative in Prussia at the moment
wrote: "The reason for not giving Hardenberg the portefeuille
is at last declared—'With him as Minister every hope of a peace
with France was lost'".

Zastrow came to office determined to take the one opening
which Napoleon had left to Prussia for the conclusion of peace.
The latest French statement on the subject had made it clear
that the Prussian king could not hope to return to Berlin until
both England and Russia had come to terms with the French
empire. This was sufficient cue to start Zastrow on a quest for
the general pacification of Europe, and since the alliance with
Russia was cemented by a very close friendship between
Frederick William and the Czar Alexander, it was obvious that
in St Petersburg the first move had to be made. Zastrow mean-

---

[1] Frederick William III to Stein, 3 Jan. 1807, in Seeley, *Life and Times
of Stein*, I, 305.

time kept in touch with the French government as though no war existed. He communicated to Talleyrand the news of his appointment, and later, of his determination to work for a general negotiation. On the 3rd of January 1807 Talleyrand replied:

His Majesty has seen with great pleasure that there has been called to the direction of affairs a man whom he esteems, whose opinion has been unvaryingly in favour of an alliance between France and Prussia, and who would have wanted to prevent if he could the events of recent times and those which may be to follow. The rapidity of events must make it apparent how important is every minute, and how useful the armistice would have been.

Talleyrand hoped that Zastrow would "neglect nothing to hasten the end of the evils of war".[1] The hint was very pointed. Zastrow, in any case, was not the man to delay. On the 22nd of December he had prepared his messages for St Petersburg, and on the following day Lieutenant-Colonel Krüsemarck, who had been entrusted with one or two previous missions to the Russian government, set out on his errand to persuade the Czar to lend his ear to Napoleon's proposals of December.

Krüsemarck carried a letter from the king to the Czar, with which was enclosed a précis of Zastrow's last conversation with Napoleon. The letter asked "if the peace proposals thrown out by the French emperor were not worth serious attention?" At the same time it protested vigorously that the king would not separate his cause from that of Russia—as though the key to the whole transaction had not been that Napoleon had repulsed all his attempts to separate his cause from that of the coalition. The arguments of this letter, combined with Krüsemarck's instructions, painted a grim picture of the immediate danger Prussia was in through an enforced retreat of the Russian armies, and the sad situation of the king who was compelled now to think of taking refuge in a foreign country. Napoleon had even threatened to dethrone the reigning house of Prussia if he defeated the Russians. The Czar was reminded that he had failed to win Denmark and Austria to his cause, and that without the

[1] In Ranke, *Hardenberg*, III, 273–4.

aid of Austria the hope of success in warfare diminished, so that the only way to prevent Napoleon from spreading more evil throughout the continent seemed to be to disarm him by a general pacification. Napoleon himself had given the opening for such a measure, and the Czar was made to see that by accepting the proposal he in no way compromised his dignity; Napoleon had taken the first step. Such an attempt to make peace would not by any means prejudice military operations. It was true that Alexander had regarded Talleyrand's overtures of the 16th of November as inadmissible, but this was a fresh offer, and it would be futile to close the door against all accommodation. Above all this new move of Napoleon's implied a concession on his part that it had been hitherto impossible to secure from him, and contained a surrender on a point for which he had always stood out in negotiations, though it had wrecked all previous attempts at peace. If the restoration of Prussia was to depend upon the sacrifices England was prepared to make, there would have to be a combined negotiation, a congress. This offer by Napoleon represented such an advance upon his former determinations—his insistence upon separate transactions with each power—that the opportunity ought not to be missed. The Prussian king, in his distress, therefore, hoped that the friendship the Czar bore towards him would dispose him to make sacrifices compatible with the interests of his monarchy for the purpose of arriving at a settlement. Napoleon demanded free navigation in all waters, the recovery of the colonies that England had captured, and the guarantee of the independence of Turkey and of the rights of that power over Moldavia and Wallachia; the restoration of Prussia was to depend upon the satisfactory arrangement of all these matters. What was asked was that the Czar should send a plenipotentiary to the French headquarters, and use his influence at the court of London to make England do the same.[1]

---

[1] Frederick William III to Alexander I, 22 Dec. 1806, in Ranke, *Hardenberg*, III, 257. Extracts from Krüsemarck's instructions and from the documents he carried, *ibid*. v, 418. Précis of military memorandum of Zastrow, showing the difficulty of defeating the French, *ibid*. v, 421.

On the 3rd of January Krüsemarck arrived at St Petersburg and on the 6th he had an audience of the chancellor Budberg. On the following morning the purpose of his mission was communicated to the British ambassador, together with the reasons "why it is impossible to listen to the present overture from the King of Prussia". The Russian court "is not averse to conciliation but can only listen to propositions brought forward immediately by France".[1]

Up to this point, then, everything has answered to expectations. The overture is made and Prussian persuasions seek to render it effective; but it comes from the wrong quarter; the recent history of Prussia, her repetition of attempts at peace, the fact that this proposal is merely the last of a series of overtures conveyed to St Petersburg, disqualify this power from fulfilling the rôle of intermediary in the present circumstances. The overture must come direct from France to gain validity. All this lies within the realm of predictable events, and is according to timetable. But within a few days the train leaves the rails and takes an uncharted course. The persevering Krüsemarck makes this possible, for he refuses to abandon the object of his mission, and combines his efforts with those of the Prussian ambassador at St Petersburg till he is rewarded with a different answer.

Ten days after the chancellor Budberg had explained to the English minister "why it was impossible to listen to the present overture from the king of Prussia" he held another conference with Stuart, who reported:

Although in the course of this interview the General constantly referred to his former language...it was not difficult to observe from his discourse the effect of a material alteration in the sentiments and decision of the Emperor upon the subject of the negotiation for peace projected and proposed by Bonaparte.

Budberg declared that his government, though determined to bring forward no overture to Bonaparte, was anxious

to show a conciliatory disposition...and try to ascertain on what grounds the French Cabinet is willing to treat, by requesting the

[1] Stuart to Howick, No. 4, 7 Jan. 1807, *F.O. Russia* 65/67.

Prussian Court, on Krüsemarck's return to Memel, to sound the French Government and learn whatever particulars can possibly throw light on the views of that power with respect to a general peace.[1]

The Russian reply to Krüsemarck's proposals is contained in a note from Budberg to Krüsemarck and the Prussian ambassador, dated the 3rd (15th) of January, and declaring:

The Emperor will...be disposed to enter into negotiation with the French Government to discuss the means of putting an end to the present war, and will invite the British Government also to take part in it. His Imperial Majesty knows too well the principles which govern the Cabinet of St James to be able to doubt of its adhesion to the proposed negotiation as soon as it can take place in a way honourable to the allied powers. But as it would be perfectly useless to set such a negotiation on foot if it did not promise up to a certain point the results that one has a right to expect from it, the Emperor desires first of all to know the basis upon which the French government proposes to treat; and as the seat of the negotiation could not be a matter of indifference by reason of the influence which one of the two parties might bring to bear upon the negotiation in consequence of the position of the respective armies, His Imperial Majesty would at the same time like a place to be selected for the negotiation in a neutral country, Galicia for example. These two points granted, the Emperor would ...gladly accept any equitable arrangement in conformity with the overtures that have just been made by His Majesty, the King of Prussia.[2]

In a letter to Frederick William, the Czar wrote: "Your Majesty will recognise, I hope, in all this, my desire to outdo your own efforts, provided only that it is compatible with my duty to my country".[3]

This is a surprising change of temper in the Czar who, riding upon the wings of rhetoric, had so recently proclaimed the emancipation of Europe.

[1] Stuart to Howick, No. 10, 17 Jan. 1807, *F.O. Russia* 65/67. Enclosed in this despatch is the note addressed to the Russian chancellor by the two Prussian ministers on 1/13 Jan. 1807, and Budberg's reply of 3/15 Jan. 1807 (mentioned below).

[2] Ranke, *Hardenberg*, v, 426.

[3] Alexander I to Frederick William III, 6/18 Jan. 1807, in Bailleu, *Briefwechsel*, p. 144. This letter was accompanied by a more formal one which was meant for the eyes of Napoleon, *ibid.* 146.

On the 28th of January Zastrow communicated to Talleyrand the reply of the Czar to the messages of Krüsemarck. Russia, he said, "desires only to know the basis upon which France wishes to treat, and she leaves to you the choice of the seat of negotiation providing only that it is established in a neutral country"; and he added that Lublin in Galicia was a likely place for a congress.[1]

Talleyrand, forwarding this to his master on the 3rd of February, commented that the reply of Russia to the overture "seemed at first glance to offer more obstacles than facilities...". But he concluded: "After all, the dispositions of Russia depend upon events, and events depend upon Your Majesty".[2] From this it appears that the movement for a general negotiation for peace has gone far enough for the present, and the French government is disposed to let it rest for a time and to wait for the chances of war to determine the next step. These are Talleyrand's words, of course, but Talleyrand is only divining the intentions of Napoleon; and there is no doubt that in this case, at least, he judged them correctly.

It was upon what Talleyrand called "events" that the entire diplomacy lay dangerously and delicately poised; for the movements of the whole negotiation registered the rise and fall of military or political happening. And what Talleyrand neatly called "events" had already broken in upon the course of the diplomatic discussions. The Russians had entered the war shouting, and their shouting had made them brave, but now their tone had lowered and their mood was somewhat chastened. The Czar, who had struck a masterly attitude in December, and had repulsed all thought of peace, was now warming to a more benevolent temper towards France, and was willing to think of sending a diplomat to a congress. He was ready to listen to an overture from Prussia which he had rejected but a week before. It seemed unaccountable to observers—this sudden softening of heart; but there was a factor behind it, for "events" were

[1] Ranke, *Hardenberg*, III, 276.
[2] Talleyrand to Napoleon, 3 Feb. 1807, in P. Bertrand, *Lettres inédites de Talleyrand à Napoléon*, No. CCXXII.

pressing home. The wild romanticisms of the Czar were coming to shipwreck once more upon grave inescapable realities. And many things had forced themselves into the picture to qualify the first ardour of his crusading.

At the end of the old year the Russians claimed to have won a victory at Pultusk; but even if they had just basis for the assertion, it was a victory followed by retreat. Napoleon might have met disappointment here, but there was nothing to make the Russians proud, no glory of pursuit, no reaping of the fruits of success. The inadequacy of Russian generalship, the quarrels and outbursts of peevishness among the Russian leaders, cancelled all that could be boasted of in the bravery of the troops, and produced everywhere a lack of faith in that army from which so much had been hoped. The Czar received a letter from Tolstoy, his representative at the Prussian army, full of complaints about the lack of discipline on all sides, and the worthlessness of the officers, and the weakness even of Bennigsen; and at this sorry story the man seemed overfaced. Replied the Czar, "Who else is there? Where is that man among us who enjoys the general confidence and at the same time combines military talents with the severity that is necessary for command? For my part I do not know him...." There seemed no remedy for the evils, and the prospect appeared not likely to be an improving one, so the Czar could only talk despairingly and bewail the "indescribable difficulties of the situation". This, in a letter to Tolstoy, at the very time when he was considering the peace proposals of Prussia.[1]

Another dismal story had recently come from Vienna telling of the failure of the final effort to persuade the Austrians to join the coalition. In the confident days before the news of Jena had arrived the Czar had been pleased to see Austria declare herself neutral, had regarded it as a happy thing that the court of Vienna had not actually joined the French.[2]   But when the

---

[1] Alexander I to Tolstoy, 3 Jan. 1807 (v.s.) in *Sbornik*, LXXXIX, p. lxxvi.
[2] Budberg to Nicolai, 9/21 Oct. 1806, No. 3, *F.O. Russia* 65/66; see also Stuart to Fox, No. 28, 30 Sept. 1806, *F.O. Russia* 65/64, for an account of the Czar's fear lest Austria should be unable to avoid an alliance with France.

Prussian disaster was announced, and more particularly when it was seen that Haugwitz still retained office and was making overtures for peace with France—doing everything, in fact, to prove that Prussia could no longer be counted upon, or trusted as an ally—the Russian minister saw that his country could not bear the whole burden of the war and declared "that this Court must now look with some degree of anxiety to Austria for support". There was no question, as yet, of inciting or luring the Austrians into the contest. "If Austria intends to act she must of her own accord come forward for self-defence and...the impulse of circumstances will more strongly shew the expediency of a measure so necessary for her situation, than the suggestion of a Foreign Power."[1] This was on the 17th of November. Two days later the situation seemed still more urgent, but even yet Budberg was proud and unbending. "It does not become the dignity of the Court of St Petersburg", he said, "to solicit the assistance of Austria"; and he thought that propositions for combined action against France should come rather from Vienna. It was Stuart, the British chargé d'affaires, who persuaded him that "circumstances imperiously demanded a mutual immediate explanation upon all the points at issue, and a speedy concert of measures necessary to check the advance of France in Poland"; and as a result of Stuart's persuasions, small scruples of pride and petty resentment were swept aside, and Pozzo di Borgo was sent to Vienna to press the Austrians to immediate action.[2] The middle of January saw the final failure of this mission,[3] and left no hope that Austria would bring early assistance in Poland: Napoleon's armies, at least for a time, found fresh security as a result.

When Stuart was informed that the Russians had given way to the arguments and suggestions of Prussia, he saw something

---

[1] Stuart to Howick, No. 52, 17 Nov. 1806, *F.O. Russia* 65/65.

[2] Stuart to Howick, No. 56, 19 Nov. 1806, *F.O. Russia* 65/65.

[3] Stuart to Howick, No. 7, 14 Jan. 1806, *F.O. Russia* 65/67: "From the moment the negotiation has been brought to bear upon the real question of peace or war the Court of Vienna has studiously avoided all appearances favourable to Russia"; see also below, pp. 114 ff.

of the connection of events, and divined the reason for the willingness of Russia to listen to discussions of peace.

I said that I feared the answer lately received from Vienna had in some measure influenced the determination of this Government. His Excellency [General Budberg] would not admit the justice of the observation, though he owned that after such a proof of ill-will on the part of Austria, his hopes of checking the progress of France must be proportionately diminished.[1]

The whole effort to create a northern confederation, and to draw powers like Austria and Denmark into the war against France, was unsuccessful.[2] Prussia had become a mere passenger in the coalition, not an effective force. England had displeased the Russian court by her slowness in arriving at an arrangement with Prussia and by her persistence in making the old quarrel of Hanover the obstacle to a real combination.[3] The Czar was beginning to resent the burden and to show his irritation with the difficulties of a war the brunt of which he felt he had to bear alone. At the same time there was a peace party in Russia; Prince Czartoryski "repeatedly presented to His Imperial Majesty memorials setting forth the expediency of an immediate peace with France"; in December he was declaring "that there (was) not a moment to be lost"; in the middle of January he was "pursuing his system steadily".[4] The proposals of Prussia,

[1] Stuart to Howick, No. 10, 17 Jan. 1807, *F.O. Russia* 65/67.

[2] The idea of forming a Northern League against France was put forward by the British government as a measure that would be much less objectionable than the Prussian scheme of a Confederation of North Germany (mentioned above, p. 12). It was hoped that "Great Britain, Russia, Denmark, Sweden and the independent states of Saxony, Hanover, and Hesse (would) be members, and Prussia (should) be not a superior or a protector but an equal" (Instructions from the British foreign office to Stuart, No. 6, Sept. 1806, *F.O. Russia* 65/64, and No. 8, 14 Nov. 1806, *F.O. Russia* 65/65). For Russian disappointment at the failure of the attempts to induce the northern powers to join the coalition, see Stuart to Howick, No. 61, 28 Nov. 1806, No. 72, 18 Dec. 1806, and No. 76, 29 Dec. 1806, *F.O. Russia* 65/65.

[3] On 11 June, 1806, England had declared war on Prussia because of the Prussian occupation of Hanover.

[4] Stuart to Howick, No. 79 (Secret and Confidential), 29 Dec. 1806, *F.O. Russia* 65/65, and No. 10, 17 Jan. 1807, *F.O. Russia* 65/67. See also Prince Adam Czartoryski, *Mémoires et correspondance avec l'Empereur Alexandre Ier*, II, 163–78.

therefore, were most opportune. Many things had happened to make them more acceptable than would have been guessed. Everything had combined to weaken the former uncompromising intentions of the Czar. In this way, in these middle days of January, there came the first stage of that process of disillusionment and conversion in Alexander that was to be consummated at Tilsit.

*   *   *   *

But if the Russians had been arrested by the gravity of things, and sobered by the thud and pressure of hard insistent realities, the next turn of the wheel, the next unrolling of "events", came as a kind of see-saw and made Napoleon himself more amenable. A battle on the 8th of February astonished Europe by its grimness, and drew lamentations from Napoleon, and stood out as one of the fiercest and most costly engagements of the age. At Eylau each side claimed a victory, but each withdrew when the fighting was over; and the campaign seemed to freeze up for a time while both armies slunk back into winter quarters. The French failed in what they were trying to do, and experienced all the anguish of defeat. The whole setting amid frosts and blinding snows, and the psychological conditions of the warfare, were of a most depressing kind, and had a particularly noticeable effect upon Napoleon. Immediately after the battle, at two o'clock in the morning, he took up the talk of peace. Tired out as he was he sent "just a word" to Talleyrand:

As to the communication which the Prussian King has made I think it may be answered in this way; say that I accept the overtures made for putting an end to the war; that far from raising any kind of difficulty concerning the place, the most natural place seems to me to be the intermediate one; that I propose Memel even; and that I will send plenipotentiaries there as soon as I am informed that Prussia and Russia have nominated theirs.[1]

So in the early days of February all parties have had time to be weary of the wasting wintry war in Poland, and all are finding it useful to talk of negotiations for peace. At last there

[1] *Corresp. de Nap. Ier*, t. xiv, No. 11,786.

has been wrung from Napoleon an explicit offer to send pleni-potentiaries to a congress. It is to be noticed that there is no mention of England, though Napoleon had brought up this idea of a general negotiation in order to fasten England, in order to hold her to a system of "compensations" and so secure the restoration of the colonies she had won from him on the sea. But in the difficult days after Eylau the ulterior problem of peace with England is less important than the predicament of the moment. It is a matter of far greater urgency to make some arrangement with Prussia and Russia, or at least to institute some parley that will give time for reinforcements to arrive. So Napoleon will send ministers to Memel as soon as the Prussians and Russians have named theirs; for his difficulties are immediate ones; he is seeking extrication.

CHAPTER II

NAPOLEON'S DIFFICULTIES AND HIS SEPARATE OVERTURES TO PRUSSIA

I T was said that the French troops marching into Poland, tramped to a satirical song which ran

> We go in search of a Kingdom
> For little brother Jerome.[1]

The fortunes of the ensuing campaign were not such as to make these soldiers change their tune. In the thaw that set in after Pultusk, observers and reconnoitring parties of both sides would remain clamped in the mud in sight of one another—symbol of the kind of helplessness in which the fighting had to be carried on. All through the month of January the reports of commanding officers told of hunger and hardship and disease that imperilled the French troops. The daily incidents of a soldier's life—the supplying of food, the marching across country, the sleeping, the pillaging and all the long weariness of winter waiting—now began to appear as things depressing and sinister. Difficulties and privations multiplied themselves for these French soldiers, far as they were from their country, and with lengthy lines of communication. And war that had been so glorious suddenly seemed insane.[2] "I see nothing for it but to die of hunger if we stay here two days", complains one general. "Send bread", is the cry of another who finds his troops falling ill through bad food and inclement weather. "The troops lack everything", wrote a third. Soult reported that his troopers had to tear thatch from the houses in order to have anything to give to the horses.[3] And another general declared: "It is evident that

---

[1] *Souvenirs du Baron de Barante*, I (1890), 175. See also *ibid.* I, 216: "Quant aux militaires leur mécontentement s'exprimait par des bons mots, avec le verve épigrammatique propre au soldat français et qui semble le préserver du découragement".

[2] See the Correspondence of the French Archives de la Guerre printed by Foucart, *Campagne de Pologne*, II (1882), *passim*.

[3] Foucart, *op. cit.* II, 128.

our soldiers have almost all a bad colour, that they are thin,
especially the older ones and the conscripts, and that anyone
who saw them in France or Bavaria a year ago, would not
recognise them to-day".[1] As they advanced they would find
houses forsaken, often pillaged already; they would come upon
villages abandoned;[2] they would find that the Russians in retreating had destroyed everything they had been unable to
carry away. After Eylau, Napoleon knew the strength of the
enemy he had to fight in a region where even the elements were
against him. His bulletins fell into an elegiac tone and this man
of countless battles began to sing the horrors of war.[3] The
"legend" of the Corsican seemed broken, and one caught a
picture of a career that was not all facile Ulms and Jenas. "It
was leaving Berlin that was the mistake", said Daru. And
Murat, a few days after Eylau, wrote despairingly to Napoleon:
"Sire, it is time that Your Majesty did something. We are here
absolutely without resources. I do not think it is possible for us
to remain forty-eight hours longer in this position, because of
our lack of provisions, and for many other reasons".[4]

The patriots of Poland had been shy of throwing themselves
in fine surrender into the war against Russia. They would not
at the call of Napoleon, and without guarantees from him, rise
up in blind quixotic passion to aid the French armies by their
insurrection. And now after Eylau the question had to be asked
again, "What will the Austrians do?" They were still arming
in the rear, and could bring new disaster to Napoleon if they
chose to come out of their neutrality. "Ah, if only I were the
Archduke Charles!" exclaimed Jomini. These Austrians were
by no means friendly at heart; their only hesitation would be
the doubt that their hour had not yet come; they were waiting
till the French should be in unmistakable straits. Napoleon
himself in after days confessed that their intervention would at

---

[1] Foucart, *op. cit.* ii, 215.   [2] *Ibid.* ii, 150, 153.

[3] E.g. *Corresp. de Nap. I*er, t. xiv, No. 11,796, Bulletin No. 58, where
Napoleon speaks of "les trophées trop chèrement payés sans doute par le
sang de tant de braves".

[4] Murat to Napoleon, 14 Feb. 1807, *Lettres et documents pour servir à
l'histoire de Joachim Murat*, v (1911), 122.

this moment have had something decisive in it, and the Austrian government came to see that in failing to join the allies it had missed its opportunity. On the morrow of Eylau, while the final decision of the Austrians was still pending, still anxiously looked for, the situation of the French was urgent and insecure.

This was not the time to think of wresting conquered colonies from England, or holding up discussions until the arrangement of a general congress. Napoleon's next move was a suspension of his large design; he dropped for the moment the idea of using Prussia as a factor in a large scheme of "compensations". This policy he exchanged for something more immediate, more adapted to the pressing moment. He made a series of attempts to win Prussia from the coalition, and lure her into a separate peace. Some negotiations now come in parenthesis; all that has gone before is held in the air for the moment: it is only after the failure of the attempt to isolate Prussia that the threads of the former policy are picked up again and the plans for a congress renewed.

And if the pride of Napoleon and of the Czar had been chastened by the weariness of the fighting, the Prussian king and his court, who had never felt hearts beat high for this warfare, were not likely to stand on ceremony in their efforts to put an end to the miseries. The wretched journeys that had been forced on them after Jena—the flight, that so often had to be resumed as a new wave of the French invaders caught up—had continued into the new year, till the Prussians felt themselves hover dizzily on the last ridge of their dominions, not knowing from day to day whether the wandering had come to an end. They had been driven from Graudenz on the 15th of November by the "alarm of the French having arrived nearly opposite the town, on the other side of the Vistula". At Osterode a week later they had refused to ratify the armistice which their plenipotentiaries had signed. Then we catch sight of them at Ortelsburg, wondering where they can find a residence in case they have to retire into Russia. Here the queen had

literally only a small, scantily furnished room, on the ground-floor of one of the wretched barns they call houses, which one can hardly step out of without getting up to the ankles in mud....The King takes a morning walk while their room, which like our own serves for sitting and bedroom, is arranged for their Majesties' breakfast.

Uncomfortable, harassed with illness, they finished December at Königsberg, "a large and dirty city, affording only very bad accommodation".

"Every apartment, however mean," wrote one of the King's entourage, "is crowded with noble fugitives, and the streets are all bustle: but everything is packed up, and the royal party are prepared for more distant flight.... I cannot help laughing when I look round the room in which I am writing, and think on the royal company I am keeping. Such a pigsty as our apartment cannot be described."

People were beginning to lose faith in the Russians who had boasted that they would bring deliverance; they waved handkerchiefs for Pultusk on the last day of the old year, but the morrow presented them with the sad realisation that they had shown their joy too soon; and in the early days of January the journeying began again. For three days in the wild northern winter, a queen ill with fever had her bed improvised in a coach, and travelled over sheets of snow and ice, sometimes almost within reach of the roaring sea-waves, till she had covered a hundred and fifty miles. The first night she spent on the way was under a roof that allowed the snowflakes to tumble upon her bed. And others who did this journey have described the confusion that came upon them—disarray of carriages waiting for room to pass, crowds of anxious people bustling to find shelter, and all amid the play of wintry weather and the din of wild sea-storms. This brought the party to Memel, the last resting-place they could have in Prussia; it was wondered if the Russians could save them; and still no one could settle down comfortably with any assurance that the wandering was at an end.

Life for that court in exile breathed no high expectancy. There was patience and resignation but no spirit for the war. On the entrance into Memel, it is true, hope had picked up again, as the sun burst out to greet the refugees and the weather began to be kind. Memel, a small clean town, with pretty houses and a pleasant sea-shore, proved a quiet, welcome shelter, where good quarters were not hard to discover. But the queen, though recovering from her illness, was plunged into deep depression as the slanders published by Napoleon overtook her. The king was a poor passenger in the place, himself part of the burden of things; was indeed "prostrate in mind and body". Even the royal family had difficulty in getting good food at times, and perhaps this helped to cause the recurring illnesses that gave so much anxiety. There was some society at Memel, and constantly new faces appeared. Besides the relatives of the king and their attendants there were many military officers who made frequent resort to the town; also a number of government servants who had faithfully followed the royal family into exile; and English, Swedish, and Russian diplomatic missions attached to the Prussian court. Constant influx of wounded soldiers, the landing of foreigners who would disembark at Memel, and the arrival of hosts of refugees, added to the population until sometimes it became difficult to find food. But Haugwitz and Lucchesini had disappeared, they had retired to their estates; and Stein and Hardenberg were gone—had stamped away like offended giants. Only the Zastrows and Beymes were near to handle the problems of politics and meet the emergencies of war.

Dreary, monotonous days there were, and time would often hang heavily; occasionally there would be depression that killed society and forbade entertainment. But life organised itself, and found a ritual for the special conditions, and took on a character of its own. Neighbouring proprietors would send presents of game to their king, and fishermen would do homage "in kind", while countryfolk would come into the town with gifts from farm and dairy. You would drive the queen to the harbour to watch a ship set sail; you would arrange sleighing parties or take tea with the Countess Voss; you would make bandages for the wounded. In this world people acted as though sorry for one another, and conspired to forget depression, and by petty occupations teased the mind out of its black broodings. Little personal touches seemed to make up the sum of life. Members of the English mission appear to have brought some liveliness into

the circle at Memel. There was George Jackson, who had shared
the successive flights and wanderings, and who in his pedestrian
way has left a record of all these days telling of how he fell ill
with the bad water at Ortelsburg, how at another place there was
nowhere to sleep save on a bed improvised from straw and
articles of clothing spread on a filthy floor, and how for some
time five men lived and slept in one room with an inadequate
supply of food. There was Lord Gower, "a handsome minor",
who played the gallant to the Countess Voss and gave her
"twelve pairs of beautiful English silk stockings". There was
Sir Robert Wilson, a stagey but irrepressible figure, a man full
of excitement, passing on his enthusiasm to all around. He would
give the queen a copy of his book on Egypt, and send wine and
tea to the Countess Voss; he would play charming chevalier to
them both; but he would desert them at times, for he was in
love with the bright eyes of danger and you could not hold him
if there were hope of a battle. Lord Hutchinson was at the head
of the party, but he had an unpleasant way with him, and he
was a shaggy-looking creature. He would talk of the greatness of
Napoleon, and pooh-pooh the hopes of victory, and shake his
head in an unbelieving way if the Russians sent good news. So
the clock beat out the solemn days. You would laugh when the
sun was shining, but it was a pathetic kind of laughing. You
toyed with trivialities and made yourself a world of little things;
it was a mere flight from the big inescapable preoccupation. You
would make jest over a tea-cup with the Countess Voss; only she,
when she found herself alone, would turn aside to her diary, and
write with vagrant touches of sadness. The whole was a kind of
stage-play, as though one danced on the edge of the abyss. And
the king—for his part, he would not dance; he had no escape
from the burden of things. You looked on him with a sort of
pity, awkward, unattractive as he was. He revolved his sad
misfortunes, and talked of sending the queen and royal children
to Riga. On the eve of Eylau it seemed that Napoleon was
pressing in. If he won the battle of Eylau he would keep his
promise to be in Königsberg on the morrow. To this king, to
this circle of luckless refugees Napoleon came now, with heavy
temptation. He offered them separate peace, and beguiled them

with words that had a lilt of former days. And the cabinet that
had to weigh and ponder his proposals, was one of which Stein
wrote soon after the battle of Eylau: " I expect nothing from the
ingredients of the Court of Memel—it is a soulless, meaningless
combination, capable of nothing but corrupt fermentation...
For myself I look for nothing from empty, slow, flat people".[1]

In the middle of January Zastrow was thinking hard, clearing
up in his mind the question of the rôle and policy of Prussia,
and formulating the situation with greater precision and em-
phasis. Haugwitz after Jena had found it useful to ask the Czar
to participate in the arrangement he was trying to make with
France. And when Napoleon had defined his policy in November,
demanding a general negotiation, Haugwitz, as was natural, had
communicated this to Russia. Now, in the middle of January
Krüsemarck was at St Petersburg, transmitting the final propositions concerning peace that Napoleon had made to Zastrow.
But in each of these contingencies the Prussians had come to a
separate decision, had sought to meet only the problem of the
moment, had taken the course that occasion put before them.
Zastrow, hammering out his problems at Memel, ran all these
into a policy. Napoleon—it was now taken for granted—would
not negotiate separately with Prussia. It had also become
obvious that the Russians were in difficulties in Poland. Zastrow
was dissatisfied with things. Lesseps, the French consul, passing
through Memel on his way home from St Petersburg, had two
interviews with the minister who expressed "the strongest desire
for peace and seemed pained at the fact that the fate of Prussia
had been bound up with that of Russia".[2] Zastrow remarked
to a British representative at Memel that it would have been
better for the Czar to tell the Prussians "to save themselves as
best they could", than to promise assistance that he was unable
to give; he came to the conclusion that the inadequacy of the
Russian efforts in Poland, and the refusal of Austria to combine
her forces in the struggle against France, and the slowness of
England to come to the help of Prussia, produced a military
situation that gave reason for alarm; he decided "that there

[1] Seeley, *Life and Times of Stein*, I, 312.
[2] P. Bertrand, *Lettres inédites de Talleyrand à Napoléon*, No. ccxxxiv.

would be nothing to gain and everything to lose by the continuation of the war"; and from all this he showed, in a Note on
the Situation of Affairs, dated the 16th of January, that the best
thing the king could do for his people would be "to secure a solid
and durable peace as quickly as possible", though he must do
it "with the greatest delicacy and circumspection" in order to
avoid offending his allies.[1] The Prussian desire for a general
peace, therefore, was not from now the event of a moment, the
result of a particular conjuncture, a separate act, a separate
decision each time; it became an attitude. In future it was a rôle
consciously adopted, a principle deliberately worked out. It was
the whole policy of Zastrow. Prussia took the cue from Napoleon
and found her place in his diplomatic system. In the heart of the
coalition and bound up with its fate she took the line that he
marked out for her, and she still played his game. Lord Hutchinson who arrived at the Prussian headquarters in December
as the official representative of the court of London, warned
General Zastrow that it was not the intention of England and
Russia to negotiate with France. "I thought it necessary to
make this declaration as I have long perceived that they flatter
themselves with hopes that England would not only negotiate
but that she was willing to make great sacrifices to extricate
Prussia out of her present difficulties."[2]

The first of Napoleon's separate overtures to Prussia was
transmitted even before the battle of Eylau. A letter of the
29th of January, direct from Talleyrand to Zastrow, put a pistol
to the head of the Prussian king, by proposing an immediate
treaty of peace and alliance between the two nations, with the
object of guaranteeing the integrity of the Ottoman Porte—and
offering the very plain threat that, if the alliance did not take
place, the next step in the execution of Napoleon's plans would
mean the dethronement of the house of Brandenburg for ever.
"Time presses", the letter said. Napoleon's own situation, it was,
that was pressing. Also he was going to rush the Prussian government, and carry his object by storm. Always, too, there was this

---

[1] Bailleu, *Preussen und Frankreich*, II, 584–6.
[2] Hutchinson to Howick, No. 6, 9 Jan. 1807, *F.O. Prussia* 64/74.

insistence upon "the integrity of the Ottoman Porte"; Prussia was to be tricked into fighting against Russia.[1] But this overture was despatched before Zastrow's note communicating the Russian acceptance of a congress had reached Talleyrand, and the two messages crossed on the way. The acceptance of a general congress was sufficient answer to the proposal for a separate peace, so the Prussians sent no reply to the latter, and Napoleon, by subsequently concurring in the idea of a general negotiation and offering after Eylau to send plenipotentiaries to Memel, withdrew to his former ground.

A few days after Napoleon had expressed his intention of sending plenipotentiaries to a congress he tacked again, resuming the attempt to draw Prussia into peace and alliance with France, repeating it in a more acceptable, more enticing form, and pressing it home with clever argument, in the overture that was brought to the Prussian king by General Bertrand.

In the Recollections of the Countess Voss the following entry appears on the date of the 16th of February 1807:

A letter from Wilson. He is pleased with the Russians but we are not all so here. A perfectly atrocious French General of the name of Bertrand arrived to-day. Klüx brought him here, and he saw the King for a moment before dinner. In the evening he insisted upon being presented to the Queen, who was as furious with him as I was. He has a repulsive countenance and ventured to say to her that "Napoleon hoped she would use her influence to hasten the conclusion of peace and hoped also that she would not keep up any unjust prejudice against him". The Queen answered him, with the greatest mildness and dignity "that women had no voice in war and peace". We were horrified at his manner and his whole proceedings....

General Bertrand had appeared at the Russian outposts on the 15th of February. The Russian commander writing to inform the Prussian king of his arrival, conjectured that his mission might have reference to the demand of an armistice by the French, and urged the Prussian king to give no thought to such a proposition. The very suggestion of the step by Napoleon

[1] Talleyrand to Zastrow, 29 Jan. 1807, in Lefèbvre, *Histoire des Cabinets*, III, 63–4. This proposal was communicated to the Czar (Douglas to Howick, No. 9, 28 Feb. 1807, *F.O. Russia* 65/68).

would be a confession of failure, thought the general, and therefore could only be an additional reason for the vigorous pursuit
of the war.[1]

Bertrand came with a proposal of peace, based on the idea
that Napoleon must have a barrier between France and Russia
—either the house of Brandenburg or some other—and that this
power must be friendly to France. If the Prussian house was to
be restored this must be under conditions that would make it
recognise that it owed its renewed existence to the will of
Napoleon; and the idea of using the good offices of Russia for
the restoration of the Brandenburg family was for this reason
inadmissible. It would be inconvenient if the Prussians became
bound to the Czar by gratitude and passed into a state of
vassalage to him. So the very thing which Napoleon had insisted upon as the condition of peace in December 1806 became
in the following February the very thing which he looked upon
—or pretended for the moment to look upon—as the disqualifi-
cation.

This argument was driven home by a score of incidental
thrusts. Russia herself, it was hinted, was slow to come to the
help of her ally—and some of the remarks and writings of
General Zastrow and others show that this reasoning would find
sympathetic ears in Prussia. Napoleon pretended that he was
dissatisfied with the Russian answer to the overture of December
1806 and with the unwillingness of the Czar to use that proposal
for the benefit of Prussia. "Besides", he wrote, "Russia has
nothing to offer in compensation for the re-establishment of the
Prussian house." All this was part of a clever attempt to rob
the Prussian government of the faith it had had in those overtures of December, and in the establishment of a congress.
Napoleon even attacked the idea directly—a congress would
bring endless discussions and delays; and, he said, Prussia would
be the loser by the waste of time, since her provinces would suffer
from the continued absence of administration and government.
He saw that he could not hope to lure Prussia into a separate

[1] Enclosed in a note from Zastrow to Hutchinson, 15 Feb. 1807, *F.O.
Prussia* 64/74.

peace unless he began by frightening her ministers with the assertion that he now considered the other method of negotiating as inadmissible.

Once this was done, the new overture could have its chance; and if M. de Zastrow would either come himself with full powers, or send a person of equal confidence, a peace could be signed immediately and the king would be reinstated in all his possessions up to the Elbe.

But it is significant that while Napoleon declared in unequivocal terms in his instructions to Bertrand that it would be contrary to his interests to see the Prussian kingdom restored by the influence of Russia, he dropped the hint that he would be willing to see the Prussian king reinstated by the generosity of England. "A few distant isles that England might cede", he wrote, "would be nothing compared with the glory that that nation would win if by means of such cessions she could know that it is to her that the House of Prussia owes its restoration." He seems to have feared that, with all his plans for a congress, England would slip from his grasp. Perhaps she would refuse to accept his challenge and would decline to regard the restoration of Prussia as an adequate indemnity for the surrender of her conquests by sea. The cool relations, the traces of suspicion that still existed between England and Prussia gave every sign that if Prussia was to find salvation in any congress it would be by throwing herself more completely than ever into the arms of Russia. Napoleon had no wish to see this.[1]

Bertrand had orders not to commit his promises to writing. The sincerity of Napoleon's offer of peace is doubtful. Beyond all question there was a trap somewhere for Prussia. She was to be a means of extrication from immediate difficulties. Afterwards who shall say what the mercy of Napoleon had in store for her?

On the 16th of February the Prussian king wrote a gracious acknowledgment to Napoleon, without committing himself to any policy, and in the evening he sent Bertrand back to his master with a letter and with a message to the effect that his

[1] *Corresp. de Nap. Ier*, t. XIV, Nos. 11,809 and 11,810.

obligations to Russia compelled him to consult the Czar before coming to a decision.[1] His first thought was to take the course he had contemplated in the autumn of 1806—to secure the assent of the Czar to the conclusion of a separate peace. On the 17th of February the Countess Voss writes: "The King sent for Rüchel, and had a conference with him, Zastrow, and Hardenberg, about the proposals of this Bertrand. God grant that they may not make any advances to Napoleon, nor give in to ill-luck". On the 20th she writes: "Another Conference. The Queen told me she had implored the King to stand firm and not to conclude peace. She was very much pleased with Hardenberg, but the other two are very wavering". There were stout patriots even among the Prussians.

The offended Hardenberg, strangely enough, was called out of his sulks to give his opinion at this moment, when once more Napoleon was asking the Prussians to desert their allies and return to dependence upon France. Hardenberg saw that here was a crisis, he jumped to the danger the king was in, he knew that there was a trap for his country; hence the importunity of his arguments in a memorandum which he wrote on the 19th of February.

He reminded Frederick William that after Jena Napoleon had deluded Prussia with a hope of generous treatment.

Can we doubt that he is deceiving us again? Has he explained himself fully and clearly on the conditions of peace that he proposes? And if he had done so, if the King were able to acquiesce in painful sacrifices, would he keep his word? Would he withdraw his troops? ...Can it be thought that in his treaty of peace he would not insert a clause hostile to England or Russia or Sweden which would straightway compromise us again?

This "so-called peace," he wrote, "even supposing we were to obtain it, which I think is very unlikely," would only be "a truce of very short duration. It would detach us from Russia and...rob us of the last shred of honour. Prussia, crossed off the list of independent Powers, would become the slave of Napoleon, either as a French province under the

[1] Ranke, *Hardenberg*, III, 308.

banner of Napoleon, or, if she opposed the least of his wishes, as the victim of his superior armies".

You might take up the argument of Napoleon and retort that the only alternative would reduce Prussia to dependence upon the Czar. Hardenberg would not flinch—he would say: Accept the fact frankly, "We cannot disguise from ourselves that we are in truth dependent upon Russia". It was useless to expect the Czar to be reconciled to the secession of the Prussians from the coalition; Russia would entertain no proposals which "would give Napoleon the opportunity of turning his best forces against her on the frontier of Turkey or in Italy"; Russia's interests would compel her to continue the fight against France in the north, "and would not the estates of the King be in that case exposed to all the evils of war?" Hardenberg saw that the overture was the result of the precarious military situation of Napoleon, and that Napoleon had made it with the object of gaining a better advantage in his war against Russia. It was not a real wish for peace, for he had refused to make a treaty after Jena and had just thrown overboard the preparations for a congress. It was a conspiracy directed against Russia. So Hardenberg attacked the idea of asking the Czar's permission to accept it—would listen to no talk of throwing upon Russia the obligation of rejecting. He would not consent to leave the decision to St Petersburg at all; to ask this, even, would undermine confidence. He dealt trenchantly with Bertrand's proposals, declared that an overture which offered anything less than a general peace was not to be debated at all, advised the king to reveal the whole affair to the Czar, and urged that Prussia should reconcile herself to a more vigorous prosecution of the war.[1]

Before the full memoir had been communicated to the king, and before he had actually seen all the arguments in writing, the overture was communicated to the Czar, coupled with an avowal of fidelity to Russia but also with the most tactless insinuations in favour of peace. The king begged his friend to give full consideration to Napoleon's offers and pressed him to ask himself if

[1] 19 Feb. 1807; Ranke, *Hardenberg*, v, 432. The whole of this was not communicated to the king until 22 Feb.; *ibid*. III, 315.

he really thought that with the means at his disposal he could hope to restore stability and independence to Europe by any continuance of the war. The difficulty of the military situation was carefully displayed. The improbability of success in the campaign without the help of Austria was insinuated, at a time when there could be little hope that the court of Vienna would join in the war. And "voluminous memoirs" were communicated to show that even if military advantages were gained the dangers that were about to result from an impending scarcity of provisions would place the Russian army in an embarrassing position. Prussia made it very clear that she was anxious for peace; in spite of her protestations of fidelity she did not make it too evident whether she was not anxious also that the Czar should acquiesce in her acceptance of Bertrand's proposals.[1] It seems to have been in regard to this overture, that the Prussian ambassador in St Petersburg reported to his government: "The Baron Budberg was astounded that the proposal was not entirely rejected and that the king should see any point in submitting it to the decision of the Emperor".[2] The British minister to Russia related at the same time that the Czar was dissatisfied with the repeated pacific overtures that were brought to him from the court of Frederick William.[3]

A still worse impression was given by the fact that the Prussian king sent a representative to Napoleon himself—and this the very day after Bertrand had made his proposals. Colonel Kleist was despatched to the French headquarters on the 17th of February. The Countess Voss curtly wrote, "I should not have done this", and she spoke for a proud minority. The mission had to be accounted for, especially to the Russian government; so it was urged that the Russian general had wished to gain time, and that this mission would give him an interval. Kleist, it was explained, was sent

[1] Ranke, *Hardenberg*, v, 430; see also *ibid.* III, 307, 311. Frederick William III to Alexander I, 19 Feb. 1807, in Bailleu, *Briefwechsel*, p. 147.

[2] Despatch of Goltz (undated, but printed along with other Russian replies to Bertrand's proposals, and referring to these or to Napoleon's previous offer of separate peace) in Ranke, *Hardenberg*, III, 335.

[3] Douglas to Howick, No. 10, 6 Mar. 1807, *F.O. Russia* 65/68.

to treat of the exchange of prisoners. He is not furnished with full powers for any other purpose. He has been charged at the same time to tell the Emperor Napoleon that the King has hastened to communicate the overtures of Bertrand to his august Ally, and that if an agreement can be arrived at with Russia the King will come to further explanations with Napoleon.[1]

Perhaps there was an idea that Kleist could obtain first-hand knowledge of the state of the French army. There was certainly no sign of giving Napoleon's offers a straight refusal. In truth the king of Prussia was pleased with this talk of peace after Eylau and wanted to hear more of it.

Kleist has left an account of his reception at the French headquarters. He interviewed the French emperor at Osterode on the 24th of February and the conversation lasted for two hours and a half. Napoleon received the Colonel graciously, but became more cool when he learned that Bertrand's proposals had been transmitted to St Petersburg. He seemed in a state of some excitement, and would break into passionate exclamation, interrupting reasoned discourse with wild menace and braggart defiance, and hurling interjections like rocks at the head of the Prussian officer.

"I must observe to Your Majesty", wrote Kleist, "that he really had the appearance of a man whose mind is greatly disturbed; and it made him distracted and caused him to keep on repeating the same thing. During the contentions which took place, the Emperor told me, among other things, that Your Majesty had a loyal character and that he was making it his duty to restore you to your lands; that he only wished for confidence from Your Majesty, and that he would do anything to please you.... Of the several boastings which he allowed himself to make, the strongest was: that if he could not come to an arrangement with Your Majesty, and if a second victory over the Russians should decide the fate of Europe, he would have to establish at Berlin a system that should be in accordance with his political views; he was ready to make war for ten years more; he was only thirty-seven, and he had grown up under arms and in the midst of affairs."

---

[1] Ranke, *Hardenberg*, v, 432; see also Frederick William III to Bennigsen, *ibid.* III, 311; to Alexander I, 5 Mar. 1807, *ibid.* III, 317; to Napoleon, 17 Feb. 1807, in M. F. von Bassewitz, *Die Kurmark Brandenburg*, I, 385.

This description agrees with all that we know of Napoleon's conduct at moments of disappointment and frustration. It represents the primitive reaction he always made to anything which thwarted him, and shows the kind of self-betrayal into which his volcanic instincts would perpetually entrap him. When in the year 1813, after the retreat from Moscow, the Austrians were preparing to turn against France and to join the Prussians and Russians in rolling back the Napoleonic empire, Metternich, who was in charge of the diplomacy of the court of Vienna, had an interview with Napoleon at Dresden, and found him in the same baffled, disappointed, petulant mood. His account of the conversation bears some resemblance to that of Kleist, though the Prussian is more reticent and concise, and attempts to illustrate the conduct of Napoleon rather than to reproduce the dialogue; also Kleist is not an egoist like Metternich, who recounts his own brilliance in the debate, taking care that he himself shall stand out dignified and dominant in the picture. Napoleon at Dresden advanced "with an affected calmness", but "his features soon darkened". Once more he bragged, and was nervously defiant; he threw his hat in a corner, and said that he did not mind if the powers compelled him to fight; he declared once again: "I have grown up on fields of battle". He showed hot indignation at one moment, and had an injured air at another; there were sudden falls from a high tone of defiance and menace and bravado to a crooning, caressing appeal and a softened persuasiveness; as though some booming wave should rear itself and crash, and then slowly trail itself out in a chastened diminuendo. The interview lasted for nearly nine hours, and Metternich called it "a series of friendly demonstrations alternating with the most violent outbursts"; finally the Emperor's tone, at the close of the conversation, became "calm and soft".[1] The whole description is reminiscent in many ways of Kleist's report, where we can see the identical Napoleon, though with not quite the same efficient foil as Metternich to fetch out his dramatic sallies and provoke his versatile mind. The Emperor in these moods would work, in fact, to a pattern, which constantly

[1] *Mémoires du Prince de Metternich* (2nd ed. 1880), I, 146–54, II, 461–3.

recurs in his letters as well as in his conversations. He would offer friendship, confidence, and soothing assertions on the one hand, threats, boasts and loud defiance on the other. It was a kind of conduct which, pursued unremittingly for a long period, must have been a formidable attack upon a man's emotional nature; for, whether he tried warm advances or sinister menace, Napoleon would explore the emotional content, the world of infinite suggestion, in each, and would leap from the one mood to the other, and practise a frenzied reiteration, in a way that could only be exhausting to his hearer. The policy he adopted towards Prussia whenever he sought to win her in the years 1806 and 1807, was precisely this alternation of friendly assurance and arrogant threat. Kleist's despatch has the marks of truth and sincerity. The sallies against the Czar and the comments upon the aggressive intentions of Russia agree with Napoleon's constant utterances in other places, with the whole character of the proposals which he sent to the king of Prussia by Bertrand, and with his mood and policy in the early half of 1807. The symptoms of agitation coincide with those which we are accustomed to find. We may take it that Napoleon was disappointed with the Prussian king's response to his overture, that he was in petulant mood as a result, and that, in fact, his situation was giving him considerable anxiety.[1]

It is evident indeed from Napoleon's correspondence that the situation was difficult for him in the February of 1807. He himself seems to have been in low spirits after Eylau, and talked in his letters of his own tiredness and of the rigours of the Polish winter. He confessed the losses he had had in the battle and declared that his distance from France made them all the more serious for him. To the empress he wrote that "the country is covered with dead and wounded...one's soul is oppressed with the sight of so many victims". On the 18th of February he declared: "I desire very much to secure a rest of a month or six weeks for (the army)". Above all he was concerned about the feeding of his troops, and his letters repeatedly express his

---

[1] For Kleist's report, dated 2 Mar. 1807, see Bailleu, *Preussen und Frankreich*, II, 586-9.

anxiety on this question. On the 20th of February he writes:
"I ask for bread and I am sent shoes". On the 26th: "It would
seem that the enemy is advancing. My greatest concern is for
provisions". To Rapp on the same day: "The only thing which
gives me some anxiety is the question of provisions. Procure
what you can for me. Spare no money for the engaging of transports". In a letter to Soult of the same date Napoleon reveals
the seriousness of the question. After describing how the food-
problem is the difficulty and how he hopes that "in four or five
days we shall be in a tolerable position", he mentions some stir
among the Prussian troops, adding: "You can see what a false
movement this is, and how, if we had bread and brandy we
could make them repent of it". All this is on the 26th of February. It was on the 24th that Napoleon had his interview with
Kleist. Here is a further confirmation of the fact that he was
genuinely disconcerted by Prussia's refusal of his overtures, and
that Kleist's account of his demeanour is authentic.

Before the interview with Kleist was finished Napoleon put
an alternative to Prussia. On the one hand he repeated the
offer of a separate peace which should be concluded within a
month and should restore to the king all his provinces up to
the Elbe; on the other hand, he declared himself willing to accept
the proposal of a congress provided the discussions were preceded
by an armistice. If military operations continued during the
prosecution of a general negotiation, he said, each side as it
gained a victory would raise its demands and the negotiation
would have nothing stable to rest upon. Once more it was
evident that whether congress or separate negotiation were
accepted, he was determined to find extrication from his immediate military difficulties. He continued his policy of attempting
to make the Prussians despair of ever finding peace and salvation
through Russia—enlarging upon the warlike character and
ambitions of the Czar, and on the difficulties England would
place in the way of any congress that might assemble. On the
26th of February Kleist returned to his master bearing a letter
in which Napoleon declared his agreement to the idea of a congress. England, Prussia, Russia and the Porte were named as the

powers that were to join Napoleon in the transaction, but a decided preference was expressed for the way of separate negotiation, and sly doubts were cast upon the pacific intentions of England and Russia.[1]

Napoleon did not soon surrender the hope of winning Prussia. At the end of the Prussian campaign of 1806 the rough and rugged General Blücher had fallen into the hands of the French, after being pursued across Germany to Lübeck. He had been treated well as a prisoner at Hamburg, being allowed liberty to move much as he liked and have intercourse with his family; and all respect had been shown to his bravery. Finally he was restored to his country in exchange for a captive French general, and on his way to his king he was interviewed by Napoleon at Finckenstein. The audience took place on the 22nd of April and lasted a whole hour. Napoleon tried every means in his power to be charming to the man—to make it impossible for Blücher to hate him: and he attempted to win the stout patriot over to the idea of peace with France. He took up the argument he had used in 1806—that Prussia and France belonged to one another; he said that warring against Frederick William was like right hand fighting left; he declared the impossibility of bringing England to reason. Blücher, however, was incorrigible; he resented even Napoleon's efforts to be charming; it was impossible to turn him pacificist. "Blücher does not speak a word of French", wrote George Jackson in his diary, "and his orders to his son, who acted as his interpreter, were never to translate to him anything that Bonaparte might say, which had the slightest allusion to a Prussian peace."

When the news of Bertrand's mission reached St Petersburg, the Czar Alexander viewed the French proposals in their true light.[2] He saw them only as an attempt to put a wedge into the

---

[1] *Corresp. de Nap. Ier*, t. xiv, No. 11,890.

[2] The Russian replies to Bertrand's proposals are contained in: Alexander I to Frederick William III, 20 Feb./4 Mar. 1807, in Bailleu, *Briefwechsel*, p. 148; Alexander I to Frederick William III, 20 Feb./4 Mar. 1807 ("Une réponse ostensible"), *ibid.* p. 149; report from Schöler (in St Petersburg) to Zastrow, 4 Mar. 1807, in Ranke, *Hardenberg*, v, 479. The Russian replies to Kleist's proposals are to be found in: Alexander I to Frederick William III,

coalition—as Napoleon's usual practice for the sundering of alliances. He put them down as a result of the difficult position in which the French armies found themselves. To him the fact that Napoleon had changed his ground and was luring Prussia with private overtures, instead of proceeding with the idea of a congress, was a proof of the insincerity of the peaceful protestations of France. He kept firm to the position he had taken up in the middle of January when he had acceded to the Prussian proposals, and he still promised to prove his eagerness for peace, once the French had given satisfaction on the two points mentioned in Budberg's note on the subject. He ridiculed "the extreme arrogance with which Napoleon imagines the fate of Prussia to depend only upon himself". He made great point of the vagueness of the French proposals. "If Bonaparte had really wished to come to an arrangement with Your Majesty he would not have omitted to inform you of the basis on which this arrangement would take place." The Prussian ambassador warned his government that the conclusion of a separate peace would "irrevocably destroy the confidence of the nation and the minister, and would put an end to the friendship the Czar had for the king". There was the alternative of a general negotiation. Napoleon had made it conditional on the conclusion of an armistice; this, said Russia, "would only serve to the advantage of the common enemy". And the fact that the French had proposed Memel as the seat of the congress, when it was "contrary to the first dictates of prudence and against the principles of war to establish in that way a point of correspondence behind the line that our armies occupy", was only a further proof of the suspicious nature of their advances. Turkey was to be admitted to the congress; but Napoleon made no mention of Sweden. At the very outset it was apparent that Napoleon was disposed to raise obstacles and find preliminary points of conflict. He himself had said that a congress would sit for years.

13/25 Mar. 1807, in Bailleu, *Briefwechsel*, p. 154; note from Budberg to Goltz, 26 Mar. 1807 (n.s.), in Ranke, *Hardenberg*, v, 490. For the attitude of Russia see also the despatch of Goltz printed in Ranke, *Hardenberg*, iii, 335, and Budberg to Alopeus, 13/25 Mar. 1807, *F.O. Russia*, 65/72.

The Russian government could not be blind to the fact that Napoleon's overtures of February were directed against Russia and against the Russo-Prussian alliance. The king of Prussia, naturally, having transmitted such proposals to St Petersburg, found himself more than ever discredited in his rôle of peace-maker; and in future the Czar was less ready to listen to his ally. "General Budberg has assured me", wrote the English ambassador at this time, "that His Imperial Majesty has expressed his disapprobation of the constant readiness of the Prussian Court to listen to proposals of negotiation".[1] In March the Russian General Bennigsen was making complaints of "alleged movements taking place at Memel to produce a disposition for peace". Zastrow was concerned to see the distrust that his policy was arousing; it was calculated to weaken the cause of Prussia even at St Petersburg. He believed that "suspicion between friends and allies is always an evil" and directed his representative with the Czar to act in an unofficial way and do what he could to counteract the complaints of men like Bennigsen.[2] The Prussians knew they had lost character. They needed to protest.

The net result of the overtures of February, then, was to remove still further the chances of a general negotiation. The check given to France at the battle of Eylau, the very fact that Napoleon had pressed strongly either for an immediate arrangement with Prussia or for the conclusion of an armistice, and therefore must have needed these things, gave hopes that his military situation would soon become desperate. The conclusion of the Czar Alexander, after the discussion of these overtures, coincided in a remarkable way with the final summing up that Hardenberg had given in his Memorandum of the 19th of February. The allies must reconcile themselves to a continuation of the war and must take steps to prosecute it with greater vigour. They must at the same time renew their efforts to persuade Austria to join forces with them and to induce England to give active assistance. Alexander did not depart from his original offers on the subject of the general negotiation. A note

[1] Douglas to Howick, No. 10, 6 Mar. 1807, *F.O. Russia* 65/68.
[2] Zastrow to Goltz, 19 Mar. 1807, in Ranke, *Hardenberg*, III, 336.

from Budberg to Goltz of the 26th of March explained his whole position:

> The Emperor is deeply convinced that the object (of the war) can no longer be obtained by any other way than that of arms so long as France does not consent to treat of the general interest simultaneously with all the powers participating in it, and to give evident assurance of her willingness to give repose to Europe—which she alone has so long disturbed—by stating finally and in a straightforward way the basis upon which she intends to begin negotiations. The Emperor cannot, in regard to this matter, go back upon the principles enumerated in the Note: Budberg to Goltz of the 3rd (15th) of January.[1]

In this way, during the winter months that open the year 1807, Napoleon still finds himself faced with that initial difficulty of the war with Prussia, and he is not comfortable. But his mind does not fret and fumble, or helplessly revolve; he is not like the Czar or the Swedish king—he is held by no obsessions; so he can reconcile himself to a retreat. He refused to think of a separate peace with Prussia in December 1806; but in February he can assert that this is the only sort of arrangement that is admissible to him. In December he had a cosmic scheme that demanded nothing less than a general negotiation for peace; within a very few weeks this is the one thing which he says he will not have. In December he is talking of a resurrection of Poland, setting hearts aflame in Warsaw; but he will not let the idea run away with him, he will not entertain it further than suits his purpose; he is not like Czartoryski, dominated by a dream of a revived Poland; he is the master, not the servant of his policies; and so, in February, we find him willing to abandon the idea altogether. Over his enemies he had this virtue of supreme elasticity, this power of adjusting himself to every turn of the shifting situation; and sometimes his sudden reversals seemed like flippancy. But in the early months of 1807 his trick had been found out, his manœuvres were uncovered. A Prussia that had recently yearned to be at his side again—that was at this very moment longing for nothing so much as peace—could

[1] Ranke, *Hardenberg*, v, 490–3. For the note of 3/15 January see above, p. 58.

not trust his fairest invitations, did not dare to put herself at his mercy once more. And the importunity of his offers and overtures to her only served to convince his enemies that the armies of France were in difficulty and danger at last.

After Eylau the troops returned to winter quarters,[1] and Napoleon soon moved to Osterode, where for over five weeks he kept at bay the wolves that yapped at the heels of his army, and exorcised those looming shapes of hunger and privation that throw a shadow of danger over a thwarted frozen army. Life in that snow-bound village was no game for Emperors; there was discomfort and hardship and the cold was cruel at times. Over and over again Napoleon would clutch at the promise of spring; the snow would begin to melt, the rivers would be unloosed, and he would send out a cry of relief; but still would winter return and harden the world up again. Savary found his master "eating, sleeping, giving audience, and transacting business, all in one apartment". But he tells us: "If the Emperor, instead of sitting in a hole like Osterode, had gone to a large place, he would have taken three months to do all that he actually did in one".

March was an anxious time. From France there came whispers of the unwelcome reception that had been given to the tidings of the battle of Eylau. Napoleon had to find antidote for ugly rumours and sinister shakings of the head that undermined confidence in Paris—had to explain away the doleful comments he himself had made after the battle; and he carefully kept his eye upon the indiscretions of his supporters, the calumnies of his foes, the vagaries of the newspapers. He gave instructions that first in the salons, then in the press, the report should be unofficially spread that Russia had no troops left to call upon, that her army was crying out for peace, that her soldiers were accusing great nobles of being in the pay of England—selling Russian blood for British gold. He reproved the newspaper "craze for copying all the English like to say about that power".

---

[1] The rest of this chapter is based upon *Corresp. de Nap. Ier*, t. xiv, Nos. 11,854–12,248, i.e. Napoleon at Osterode, 22 Feb./31 Mar. 1807.

He watched the mood of France, told the Empress to set an example of gayness, bade her play a royal part just as if he were at her side in Paris.

From Vienna there were disquieting reports of armaments and equivocations and unavowed hostility. Napoleon met Austria with a show of power, played the nonchalant braggart, advertised the numbers of his troops, proclaimed his recent levies of new conscripts, pointed to his organisation of fresh reserves, and ordered it to be spread abroad "that if it is imagined in Austria that I am in difficulties, I ask nothing more than to pass my army of Brittany and Normandy in review before an Austrian officer, who will see with his own eyes how many troops I can send into Bavaria within a month". He commanded Prince Eugene in Italy to "keep an eye on Austria, and let General Marmont be told to do the same—not in writing in case the letter should be intercepted". "I have no reason to believe that this power wishes to make war, but she is arming and we must always be ready." Eugene had his orders to be prepared; "but carry out your dispositions gradually, and without precipitation", for the Austrians must not be reduced to panic. "You must be careful", wrote Napoleon to Talleyrand, "that M. de Vincent does not raise alarm in his reports to Vienna; he must not perceive that we have any resentment against Austria. We must continue to talk of our project of alliance."[1]

On the side of England there were still more apprehensions, for she might create a diversion on the continent, or send an expedition against the coasts of France. Napoleon multiplied preparations, placed Antwerp and Brest in a state of siege, created a strong army of observation in Germany, and made anxious enquiries for news from the Baltic and the North Sea towns. "If the English send an expedition I think they will send it to the Baltic", he wrote. Twenty to twenty-five thousand men, he believed, would be the limits of its strength. He ordered the fortresses of Stettin, Cüstrin, Glogau, Magdeburg and Hameln to be prepared to withstand a siege. "Whether the enemy makes a very large invasion at the estuary or at Stralsund, he

---

[1] *Corresp. de Nap. Ier*, t. xiv, No. 12,181.

may possibly become master of Berlin for a short time, if he has very strong forces. Frederick himself did not defend his capital." At the end of March there seemed a prospect of an expedition being sent against Brest. Napoleon's empire was beginning to need an extensive system of defence; it was a sprawling thing to cover; the coasts of Italy might be attacked; and above all the army in Poland was to be prepared against a diversion in its rear. Napoleon could not know how the British government would let its opportunity slip by.

But the greatest of all his difficulties—his grand preoccupation at this time—was the condition of his armies in Poland. "If I had had bread, and if the bad weather had not come, I should have reached Königsberg before [the enemy] and defeated them in detail." Again: "My greatest anxiety is for food". When Ney reported the privations of his troops, Napoleon could only write, "I am pained to hear of all you are suffering. You must still have patience. Provisions are ready here for your corps; it is the transporting that makes the difficulty". And, "I must organise my provisions. It is a game of lottery to do anything in March or April". He commissioned Talleyrand to see the provisional government of Poland, and enlist their assistance in this matter. "Make them understand that the problem to-day is less a military question than a matter of provisions; and they must use all the means in their power, and arouse zeal and patriotism.... They must look after transport and procure me what I ask. I shall not grudge the paying.... Money is not lacking, and I count it nothing if only provisions reach me and my army is supplied with food." Again he wrote to Talleyrand: "Work miracles. To fight the Russians is child's play if only I have bread....If the patriotism of the Poles can not rise to this endeavour they are not good for much....The importance of the charge I am committing to you is greater than all the negotiations in the world". Talking of clothing for his troops and mounts for his cavalry he declared: "There is no money better employed than that which is lavished on these objects". Shoes he ordered; bakeries he built; he raised bridges, he organised his transport. To stop the congestion of the

hospitals he removed the wounded, whenever possible, back to
Breslau and Glogau. He called upon the Senate for more troops.
There was disorganisation among his Polish levies; generals and
officers had quitted their post; and the soldiers had lost heart.
He set himself to restore order. And when Marshal Lefèbvre,
sent to open the siege of Danzig, was all alarms and full of grave
misgiving, Napoleon had to be inspiration to his leader, warming
him with words of encouragement, disparaging his fears and
winning him with promise of fame—had even to send Savary to
put heart into the Marshal, and discover if the situation were so
difficult and disquieting as the reports made it appear.

Small wonder that he declared to Austria: "The upshot of all
this will be an alliance between France and Austria or one
between France and Russia; for there will never be peace for
the peoples—the peace they are all in need of—except by such
a union".[1] It is tempting to dwell on this assertion, where
Napoleon is speculating about alliances, with his mind seeming
to veer towards Tilsit. Yet the hint of union with the Czar is
rather a stick with which to waken the Austrians. "An alliance
with Austria, if it is possible", says Napoleon, "would give at
least a period of tranquillity. I am sufficiently inclined towards
this to be prepared to make some sacrifices for it." Even in
pressing his advances to Vienna perhaps he thought rather of
lulling her fears, and fixing her in her neutrality than of actually
drawing her into his system. And as for the talk of Russia, this
must not be taken too seriously. "I think that an alliance with
Russia would be very advantageous, if it were not a fantastic
idea, and if any dependence could be placed upon that court."[2]
At this moment he is rather more earnest, and seems more
pressing in his offers to Prussia. He is waiting for her answer to
the proposals he sent by Colonel Kleist. For he has stretched
out his arm to the Prussian king with an offer of renewed friendship, and if there is talk of refusal he growls something about
dethronement.

[1] *Corresp. de Nap. Ier*, t. xiv, No. 11,977.
[2] *Ibid.* t. xiv, No. 12,028; cf. J. Holland Rose, *Life of Napoleon I*
(1924), ii, 127.

CHAPTER III

THE ATTITUDE OF ENGLAND TO THE PRUSSIAN PEACE MOVE

THE peace proposals that Krüsemarck carried to St Petersburg at the close of the year 1806 were to be passed over to England after their acceptance by the Russian cabinet; and the Czar fulfilled the promise he had given to support them with his persuasions at the court of London. The Prussian minister of foreign affairs also took up the theme, and when a new British representative came to Memel, with instructions to fasten Prussia to a vigorous, warlike policy, Zastrow, having the courage of his cowardice, dared to greet him with this reddest of all red rags and whisper the forbidden word of "Peace". "He dwelt strongly on the offer which Bonaparte had made to negotiate conjointly with Russia and England, and he seemed to think it would not be unadvisable to assemble a general congress for the purpose of forwarding so desirable an object."[1] Distance, however, prevented the English ministers from keeping pace with continental affairs, and they did not reply to the overture until the 7th of March.

These English ministers were not likely to be slow in piercing the meaning of the offers of Napoleon. Stuart, in sending from St Petersburg his report of Budberg's action, had put the position plainly to them:

"The fact is", he wrote, "that the sole Balance in the hands of the powers waging war with Bonaparte, which can offer solid ground of negotiation is comprised in the Colonies conquered by Great Britain from France and her Allies, and this compensation according to the argument of the Russian Government must ensure the restitution of the territories wrested from the King of Prussia.... From the language of Bonaparte to M. de Zastrow it is generally understood that the evacuation of Moldavia and Wallachia will not induce the French Government to cede objects of real value in the eyes of the Allies."[2]

[1] Hutchinson to Howick, 23 Dec. 1806, *F.O. Prussia* 64/74.
[2] Stuart to Howick, No. 10, 17 Jan. 1807, *F.O. Russia* 65/67.

Lord Hutchinson after speaking with the Prussian minister announced that the hope of Zastrow "as well as that of every other man in Prussia is that they may be enabled to obtain peace on tolerable terms by the cession of captured colonies which England is to make to France".[1]

Now, at the moment when the invitations were sent to London, England had not even made peace with this Prussia for whom she was asked, out of her charity, to cede the spoils of victory. Lord Hutchinson had recently arrived at the Prussian headquarters to put an end to the state of war, and his instructions were headed with the peremptory command: "You will first satisfy yourself that all negotiations for peace with France are at an end".[2] There was no predisposition in favour of Prussia, at all, among Englishmen, and the reception of an overture of any sort from Memel was only calculated to confirm lingering suspicions. After the battle of Jena things like this were said in England: "That Prussia had fallen a sacrifice to her want of a good principle and that if that Monarchy should be abolished it must be recollected that it was but a new one". One magazine could write: "For our part, if she alone were to suffer by the event, it would be a subject of rejoicing to us, to see the regicidal flag of France on the towers of Berlin, and a Corsican Viceroy master of the palace of Potzdam". The English ministers were jealous of all the things for which the Prussians had quarrelled with Napoleon. They did not wish to see the armies of Berlin lording it over the north of Germany. Not any more than Napoleon did they like the idea of a confederation of states under the hegemony of Prussia. George III's interests in Germany ran counter to those of Berlin and it did not soften his anti-Prussian heart to learn that Frederick William had gone to war with France after Napoleon had promised Hanover to England. Whigs and Tories alike had learned the weakness of the ruling spirits at Berlin, and, in recent tenure of office, had had bitter experience of their treachery. When it was known that Zastrow was chosen to be the new foreign

[1] Hutchinson to Howick, No. 8, 29 Jan. 1807, *F.O. Prussia* 64/74.
[2] Howick to Hutchinson, No. 1, 20 Nov. 1806, *F.O. Prussia* 64/74.

minister at Memel the appointment was taken as a promise of further feeble policy, this time preconsidered and forechosen.[1] There was no mood for making excuses and allowances, and Stuart at St Petersburg jumped to the reasoning that would go straight to the English heart, when, on hearing of the new proposal for peace, he declared, " It is evident that the Prussian Monarchy regenerated by Bonaparte will be no less subservient to the views of France than a Dynasty of his own creation placed on that throne ".[2]

In England the ministry of the day was distinguished only by a certain lack of cordiality in its relations with the continent, and an evident disinclination to work hand in hand with the other powers of the coalition. So long as Fox was at the foreign office his general humanity tempered what might have been harsh and insular in the attitude of the party in power, his personal qualities won esteem abroad and he infused a warmth into his intercourse with foreign powers. When he died in September 1806 he was universally regretted, and the fear was expressed repeatedly at foreign courts that English policy would make a change for the worse.[3] But the rupture of the peace negotiations and the new need for vigorous action brought out the weak side of the Whigs. Lord Grenville seems to have been an unfortunate influence in the ministry showing himself in foreign policy more whig, more averse to the methods of Pitt, than even the Foxites themselves. He had entered office in desponding mood and never recovered his energy; and his ascendancy in matter of policy was heightened when Lord Howick, who was new to diplomacy, found himself transferred to the foreign office. The situation was certainly not encouraging; recruiting was low, finances were embarrassed, and there was

---

[1] Hutchinson to Howick, 23 Dec. 1806, *F.O. Prussia* 64/74. On the 29th of December Hutchinson wrote: "There is something in the conduct of this court, whether arising from fear or some other weak or foolish motive, which leads me to suspect that negotiation, or at least desire of negotiation with France is not entirely abandoned.... The sincerity of Prussia is still, in my opinion, doubtful" (*ibid.* Despatch No. 2).

[2] Stuart to Howick, No. 10, 17 Jan. 1807, *F.O. Russia* 65/67.

[3] E.g. Stuart to F.O. No. 31, "31 Sept." 1806, and No. 35, 11 Oct. 1806, *F.O. Russia* 65/64.

every temptation to minimise the responsibilities and commitments of England. The budget of 1806 had been drawn up with the greatest possible economy, and all the preoccupation with peace-making during this year had made the government overlook the necessity of preparing new enterprises of war. Howick, though he was greatly distracted by his work as party leader and by the demands of internal politics, and though he had the reputation of being hot and ill-tempered and difficult to manage, seems to have been happy in his personal relations with the ministers of foreign powers, and he won their approbation; but this may have resulted from nothing more than his agreeableness in conversation, and his power of stating his case in interviews.[1] He did not succeed in justifying British policy before foreign courts, or in infusing geniality into British foreign relations; while the king, who as elector of Hanover could have little love for Prussia or for transactions that centred in Prussia, was disposed to encourage still further the things that were harsh and unsympathetic in the measures of the reconstituted ministry.

That ministry became proverbial for its slowness and indecision; and, rightly or wrongly, its parsimony became a byword in Europe. The enemies of Napoleon perpetually spoke of the need of winning Austria to their cause, and the need of rousing England to activity, in the same breath. Starhemberg, the representative of Austria, wrote in the highest terms of Howick when that minister stood out in the early months of 1807 as the one man of energy and determination in office; but all the time he described the slackness of the cabinet, declaring that "Napoleon must count very much on this indifference".

Grenville's "own unsleeping distrust of foreign governments,

---

[1] E.g. Starhemberg to Stadion, No. 20, 24 Mar. 1807, *W.S.A. Berichte aus London*: "Le successeur de M. Fox ne laissait rien à désirer et c'est avec autant de satisfaction que de vérité que je puis avoir l'honneur d'assurer Votre Excellence que depuis 14 ans que je suis en Angleterre je n'ai point vu de Secrétaire d'Etat qui ait autant réuni les suffrages de tous ceux avec lesquels il avait à faire et dont quoique toujours bien avec tous, j'ai eu plus personnellement raison d'être content". Perhaps Howick's policy of not pressing the Austrians to join in the war (see below, p. 110) may account for this pleasant relationship with Starhemberg.

to whose treachery or incapacity or cowardice he attributed, often most unjustly, the successive defeats of coalitions against France", showed itself in Howick's cold and ungenerous despatches. Small points of difference were worded with too little regard for the susceptibilities of foreign powers, and were exaggerated by representatives abroad who often misconceived the nature of their office. There were men like Canning at home who had resented Fox's policy of declaring war on Prussia in the summer of 1806; for it had merely given triumph to Napoleon's plan of sowing dissension between the powers. But there were louder protests when, after the Prussians had entered the field against France, the ministry still refused to forget old resentments and co-operate in the war.[1] Even after Jena the government did not relent, but made it the burden of their song that they had had no share in the mischievous counsels which had hurried the Prussians into an imprudent war—they were not in any way responsible for the misfortunes of that unhappy country. Still they persisted in their distrust, while the Russians stormed at them for their delays; still they shouted "Hanover" and cried out for guarantees, carrying their suspicions to the point of demanding that the Czar should add his pledge to the promises of Prussia in the treaty that was to settle their affairs with the court of Berlin.

All this created irritation between the allies, and the Czar for some time refused to give any of the guarantees that were asked of him.[2] Moreover, a commercial treaty with Russia that worked to the great advantage of English merchants was on the point of expiry, and the importunity of the British government, its eagerness to see the treaty renewed without any curtailment of

---

[1] Writing to Nicolai on the 9th of October 1806 v.s. (despatches communicated to the British government and to be found in *F.O. Russia* 65/66) the Russian Chancellor urged England to postpone all discussion of the Hanoverian question, which was an obstacle to peace and co-operation with Prussia, and refer the fate of the electorate to the general pacification of Europe. Budberg declared the Czar's dissatisfaction with England for her unwillingness to move to the help of Russia.

[2] Stuart's cypher despatch, No. 41, to Howick, 28 Oct. 1806, *F.O. Russia* 65/64, reports the Czar's positive refusal to give the required guarantee.

English privileges, only increased the friction. Russia and Prussia again and again urged that an English force should make a diversion on the continent to relieve the pressure of the French armies in Poland, but Starhemberg wrote to his court: "I see secret plans of diversion adopted one after the other and abandoned for the sake of economy".[1] Napoleon took precautions to guard his frontiers against an expedition that did not arrive; the English ministry preferred ventures like the taking of Buenos Ayres which would work to the profit of Great Britain in some far corner of the world, rather than serve the combined cause; and the result was, that not only did the Grenville government fail to despatch a force themselves, but they made it difficult for their successors to carry out a plan when it was decided to send relief to Europe.[2] It was reasonable that on the question of subsidies they should take the line of declining to incite powers to war with Napoleon by the offer of pecuniary grants, that they should refuse to buy enemies against France when self-interest or self-defence did not determine the powers to take up arms in their own cause; but they carried the reaction against Pitt's subsidy policy too far, refusing to give grants to an ally who merely defended his own territories,[3] measuring their offers to the service which each power rendered to the general interest, with the result that Prussia, incapacitated and reduced to dependence, might be argued to be no subject for aid at all. Then they delayed the grant of money, and, having at last decided to give it, they still desired to strengthen their government by refraining from great financial commitments, so they limited their offer to an amount that startled and dismayed their allies. When the Czar asked them to guarantee a Russian loan in London they remembered the evil effects of such a measure in the time of Pitt, and declined in an ungracious

[1] Starhemberg to Stadion, No. 1, 1 Jan. and No. 9, 7 Feb. 1807, *W.S.A. Berichte aus London*.

[2] Communications from Alopeus, the Russian minister in London, to the new foreign secretary, Canning, 19 Mar., 17 May, 5 June 1807 (v.s.), on the subject of a military diversion, *F.O. Russia* 65/72.

[3] See Howick to Adair, No. 1, 13 Jan. 1807, *F.O. Austria* 7/83; Howick to Pierrepoint, No. 4, 2 Dec. 1806, *F.O. Sweden* 73/36.

manner, saying that Russia might at some future time make war against England, and repudiate the loan. All these things had an influence on the question of peace at a later date, and fill a large space in the Czar's excuses for the treaty of Tilsit; but, although the Czar in January was beginning already to adopt the air that "he was deserted by his allies", that "he had no ally", and the Russian chancellor was already showing that irritable disposition, that withholding of confidence, that became very marked at a later date in his relations with the British ambassador, the real evil effects of the attitude of the English government came out more plainly in the summer.[1] What is more important at the moment is the fact, of which all these measures are a symptom: the lack of cordiality and of rich sympathy in the relations of England with the continent.

The ministry was served very badly by its agents in the most important stations abroad. Lord Morpeth had been sent to negotiate peace with Prussia and had caused a great hitch by abandoning his mission, escaping with the wave of fugitives from Jena;[2] Englishmen and Prussians alike who were on the spot declared his successor, Lord Hutchinson, unfitted for the charge. He was an indolent, unsociable man, with an ungracious manner, and violent temper—"improperly neglectful of his personal appearance, hair uncombed, clothes unbrushed". He had played an important part in the Egyptian campaign of 1801 but had been unpopular among his brother-officers there. At Memel his suite regarded him as a disagreeable person. A military man, with a high opinion of the powers of Napoleon, he had no faith in the cause which he was serving; and in his counsels at the Prussian headquarters he had nothing but discouragement to give. He sent to his government reports that only increased the suspicions against Prussia and did nothing to reconcile and unite; so that a contemporary rhymist could tell of

> Hutchinson, sent out the Lord knows where,
> To write us long despatches of despair.

[1] E.g. Douglas to Howick, No. 1, Jan. 26, 1807, *F.O. Russia* 181/6.
[2] The British ministry expressed its disapproval of Morpeth's desertion; cf. *Private Correspondence of Lord G. Leveson-Gower*, II, 224–6 and 231.

Altogether he confirmed the English ministry in the weak points of its foreign policy.[1]

Lord Douglas, who went to St Petersburg at the new year, was "a perfect novice in politics" and had been given his post purely for party purposes, in return for votes registered against Pitt. He was totally ignorant of diplomacy. After haggling about the conditions and the payment of his mission and "loitering away his time in England in choosing his service of plate and stocking his wardrobe", he set out for Russia, where he conducted himself in strange fashion. His appointment was unpopular in England, and the papers described how he rode about St Petersburg "in a dress compounded of every costume in the known world", till he became the standing jest of the natives.[2] Perhaps he was maligned for party purposes,[3] but his diplomacy was certainly unsound. He was instructed to secure the guarantee of Russia to the claims of George III over Hanover, and to bring about the renewal of the expiring commercial treaty; and from this he seems to have gathered that his whole duty was to complain. He carried out his mission in the spirit of an enemy spy and wrote hostile accounts of transactions in St Petersburg. When the Russians at last promised to guarantee that Prussia should not have Hanover, he demanded a further guarantee against France, till he was instructed that this had not been the intention of his government.[4] On one occasion the British merchants in Russia sent him a statement

---

[1] Howick, writing to Hutchinson on the 20th of February 1807 (*F.O. Prussia* 64/74, No. 1), said: "Nothing can be more afflicting than the representations made by Your Lordship not only of the state of the Prussian court but of the divisions among the Russian generals". On the 22nd of February the Prussian king informed his minister in London that "je suis fâché que nous ayons à faire ici à un homme aussi peu communicatif que le Lord Hutchinson" (intercepted despatches, *Add. MSS.* 32,273).

[2] See e.g. *Anti-Jacobin Review*, Nov. 1807, "Plain facts—or a Review of the condition of the Late Ministry"; *Farington Diary*, vol. IV, under "April 16, 1807".

[3] See De Maistre, *Mémoires et Correspondance*, p. 311: "On l'a turlupiné dans les papiers anglais sur quelques ridicules extérieurs qu'il s'était donnés ici et que nous n'avons pas vus. Son véritable tort est qu'il parle trop bien français et italien...et qu'il pourrait fort bien ne tenir à l'Angleterre que par son nom et ses droits".

[4] Howick to Douglas, No. 8, 7 Mar. 1807, *F.O. Russia* 65/68.

of grievances, expressing in strong terms their resentment against the conduct of the government there. Instead of turning this into a diplomatic paper, smoothing over its crude attack and presenting all its complaints in less repellent guise, he despatched the document itself, making its bitterness his own. This so offended the Czar that the man's position became impossible at the Russian court. Budberg refrained from treating with him, spoke of him only with irritation, and left him to gather his political information from indirect sources. And when Alexander and his ministry finally left St Petersburg to join the Prussians at Memel, the ambassador was not granted an audience and was not allowed to follow—"A very humiliating position for a British ambassador", he wrote.[1] Canning, on becoming the new foreign secretary in March, saw that he had annoyed the Russians with "unreasonable and unnecessary demands, urged in no very becoming manner", so immediately recalled the man without giving a word of appreciation of his services, and ordered his successor to make apology for him. Douglas, in truth, was little of an Englishman; hence his unpopularity at home. After he was superseded at St Petersburg he showed no desire to return to his country, but lingered in Russia, long after the treaty of Tilsit, ingratiating himself with the enemies of England by expressing his admiration of Napoleon and declaring that his government ought to make peace.[2] And when he departed from Russia he made his way not to England, but to France.[3]

Hutchinson and Douglas were unfortunate ministers to have in charge of British relations with the coalition powers. Neither could be on terms of intimacy with the government to which he was accredited; neither was treated with confidence on the subject of the French overtures; neither received anything more

---

[1] *Dropmore Papers*, vol. IX, Introduction, pp. xxxviii–xxxix.
[2] Despatches of Caulaincourt, in Grand-Duke Nicholas Mikhaïlovsky, *Relations diplomatiques de la Russie et de la France*, e.g. II, 139, 246, 252.
[3] P. Bertrand, *Lettres inédites de Talleyrand à Napoléon Ier*, No. cccxxx. On the 12th of August 1808 Douglas described to Canning the pacific dispositions of the French government and advised the opening of discussions (*F.O. Russia* 65/74).

than a limited and partial communication of the content of
Napoleon's proposals or even of the reception that was given
to these; each therefore saw movements for peace, half-concealed,
and regarded them as objects of suspicion; each wrote to his
government of doubtful transactions and negotiations, and
complained of confidence withheld.[1] A certain M. de Lützow
arrived in St Petersburg from Prussia; Douglas was merely
allowed to make conjectures as to his mission, but the man
"announced on all sides the favourable opportunity of making
peace at present with Bonaparte". When he was leaving,
Budberg informed the ambassador that an offer of a separate
peace had been made to Prussia, as well as proposals of a wider
negotiation, but that "little attention had been paid". "I have
no right to doubt these assertions", wrote Douglas, as he saw
the arrival of still another Prussian messenger in St Petersburg,
"but...if I allow myself to reason upon circumstances I am led
to suspect".[2] In April Douglas heard of Bertrand's mission and
the succession of offers that Bonaparte had made, but he learned
them from the Prussian minister, Goltz. "None of these various
papers have ever been confided to me by this government", he
wrote.[3] The British ministry, therefore, at one moment envisaged Prussia as stealthily working for a separate peace; at
another moment took alarm lest the Czar, out of friendship,
should succumb to the pacific persuasions of king Frederick
William. It refused to send help to Prussia until it should be
reassured on the subject of that separate peace; it only learned
the fidelity of Russia as Alopeus, the Russian minister in London,
communicated the French overtures and stated the intentions
of his government.[4]

The truth was that the whigs themselves had no diplomats to
send to important posts in Europe and the demands of party

---

[1] Hutchinson to Howick, No. 6, 9 Jan. 1807, *F.O. Prussia* 64/74: "Everything they say and everything they do is enveloped in such doubt and
mystery that it is impossible not to be suspicious".

[2] Douglas to Howick, No. 9, 28 Feb. 1807, *F.O. Russia* 65/68.

[3] Douglas to Howick, No. 15, 3 Ap. 1807, *F.O. Russia* 65/68.

[4] Budberg to Alopeus, 13/25 Mar. 1807, and other documents communicated by Alopeus, *F.O. Russia* 65/72.

prevented them from making use of the experienced men who had seen previous service.[1] The distance of England from her allies, and the slowness of communications at that period, were sufficient in themselves to hinder the intercourse of England with the continent; but the inadequacy of the diplomatic service greatly increased the isolation. It prevented the cabinet of London from quite realising the estimation in which it was held abroad, at a time when men muttered ugly things about this country—when even the patriotic Englishman away from home had become angry and ashamed. It prevented the cabinet also from visualising the situation on the continent, and it delayed the assistance of England in the campaigns on the mainland of Europe. So it came to be easily believed that the government had no heart in the war, and was on the point of reversing its policy; the rumour quickly caught that England was meditating a system of "isolation". The British government seemed to have no interest in the continent; it fought rather for Buenos Ayres and Egypt, collecting more maritime plunder for itself. The spirit of Pitt seemed dead.

Lord Howick sent his reply to Krüsemarck's peace-proposals in a despatch to Lord Douglas dated the 7th of March. He supported the Czar's demand for a formal statement of the French bases of negotiation as a preliminary to the assembly of a congress, and only disagreed with his suggestion of a seat for the proposed meetings. The subject was important to England because of the difficulties of communication; a town in Galicia would be too far distant. Howick suggested Copenhagen as more central; though he had no objection to Hamburg or Dresden provided that the French garrisons were withdrawn from these places, and that unmolested communications could be guaranteed. When it came to the principles of the negotiation, he expressed himself at length on the system of "equivalents" for which Napoleon had stipulated in December. He answered to the expectations of Europe and confirmed Napoleon's fears by attacking the implied basis of the whole overture for peace

---

[1] Besides the above notes on Douglas and Hutchinson, see below, on Adair, English minister to Vienna, pp. 117–18.

and refusing his concurrence to the particular scheme of compensations to which the negotiation was pointing.

"An apprehension that Prussia may indulge a mistaken hope that His Majesty can ever be induced to admit such a principle of exchange makes an early and frank explanation of the Sentiments of His Majesty's Government on this head, indispensable...."

...The English objects in negotiating would be, "first the honourable fulfilment of all engagements to (her) allies by the restitution of the territories of which they may have been dispossessed, or an indemnity for the losses which they may have sustained in (her) cause; and, secondly, the re-establishment as far as it is found to be practicable of some equilibrium of power which may tend to insure the tranquillity and independence of Europe. To attain these objects His Majesty would always be willing to make great and important sacrifices."

But the second of these aims would not be furthered by

the restitution of territories which France could at will resume with equal or greater facility than she originally overran them. Governments which owe their existence to the mere articles of a Treaty and which possess no military frontier towards France, must even in time of peace fall into a state of dependence upon that power....Your Excellency will therefore state that His Majesty, though satisfied with his colonial possessions and far from designing to add to them, cannot consent to restore to France or her immediate dependencies those acquisitions obtained by his arms in return for the insecure restitution of Conquests on the Continent which France can at pleasure regain. To increase the power and to multiply the resources of the great Continental states of Russia and Austria, could it be accomplished without any injustice to other powers, His Majesty would willingly do much, but he does not feel equally disposed to surrender Conquests for the reinstatement of princes who have been dispossessed of Dominions which they were unable to defend, and who have no claims founded on specific engagements or arising out of general friendship and alliance.[1]

The Czar of Russia, out of friendship, gives his sanction to a movement that promises to lead to the restoration of Prussia. Howick replies that the claim of friendship does not commit England in this way to Prussia. He regards the question in the colder light of policy. England, it is true, wishes to use her

---

[1] Howick to Douglas, No. 9, 7 Mar. 1807, *F.O. Russia* 65/68.

colonies to raise up a barrier and a safeguard against France. But Alexander, with some cause of irritation against the court of Vienna, and with one possible source of hostility against Austria in the Ottoman Empire, finds nothing to discount the policy that his friendship for Prussia suggests; while England has no desire to see Prussia raised to a great power in the north of Germany, and has not forgotten the history of that court of Berlin which was "unable to defend itself", and "even in time of peace fell into a state of dependence upon France". She therefore chooses Austria, rather, to be the barrier against French aggression. This is an issue between the allies. This is to be the stumbling-block in all future talk of peace. But England holds the colonies, so she has a decisive voice. The history of the ensuing weeks, when the peace-negotiations advance and the aims of the enemies of Napoleon find clearer formulation, shows this cleavage growing more deep as Canning and the new ministry prove no less insistent and unequivocal in the matter than were the men of "All the Talents".

The Austrians were counting on this—were sunning themselves with the expectancy. For Austria—as well as Prussia—was looking for England to bring back her power, and she too hoped that British maritime conquests would be used to buy her restoration. Without joining in the war she nursed her claims, hoping that the map of Europe would demand her exaltation, trusting that the "balance of power" would cry out for her aggrandisement. Surely she alone could be that barrier against France which England demanded as security for the repose of Europe—and without which the British government would refuse to disgorge its conquests. Yet the conduct of the whig ministry gave her, also, apprehension at times. She would call on the British minister to see if England was changing her policy.[1] In March Lord Douglas at St Petersburg was indulging in more of his indiscretions, glorying in new mischief; lately arrived in Russia, he conversed at length with the Austrian minister there, in terms that implied a reversal of English policy. His remarks were "based on a system of isolation that England

[1] E.g. Adair to Howick, 24 Feb. 1807, in Adair, *Historical Memoir of a Mission to the Court of Vienna in* 1806 (1844), pp. 190–1.

had adopted in the present conjuncture and according to which
she was determined not to sacrifice any of the advantages she
had obtained in the maritime war for the general utility or the
amelioration of Europe". The Austrian government was greatly
concerned to hear "this opinion enunciated by a new diplomatic
agent at the moment he had received his instructions".[1] The
conduct of Lord Hutchinson at Memel and the refusal of the
court of London to consent to a Russian loan, seemed to confirm
the words of Douglas. There was some disquietude at Vienna.
The chancellor remarked that no sign was yet apparent of the
preparation of an English expedition to the continent; and that
England had manifested "no intention of endeavouring to
obtain at a general peace securities for the Continental Power
by the restoration of (her) conquests".[2] Incidental occurrences
reinforced the apprehension. The Austrians, though they were
crying "neutrality" from the housetops, trembled for their
interests in a future settlement of Europe. Though they were
inactive, they could not be indifferent.

In fact, at this very moment, the veil was beginning to lift from
the mysterious and silent purposes of the cabinet of Vienna.
While Napoleon was still waiting for the reply to Kleist's communications—a reply which was to come later after a good deal
of rumination; and while the promotion of a general negotiation
by Prussia was held in long suspense—to be resumed in time,
however, with more precise plans for a congress—the Austrians
made an important move, and offered their mediation. It was
their contribution to the problem of peace in Europe, though it
came as an added complication. It interpolates at this point,
and brings a large parenthesis, but it by no means destroys or
displaces the Prussian plans for the assembly of a congress.

---

[1] Stadion to Starhemberg, No. 2, 5 Ap. 1807, *W.S.A. Weisungen nach
London*. Adair to Douglas, 3 Ap. 1807, in Adair, *Historical Memoir*,
pp. 384–6. Douglas defended himself in his despatch No. 17 to Canning,
16 Ap. 1807 (*F.O. Russia* 65/68), and in a reply to Adair, 11 Ap. 1807 (Adair,
Historical Memoir, pp. 386–9). The misunderstanding gave the British
government an opportunity to make many profuse protestations of fidelity
to the continental powers.
[2] Adair to Howick, No. 24, 4 Ap. 1807, *F.O. Austria* 7/83 (omitted
from the *Historical Memoir* of Adair).

BOOK TWO

THE INTERVENTION OF AUSTRIA

CHAPTER I

THE POLICY OF AUSTRIA AND THE OFFER OF MEDIATION

IT was supposed, in the summer of 1806, that it would be the Austrians rather than the Prussians who would soon be at war again with Napoleon.[1] There had been boundary difficulties to be settled in Italy, where the French were making encroachment; and Napoleon had been mortifying these long-suffering Austrians by a succession of miscellaneous demands of an irritating kind. The Emperor Francis was having to sacrifice his ancient titles, his proudest dignities, and put away all the fading glories of the "Holy Roman Empire"; he had found himself confronted with drastic changes in Germany, which gave France a ruling influence there; and he was expected to disown his relatives and allies by assenting to the claims of the usurping ruler at Naples. The Austrians themselves had been inviting animosity by their connivance at the Russian occupation of Cattaro—the key to the Adriatic territories which they had ceded in the treaty of Pressburg; and they were creating successive diplomatic crises for themselves by their evasions and procrastination when they were pressed to take steps for expelling the Russians and handing over the port to Napoleon's troops. Napoleon in revenge was keeping his armies in Germany and each side complained of the non-execution of the recent peace treaty.

M. de Larochefoucauld, the French ambassador at Vienna during the year 1806, had no love for the Austrian chancellor with whom he had to transact business. He found the man evasive in interviews, and detected a guilty embarrassment in his manner, and in time came to feel him untrustworthy and secretly hostile, too much engaged in "caressing the Russians". "As to Count Stadion", he wrote, "I have waited a long time

[1] See e.g. the second despatch from Budberg to Nicolai, 14/26 Aug. 1806, in *F.O. Russia* 65/66.

to fix my opinion of him, but there is no concealing the fact that he is absolutely Russian and his policy is diametrically opposed to France."[1] The time came when he would write "I cannot vouch for the veracity of this minister", after Stadion had been insistent in his declarations and promises.[2]

To confirm his view he produced specimens of the instructions that had been sent by the Austrian government to its servants abroad—despatches in which Stadion had talked of the "excessive power" and "unbridled ambition" of France; had described Bonaparte as one who "without the least respect for the rights of men or for justice or humanity, only seeks to augment his sway for the advancement of his family and his minions"; and had shown Austria's true policy to be the quiet cultivation of confidential relations with England and Russia, with careful avoidance of any step that might awaken French suspicions. The Austrian government, it appeared, was slowly and secretly gathering up its forces in readiness for the war that would come when the convenient moment should arrive.[3]

On the 13th of August 1806 the Austrian chancellor declared that the farthest limit had been reached in submission to Napoleon, and, "in the strictest confidence", outlined to the British minister, Adair, "the course which His Imperial Majesty intended to pursue in future", saying that the emperor would follow a defensive system, would not even oppose the passage of French troops through his territory, but, at the same time, would not be the first to dishonour himself by recognising Napoleon's new arrangements at Naples, would make no further sacrifices of territory, and, if attacked, would avoid a general action, and make a retreat into Hungary. Count Stadion gave assurances that preparations were very forward.[4]

---

[1] Larochefoucauld to Talleyrand, No. 55, 23 July 1806, *A.A.E. Autriche*, t. 379.

[2] Larochefoucauld to Talleyrand, 14 Oct. 1806, *A.A.E. Autriche*, t. 379.

[3] Passages from the instructions of Stadion to the Austrian minister to Spain and the Austrian chargé d'affaires in Würtemberg, intercepted by Larochefoucauld and enclosed in his despatch No. 55; see above, note 1.

[4] Adair to Fox, 13 Aug. 1806, *F.O. Austria* 7/80. This passage is deleted from the document published in Adair's *Historical Memoir*, p. 120.

Yet the Austrians had no intention of going to war if diplomacy could prevent it.

At this very moment Count Stadion was making advances for closer intimacy with France. A few days before his pronouncement to Adair he had stated to Larochefoucauld, the French minister, his desire for a closer union between Austria and France, affirming that

he had given instructions to Count Metternich (the new minister in Paris) to use every means in his power to put an end to a state of distrust that was so disagreeable to him personally; he was of opinion that the welfare of his sovereign lay in binding himself more closely to the Emperor Napoleon, and he would welcome everything that might further this.

Larochefoucauld, with more insight than Adair, divined the real significance of the overture, and reduced the situation to its proper terms. The fact was that the Austrians were nervous and conscience-stricken and had a feeling of insecurity. They had recently heard of the signing of Oubril's treaty,[1] and they knew that the Russian peace would make their position a precarious one. Stadion confessed to Larochefoucauld that the news had come as a surprise; he showed signs of disappointment; and he added that he was all the more anxious and in suspense because Napoleon had made no reply to the letter the Emperor had last written him. The Austrians, left in the lurch, dreaded these long, ominous silences of Napoleon, and feared that fresh injury, new hostility, were brooding. Larochefoucauld saw his advantage, deliberately avoided giving reassurances, and heaped up the agonies of the Austrians, playing on their anxieties and lashing their fears. He reminded them that their present principles and policy were known to be the same as ever—only more "disguised"; they had learned nothing from Ulm and Austerlitz. He tore away the veil from their double-dealings, and whipped them with frank recapitulations of their lack of faith. And he comforted them with the conclusion that "it seemed impossible to him that any confidence at all could be placed by the

[1] The treaty between Russia and France signed by Oubril in July 1806; see above, p. 33.

government at Paris in the conduct of the court of Vienna".[1] Little wonder that Stadion thought he heard the distant rumblings of war in it all, and put himself in the hands of Adair.

This nervousness of Austria is the key to her conduct for the whole of the ensuing year, and is the explanation of all the contradictions and evasions and equivocations of her policy. It was a definite factor in the European situation; and as part of the fatalism of events it had to be accepted and allowed for, like the bad weather in Poland.

England, though anxious to see Austria engaged against France, did not hurry her, was unwilling to press her to act against her will, and refused to bribe her in any way. Lord Howick in November 1806 showed no disposition to alter this policy, and wrote:

> It may be doubted whether it would be prudent in all the circumstances of the moment to urge the Austrian Government to measures which a conviction of its own necessity and a sense of its own honour do not inspire it with the courage voluntarily to adopt. All that can be done therefore is generally to continue the assurances which you have already been instructed to give, of support from His Majesty whenever circumstances shall permit the King to give and Austria to accept his assistance.[2]

The Russians, it has been seen, adopted a similar attitude at that period; for their mood was ruffled and prickly, and they would do nothing that had the appearance of crying for help.[3]

It was Napoleon who first betrayed anxiety about Austria, as his differences with Prussia developed. Immediately he changed his tone, and abandoned his threatening attitude. "It is absolutely necessary to remove every difficulty with Austria", he wrote, "by fixing our boundaries in Italy." When the Czar repudiated the peace treaty which Oubril had signed for Russia, the crisis which released a score of waiting plans, and struck off a host of new sparks of thought in the mind of Napoleon, brought out the project of an alliance with Austria, and he wrote a

[1] Larochefoucauld to Talleyrand, No. 61, 6 Aug. 1806, *A.A.E. Autriche*, t. 379.

[2] Howick to Adair, No. 7, 14 Nov. 1806, *F.O. Austria* 7/80.

[3] See above, p. 61, and below, pp. 114–15.

friendly, fervent letter to the Austrian Emperor. After this, over and over again, in his correspondence with Eugene, the commander of the army in Italy, he reiterated that he was on good terms with Austria, that the language of newspapers and of conversation must be entirely pacific and that nothing must be done to alarm the court of Vienna; while in letter after letter he betrayed his anxiety on the point and ordered precautions to be taken. And time and again, with all the wearisome insistence of the most frantic suitor he made advances and pressed for an alliance, exhausting the arguments by which to conjure and beguile, now luring with smooth words, now playing the braggart and hinting possible menace, one moment calming the Austrians with reassurances, next moment redoubling their fears, then offering them fairest promise and richest bribe, or if these failed, resorting to some trick that would entrap—all the while neatly rattling that dreadful sabre of his, till the Austrians, with their coy replies and the cold neutrality, and their evasive promises of friendship, began to show obvious symptoms of embarrassment, and feared that their unresponsiveness might be construed as hostility.

It began in the middle of September when Napoleon proposed to the court of Vienna the conclusion of an alliance, grounded on the basis of the treaty of 1756, stipulating the integrity of the Ottoman Porte and the independence of Saxony, and therefore directed against the courts of St Petersburg and Berlin. It was explained that Prussia was going to war to assert undue pretensions over Germany, and every chord was touched that would set Austrian jealousies vibrating. When an evasive reply was received Larochefoucauld was ordered to renew his efforts " as of your own accord and not as though you were acting under instructions", and was told to threaten that in case of refusal an alliance would be made with Prussia. He was further recommended to warn Stadion that if he allowed this opportunity to slip, he, and he alone, would be responsible for any disaster that might fall upon Austria; it was a risky form of argument, Talleyrand admitted, "but", he wrote, "nobody is more capable than you, Ambassador, of putting into dangerous reflexions all

the nuances and all the delicacy necessary for their efficiency".[1]
The elector of Würzburg was made the intermediary of a further
overture. Still the Austrians made evasive replies and paraded
their neutral intentions. On the eve of Jena they almost persuaded the English minister at their court that they were preparing to join the coalition;[2] though the defeat of Prussia dashed
these hopes to the ground,[3] and drove Stadion to the side of the
French minister. The chancellor became more ingratiating than
before, and held many, and long, interviews with Larochefoucauld. "He told me a host of things that might be taken for
certainties if words sufficed in politics", wrote Larochefoucauld;
and he added: "I keep up the appearance of having no distrust".[4] He had succeeded in persuading Talleyrand that the
Austrians felt the advantages of the alliance proposed by
Napoleon, but were unwilling to become involved in the existing
war.[5] The two ministers attempted to induce Napoleon to
exempt Austria from engagements that would involve her in the
war with Prussia, and rather to concentrate on the eventual issue
with the Czar; but Napoleon would have no exceptions, insisted
on the immediate present, enlarged on the opportunities of the
flying moment, played with the idea of a partition of Prussia
as an inducement to the Austrians, threatened to make some
alternative alliance, and became every day more impatient,
more pressing. At the beginning of November he learned after
long uncertainties that the Russians were marching to meet him
and that he was faced with a campaign in Poland. The army
with which the Austrians were proposing to guard the neutrality
of their states had hitherto given him little concern, but henceforward it would be in a position to threaten his rear. Now, in
a flash, he revealed himself in his most alarming mood. He had

---

[1] Talleyrand to Larochefoucauld, 12 Oct. 1806, *A.A.E. Autriche*, t. 379.
[2] Adair to Fox, No. 18, 13 Sept. 1806, in Adair, *Historical Memoir*,
p. 128, and Adair to Fox (separate), 24 Sept. 1806, *F.O. Austria* 7/80
(omitted from the *Historical Memoir*).
[3] Adair to Howick, 24 Oct. 1806, in Adair, *Historical Memoir*, p. 143.
[4] Larochefoucauld to Talleyrand, No. 83, 25 Oct. 1806, *A.A.E. Autriche*,
t. 379.
[5] See e.g. Talleyrand to Napoleon, 9 Oct. 1806, in P. Bertrand, *Lettres
inédites de Talleyrand à Napoléon*, No. cxcix.

already filled the Austrians with apprehension by appointing a military representative, Andréossy, to replace Larochefoucauld. He followed this step by issuing peremptory demands for Austrian disarmament. Coupling his anger with reassurances he repeated his call for an alliance, calmed any doubts the Austrians might have concerning the fate of their Polish provinces in the forthcoming campaign, and ordered Andréossy to "bring up lightly the question of the exchange of Galicia for Silesia".[1] The court of Vienna ceased its armaments but made no response to the renewed overtures. On one occasion the French minister met their refusal "in a tone of menace".

The suddenness and completeness of the victory of Jena— a victory for Napoleon over a new enemy and over a power that since the time of Frederick the Great had lived on a tradition of military glory—and the astonishing collapse of a whole monarchy which crumpled up in a way that was new to modern history, made the march of Napoleon seem like a cataclysm in nature and, more than anything else, was the type of achievement calculated to create a Napoleonic legend. Upon Austria, whose counsels had so long been confessedly ruled by timidity, the effect could only be disastrous. From this time the court of Vienna may spread hints that she intends joining the coalition, and may delude the ministers of Russia and England by judicious suggestions that she is always about to come to an energetic decision, but however much she may desire the downfall of France she is never sure that the opportunity has really arrived and she is haunted by the fear that if she makes a false move Napoleon will turn aside to finish with her before coping with Russia and will destroy her by some rapid stroke before her allies can come to her aid. If she is told that French designs in Poland are a menace to her own Polish provinces, she finds that Napoleon has anticipated her apprehensions and is ready with every assurance. If she is informed that Napoleon is always the enemy of Austria and will deal with her in turn, Napoleon points out Russia as a possible menace, too, and by every insinuation turns the eyes of Austria

---

[1] See the correspondence between Talleyrand and Andréossy printed in Handelsman, *Napoléon et la Pologne*, pp. 215–18.

upon the issue in Turkey. When the allies press for her co-operation she replies that her armaments are not ready, that her finances are exhausted, that she must have time to recuperate; she makes capital out of these difficulties and advertises them, and the Austrian Emperor will lay the responsibility for his decision at the door of the Archduke Charles who is resolutely opposed to war, while the Archduke Charles will say that the decision is not his, that he is not Emperor. Russia must concentrate her forces upon the struggle with Napoleon himself, and not discount her chances in this campaign by making diversions against Turkey; the Czar has not enough men in Poland—these are the objections of Austria, and if one victory is gained over the French, she says that two more must be won before she will risk a declaration of war. And all the time Napoleon entreats and makes promises and tries plan after plan, overture after overture, even repeats his threats at times, in an attempt to bring the government of Vienna into some engagement with France, and he too is met with evasions and delays and perpetual suggestions that a favourable decision is *about* to be announced, till he asks in despair, "What is the House of Austria after?"

At the close of the year 1806 the enemies of France set out seriously to win Austria to their side and to rescue their shaking cause; for the Austrian intervention, that was of such moment to Napoleon, had become a matter of unconcealed urgency to his enemies after the Prussian collapse had put an end to their first rash and over-confident hopes. The battle of Jena had reawakened Austrian terror of France, and minor points of complaint that had previously disturbed the relations between the courts of Vienna and St Petersburg, now came into light again, and old quarrels and jealousies broke out anew, intensified by the conduct of the Austrian minister in St Petersburg, a certain General Merfeldt who "mischievously exaggerated and inflamed every topic of dissension".[1] Strangely enough, the

---

[1] Adair to Howick (Private), 29 Jan. 1807, *F.O. Austria* 7/83. This passage is omitted from the close of the despatch as it is published on pp. 180–1 of Adair's *Historical Memoir*.

Austrians had just been complaining that the Russians did not "speak out to them", and had been excusing their inactivity by saying that they were kept in the dark concerning the Russian efforts in Poland and the Czar's attitude to themselves;[1] when, within four days, there arrived in Vienna one of the cleverest of the agents of the coalition. The Corsican, Pozzo di Borgo, in the service of the Czar, was pursuing Napoleon with all the passion of a vendetta, and the Russian government, making every attempt to prevent recent bickerings with Austria from leaving obstacles in the way of understanding, had released this man upon Vienna allowing him to draw up his own instructions.[2] He carried a letter from the Czar to the Austrian emperor, which declared that the Russians had no aim in fighting but that of self-defence, and showed in the strongest terms the necessity for co-operation. He carried also a flattering letter from the Czar to the Archduke Charles.[3] His object was to persuade the Austrians to grasp the favourable moment and intervene immediately in the war, and he was to propose the exchange of a declaration between the two powers to the effect that the war should be carried on to the utmost extremity, that no peace should be concluded unless by mutual consent, and that in case Prussia should abandon the common cause her neutrality should not be respected. Such was the distrust of the Prussians at this time, that, on the suggestion of the British minister in St Petersburg, even they were not allowed to pierce the secret of this mission, in case they should seek to win favour with Napoleon by betraying the move to him. "The fate of Europe", wrote the Czar to the Emperor, "will depend upon the decision you are about to make."

Pozzo di Borgo when he had at last helped to hound Napoleon from the continent was destined to be a creator of the tyranny that took his place, an apostle of the Holy Alliance, the incarnation of the policy of reaction. He became a kind of potentate

---

[1] Adair to Howick, 14 Dec. 1806, in Adair, *Historical Memoir*, p. 157.
[2] Stuart to Howick, No. 58, 28 Nov. 1806, *F.O. Russia* 65/65. Stuart to Adair, 26 Nov. 1806, in Adair, *Historical Memoir*, pp. 347–8.
[3] Printed in Beer, *Zehn Jahre österreichischer Politik* (1877), pp. 472–6.

in Europe till, to the minds of Englishmen, his name came to mean something crooked and sinister. In 1807, however, he was still on the side of the gods, servant of Liberation. Astute in diplomacy, subtle and smooth in speech, skilled in all the pleasant ways of courts, he seemed the very man to make his cause plausible and telling. With his social gifts, his love of deft intrigue, his graces of the "ancien régime", he was fitted for the old-world court of Vienna. This was a cause in which his personal feelings came to reinforce his zeal for the general good, the private hatreds of his passionate nature were at one with the motives of his public service, and the vanity and selfishness and ambition of the individual and the things in his make-up which were the most mean and corrupting, only added fuel to his desire to achieve the purpose of his mission.

Pozzo was seconded by Razoumovski, the Russian ambassador, and most influential of the foreign ministers in Vienna at this period. By his great wealth and social prestige Razoumovski had acquired an admitted ascendancy in the Austrian capital. He had rooted himself in the place, entwining his interests round it, becoming himself rather an Austrian than a Russian, and it was known that even should his official mission cease he would not return to his own country. His recall had been announced and his successor appointed in the summer of 1806, but his removal was a manœuvre of palace intrigues and the change was long delayed.[1] Napoleon was waiting for this, the Austrians were crying out against it, and when it should happen all the world knew that it would mean a tremendous weakening of the influence of the coalition in the counsels of the Austrian government; for though he was charged with having vested interests in Austria, and with neglecting the cause of his own government, and though he was even held culpable by many people for not having prepared the court of St Petersburg for the disastrous collapse of Austria at the close of 1805, he was a

---

[1] Czartoryski's protest against the removal of this minister is printed in *Sbornik*, LXXXII, 312–14. Budberg condemned the recall of Razoumovski as "the consequence of a court intrigue before he came into office". Stuart to Adair, 26 Nov. 1806, in Adair, *Historical Memoir*, Appendix, p. 347.

good "coalition" man. In society, above all, he succeeded in doing what it was impossible for anybody to do in official intercourse with the government at Vienna, and it was due to him more than to anyone else that the French minister in his despatches to Paris had to complain that the people of Vienna were loud in their sympathy with the coalition, that they rejoiced to hear news of reverses to French troops, that they were waiting to fall treacherously on the rear of Napoleon if the opportunity should occur, and that the situation was such as to make a Frenchman's position delicate and embarrassing.

Pozzo and Razoumovski found an ally whose assistance seemed likely to add weight to their efforts. This was the English minister at Vienna.

The English tory newspapers were never weary of insisting upon the fact that

At the court of Vienna, a court which, however fallen in dignity, still prides itself in the antiquity of its nobility, the splendour of its appearance, and the forms of its ceremonial, the son of an army surgeon was commissioned to represent the dignity of the British nation.

But the wits retorted that, son of a famous surgeon, he was "le fils du plus grand saigneur de l'Europe". The surgeon was the man who was hero of the Scottish version of "Robin Adair", and Robert, the son, did not go unsung, for he was the subject of famous parodies in the *Anti-Jacobin Review*, and was the favourite object of ridicule of the enemies of the Whig party. He had no experience in diplomacy, though at a critical period in the history of Anglo-Russian relations he was charged with acting as representative of the English opposition at the court of the Czarina Catherine II, and the mysterious journey that he made to St Petersburg, the attitude he adopted towards the English minister there, and the uneasiness he gave to the British government at the time, brought him into disrepute. The incident provoked the lines about

the youth whose daring Soul
With *Half a Mission* sought the Frozen Pole.

He seems to have been an easy, impetuous, light-headed fellow, firm friend of Fox. But he was married to a French woman, who was "suspect", and he was never allowed to escape from the handicap which this gave him. According to Starhemberg the French wife "was the only reason which prevented Fox from nominating Adair as under-secretary for foreign affairs". As it was, he went to Vienna—the appointment was an acknowledged "job"—retaining the post on the condition that Mrs Adair stayed in England. Howick, when he came into office, repeatedly said that "if she went to Vienna her husband would be recalled on the spot".[1] Everything gave the idea that his was a precarious appointment, from which the interests of England would suffer. And yet when the tory ministry came into power in March and talked of replacing him by a person of dignity and worth, more adequate to a court like the Austrian, there came from Vienna one strong insistent line of protests. "We could not be anything but annoyed if M. Adair were recalled."[2] From the allied headquarters at Memel the new ambassador to Russia, Lord G. Leveson-Gower, wrote strongly to the ministry in order to prevent the change.[3] And although a new minister-plenipotentiary was despatched and reached Vienna, Adair did stay on—stayed after his wife had outraged the English government by making the forbidden appearance in the Austrian capital—and only returned to England when the British diplomatic missions were driven out of Europe after Tilsit.

Adair had been strongly warned, in his instructions, of the inadvisability of any attempt to urge the Austrians to declare war, unless they could see for themselves that this was the policy their own interests dictated to them; but when Pozzo di Borgo reached Vienna and the two Russian ministers called for Adair's

[1] Starhemberg to Stadion, No. 78, 7 Oct. 1807, *W.S.A. Berichte aus London.*

[2] Stadion to Starhemberg, 28 Ap. 1807, *W.S.A. Weisungen nach London.* Stadion, in despatch No. 4 of 5 Ap. 1807, had described the interest he took in seeing that Adair "soit fixé ici d'une manière plus solide qu'il n'a été jusqu'à présent et qu'on le récompense en quelque façon des services qu'il rend à son souverain." See also Stadion's despatch No. 5 of 11 July 1807, but cf. p. 123 below.

[3] *Private Correspondence of Lord G. Leveson-Gower*, II, 296.

co-operation, he sent arguments, excuses, and apologies to his government and threw himself into the endeavour.[1] These three men consulted and combined together and began a vigorous organised campaign to break through that stubborn neutrality which was working so much to the advantage of Napoleon, and to combat that obstinate perversity which was the paralysis of the Austrian counsels.

Their failure, coming at a moment of pessimism and disquietude, was the greatest of all the disappointments of the campaign. So soon as Pozzo di Borgo brought the court of Vienna to the direct issue of intervention or non-intervention, all hints and suggestions of an impending decision vanished, and Count Stadion, faced with the logic of the situation, resorted to the wildest fencing, to arguments that ceased to be even plausible, rather than recede from the position he had taken up. The Austrians had no love for France, but, wrote Pozzo di Borgo, "their hearts are frozen with fear, it is the master-motive of their conduct".[2]

The situation would have been much more simple if Austria could have been indifferent to the issue of the war in which she refused to take part. But hers was not a disinterested neutrality, her own fate was being hammered out while she stood watching, and it soon became evident that the longer she dallied and made attempts to flirt with both parties, the more difficult it would be for her to come to terms with the victor. She dreaded a victory for France which would enable Napoleon to turn upon her with punishment for her equivocations; she was anxious lest the Russians in despair should make a self-regarding peace with France, ignoring the salvation of Europe which they had set out to secure; she was nervous about England—for England might win a selfish advantage by coming to a private arrangement with Napoleon. These powers soon learned how to tease the Austrian government by threatening to leave its interests

---

[1] Adair to Howick, No. 33, 30 Dec. 1806, *F.O. Austria* 7/81. The parts of this despatch referred to above are printed in Adair, *Historical Memoir*, pp. 162–9.

[2] Extracts from Pozzo's despatches are printed in A. Vandal, *Napoléon et Alexandre Ier* (1911), I, 17–22, 39 *et seq.*

out of any future settlement of the affairs of Europe. Secretly praying for the downfall of France the Austrians felt the dangers of the attitude they were adopting, and dreaded the contingency that might come to force their hands. On the 30th of December Count Stadion "admitted that it was morally impossible in the present state of things to look forward to neutrality as a permanent system".[1]

In these circumstances the declaration of policy that Napoleon made on the subject of a general peace, came as a welcome suggestion to the court of Vienna at the close of the year 1806; for it not only gave the hope that a pacification would put an end to the dilemma that was before Austria, it provided her with a rôle and a purpose, it gave her some fixity of aim in the existing difficulties, and it enabled her to evade the problem of intervention that was daily pressing more closely upon her. On the 6th of December Adair reported to London that "the communication made by M. Talleyrand to Count Lucchesini on signing the armistice on the 16th [Nov.]...will, I have reason to believe, be productive of an offer from this Court of its mediation for a General Peace".[2]

Adair's first thought, when he became aware of the Austrian intention, was that this premature talk of peace, when the Russians had barely come to grips with Napoleon in Poland, would have a restraining influence upon the prosecution of the war. Immediately he wrote to the English minister, Stuart, informing him of what the Austrians proposed to do, and "cautioning him against the effect such a measure may have in relaxing the exertions of the court of St Petersburg".[3] His information, arriving at a time when every message from Vienna was giving anxiety to the Czar, drew out the Russian chancellor to a declaration of opinion. Stuart "observed that such a measure would afford time for the French government to ripen and combine her military and political operations"; he thought

---

[1] Adair to Howick, No. 33, 30 Dec. 1806, in Adair, *Historical Memoir*, p. 168.
[2] Adair to Howick (Separate), 6 Dec. 1806, in Adair, *op. cit.* p. 156.
[3] *Ibid.*

that Austria "without really forwarding the peace" was merely delaying the time when she would be called upon to take action, trying to create an excuse for disbanding the troops she had already assembled in Galicia and Bohemia. Budberg declared his agreement but added that

in case the offer should be submitted to the Court of St Petersburg it would be necessary to shew the sincere wish of His Imperial Majesty to conciliate all existing differences by patiently and temperately hearing what conditions the French Government may propose as a basis of negotiation; but that this Power would not on that account desist from any military enterprises or cease to press the armaments which there is reason to believe have already commenced in Austria.[1]

With this plan slowly forming and defining itself in their minds, the Austrian government could more easily and comfortably resist the pressure of Pozzo di Borgo and his colleagues; the importunity of the demands for the intervention of Austria only confirmed the court of Vienna in its adoption of a policy which provided such a plausible means of escape. The final answer of Stadion to Pozzo was

that, after everything else had been tried, the measure that had been adopted, that is to say the offer of mediation and the desire to take part in the promotion of peace, was the only one which could be reconciled with the differences of opinion here, particularly between the Archduke and the Emperor.[2]

Stadion gave it to be understood that such a step was the only one which could possibly allow any chance of the eventual entry of Austria into the war. He declared his intention of supporting the mediation by a great display of forces. He pointed out that if Napoleon should refuse to consent to a general negotiation, his obstinacy would put him so obviously in the wrong, that Austria could have no choice but to turn against him; while, if Napoleon accepted, things would happen during the discussions which would make Austria range herself on the side of the allies, and gradually drift from mediation into war.

[1] Stuart to Howick, No. 77, 29 Dec. 1806, *F.O. Russia* 65/65.
[2] Despatch of Pozzo di Borgo 14/26 Jan. 1807, quoted in Vandal, *Napoléon et Alexandre Ier*, i, 40.

As a preliminary to the offer of its good offices the Austrian court sought to secure a statement of opinion from Russia, and instructed Merfeldt, its minister at St Petersburg, to sound the disposition of the Czar and discover in what way the measure would be received. After several conferences with the chancellor Budberg, Merfeldt was able, in the middle of February, to send a very favourable report to his government. Budberg explained to him that on the rejection of Oubril's treaty he had looked to France to make the next move in negotiation, but that each power was afraid of compromising its dignity by suing the other for peace. The mediation of Austria, he thought, would remove any obstacle caused by the unwillingness of both France and Russia to make the first advances. Prussia had recently sent Colonel Krüsemarck with a similar proposal, but Austria was in a far better position than Prussia to act as peace-maker on this occasion. She had the same interests in seeing a limit placed upon the power and aggressions of Napoleon and in securing the independence of Germany, but she had the advantage in that she could support her mediation by a large army and with the resources of a great power. Prussia, also, by the very fact that her whole existence depended upon her efforts for peace, had an interest in exploiting every chance of negotiating, and so was unfitted for the serious rôle of peace-maker, being unable to exert the same persuasion and invite the same response as the court of Vienna could do. The Czar, added Budberg, also desired that the intervention of Austria should put an end to his differences with the Porte; he wished to leave to Turkey all the territories and all the rights which her last treaty with Russia had secured to her; all that he would insist upon would be the maintenance of the treaties. He desired nothing so much as the re-establishment of the former relations with Turkey under the guarantee of Austria and England; but he wanted the destruction of the French ascendancy in the Divan.

General Budberg, while accepting the proposal of mediation, sought to fasten the Austrian government down to the interpretation of it that Stadion had given to Pozzo di Borgo. He insisted that the mediation should not be the excuse for a weak and pacific policy on the part of the court of Vienna. He pointed out the advantage that would result from effective armaments which would give weight to the mediation, and he explained how, under cover of the negotiation, Austria could advance and hasten military preparations without raising suspicion or compromising herself with France.[1]

Nor during this period did the Austrians cease to raise the hopes of the allies by hints of their intention of entering the war. Once more, on the eve of the battle of Eylau, the government sent round a whisper—it wished to enter into explanations with the coalition, and everybody was on tiptoe to see the desired event. Adair reported, in cypher, secret communications between Stadion and Razoumovski, Pozzo di Borgo, and himself, and described how Stadion's brother had acted as intermediary.[2] He gave optimistic accounts of the condition of the Austrian army, related even the conversion of the Archduke Charles, and declared that everything would be ready within a few weeks. Adair listened readily to such flowery tales. Perhaps this explains why his presence was so welcome at Vienna. Later he must have recognised the excess of his enthusiasm, for when he published his despatches in his *Historical Memoir of a Mission to Vienna*, a large number of excisions that he made consisted of passages where he had been over eager to promise or predict a forthcoming intervention of Austria. M. Andréossy, French minister in Vienna, did not at this period allow himself to be so deceived, "It is easy to see...", he wrote, "as I have often had the honour to inform your excellency, that in completing the organisation of her army, in adopting a warlike tone, and in making military dispositions, Austria was only seeking to delude both parties."[3] Disillusionment soon came to the allies. Eylau, which should have brushed away the last obstacle and convinced the Austrians of their opportunity, produced a contrary effect,

[1] Merfeldt to Stadion, 4/16 Feb. enclosed in Stadion to Starhemberg, 5 Ap. 1807, *W.S.A. Weisungen nach London*. Budberg also declared his opinion in a despatch to the Russian minister in Vienna, dated 24 Jan. 1807 (v.s.) See Alex. Wassiltchikow, *Les Razoumovski*, t. ii, 3me partie, p. 85.

[2] Adair to Howick, No. 7, 28 Jan. 1807, *F.O. Austria* 7/83; see also No. 3, 14 Jan. 1807, *ibid*. The passages referred to are omitted from the documents printed on pp. 172 and 177 respectively of Adair's *Historical Memoir*.

[3] Andréossy to Talleyrand, No. 23, 10 Mar. 1807, *A.A.E. Autriche*, t. 380, but cf. pp. 162 *et seq*. below.

and seemed to come itself as a discouragement. Now it began
to appear that not France only, but Russia, was being regarded
as a possible menace.[1] People shook their heads and feared that
these Austrians were anxious about Turkey and jealous of the
movements of the Czar, and that they would be happy to see
Russia and France break against one another, and wear themselves out in the contest, until both should cease to be a menace
to their neighbours.[2] At the same time, the court of Vienna was
anxious concerning the future of Germany, and looked with cold
distrust upon the ambitions of the Prussian ministers. "Shall
I tell you what people are thinking here?", said Stadion to the
Russian ambassador: "They are thinking that you are carrying
on the war for the interests of Prussia."

Away in Warsaw another special agent, General Vincent, was
conducting an evasive diplomacy. The Austrian government had
despatched him in January to the French headquarters, "for no
particular object", so it declared, "beyond that of obtaining
correct information of what is going on there". His stay in
Warsaw caused some apprehension by reason of the mystery
that surrounded it, and the reticence that was shown concerning
its purpose. For a long time he waited, playing for time, without
coming to any point, and in March Talleyrand was writing that,
though "the time which has elapsed since Vincent has been in
Warsaw might give to suppose the existence of active negotiations and perhaps of an arrangement between the two powers,
there has been nothing but discussions which as yet have been
fruitless".[3] Adair saw that the object of the mission was "kept
a most profound secret",[4] but guessed that it was concerned with
the proposed movement for peace.

"I cannot dismiss my suspicions", he wrote, "that although
Austria would be sorry to see a separate peace concluded by Prussia,

[1] Adair to Howick, No. 15, 26 Feb. 1807, *F.O. Austria* 7/83 (passages
omitted from the document published on p. 191 of Adair's *Historical
Memoir*).

[2] *Ibid.*; see also P. Bertrand, *Lettres inédites de Talleyrand à Napoléon*,
No. CCXLV.

[3] Talleyrand to Andréossy, 8 Mar. 1807, *A.A.E. Autriche*, t. 380.

[4] Adair to Howick, 21 Jan. 1807, in Adair, *Historical Memoir*, p. 174.

or even a peace concluded at this moment by Prussia and Russia together, she would seize with eagerness any opening that might be afforded to be the mediatrix of a general peace, in the discussion for which her own interests might be likely under such circumstances to be considered."[1]

Stadion informed the Austrian minister in London of the motive of this mission. Vincent had been sent, he said, to deal with the problems that were bound to arise from the proximity of the belligerent armies to the neutral frontier, but he had also been charged:

not only to sound the dispositions of Napoleon with regard to a negotiation of peace by means of a Congress of the powers concerned, such as he himself had suggested, but also to declare how much our August Master wishes to contribute to the promotion of a just and lasting peace.[2]

Until the Russian government replied to the first hint of the proposed mediation, Vincent did not seriously press the subject in his conversations at Warsaw, but concerned himself with gaining time, patiently listening to offers of alliance from France, quietly transmitting them to his government, carefully avoiding every commitment, until Napoleon despaired, could not think what Austria was wanting, even talked of offering part of Silesia as a bribe to her, though he saw it was a "hazardous" move.[3] At the beginning of March Vincent secured from Napoleon a declaration of his intentions and a statement of the plans he had for Europe, the basis he desired for a future peace.[4] In reply to his overtures Napoleon declared that the integrity of the Porte and the restoration of Prussia, which implied, he said, the abandonment of his views on Poland, were the objects he had in view. He asked Vincent to state what he, on his part, would demand for Austria, he invited him to conclude a treaty on

---

[1] Adair to Howick, 28 Jan. 1807, in Adair, *Historical Memoir*, p. 179.

[2] Stadion to Starhemberg, 21 Feb. 1807, *W.S.A. Weisungen nach London*.

[3] Talleyrand describes his conversations with Vincent at Warsaw in letters to Napoleon (P. Bertrand, *op. cit.* pp. 302–464 *passim*) and in despatches to Andréossy (*A.A.E. Autriche*, t. 380 *passim*).

[4] P. Bertrand, *op. cit.* No. ccxxxix, where Vincent is described as perpetually saying, "Ne voulez-vous rien faire avec nous, ni par nous?"

these terms and he made it known that there could be no peace, no stability, until France and Austria or France and Russia combined to guarantee it to Europe.[1] At last he imagined he had fastened Vincent to something definite; he interviewed the man in person, and sent instructions to Talleyrand at Warsaw and to his ambassador in Vienna. Vincent drew him on. He could not disguise from himself, he said, that the proposed basis seemed satisfactory. The offer to restore Prussia would particularly remove the uneasiness his government had felt. When pressed to say what the court of Vienna would demand in the proposed peace he declared that great value would be set upon the possession of part of the Adriatic coast and of Dalmatia, but he made it understood that his court expressed desires rather than demands or even hopes in this matter. What he considered as far more necessary, and as being essential to the security of peace, was that Napoleon, having arranged the continent, should keep only a stipulated number of troops in Germany until the maritime peace should be concluded. Napoleon even showed himself disposed to grant this point. Vincent had no powers to sign anything on the spot, but he would write home for fresh orders. It was not until Talleyrand enquired if, once these terms of peace could be agreed upon, Austria would help to win and conquer such a peace, that the futility of the discussions became apparent. Vincent pretended not to see that Napoleon was working for an alliance of that kind; in his naïve way he explained that he had been talking of peace, not of war, and that his court would make no engagement binding Austria to join in the war, and that Austria would use persuasion and influence, but nothing more, to bring the belligerent powers to reason. He had played a deep game, but he had won from it a statement of the dispositions of France in regard to a future settlement.[2]

Napoleon was angry when the news of the failure of this negotiation and the reports of the continual armaments of Austria seemed to suggest that that power was contemplating

[1] *Corresp. de Nap. Ier*, t. XIV, No. 11,977.
[2] P. Bertrand, *op. cit.* No. CCL. Talleyrand to Andréossy, 12 Mar. 1807, *A.A.E. Autriche*, t. 380.

hostilities against France. He made a show of force and assumed a threatening attitude, but repeated the same offer of alliance and pointed out the splendid rôle that Austria could play in thus contributing to the cause of peace. Even England, he said, desired peace at bottom, and could not bear the immense financial burden of the war.[1] This communication reached Vincent at an opportune moment and he was in a position to use it to advantage, for before it arrived he received new instructions. These were sent from Vienna on the 11th of March, when it was known that the Czar had given a favourable answer to the tentative proposal of Austria. On the 18th of March Vincent informed Talleyrand of the intention of his court to contribute to the cause of peace by mediating between the belligerent powers, and he supported his offers by describing the reception they had received at St Petersburg. The overture was unofficial and Vincent was unable to grant Talleyrand's request for a written communication on the subject. Talleyrand criticised the answer of Russia to the proposal. He saw that the Czar considered his war with Turkey as being separate from his war with France, and was disposed to conclude it by a separate transaction. He saw too, that although the Russians had stated the basis upon which they would consent to negotiate with the Ottoman Porte, they had not shown the same frankness with respect to a peace with France but had merely declared an intention of treating. He explained that while the Russians stipulated for the maintenance of ancient treaties in their settlement with the Porte, Napoleon demanded more and insisted upon the complete independence of Turkey. Vincent however slurred over the objections and made it understood that the present overture was merely a preliminary one and that modifications could be made at a later date.[2]

Napoleon refused to allow an official reply to be made to this overture before it had been officially opened to him by Austria, but he ordered Talleyrand to give an intimation that his answer

[1] *Corresp. de Nap. I*er, t. xiv, Nos. 12,028, 12,082.
[2] P. Bertrand, *op. cit.* No. cclxv. Talleyrand to Andréossy, 22 Mar. 1807, *A.A.E. Autriche*, t. 380.

would be favourable provided that Austria did nothing to cause him uneasiness or alarm. He immediately seized upon the fact that the Russians had accepted the offer of mediation because it seemed a means of dragging the court of Vienna out of its isolation and of engaging it to join the coalition. Therefore as a condition of his acceptance he demanded that Austria should not arm, and should adopt no hostile attitude. She must sincerely take up the part of peace-maker, and Talleyrand was to show her what a fine rôle this was.[1]

Talleyrand informed Vincent of the attitude of Napoleon and wrote also to Andréossy at Vienna, ordering him to act, if the matter were broached to him, as though he were "not certain, but had an idea that France would not be unwilling to accept the intervention of Austria for the establishment of a peace in which Turkey should be comprised".

"If there is talk of an armistice", the instructions went on to say, "You must remark that in the despatches which I write to you there is no mention of this topic; you do not see any reason why the Emperor should desire an armistice; you do not think the matter has entered his head; it does not seem to you that such a proposition should come from him; the power which has been allowed to intervene as mediator is the one to do this, if it thinks proper; still, it is your private opinion that a suspension of arms is not only natural but necessary in the event of a negotiation. To negotiate while fighting would be to work upon bases which would shift every day with the movement of events; consequently it would be fruitless."[2]

Napoleon declared that a proposition like the following would be acceptable to him:

There shall be a suspension of arms of three or six months' duration between the belligerent powers, and it shall be based upon the actual status quo; negotiators on behalf of Russia, Turkey, Prussia, England and France, shall meet at Vienna to work for peace under the mediation of Austria.[3]

It was a repetition of the proposal of a congress that Napoleon had made to the Prussian Colonel Kleist a month before, with

[1] *Corresp. de Nap. Ier*, t. xiv, No. 12,098.
[2] Talleyrand to Andréossy, 31 Mar. 1807, *A.A.E. Autriche*, t. 380.
[3] *Corresp. de Nap. Ier*, t. xiv, No. 12,181.

Vienna instead of Memel as the seat of negotiation, and with the admission of Austria as mediating party. An armistice was wanted and was to be put forward with the same arguments as before, only Napoleon was unwilling to ask for it directly, this time, and did not even wish the question to be raised as yet. Talleyrand was ordered not to mention it at all to Vincent until later. Meanwhile Austria would have something to keep her quiet.

At some times Napoleon would have growled at the Austrians and pushed their mediation down their throats, or dismissed it with a swagger. But now he was rather in a mood to humour them. In a way he was not sorry to see them adopt a rôle which would prevent or at least postpone their entry into the war against him. He had every motive for gaining time and beginning a negotiation which might relax the efforts of his enemies or provoke differences and dissensions among them. If he could not have his way with the Austrians, yet at least they had given him something to juggle with. He had forgotten none of his old tricks and manœuvres; as his response to the offer of mediation clearly proved. Everything was buried in suggestions and stipulations that hinted no generous gesture from him, no desire to meet his enemies half-way. Everything was worded to announce that though they offered themselves as peace-makers, the Austrians were expected to come as a secret support against the Czar. Again there was that harping upon "the integrity of the Ottoman Porte"; the phrase had become a wearisome obsession with him; he knew that no words could have been more charged with menace to the proposed negotiation, no cry could have been raised better calculated, behind its plausibility, to challenge and inflame any discussions that might be contemplated. The Austrians might have their mediation to play with, but it must spoil no plans, and Napoleon must have a free hand to turn it, as he had turned his overtures to Prussia, into a conspiracy against the Czar.

It satisfied the Austrians that the Czar disclaimed all pretensions against Turkey, and that Napoleon was promising to restore the Prussian monarchy and abandon his Polish schemes.

They did not look too closely at the further inconsistencies in the respective demands of the two monarchs, and they declared themselves encouraged in their purpose. The way was now clear for another advance, and they came forward with an official offer of their good offices on behalf of peace. It was important that they should prescribe unobjectionable bases for the negotiation they had in view, in order to give no loophole to unwilling powers. A month before their offer of mediation, Stadion had in an unofficial way given an outline of the principles which he would wish to lay down for a proposed congress. He had declared that Poland must be left as before the war, that the affairs of Germany and Italy—in which the Austrians had many interests—should be the subject of general revision and negotiation, and that the question of the Ottoman Porte should be settled according to former treaties.[1] There was an obvious anti-French bias, however, in these stipulations and Napoleon had recently announced his refusal to accept that renewal of the old treaty arrangements in Turkey. Therefore the Austrians took refuge in pious vaguenesses, and drew up a note that could be accepted by all parties, demanding only that the negotiation "should extend over the reciprocal interests and essential relations of the Powers taking part in it", and that a secure and stable settlement should be made for the future.[2] No particular method of pursuing the negotiation was laid down, but a town in Moravia or Bohemia was offered for the assembly of a congress.

To the enemies of France the Austrians sent with these proposals some footnotes of explanation. They could not grant a place in Galicia as the seat of a congress, they said, since Napoleon might see an opportunity for abusing their invitation and filling the province with his emissaries or attempting to spread his Polish insurrection there. It would be easy to stir up discontent in a territory so recently acquired by Austria.

[1] Adair to Howick, 14 Mar. 1807, in Adair, *Historical Memoir*, p. 203. See also despatch Razoumovski to Budberg 20 Feb./4 Mar. 1807, in Alex. Wassiltchikow, *Les Razoumovski*, t. II, 3 me partie, pp. 100–2.

[2] Starhemberg to Canning, 18 Ap. 1807, in *Parliamentary Debates*, x, cols. 100–2.

Stadion also took the view that Turkey was outside the system of Europe and not concerned in the questions at issue in the negotiation. If a Turkish minister took part, he explained, the man would be under the complete influence of France whenever the discussion touched on the larger European issues. Constantinople was merely notified of the mediation, but not invited to join in the congress.[1] When the court of Vienna asked the views of Russia and France on the expediency of an armistice, it turned aside to explain to the Czar that Napoleon would in all probability demand a suspension of hostilities in order to gain time for military preparations and reinforcements. Though not acquainted with the precise opinions of the Russian government, Stadion wrote that he had

reason to suppose that the Cabinet of St Petersburg will see no advantage in an arrangement which would apparently leave France in possession of all the conquests she has made over Prussia, and on the other hand keep the Russian troops almost on their frontier. It appears that if there is to be question of an armistice it can only be on terms which would establish some equality between the positions of the respective armies or which, at any rate, would not make the situation of things worse by perpetuating it.[2]

But with all their whisperings and safeguards and manipulations the Austrians knew that their schemes might be ruined and all they had hoped to secure from their mediation thwarted, if one power proved intractable—and that power the one which had offered no hint of the reception it would give to their proposals. The Austrians had not merely decided upon mediation in order to escape warlike commitments and evade the dilemma afforded by the war of the fourth coalition; they had adopted it as a device for securing a voice in the future settlement of the continent. All would be ruined if England scorned their mediation and refused to make this her opportunity for contributing to the salvation of Europe. All would be hopeless for them if

[1] Stadion to Starhemberg, 5 Ap. 1807 (No. 1), *W.S.A. Weisungen nach London.*

[2] Soltikof (acting foreign minister at St Petersburg), describing his interview with Merfeldt, in a letter to Budberg 6/18 Ap. 1807, in *Sbornik,* LXXXVIII, 35–8.

England clung to her maritime plunders and left them to pursue the master of the continent empty-handed.[1] The matter of highest moment was to enlist the British government in the Austrian cause, and secure its colonial conquests as objects of negotiation. Yet what was England doing? the continent was asking. It had even been rumoured that she was resuming separate negotiations at Paris. On the other hand if she refused to join in the arrangements for peace in Europe and persisted in the war, matters would be still worse, the pretext would exist for the continued retention of French troops in Germany, and the source would still remain for future wars and disturbances in Europe. Count Stadion expressed his uneasiness when he communicated the offer of mediation to London. In his despatch to Starhemberg he recalled those mischievous words by which Douglas at St Petersburg had insinuated the adoption of a "policy of isolation" by England. His instructions were pressing.

"It seems to us impossible to reach the goal", he wrote, "unless England takes a principal part and joins a maritime peace to the Continental Peace. There is nobody but the British Ministry at present in a position to negotiate on equal terms with France; there is nobody but England able to offer real compensations for the objects which would be necessary for the establishment of any sort of balance in Europe; she alone can induce Napoleon to withdraw all his troops to France, she alone can contribute with real efficacy to the security of the future pacification."

Stadion appealed to the interests of Great Britain herself, and added "whatever may be the political opinions of the Cabinet of St James's, it could never cut itself asunder from the general system of Europe".[2]

With all these preparations and safeguards the Austrian mediation put out to sea, for the four winds of heaven to blow upon it.

---

[1] "Il n'y a que le Cabinet Britannique qui soit dans le moment en position de pouvoir négocier avec la Cour de France à avantage égal; il n'y a que lui qui puisse offrir des compensations réelles...." Stadion to Starhemberg, 5 Ap. 1807 (No. 1), *W.S.A. Weisungen nach London.*

[2] *Ibid.* The official offer of mediation is printed in *Parliamentary Debates*, x, cols. 101–2, with covering letters from Starhemberg to G. Canning, 18 Ap. 1807, cols. 100–1.

CHAPTER II

THE REVIVAL OF MARTIAL ARDOUR IN ALL PARTIES

THE Austrian mediation came to the powers at war at the moment when they were beginning to regain their liveliness. The campaign seemed to unfasten itself. All was galvanic again. With the passing of March things seemed to loosen and thaw, and something of the change of weather passed into the combatants, and you began to discover that though Napoleon might still talk of an armistice, he did not want it yet—the Russians might consent to negotiate, but they were exchanging whispers about "driving the French beyond the Rhine". England at last awoke and picked up a score of lost threads of activity. And the Prussians not merely gained confidence along with the rest of the powers, but became the most aggressive and boastful of them all. On the one hand Napoleon began to talk more loudly, more hopefully of the campaign; on the other, all his enemies leapt up at once to put energy into the coalition. The Austrian intervention was not very fortunately timed.

On the 1st of April Napoleon left his dreary quarters at Osterode, and moved to a neighbouring village. Here he found comfort, for he lived in the castle of Finckenstein, the residence of a Prussian court official. For two months he stayed in the place, having walks with Murat in the garden, attending a daily parade of troops in the grounds, and riding off on tours of military inspection. Every day he would sit before masses of correspondence from his marshals and his ministers in France, from Talleyrand at Warsaw and the chief of police in Paris, from the vassal kings of Naples and Holland, and other members of his family; then pacing the room with slow and measured tread, bursting out on occasion with angry or passionate gesture in those terrible tempers of his, he would dictate the letters that directed the movements of an army and the destiny of an empire but only half revealed the soul of the man—letters crisp and pointed, full of abrupt ejaculations and neat colloquialism, not without moments of acid reproof and stinging concentrated criticism—not without open-hearted generosity and stirring trumpet-calls. To Finckenstein Napoleon's officers would come to report or to receive his orders; and Blücher came, as we have seen, surly and rugged and cold, determined to resist the charms and blandishments of his attractive foe; an ambassador from Turkey who had been waiting for over a month in Warsaw arrived, not so eager as could be desired to promote the French alliance, and not at all pleased to find that there was an envoy from Persia as well; Talleyrand also came, when Napoleon could not quite trust him in Warsaw talking too freely with an Austrian minister; came also—not Josephine, for Napoleon would not hear of it—but the Countess Walewska, who perhaps was not yet disillusioned in her hopes of promoting the salvation of Poland.

One would like to have been at Finckenstein, to catch a glimpse of that short, uniformed figure, now beginning to grow stout—getting stouter in the thick of campaigning—not as handsome as he once had been, but with those strange irresistible eyes. Never was his mind more masterly or his genius more sure than in those weeks that preceded Tilsit, when he rescued the situation in Poland and once more organised astounding victory. Already when he moved to his new quarters he had caught a hint of the better weather that was approaching and he was not the one to be slow in making dispositions for the event. Already he was shaking the snow from his coat, and one could catch the first rumblings of the adjustments and preparations that were soon to set his gigantic machine in motion once again. Danzig had been invested, and he was beginning to press the siege with vigour. He moved against the Swedes and compelled them to make a truce. He took a sultan under his wing and directed the efforts of the shah, signing a treaty with Persia, finding it prudent to delay commitments with the Porte. He rejoiced to hear the failure of British ships which had sought to dictate policy at Constantinople; he became satisfied, after long doubting, that the Turks were really ready to co-operate with him; he even talked of enterprises in India. "Make

preparations at Brest", he ordered, "which will give an idea
that there is to be an expedition to Ireland. Speak of this to
Irishmen themselves and see that the news spreads."[1] From
Stralsund to the bounds of Persia his eye swept the whole line;
and he was co-ordinating a great effort and seemed like organising
a grand confederacy to bring the Russians to heel. Still it was the
Russians who were the focus of his thoughts, and nothing at all
breathed expectancy of peace.

He watched the drift of opinion in Paris and caught the
flying rumours. His eye was on the columns of newspapers, and
the conduct of theatres in the capital. If anything of the gossip
of salons or the talk of cafés touched the political situation, he
would get wind of it. Occasionally he would turn round as though
something was tugging at his coat; some element in French
affairs would demand his intervention. It annoyed him that the
public seemed incorrigible on the subject of Eylau; people
persisted in taking too seriously the bulletin he had issued after
the battle;

"Never has the position of France been greater or finer than to-day",
he wrote. "As for Eylau I have said time and again that the bulletin
exaggerated the losses....As for the letters that some officers may
write, it must not be forgotten that they do not know what is going on
in an army any more than the people who walk in the garden of the
Tuileries know what is going on in the Cabinet."[2]

There had been a new call for conscripts; more murmuring, more
complaints. Napoleon would try to make answer—to stop the
foolish speculations of his subjects. "There is no point in always
talking of peace", he would say. "That is just the way not to
get it."[3] He would have peace, he said, though he had to fight

---

[1] *Corresp. de Nap. Ier*, t. xv, No. 12,486; cf. No. 12,362.

[2] *Corresp. de Nap. Ier*, t. xv, No. 12,361. The effect that the news of Eylau
produced in Paris can be appreciated from a remark in a report from the
Austrian chargé d'affaires in Paris, Le Fèvre Rechtenberg, to Metternich
dated Paris, 23 Nov. 1912: "La bataille du 7 Sept....fut d'abord assez
généralement représentée à Paris comme une seconde bataille d'Eylau.
La consternation de grand nombre de familles qui avaient des craintes à
concevoir, s'était alors étendue à la généralité". *English Historical Review*,
xvi (1901), 515.

[3] *Corresp. de Nap. Ier*, t. xv, No. 12,382.

for it. It was the true military man's way of murmuring Peace
with his hand on his sword. He was his former self again, and
old familiar strains were returning to his utterances—echoes of
passed campaigns. It was exaggeration perhaps, but it was not
a mere hoarse boast and it came with the authentic Napoleonic
ring, when he wrote: "It is probable that within a fortnight
I shall have defeated the Russians".

Yet if we are to see Napoleon in his giant days at Finckenstein
and form the least conception of that brain which was teeming
with ideas, racing with utmost fertility of expedients—every
new conjuncture striking off more sparks as from a perpetually
live wire—we must give a glance at the things he did in aside,
the threads of government which he followed up, as it were, in
parenthesis, when for a moment he could turn his head from the
grand preoccupation. We see then the summary way in which
he could dispose of the sundry by-problems that came to side-
track him, we realise his mastery of touch in the most casual
matters, and we can gain an impression of the agility with which
he could bring the focus to every new question that confronted
him, the versatility of his mind in the face of a complexity of
problems, the clearness with which he would sort out the issues
from a confusion of events, and the certainty with which he
could swoop down upon his objective. These are the things
which make the impressiveness of Napoleon's genius and give
it the imperial range. Amid all the labours of war and of
diplomacy he had time to quarrel with the Pope, or play
"paternal government" to necessitous industries in France. He
would go into a lengthy discussion about the founding of a
special school of literature and history, or give comprehensive
regulations for the education of girls. Not merely the broad
direction of policy but the intricacies of small detail came under
his careful scrutiny. "It was he who called attention to the
omission from a return of two regiments which had been overlooked at Luxembourg; it was he who, by comparing hospital
with the regimental returns, discovered how many of his men
were marauding all over the country." It was he who informed
his minister of police of what Mme de Staël was doing in Paris,

when the minister had announced that she had actually left the city. Further he would give lessons in government to his brothers, tirelessly reiterating and ringing the changes on the text: "A prince who in the first year of his reign is held to be good, is a prince who will be laughed at in the second". He would attempt to heal family quarrels, and write to his brother: "You treat your wife in the way one would lead a regiment". And when little Charles Napoleon died, and his mother, Queen Hortense, proved inconsolable, it was the Emperor who, father of all the Bonapartes, concerned himself in her grief and showed unceasing anxiety on her account, and took measures to provide for her amusement.

Napoleon at Finckenstein was no ineffectual optimist, lost in a tangle of dreams, but a master-mind, about at its zenith, exulting in the fever of action. When he found again his zest for the fight and felt himself riding to victory there was something positive and real in his change of mood, something more than self-delusion; for he had new plans afoot and was beginning to see a way out of his distresses. If he reared himself more proudly and spoke less pressingly for peace, it was all part of the game of chess that he was playing, and not for a moment did his passions run away with him. But coinciding with all this there was a revival of confidence in the ranks of his foes, and a wave of optimism came over them that reached heights of rashness and enthusiasm for which it is not so easy to find a basis. There was a decided attempt to tighten the coalition against France, a determination to pursue the war with vigour, but no positive grounds can be discovered for the extravagant hopes and self-congratulations with which the Russians and Prussians amused themselves at this period. As usual they allowed Napoleon to be the first to come out of the winter's inactivity and to spring upon them with a fresh assault. All the time the threat to Danzig was giving their military leaders alarm. Yet it is interesting, in watching these people, to see how some trick that their own minds played with them, carried them to ecstasies of confidence and ambition, while no very definite military advantage or military prospects created or confirmed their ardour

—rather their own psychology fed them with it; with the result that for many weeks we are dealing with men who are, so to speak, in a dream, who, having achieved some sort of buoyancy in themselves, have lost touch with the hard earth and become unanchored in their thinking.

The arrival of the Czar in person at Memel gave the start to the new rush of hope and ardour. He in whom all had pinned their faith, came like a ray of light into the dreary life of the place. Like the hero of a poem he appeared, giving a romantic touch to the days of that court-in-exile, drinking tea with Queen Louisa, riding horseback, reviewing troops, discussing matters of state and measures of war with statesmen and soldiers, hammering at Lord Hutchinson for English subsidies, and defeating Napoleon in cabinet talks. The emperor was with his army, the saviour of Europe was on the spot, those quarrelsome and inefficient Russian generals had a master close at hand —the thing had a look of vigour, it seemed like determination, it gave the illusion of success. The Czar had left St Petersburg at a moment when the overtures of Bertrand and Kleist had made Russia more warlike, more assured that the French were in sore straits. He brought with him to Memel that confidence grounded on Napoleon's difficulties of the winter. Everything was staged for mutual compliments and congratulations. Everything was calculated to make all the illogical things in the minds of men play traitor to reality.

That the Prussians soon gained heart from the event is proved by the first achievement of the Czar after his arrival in Memel. This, too, had a spectacular appeal, and was the satisfaction of a hope long deferred. On the very day of Alexander's coming, Hardenberg wrote him a letter complaining of continued exclusion from office, and attacking the policy of Zastrow.[1] Vainly for a long time Hardenberg had been urging his king to a more hearty prosecution of military measures, a more welcome acceptance of war, and a more cordial union with Russia. The Czar talked with Lord Hutchinson, found that he was "authorised to speak on

[1] Hardenberg to Alexander, in Ranke, *Hardenberg*, v, 483.

behalf of England",[1] and catching the rising tide of confidence and enthusiasm at Memel, he renewed his attempts to secure the dismissal of the unpopular ministers. Very soon his wishes were granted, and Hardenberg was restored to power.

From this point Hardenberg and Alexander moved hand in hand. Their names had become a legend for passionate hatred of Napoleon. Each of them independently had come to be to the enemies of France the symbol of a creed and of a cause. It was an encouraging sight for all—these men, putting heads together, organising the salvation of Europe. They had been at one in the deductions they had made from the pressing peace overtures of Napoleon in February. From now they set themselves to carry a stage further the same kind of thinking to advance their previous conclusions, to intensify their former confidence. Alexander picked up the thread of the argument he had used in rejecting the peace offers of France; Hardenberg jumped into the same line of thought, which was the policy he had urged at the time of the proposals of Bertrand. Too sympathetic in their aims and ideals, perhaps they allowed their ardour and goodwill to carry them away. Perhaps it was easy for them to run into the kind of thinking that was pleasing to one another. Each seems to have imparted some of his enthusiasm to his friend, each seems to have outstripped the other in his flight, each incited the other to the logical development and elaboration of views arrived at previously. Very pleased with themselves, both soon went riding into the sky, conquering the French from a broomstick, reorganising Europe as though Waterloo had already been won, and inaugurating a period of optimism and ambition that may have suited the unbalanced imagination of the Czar but seemed strange and utterly unreal in the counsels of a state like Prussia.

At one time the Prussian king had put a challenge to the Czar, questioning whether he had the means sufficient to secure the objects for which he was fighting and to achieve "a peace, general and solid, such as would not only re-establish the King

[1] Lord Hutchinson to Lord Howick, No. 17, 10 Ap. 1807, *F.O. Prussia* 64/74.

in full possession of his lands but free Germany from the French yoke and drive Napoleon beyond the Rhine".[1] The context of these words had been sufficient to reveal that they were intended to dishearten the Russians by magnifying the task that was to be accomplished. Alexander had accepted the challenge, had agreed that such was the kind of peace that he was fighting for, had taken up that cry of "driving Napoleon beyond the Rhine"; and he had added, "I do not doubt that we shall succeed in this, if we stay united until the end".[2] Alexander came to Memel to promote the union of the two powers, and to be near his armies —altogether, to stiffen the resistance to France. But the vision had been conjured into existence of a Germany freed from the yoke of the usurper, and in this there was an idea that simply cried out for elaboration and development. It was a thought that figured large in the conversations that took place when the Czar had his meetings with the king and ministers of Prussia. And it led to the most pretentious statement of policy and aim that the coalition had yet put forward.

On the 7th of April Hardenberg gave an outline of his views in a statement, addressed to the Prussian king and the Russian Czar. The enemies of France must draw together in concerted operations. Austria must be pressed to join immediately in the campaign—so much homage he paid to the necessities of the military situation. But where he blossomed out, spread himself, and waxed lyrical, was on the subject of future peace. He urged the adoption of a political scheme, a statement of what the allies were fighting for, a "platform" that should bring the powers into line with one another so that no suspicions or dissensions might make cleavage in the coalition. And having shown the necessity for this instrument he forthwith produced his programme.

You were to seek the "general good" of Europe, Hardenberg admitted; he would not dare to scorn or to forget such a pious phrase; yet "in so far as this allows it, the political plan should favour the particular interests of the allied powers, in a way that

[1] Ranke, *Hardenberg*, v, 431.
[2] Alexander I to Frederick William III, Feb. 20/Mar. 4, 1807, in Bailleu, *Briefwechsel*, p. 152.

will realise the general good, so that out of it will emerge a force able to counter-balance that of Bonaparte and maintain the independence of Europe". Certainly you were to promote this "general good" and further the universal cause, but you would do it by advancing the particular interests of the allies, making the two, as far as possible, coincide. Hardenberg went beyond this and proceeded to show how you might ensure the desired security of Europe and promote the views of the coalition by favouring the particular aims and interests of one power among the allies—namely, Prussia. You were to see the Prussian and Russian governments in consultation with Lord Hutchinson coming to some arrangement on the lines Hardenberg had to suggest. They would not only draw up a statement that would represent the views of the existing coalition against France, they would make arrangements for the benefit of the court of Vienna, and secure the adhesion of Austria to the proposals—for, said Hardenberg, they were sufficiently acquainted with the views of Austria to speak on her behalf and to work out her own interests for her. Austria, indeed, was the rival to be feared on this very question of post-war reconstruction; she was the competitor of Prussia; very fortunate that she was not on the spot to press and supervise her own cause, very clever of Hardenberg to arrange that here at Memel should be decided how Austrian interests were to be catered for in the reorganisation of Europe.

According to Hardenberg's plan the Prussian king was to be restored to his estates, and something was to be done to strengthen his position and improve his frontier. He declared the very weakness of Prussia a reason for increasing her power. "It would be impossible for Prussia to withstand the slightest blow from France if she were not made stronger, not so much by augmentations of territory, as by the rectification of her frontiers." And he showed how you could secure this object by transplanting the king of Saxony into Poland.

When he came to discuss the large problem of the future stability of Europe, Hardenberg could pursue the question in an unhampered fashion, for his country had no solemn engagements which bound it first of all to secure redress for the victims of Napoleonic conquest; it had not, like Russia and England, a point of honour at stake in this matter. Therefore, without being too much harassed by such points as the claims of the kings of Naples and Sardinia, he was able to concentrate upon his favourite well-fondled scheme of raising up in central Europe a power that would arrest the devastating career of the Corsican usurper.

Here Hardenberg pronounced the magic name of "Germany". He could not fly in the face of England, whose conquests were the one thing in the hands of the coalition that could be offered to Napoleon in negotiation. He could not ignore the Austrians, who had held the legacy of Holy Roman Empire. Therefore he dodged like a diplomat and took refuge in an evasion. "Germany" should be the buttress of the reorganised continent. Not the old Germany, however, with its effete institutions and cloudy dignities and dust-ridden formalities, not the Germany of mediaeval empire and Austrian hegemony—this had been incapable of meeting the French onrush. The Germanic system should be remoulded, it should be strengthened and organised into a confederation; and this, placed under the guarantee of Russia and England, should be the mainstay of the new Europe.

Then appears the reason why the "general good" that is to be promoted must be achieved by the advancement of the private interests of the allies, why the erection of a bulwark in Europe must take precedence over the claims of unfortunate monarchs of Naples or Sardinia, why everything is to be subordinated to the creation of a powerful Germany. Austria is not to return to the primacy that Napoleon had usurped; Prussia is to be advanced to a share with her in the leadership. She, along with Austria, is to control the destinies of the new confederation. The problem of the heritage of the obsolete Empire is to be solved by a division. One will not be over-tender with the rights of the minor princes of the old imperial system in working the reconstruction—nowhere do Hardenberg's proposals fall into a fond solicitude for the small and weak.

"On the independence of Germany", he writes, "hangs that of Europe. But it cannot exist so long as a large number of little courts have divided interests and are at cross-purposes. Sovereignty must disappear for them in matters of war and peace, and must only belong to the heads of Confederation."

And if it should be objected that the problem of Germany was not solved by a division between Austria and Prussia, or that at least a fresh difficulty was raised by it, if it was argued that according to this plan Germany would still be divided against itself and its two great powers would find the new situation more rife with jealousies and mutual conflict than before, Hardenberg was ready with an answer that belongs rather to the politics of the copy-book than to serious statesmanship; he said that Austria and Prussia must not quarrel, but must work as allies, and be good.[1]

One cannot for a moment be blind to the stupidity and infatuation of these Prussians. It is impossible not to condemn the basic principles that underlay their policy—the ardour with which they made everything turn to the benefit of themselves, the readiness they showed to equate the good of mankind with the private advancement of Prussia. Ambition for domination in north Germany had become a growing obsession with them; it commanded their minds whenever for a moment they could forget that the French had hunted them to the farthest corner of their land. It had been their secret purpose when they had become allies of France in 1806; it had made them eager to occupy Hanover and organise a confederation of the north. For its sake they had later come to quarrel with Napoleon and had shown themselves more exacting in negotiation, more ready to plunge into war; with the result that Napoleon found it easy to make it his case that he fought the campaign of Jena to save the smaller German states from domination. All the time the British government, alert for its interests in Hanover, and made alive with jealousy, saw what was at the heart of these Prussians and stood watching them with irreconcilable distrust.

These were the people who had fawned and cringed before Napoleon, and then had become a dead weight in the coalition. Wavering, irresolute, fear-driven they had feinted and twisted, and left friends in the lurch. In the contest that cracked a

[1] Ranke, *Hardenberg*, III, 341–4.

continent they had shuffled their way with nothing of grandeur, had sided in turn with both parties, had often double-crossed both, now sending piteous calls for help to their allies, now making pathetic manœuvres for peace, never winning for themselves a title to the greatness they were pursuing or forging an excuse for the ambitions that they had in contemplation. Looking on what there was of selfishness and ruthlessness in their policy, as it appears in that gigantic piece of self-betrayal which Hardenberg wrote at Memel, one begins to think more kindly of this Napoleon who had such men arrayed against him, and one can view his career of conquest with more equanimity and less pain. Early he had come to an encounter with Austrians and Prussians and the like, and had learned their unfaithfulness and double-dealing and cowardice; and nobility and kindness that had been in the rising youth might well have withered at the contact. Little wonder if he came to think all the old governments contemptible, and accepted everything in diplomacy as crooked, and counted every royalty a mean and ragged thing. These people had menaced him with their feigned friendship and secret conspiracies. On every side of him were governments selfish, effete, corrupt. If he thought it a little matter to wipe them out and clean away the crusted relics of degenerate mediaevalism, who can say that it was not a service? If his diplomacy was cunning and clever, what else could have prospered against the methods and devices of Vienna? Many of these enemy governments had taught him something in selfishness and treachery, and some could have very little to urge in defence of their own utility; if he hardened his heart against them and became too like themselves, perhaps it is not mere weary waste of pity to reflect on the world that moulded him— to recall the youthful Bonaparte who, as a subordinate officer, had been willing to starve for the sake of his family—and to glance at times, in aside, at the Napoleon who could forgive generously, who was the cherished friend of his soldiers, who organised the welfare of peoples, and who bewitched with charm of personality every person who came near him. In all their ambitions the Prussians had nothing of his grandeur, and when their characters had room to play, never for a moment did they show his generous impulses; while along with his passion for rule, his insatiable greed of conquest, there went a gift of efficiency and a reforming zeal that left their mark from Dalmatia to the farthest edge of the German dominions—beside which the Prussian craving for power is a pretension and an offence, and seems selfishness unredeemed.

While Hardenberg was occupying himself with his masterly remappings of Europe there arrived from London a despatch which was a challenge on the question of the re-establishment of Germany. It was a reminder that England had a hand in the matter, that there was vexation in store for the men who were to remodel Europe, and that even with Napoleon beyond the Rhine the strife and perplexity would not be over. It was Howick's reply to the peace proposals which had come to him from St Petersburg at the beginning of the year; and it arrived conveniently at the moment when the Russians and Prussians were engaged in discussing their intentions in personal conferences.[1] The point on which the British government seemed disposed to create the greatest difficulty related to the erection of a bulwark that would keep France in check for the future. England had made it plain for a long time that she had fixed upon Austria for the rôle, and that she would tolerate no aggrandisement of Prussia. Howick's despatch did not mention Prussia by name, when it declared England's refusal to use her maritime conquests in the way that was desired at Memel; but it clearly designated a certain state which was considered to have no claims upon England by reason of any friendship or alliance and it mentioned the futility of restoring a prince who had been unable to defend his own dominions—who even in time of peace had fallen into dependence upon France. It was further at issue with Hardenberg's proposals in that it gave a priority to the claims of the minor victims of Napoleon and

---

[1] See above, pp. 101–2. The despatch was addressed to Lord Douglas at St Petersburg but a copy had been sent to Lord Hutchinson at Memel and he communicated it to the Russian ministers. Hutchinson to Howick, No. 17, 10 Ap. 1807, *F.O. Prussia* 64/74.

recognised England's obligations to the dispossessed princes. Here was much matter for discussion and the conversations at the allied headquarters in Poland were continued. It was agreed that the correspondence with Napoleon should be taken up again, the negotiations for a congress resumed. It was arranged that the aims of the proposed concert of the powers at war with France should be modified according as England, Austria and Sweden agreed to subscribe to the treaty. Finally, the proposals of Hardenberg were diluted and wrapped in generalisations, and robbed of any sting that they might have, in a convention concluded between Prussia and Russia at Bartenstein on the 23rd of April.

That convention was not merely an engagement, but an appeal; it was drawn up in a way intended to make it not merely accept-able, but inviting. It was an attempt, also, to find a common formula for diverse points of view. It was therefore conveniently vague on matters that were likely to cause disagreement. It was a document based on the optimism of the moment and proposing to set limits to the power and aggressions of Napoleon, to free Germany from the oppressor, to raise a barrier against France for the future, and to separate the Crown of Italy from the Crown of France.

Nothing in it contradicted the proposals of Hardenberg of the 7th of April; nothing in it suggested that that minister had modified or abandoned any point; nothing was mentioned that would forbid the interpretation of the convention in the light of Hardenberg's programme or would give final reassurances to any person who had had reason to be alarmed by the Prussian ambitions. Everything in fact supported the reading of the one into the terms of the other. In the convention of Bartenstein, a restored and reconstituted Germany was to form a barrier against France, the independence of Europe was again declared to rest upon that of Germany, and the obsolete Holy Roman Empire was to be replaced by a strong federation; but the more precise features of Hardenberg's plan were omitted out of delicacy; to have talked openly of abolishing various powers of sovereignty enjoyed by smaller rulers, or even to have declared in plain words the combined supremacy of Austria and Prussia, would have touched delicate interests, or would have demanded from the signatory powers commitments that as yet were far too definite. These things could not be hauled into the common formula.

Even as it was, the convention bore signs of its Prussian origin. By its terms Austria was to be consulted in the reorganisation of Italy, but she was not mentioned in connection with the future of Germany. Vague promises of territory were held out to powers which should join the concert; in the case of Austria these took more precise form; she should receive the Tyrol again and have a frontier on the Mincio. Austria was envisaged, that is to say, in her connection with Italy, not in the light of her former relations with Germany; and this in a political statement that was intended to be inviting to her.

Prussia was to be restored completely to her former power, with compensations for any territory not returned to her, and with the advantage of a better military frontier. Another of the Prussian objects of the war was guaranteed in a clause which promised indemnities to the Prince of Orange for his losses in Germany and Holland. Russian ambitions did not assert themselves in this document. The independence of Turkey was guaranteed.[1] The Czar, who had a habit of making surrender to personalities, and was impressionable when he could be met in personal interviews, seems to have given Hardenberg free scope and to have satisfied himself with the joy of being the deliverer of Europe. He is all benevolence, and it is Prussia that is haughty, self-confident, exacting.

The king of Sweden was hauled into the movement that was to tighten up the coalition. He took the opportunity to strike another of his romantic attitudes, and he played up to his part of crazy knight-errant. A military convention, concluded at Bartenstein on the 21st of April, brought him into the group and marked out a plan of co-operation with Prussia, by which he was to lead a joint expedition of Prussians and Swedes against

[1] The convention of Bartenstein is printed in F. de Martens, *Recueil des traités*, VI, 409.

the French in Prussian Pomerania. Gustavus, however, having come to this agreement, thought he had done enough, and regarded himself as absolved from further commitments with his allies, and saw no necessity for acceding to the other, the political, convention of Bartenstein. Although he was heartily in favour of its spirit and of the intention of vigorously continuing the war, he was not in full agreement with its politics.

"Nothing will give me more joy", he wrote to the Prussian king, "than to be able to join with you in the secure re-establishment of order and independence; but to reach this important aim, it is necessary, I think, to turn our attention to the cause of Legitimacy, the Bourbon cause, and to declare ourselves publicly in its favour, and not to lose sight of the principles upon which the existence of all legitimate governments and of their subjects, is based."[1]

He was the "die-hard" of the coalition, and all the adjustments and balancing of forces were wasted upon him. That was why he regarded the political convention of Bartenstein as "superfluous" and as "having relation to objects entirely foreign to our present efforts and cares".

While the continental enemies of France were arriving at these measures of more effective co-operation and more determined energy, England was arising out of the "apathy" that had brought her into universal reproach, and was sharing and anticipating the aims of her allies. Events in domestic politics produced a change of ministry. The occurrence was at first unpopular in Europe; the Austrian government declared it little calculated to inspire confidence; it was remarked that the ministers were personally more feeble than the men whom they replaced, and it was feared that they would find difficulty in facing the House of Commons. Various matters—the demands of home politics at a critical moment, and a short illness of Canning's that had been hastened by over-work—prevented for some period the dissipation of this opinion, and caused a continuation of the delays of which the British government had been guilty. The slackness of the retiring cabinet projected its

---

[1] The letter is printed in Koch and Schoell, *Histoire abrégée des traités de paix*, VIII (Paris, 1817), 456–7.

evils for a space into the regime of the new government and made it impossible for the succeeding ministers to come out with an immediate display of energy. And the distance from the continent postponed any appreciation of the effect that the constitutional change could have upon the European situation.

But gradually there emerged from the array of uninspiring names, one that had the compelling, unmistakable marks of strength. He was one of those personalities that are winning and yet at the same time must be unpopular. He had that sort of witty tongue that makes a man hated for his wit. Nimbleness and versatility gave a swiftness to his mind and there was something so palpably clever about him that he could not but be distrusted. Quick, sensitive, short-tempered, he could display a haughty or quarrelsome or trenchant side, and these moods which would bring out "the flash of his eye, and the scorn of his lip", were the times that found him most brilliant. Taunted as the son of an actress, famous as author of skits and epigrams that had had a smart and a sting, gifted with an eloquence that was almost considered a crime, George Canning brought to the Foreign Office an application, an energy and a practical ability that set off those more "flashy" arts which had brought him into a sort of paradoxical disrepute. Coming into office with a strong notion that British foreign policy was in need of a grand awakening, he very soon produced a series of instructions that swept the length and breadth of the political situation. In despatches that would glow with heat and passion, breaking out often in impetuosity and wrath, and sometimes surprising the reader with their betrayals of flaming personality, he sought to give England a more masterly hand in the politics of Europe. Finding his country suspected of insularity by her continental allies, he took the opportunity of his appointment to circulate the strongest assurances that this was a misapprehension; he induced the king to write a personal letter to the Czar in confirmation of his assertions,[1] and when the Austrian complaints reached him concerning the language of Douglas at St Petersburg,

[1] George III to Alexander I, 10 Ap. 1807, *F.O. Russia* 65/72. The reply of Alexander, 7 May 1807, is in the same volume.

and the fear of an impending system of "isolation" on the part of Great Britain, he was ready with the most convincing disavowals. He quickly instructed his ministers "to counteract the notions known to have been entertained and not sparingly insinuated...with respect to the imputed selfishness of the enterprises and military achievements of this country".[1] He ordered Lord Hutchinson to proceed to Sweden to discuss the question of a joint expedition, and he set on foot a negotiation with Sweden that led to the conclusion of a military convention. And when the Russian minister, in a particularly angry note, complained of continued delays in the execution of a military diversion, he was able to show a righteous wrath and came out with a vigorous retort:

But surely, Sir, it was not in a Note from you to me that I should have expected to find the reproach that the British Government was not prepared with such an expedition two months ago, apprised as you are of all the difficulties which the present administration have had to surmount in making the preparations for it.[2]

Immediately on entering office, Canning recognised the feebleness of England's diplomatic representation on the continent, and saw the special necessity of having a competent minister with the monarchs at the allied headquarters. He promised the early departure of "a person invested with the highest diplomatic character and furnished with the most ample instructions and powers" who should be attached to the Czar. He informed the allies that the government was engaged "in ascertaining the highest amount to which it will be possible to carry the pecuniary exertions of England",[3] and he gave it to be understood that the new minister would be able to deal with the question of subsidies immediately on his arrival; only he insisted that Prussia should conclude a treaty of concert that was much belated and give a guarantee that she would come to no separate arrangement with France, before she should receive any money from England.

[1] G. Canning to G. Leveson-Gower, No. 5 (Secret), *F.O. Russia* 65/69.
[2] G. Canning to Alopeus, 18 June 1807 (replying to the note from Alopeus 5/17 June 1807), *F.O. Russia* 65/73.
[3] G. Canning to Hutchinson, Nos. 3 and 4, 5 Ap. 1807, *F.O. Prussia* 64/74.

The first of Canning's instructions for the new minister who was to go to the allied headquarters did in fact direct that a treaty should be concluded with Russia "of which the object shall be the joint prosecution of the war until the conclusion of a general peace which shall comprise and secure the interests of all the powers engaged in the contest".[1] All the enemies of France were to be invited to accede to it; and Canning thought that the proposal would destroy any impression that prevailed concerning the insular policy of England. But Canning came into office with an intense distrust of the policy and practices of the ministers at Memel; his early despatches to Lord Hutchinson show that he seriously feared the conclusion of separate peace by Prussia; the idea of the treaty of concert appealed to him as a way of tying her hands in future.

The day after the instruction was drawn up the English government received the news that the very kind of convention which it desired had already been concluded at Bartenstein; Canning was asked by the Russian minister to accede to it. The new English representative was informed of the event which cancelled his first instructions, and he was told that "as the principles upon which it was founded were consonant to the orders he had received", England would probably join the concert; but, it was added, "it is probable indeed that His Majesty's accession will be accompanied with a reservation making that accession conditional upon His Imperial Majesty's consenting to guarantee the literal execution of the Treaty of Renunciation signed at Memel on the 28th of January".[2] Canning, like his predecessor, had an instinctive distrust of Prussian policy, and meant to make the Czar the pledge against the danger of Prussian ambitions. England in 1806 had been antagonistic to the Prussian scheme of a northern confederation, by which that power had intended to share with France the

---

[1] G. Canning to G. Leveson-Gower, No. 1, 16 May 1807, *F.O. Russia* 65/69.

[2] G. Canning to G. Leveson-Gower, No. 12, 17 May 1807, *F.O. Russia* 65/69. The treaty of Memel, by which peace was concluded between England and Prussia on the 28th of January 1807, is printed in the *Annual Register* (1807), p. 712.

leadership of Germany and balance the Confederation of the Rhine. Canning came down with redoubled anger on Hardenberg's new proposals, and wrote heatedly to the new minister concerning the renewed pretensions of the cabinet of Berlin.

"I have received private intimations", he wrote, "that M. de Hardenberg immediately upon his restoration to Power has been busied in framing a plan of pacification for Germany, which is founded upon the idea of placing all the states of the North, under the superintending Protection and military authority of Prussia—and that Hanover is specially intended to be comprised in this arrangement."

He set it down as an "extraordinary idea"; said that Prussia was trying to treat her neighbours as France had done, and commanded:

Your Excellency will not hesitate to declare in the most unequivocal terms His Majesty's determination not to consent to the creation of such a predominant power in Prussia, and the resolution of the British Government not to suffer the electoral dominions of His Majesty to be incorporated.... The experience which Hanover has had of the exaction and tyranny belonging to the military laws of Prussia, especially when enforced upon neighbouring states, has excited in that country a repugnance to Prussian Protection which makes any arrangements founded upon that principle in the highest degree distasteful.

Canning was not hostile. "His Majesty is perfectly ready to co-operate for the restoration of the Prussian monarchy to all its own estates", he wrote; he even showed a willingness to see the Prussian system strengthened in a sound political way; but he was merciless when it came to the restoring of that military system "of which the vice and weakness have been unfortunately made too manifest to all the world", and he considered that

to attempt to re-establish that same fictitious power and to give it strength and support by subjecting to it in a great degree the neighbouring countries which are as much entitled as Prussia to the recovery and maintenance of their independence is a project in which there would be as little of policy as of justice....

He shouted and harangued where Howick had delicately insinuated, and he returned more than once to his text, that

Prussia was "a power who has shown herself unequal to her own defence, but who would repair that instrument which has broken short in her own hand, at the expense of her neighbours, and then call upon them to trust exclusively to it for their protection"; once again you were met with that terrible "flash of his eye and scorn of his lip", and a diplomatic despatch became eloquence in his hands as he enlarged upon the point. He explained the arrangements which he would be willing to accept for the future of Germany. He would have a federation in the north in which the states should bear their part "not as subordinate vassals, but as great and independent members", acting not under compulsion, but out of free-will. And he demanded that the Czar should check these vagaries of Prussian ambition.[1]

In the middle of May, when Canning sits down to write despatch after despatch, he makes it clear that he is ready with an active policy and that it was not for nothing that he called himself the disciple of Pitt. Foreign ministers in London soon found him more determined than his predecessors in the energetic prosecution of the war. Distrust of the Prussians and anger at the Hardenberg proposals, determined Lord Hutchinson to refuse to have anything to do with the convention of Bartenstein, when it was put before him for his accession. Canning would not allow these things to ruin the concert. He blustered —threatened to refuse to accede if the Czar did not guarantee to check the Prussian designs; but everywhere he declared the convention agreeable to England, he officially communicated to the Austrian minister his intention to accede, and he urged the court of Vienna to follow his example.[2] If he did not actually sign, the fault was not on the British side. The Russian minister in London was furnished with powers for the transaction. Everything waited in readiness for the arrival of Colonels Engelmann and Krüsemarck, the emissaries of Prussia for the

---

[1] G. Canning to G. Leveson-Gower, No. 6, 16 May 1807, *F.O. Russia* 65/69.

[2] Starhemberg to Stadion, No. 44, 20 May, and No. 46, 26 May 1807, *W.S.A. Weisungen nach London.*

purpose. English observers at the Prussian headquarters commented on the delay of the departure of these men and could not understand it. When eventually they did reach London, it was the 28th of June, and two days later, before anything had been done, rumours came through of a great battle lost at Friedland.[1] This was an end of combinations and conventions and attempts to tighten the coalition.

[1] G. Canning to G. Leveson-Gower, No. 20, 29 June, and No. 21, 30 June, 1807, *F.O. Russia* 65/69.

CHAPTER III

THE RECEPTION OF THE AUSTRIAN PEACE PROPOSAL

IT was at the moment when the campaign was awakening once more and when all the powers were recovering the warlike mood, that Austria came with her proposals for peace. In the Prussian headquarters there was confidence untimely and excessive. Even the Russian commander, the grumbler Bennigsen, who had been frowned at for his pessimism and his lack of enthusiasm could scarcely be refrained, it was said, from proclaiming his master king of Poland on the spot. The Swedish king was shouting for the Bourbons; London was the scene of unfamiliar activity. And Napoleon was beginning to slip and slant as in former days, and take refuge in indirectness—to do everything in fact to prove the falsity of his various pacific assertions. The Austrian mediation, instead of falling among chastened people, weary with the war-ridden times, dropped into a gang of rowdies, who were in a mood to bellow and brag. Russia had promised to receive it kindly—but on the condition that behind it there should be an imposing show of power; Napoleon would not turn it out of doors, he said, if Austria would abandon her armaments, and display nothing but an olive-branch. The Austrians were deluded if they imagined that mere diplomacy could straighten out this situation.

George Canning had always asserted that the only conditions to which England could listen in any proposal of peace or mediation were such that Napoleon would be certain to reject. When he found the basis of the Austrian proposals satisfactory he swore that France would have nothing to do with them unless she received another check, and even in that event he declared that Austria would do better to play an active part, taking it as her opportunity. When he heard that France had actually accepted this very mediation—agreed to throw Italy and Germany into the discussions of a congress—it was nonsense to him, the insincerity was palpable, it was a trick to gain time, Napoleon was bent only on trapping the allies into the granting of an armistice. Starhemberg saw that England attached to the proposed Austrian intervention the idea of an "armed mediation"; she "divined the intentions of the Russian government" on this point. But, after all, the court of Vienna had the satisfaction of learning that England accepted its good offices, on the condition that her allies did the same—stipulating only that the seat of any negotiations which might be set on foot should be a place remote from the immediate influence of the campaign and should be so situated as to "afford His Majesty in an equal degree with all the other powers concerned the opportunity of a prompt and uninterrupted communication with his plenipotentiaries".[1]

Canning had a commentary to make on this acceptance, and he did not address it to Austria.

"In giving this answer", he wrote in a despatch to the new minister to the Czar, "the King has done no more than refer the decision of the question to the Emperor of Russia, without whose perfect concurrence it is obvious that Prussia cannot take any step whatever, and who in proportion as he bears the brunt of the Continental War is best qualified and best entitled to judge of the course which it may be fit or necessary to pursue in the acceptance or rejection of any overture for pacification."

Canning touched on the inconvenience of the mediation; the thing could be welcome to nobody but there was advantage capable of being derived from it "if Austria [could] be induced to support its offer of Mediation or resent its refusal". Let the Czar listen to no proposal of an armistice, in any event; far from leading to peace it would be "calculated only to afford time for the power of Buonaparte to strike its roots wide and deep in the country of which he at present has military possession". As to a naval armistice, Canning declined "in the most unequivocal manner" to entertain the idea. And he gave his full concurrence

[1] G. Canning to Starhemberg (with covering note) 25 Ap. 1807, printed in *Parliamentary Debates*, x, cols. 102–4 (No. 11).

to Alexander's decision "that a previous settlement of a basis of negotiation acceptable to all parties is essentially requisite before a Congress can be opened with any prospect of useful discussion".[1] To the British minister in Vienna, Canning revealed his real opinion of the whole transaction.

> But it does appear truly inconceivable that the delusion which the Court of Vienna is too probably practising upon itself in this Parade of a splendid and imposing Mediation should so entirely have got possession of the Austrian Cabinet as not to permit them to see that no party can in truth be thankful to them for this interference whatever motives of policy may prevent either from actually declining to accept it.[2]

This mediation, accompanied by the armaments Austria had been making, could not fail, argued Canning, to arouse some resentment in Napoleon; and if he should win another victory, Austria lay at his mercy. Russia could only regard the whole affair as an evasion of the plain duty that was before the court of Vienna; and if the next engagement proved as indecisive as the others, the emperor of Russia, "having fully redeemed the credit of his arms and seeing no further probability of effecting the ulterior objects of the war without the co-operation of Austria", might see nothing to prevent him making peace for himself and Prussia, and leaving Austria to her own resources. How could this power expect her welfare to have consideration from the allies if she "held out no encouragement to expect that she would concur with them in contending by force of arms" for the objects in view? Even should a congress assemble there could be no reason for complaint on her part if the allies arrived at a settlement "omitting only those points in which Austria feels vitally interested". Scenting the real apprehensions of the Austrians, taunting them by a parade of their own worst premonitions, conjuring up the possibilities with which they had been tormenting themselves in their most dreadful times of

---

[1] G. Canning to G. Leveson-Gower, No. 2, 16 May 1807, *F.O. Russia* 65/69.

[2] G. Canning to Adair, No. 5, 9 June 1807, *F.O. Austria* 7/84.

uncertainty, Canning resumed the coward's arguments for being brave at such a moment, and summarised the selfish reasons for Austria's enlistment in the common cause. One course was open to the court of Vienna—to accede to the convention of Barten-stein; the powers "might otherwise accept disadvantageous offers from France, considering that acceptance (however inadequate to greater objects) as a less evil than the hopeless continuance of a protracted contest". And unless this was done, without delay, Austria's "good offices for the establishment of peace would be fruitless".[1]

Starhemberg, the Austrian minister, gleaned from his con-versations with Canning some hints of the kind of peace that would be acceptable to the British government. "As to the Prussian Monarchy", he wrote, "it is easy to guess that England attaches no other value to its existence and re-establishment than what the general interests of other powers might demand. The conduct of Prussia has destroyed all kind of attachment to her in England."

"I do not think that it is the same with Russia", adds Starhemberg. And later he refers again to the subject. "It is possible that Russia, concerned above all with the interests of Prussia, will neglect the interests of Austria."

Although he received no official communication on the subject, Starhemberg, from these conversations with Canning and from his observations in London, was able to deduce and divine the objects that England would seek to promote in any negotiation for peace. The English ministry, he said, desired a treaty that would organise the interests and relations of all the powers and would have the guarantee of all. It wished to see Austria in a position to stand by such a treaty, and was ready not merely to allow her to recover most of her losses, but to see her acquire an augmentation of territory in the Tyrol or Bavaria or Prussian Silesia. Like Alexander, the English ministers regarded it as important that the Germanic system should be restored to order and independence, and that to this end the Confederation of the

---

[1] G. Canning to Lord Pembroke, No. 2, 15 May 1807, *F.O. Austria* 7/85. G. Canning to Adair, No. 5, 9 June 1807, *F.O. Austria* 7/84.

Rhine should be abolished; but they would not give Prussia the same place in that reorganisation that the Czar was willing to allow. Like their predecessors they refused to put into the background the claims of those rulers who had been the victims of France, and they stood out plainly for the re-establishment of the kings of Naples and of Sardinia; and they stipulated for the independence of the Ottoman Porte. Starhemberg declared "with certainty" that they were "ready to make the greatest sacrifices in order to bring about a peace of this nature, and that none would be too costly for them provided that the honour and superiority of the British flag were not compromised".[1] Stadion, learning this, asked for more precise information as to the extent of the sacrifices which England was disposed to make for the attainment of peace, but Canning would not declare his intentions at the moment, urging that he must first be accurately acquainted with the principles upon which the negotiation would be conducted and the basis upon which France would be prepared to treat. His Majesty "must reserve to himself to proportion [those] sacrifices to the importance of the restitutions to be made by France and to the degree of security which may appear likely to be obtained for the continuance of tranquillity in Europe".[2] Canning is very careful to keep the conquered colonies up his sleeve; he will not put all his cards on the table; he will first satisfy himself that the peace is going to be to his liking. The conquered colonies are an important lever for the English politicians.

But all this matters little as yet. The mediation will defeat its own purposes—this is the seasoned opinion of Canning. The proposal is as unwelcome to him as it can be to any of his allies; only he will not be the one to toss it by with a refusal—he must show that England is not sulking or playing a lone hand. Therefore he will pass on the obligation and transfer the unpleasantness to Russia; for his own part he accepts the good offices of Austria, on the condition that his partners are willing.

---

[1] Starhemberg to Stadion, No. 36, 28 Ap. 1807, *W.S.A. Berichte aus London*.
[2] G. Canning to Adair, No. 6, 26 June 1807, *F.O. Austria* 7/84. Starhemberg to Stadion, No. 53, 27 June 1807, *W.S.A. Berichte aus London*.

Russia in turn moves it one step further on to the shoulders of Prussia. The Czar had already expressed satisfaction with the Austrian intention to mediate, and his original answer to the proposals of Merfeldt had been communicated to all the powers concerned. He could not draw back at this point. He merely took up the attitude he hâd maintained throughout the whole year, and held to the principle which Howick and Canning had cordially approved and confirmed; he accepted the mediation, provided only that Napoleon should state the bases upon which he proposed to treat.

It was left for the Prussians to catch up the tale and make out the rest of the argument. Napoleon would not give satisfaction on this question of bases, they said, and they addressed their reply to this subject, "[The king's] natural moderation would induce him to accept without scruple the offer of His Imperial and Royal Majesty if he could convince himself that the basis which France would consent to in a negotiation would be such as his honour allowed him to accept".[1] Now it is true that the Prussians could have no desire to see a peace concluded under Austrian auspices. Their ambitions in Germany ran too much counter to those of Austria and they had disliked the mediation from the start. Before the close of the year 1806, when Lord Hutchinson had first raised the subject, the foreign minister Zastrow had "regarded the idea with great indignation and said that the interference of Austria was not only not desirable but might probably be mischievous".[2] It is moreover certain that, at the time when the offer of mediation was actually made, the Prussians were showing themselves the most unreasonable and arrogant of all the powers. But it is difficult to imagine that the Czar and the king who were so closely co-operating in Prussia, so firmly united at Bartenstein, would draw up, without connivance or mutual comparing of notes, their respective replies to this mediation which so nearly concerned the very matters they had had under discussion. The Czar in his subsequent

---

[1] *Annual Register* (1807), p. 730.
[2] Hutchinson to Howick, No. 2, 29 Dec. 1806, *F.O. Prussia* 64/74. See also Hutchinson's despatch of 23 Dec. 1806.

conduct acted up to the Prussian reply, and followed this with measures that revealed the Prussian attitude to be really his own. The answer of the king of Prussia was despatched with a copy of the convention of Bartenstein to the Prussian minister at Vienna. The answer of the Russian government was sent to the Russian minister there, "accompanied by an instruction to press Austria in the strongest manner to accede to the above convention". Later, these two ministers received parallel instructions asking for an immediate categorical answer from Austria on this subject.[1] Both powers moved in step, and showed that they were acting in concert. Prussia in sending the convention of Bartenstein as her answer to the mediation was really speaking for Russia as well as for herself—speaking also for England.

Prussia, then, was made the scapegoat, hers was the burden of communicating the new intentions of the now confident allies; she voiced the real answer of the coalition when she wrote:

His Imperial and Royal Apostolic Majesty will easily see that the noble object which he had in mind when he offered his mediation to the powers at war, will be beyond all doubt sooner and more fully attained by his accession to the above Convention than by the employment of his good offices.[2]

The Austrian mediation which was so unwelcome to the powers of the coalition was a matter for serious anxiety to Napoleon, who had so often declared himself bewildered by the politics of the court of Vienna. He feared now that sharp practices were afoot, and he suspected the connivance of his enemies. Not until June could Talleyrand write to say that the Russians themselves had been displeased with the Austrian proposal and that "this puts aside every idea of a secret understanding between Austria and Russia".[3] In the weeks that preceded the offer of mediation Napoleon's relations with the court of Vienna had become more and more mystifying and strained, partly because the conduct of

[1] Adair to Canning, 29 May and 3 June 1807, in Adair, *Historical Memoir*, pp. 241, 244.

[2] A. Lefèbvre, *Histoire des Cabinets* (1866), III, 74.

[3] P. Bertrand, *Lettres inédites de Talleyrand à Napoléon Ier*, No. cccxvi.

the Austrian ministry had itself been equivocal, partly because the French minister in Austria had shown himself unfitted for his post.

"No appointment could more fully prove the hostile intentions of Bonaparte nor be more disagreeable to this court",[1] wrote Adair, when Andréossy was sent to Vienna; and Andréossy himself reported: "My nomination has caused the court and ministry the most lively disquietude".[2] In the society of the Austrian capital he found the atmosphere hostile and felt his position delicate and embarrassing; he had reason to envy his Russian colleague Razoumovski. From the beginning he took his rôle to be that of a rather unfriendly observer, and adopted a policy of "extreme reserve". It was easy for him to take alarm at the tone of conversation in the city, and to end by confusing it with the reasoned policy of the government, and his petty social vexations would make him a more jealous observer. From the middle of March 1807 he kept Talleyrand puzzled and perturbed by his reports of Austrian military preparations, and by his sinister comments on the secret intentions of the Austrian government.[3] Talleyrand sent to him a despatch in cypher recommending him to inspire or to increase confidence in his relations with the chancellor, Stadion, but also to keep a constant watch over any movements that might take place in the army, and to send reports concerning these in cypher.[4] The news from Vienna became more and more disquieting. On the 20th of March Andréossy gave his opinion

that Austria does *not wish to do anything* for the moment, but that she *would like* an opportunity to present itself when she might without risk join hands with the other Powers with whom she is tacitly making common cause though without compromising herself....Her estrangement from France is unremediable....I see no political method of winning over this power; her line is taken; the fact is indubitable.[5]

---

[1] Adair to Howick (Separate), 16 Nov. 1806, *F.O. Austria* 7/81. (This passage was deleted from the document published in Adair, *Historical Memoir*, pp. 151–2.)

[2] Andréossy to Talleyrand, 25 Nov. 1806, *A.A.E. Autriche*, t. 379.

[3] P. Bertrand, *op. cit.* pp. 339 *et seq.*

[4] Talleyrand to Andréossy, 19 Mar. 1807, *A.A.E. Autriche*, t. 380.

[5] Andréossy to Talleyrand, No. 26, 20 Mar. 1807, *A.A.E. Autriche*, t. 380.

Soon afterwards, carried away by his idea that the Austrians were nursing a "secret desire and hope" for the "annihilation" of France, Andréossy picked up an alarmist rumour and wrote to his government in a scare. Long and frequent cabinet meetings were being held in Vienna, he related—and couriers were flying to St Petersburg and Constantinople, and there was an unaccustomed liveliness of correspondence. The Emperor had told the Russian minister that he would declare against France once the allies had secured two victories. A "secret connection" existed between Russia and Austria, Napoleon was about to be the dupe of a conspiracy; and—here was the key to the riddle, the explanation of many suspicious happenings—there was a surreptitious scheme afoot for the dismemberment of the Ottoman Empire.[1]

Talleyrand did not believe the story, but he showed that he was not without uneasiness. The total sum of the information against Austria was difficult to explain away. He searched out the inner inconsistencies of the various rumours—showed that the report of designs against Turkey did not tally with the alleged disposition of the Austrian troops; and he secured denials from General Vincent, who contradicted the rumours of military activity and repudiated the suggestion that his government had formed connections with other powers.

"General Andréossy seems to have set himself to believe everything which is calculated to raise our suspicion of the intentions of the Court of Vienna", wrote Talleyrand. "...General Andréossy and Count Stadion have no confidence in one another and from their connection it will be difficult to derive anything that will lead to a rapprochement."[2]

Talleyrand compared this strained situation with the happy relationship that existed at Warsaw, where he and General Vincent were "on the best of terms". But perhaps Napoleon did not follow his minister so far; he does not seem to have been

---

[1] Andréossy to Talleyrand, No. 29, 4 Ap. 1807, *A.A.E. Autriche*, t. 380. See also No. 28, 28 Mar. 1807, where Andréossy shows himself irritated because the people of Vienna had betrayed their disappointment on hearing news of a British defeat near Constantinople.

[2] P. Bertrand, *op. cit.*, No. CCLXXXIII; see also, especially, No. CCXC.

quite so assured; those conversations at Warsaw—Talleyrand and an Austrian general "on the best of terms"—did not leave him free from uneasiness. Time came when he put them at an end.

Napoleon had learned months before, from intercepted despatches, the very truths that Andréossy was trying to bring home to him—that the Austrian government was merely nursing its hatred and gathering strength for a favourable moment.[1] The point to be discovered was: with what immediacy did the warlike intention now present itself to the court of Vienna? Talleyrand imagined that his own theory on this matter was confirmed and his whole argument clinched—he seems to have assumed that Andréossy ought to make an embarrassed retreat from his position—when the Austrian emperor made a formal offer of mediation to the powers at war. This, taking place in April, came at the very time when Andréossy's panic was at its height. Napoleon, however, had been in the utmost anxiety during the whole difficult winter campaign; he could see that Talleyrand was arguing in a circle and he was inclined to agree with his minister in Vienna.[2] At the moment when the official note arrived, with the offer of Austria's good offices, he felt the situation a delicate one. It was important that he should not offend the Austrians. Yet he had no intention of foregoing any of his desires for their sakes. He declared his opinion to Talleyrand.

It is of interest to me to gain some time. A negotiation without armistice is ridiculous, since there would be no basis for it to rest upon; but to make an armistice before I have taken Danzig would be difficult. Now everything gives me to hope that Danzig will be taken in a fortnight....[3]

He exchanged ideas with his minister and gave much thought to the reply which was to be made to the Austrian overture. Taking great care with the phrasing, making many subtle verbal

---

[1] See above, p. 108.

[2] Cf. P. Bertrand, *op. cit.* Nos. CCLXXXVIII and CCXC with Napoleon's letters Nos. 12,450 and 12,453 in the *Correspondance*, t. xv.

[3] *Corresp. de Nap. Ier*, t. xv, No. 12,341.

corrections, and manipulating cleverly the implications of words, he finally concocted a note, accepting "for himself and his allies" the "friendly intervention of Austria". He explained to Talleyrand that if it should be asked who the "allies" might be, he must reply "Spain, etc., the Porte, and Persia".[1] None of these auxiliaries had been invited by Austria to join in the negotiation. Talleyrand had already noticed the glaring exclusion of Turkey, but Vincent had been all smoothness, for he had had instructions from Vienna, stating that "if our intervention is accepted on the express condition that Turkey shall take part in the negotiations, there will be no difficulties about that, we are sure, on either side".[2] It did not matter that at this very moment the Austrians had been making credit with the Russians by giving the assurance that the Turks would be kept out of the negotiation. This was all part of Austria's double-barrelled policy.

Even in his official acceptance of mediation, Napoleon could not deny himself the opportunity of a fine sortie against England. He only feared, said he, "that the power which up to this time seems to have made it a system to found its greatness and strength upon the divisions of the Continent, will use the Congress to raise bitterness and bring out new causes of dissension". It was curious, too, that he should find this moment when peace was under discussion and mediation was being accepted, "a natural and clear occasion" for renewing his offers of alliance to Austria.[3]

Having met the uncomfortable proposition with a reply calculated to bring controversy and delay, Napoleon carefully laid out the policy Talleyrand should then pursue in regard to the Austrian mediation. He explained the course that should be taken in the discussions with General Vincent, and from Finckenstein he closely supervised the conversations that took place in Warsaw. It would seem that he did not feel too sure of these ministers who were "on the best of terms".[4] "To all the

[1] *Corresp. de Nap. Ier*, t. xv, Nos. 12,341 and 12,390. P. Bertrand, *op. cit.* Nos. CCXCIV and CCC.

[2] P. Bertrand, *op. cit.* No. CCLXXXVI.

[3] The French answer to the official offer of mediation is to be found in Adair, *op. cit.* p. 227; translation in *Annual Register* (1807), p. 712.

[4] See *Corresp. de Nap. Ier*, t. xv, Nos. 12,389 and 12,488.

observations of General Vincent", he commanded, "you must reply: 'We shall make no difficulties about incidental points'. Also, in conversation, fall back frequently on the fact that, at this distance, you cannot tell what my intentions are."[1] More than once Napoleon sought to restrain his minister. "It remains for the present to wait in silence and with the greatest circumspection for whatever may turn up."[2] It was important, above all, that the question of an armistice should not be raised at this point. "If peace is really desired, there will probably be a demand for an armistice, and then things will take on a more sincere character; for at bottom Russia and even England can find no pleasure in seeing me enjoy the revenues of Prussia for five or six years....But wait for events."[3] Incorrigible Talleyrand, however, seemed bent on making things "take on a more sincere character". He allowed Vincent to draw him into conversation about a suspension of arms, and went so far as to say that Napoleon would require that any armistice which might be concluded should be based on the dispositions of the respective armies at the moment of signature. Napoleon, jealously watching every move, came down with a sharp reprimand.

It seems to me that you were in too much of a hurry. I have recommended to you, and still recommend, the greatest circumspection. You know that first of all I must have Dantzig; it is even possible that I must have Graudenz also. You have therefore committed a very great error. You ought to have held to your first statement—that you know nothing of these things. Why play with explanations of this kind when we do not know whether the powers have accepted the mediation or not?...There are no circumstances under which it could be more necessary to move carefully; the less you say, the better....You must be absolutely ignorant of military operations... this is not your business.

Then Napoleon revealed his real opinions and intentions:

I regard the intervention of Austria in this affair as a misfortune. I have replied to it because I did not wish to give her any complaint against me at the present moment. It is necessary, therefore, to be

[1] *Corresp. de Nap. Ier*, t. xv, No. 12,390.
[2] *Ibid.* t. xv, No. 12,450; see also No. 12,453.
[3] *Ibid.* t. xv, No. 12,390.

circumspect, to go quietly, and to watch things happening. We must commit ourselves to nothing in any way—not a jot more than is written in the Note; the very place where a Congress is to be assembled must, if it suits, become an excuse for delays and discussions. I recommend you to let all this sink in, as it is of the greatest importance.[1]

In his quick trenchant style, with its touches of frankness, its semi-colloquial lapses, and its insistent repetitions, Napoleon drove home his policy and administered his rebuke.

Still he was not satisfied. The affair was too big for trifling. So although Talleyrand protested that he was saying nothing to Vincent, Napoleon called him to his side, out of range of the man. He might inform Vincent of his departure, and promise to return in a few days; this would have the advantage of making it appear that there was nothing to hide. Also, "You might tell M. de Vincent that it is possible that an overture has been made to me; that this unexpected call would give you to think so, but that you do not know anything".[2] But the few days passed by, and Talleyrand made no return. "During the whole month of May Baron Vincent attempted to get into touch with the French Headquarters. It was in vain. And he was very hurt by it."[3]

The Emperor and minister were having one of their differences of opinion at this time, and the long alliance between the limping, humorous, courtly aristocrat who had been bishop, exile and diplomat in turn, and the Corsican adventurer, "so badly brought up", who had leaped from the dismal lodgings of an impoverished subaltern to a grandeur that outshone the royalty of Louis XIV, was fast coming to a close.[4] Napoleon was essentially a man of visions and impulses, every conjuncture, every trick of circumstance only prompting him to more grand designs, only luring his eye to more untrodden hills. But Talleyrand could not go with him all the way, and, aristocrat at heart, would not consent to be a mute unreasoning tool. Talleyrand's thought was of that withering kind that was so

[1] *Corresp. de Nap. Ier*, t. xv, No. 12,453.
[2] *Ibid.* t. xv, No. 12,488.
[3] Driault, *Tilsit*, p. 111.
[4] See *Revue Historique*, t. cxlvi (juillet-août, 1924), pp. 222–30.

fashionable and attractive in the gilded world of his youth. He talked with a wink and a smile, his sarcasm would charm a salon, and, in repartee, he would cover a sword-thrust with velvet; but always his was the talk of the sceptic rather than the enthusiast, the critic rather than the dreamer; he could be delightfully oblique, he was never daringly grand. He thought best when on the defensive. This is where he differed from his master. This is why he was able to play a sort of second critical self to Napoleon, checking his flights of ambition, softening his intemperate expressions, and moderating his indiscreet outbursts—and, on the positive side, furnishing him expedients rather than grand designs. Hence he was perhaps the man to know Napoleon, and realise the true situation of affairs, better than Napoleon himself.

So, while his master was riding away on the wings of some new inspiration, Talleyrand kept his ear to the ground and caught any rumbling that promised danger. He had the instinct of self-preservation developed to its highest power. At the close of 1805 he seems to have felt that Napoleon was over-reaching himself, over-straining the power of France in the attempt to carry out his unbridled ambitions; and he made great point, after the battle of Ulm, of a scheme by which the beaten Austria should be won into alliance with France and, by the cession of Danubian territory, should be induced to direct her ambitions towards Turkey and the east, leaving Napoleon a free hand in Germany and Italy. Napoleon scorned such moderation, used his victory to despoil and enfeeble Austria, and so left that country bitter, and secretly hostile, ready to avenge herself if ever opportunity came. Throughout the year 1806 Talleyrand faithfully served Napoleon in the attempts to make peace with England and Russia, and to avert the Prussian war. But after the battle of Jena Napoleon seems again to have feared, or to have desired to prevent, Talleyrand's moderating counsels, and the minister was carefully excluded from the whole negotiation with Prussia. It was the opinion of many people that his intervention was the only thing which could have saved Prussia and bridled the anger of Napoleon. The story of Napoleon's attempts to make a separate peace with Prussia in the early months of 1807, when it was too late, prove that a restraining influence would have been useful and profitable to him in the days after victory had come to him too easily at Jena. Metternich, in a despatch to Stadion in the year 1808, traces Talleyrand's opposition to his master to the closing months of the year 1806, and the fall of Prussia. From that time, at any rate, Talleyrand seems to have been neither happy nor contented. He hated the Poles, hated the life he was compelled to lead in Warsaw.[1] On the 27th of April he wrote: "Nothing can compensate for our stay in this country, where it snows and rains, and one gets wearied. And all Poland is not worth one drop of the blood which we are shedding for it".[2] Napoleon at St Helena declared that his minister condemned his Polish policy—even ventured to suggest that he might have helped to thwart it.[3] It is said that Talleyrand never looked more pleased than after Eylau when Napoleon was in difficulties and had to put forward offers of peace. Even after Friedland the man could not resist the temptation to thrust his views, when writing to congratulate his master: "I like to think of [this victory] as the last which Your Majesty will be obliged to win. That is why I value it so much".

All this will help to explain why Napoleon distrusted the freedom which Talleyrand allowed himself in his discussions with General Vincent. Talleyrand had leanings towards Austria, had a bias in favour of moderation, had a hankering after peace. And, when convinced that he was right, he was none too scrupulous in the measures he would take to force his master's hand. So Napoleon put him out of reach of Vincent, and kept all the threads in his own fingers.

There is a memoir which Talleyrand wrote with much care and thought—many erasures and alterations—on the 4th of June 1807. The man was still looking for peace, and thought the moment favourable. He considered the new ministry in England

---

[1] E.g. Jomini, *Vie Politique*, II, 328; *Mémoires du duc de Rovigo*, III, 116; Blennerhasset, *Talleyrand* (Eng. tr. 1894), II, 117.

[2] Talleyrand to Clarke, 20 Ap. 1807, in Lefèbvre, *Histoire des Cabinets*, III, 44.

[3] *Corresp. de Nap. Ier*, t. XXXII, pp. 443–4 (quarto ed.), p. 358 (octavo ed.).

to be so weak in parliament, so much distrusted by the public, that it would wish to offer to the English people the bribe of a peace with France. He saw that Prussia, in her present position, would welcome any settlement. He was of opinion that Russia was only waiting for a not too costly escape from a war which was such a burden to her. He himself desired peace then and there, without waiting for new victories to compel it.

"Your Majesty", he wrote, "will prefer to owe it to milder methods, which although they may take more time, will give a more complete and secure result. In fact, if Prussia and Russia are compelled to make peace alone, without being able to reproach England with having abandoned them, England will preserve all her influence over them. She will gain by it, for she will be able to make her own peace with less sacrifices—and, consequently, to our disadvantage. And if she goes on with the war in the new conditions, she will be able to hope to find allies yet on the Continent."

Talleyrand, it is plain, did not desire any more of those sweeping Napoleonic victories that would only lure the French armies to more distant wars. And he had no wish for a peace which would strengthen Napoleon in Europe, and confirm his vast designs, while leaving England at war, ready to raise new coalitions at the first opportunity. He desired a congress and a settlement. He had quarrelled with Napoleonic diplomacy.[1]

Now Napoleon, from the very time when the Austrians made their official offer of mediation, seems to have had little real desire for peace; and, even when he was talking of negotiation, even while he was taking steps for the promotion of a general congress, he appears to have returned to his former preference for separate discussions and arrangements with individual powers; he desired once more to create division among his enemies, and dissolve the coalition by making private treaties with single members of it. When, in March, he wrote to Talleyrand, intimating that he would be inclined to accept the mediation of Austria if it should be offered, he added that in three months his troops would be ready, and that by September he would have 80,000 men.

[1] Vandal, *Napoléon et Alexandre Ier*, I, 44–5.

"Not that I do not want peace with Russia", he went on, "for I think that this would lead to peace with England; but I think also that when two powers like France and Russia wish to make peace, the best way of doing it is for them to treat with one another directly."[1]

On that very day Napoleon sent a new message to the Senate:

"Our policy is fixed", he declared: "We offered peace to England before she engineered the Fourth Coalition; this same peace we still hold out to her....We are ready to conclude a Treaty with Russia on the same terms that her negotiator had signed—terms which the intrigues and persuasions of England induced her to reject. We are ready to give tranquillity to those eight millions of people whose country has been conquered by our arms and to restore to the King of Prussia his capital."[2]

It is significant that, at a moment when he was declaring his willingness to accept the mediation of Austria, he took great care that the court of Vienna should not remain ignorant of this "Message to the Senate".[3] And it is significant that in a document that is intended to advertise his desire for peace, he speaks once more in the language of separate negotiation, he offers England and Russia the terms they have already indignantly refused, and to the Prussian king he only renews the promise of restoration to his estates, for which that king has recently more than once declined to desert his allies. A little later he addresses the king of Sweden, and, behind him, speaks to the Swedish people, in deprecation of the war which was so ruinous to them.

Peace, even a truce, accorded to Sweden, would answer the dearest desires of the Emperor, who has always felt a true grief at making war on a nation brave, generous and both historically and geographically, the ally of France. And, in fact, ought Swedish blood to be shed to defend or destroy the Ottoman Porte? Ought it to be shed to maintain the freedom or enslavement of the seas? What has Sweden to fear from France? Nothing. What has she to fear from Russia? Everything.[4]

Austrian mediations might come and go—and Napoleon would bow politely to them as they passed—but he was not inclined

---

[1] *Corresp. de Nap. Ier*, t. xiv, No. 12,098.
[2] *Ibid.* t. xiv, No. 12,100.   [3] *Ibid.* t. xiv, No. 12,099.
[4] *Ibid.* t. xv, No. 12,459 (*72nd Bulletin*).

to meet the powers and clear up the whole situation in a congress. His words and actions were full of contradictions, and one cannot listen to his peace talk at all seriously. Perhaps, as usual, he did not know himself just what he intended to do, and carried on the discussions for a congress till the military situation should become clear, throwing out offers of separate peace by the way, in case one should find response, and so playing with the alternative courses open to him, until "events" should give him his cue.

The Austrian government was satisfied with the English response to its overture;[1] for it did not know the full implications of Canning's attitude, it did not realise that England had merely passed on to her allies the unpleasantness of turning down this most unwelcome proposal. When the Austrian minister Starhemberg informed the British government of the answers of the other powers, Canning showed some surprise at the news that Russia and more especially Prussia had given disappointment to the court of Vienna, and Starhemberg had to report that "the English cabinet finds the two replies perfectly conformable to that which it made itself".[2] On the other hand, the Austrians were "disagreeably surprised" to find a "sortie" against England in the note by which Napoleon gave his consent to the mediation. "I did not expect, either", wrote Stadion, "to see in a reply to a pacific measure a kind of offer of rapprochement or alliance with us."[3]

The Austrian government, however, did not entirely abandon its plans, and gave it to be understood that an attempt would be made to persuade the French cabinet "to enter into some explanations of the sort which the two Courts [of Russia and Prussia] demanded".[4] Vincent was ordered to communicate the

---

[1] Stadion to Starhemberg, 30 May 1807 (No. 1), *W.S.A. Weisungen nach London*.

[2] Starhemberg to Stadion, No. 54, *W.S.A. Berichte aus London*.

[3] Stadion to Starhemberg, 7 May 1807, *W.S.A. Weisungen nach London*; see also Adair, *op. cit.* p. 234.

[4] Stadion to Starhemberg, 30 May 1807 (No. 1), *W.S.A. Weisungen nach London*.

replies of the allied powers to Talleyrand and to accompany them with some verbal explanations. For a long time he waited for an opportunity of interviewing the French minister, but Napoleon had taken care that Talleyrand should be out of reach, and at last, on the 16th of June, Vincent gave up the hope and merely despatched copies of the English, Russian and Prussian notes to the French headquarters, with an earnest appeal for the return of Talleyrand to Warsaw. But by this time Friedland had already been fought.[1]

In this way the Austrian mediation flickered out. Perhaps it had served its purpose. At least it had covered the weakness of Austria's policy; it had assisted, it had excused, the protraction of her neutrality. It had been her reply to the importunity of both Napoleon and the coalition—her escape from all the traps that were being laid to embroil her in the war.

[1] Driault, *Tilsit*, pp. 111–12 (two letters from Vincent to Talleyrand, 16 June 1807).

CHAPTER IV

THE RESUMPTION OF THE PRUSSIAN NEGOTIATION FOR A CONGRESS

WHILE the Austrians were making their hopeless attempt to proceed with their mediation, a parallel negotiation was seeking to promote a general congress and was being carried on between the belligerents themselves. It was conducted with more smoothness and honesty, and seemed to approach more closely to the desired end, than the twisted and profitless transaction that the mediation had come to be; and on the eve of Friedland it appeared to have reached astonishingly near its goal. It was a continuation of the original discussions that had been carried on since December 1806 when Krüsemarck had ridden to St Petersburg to convert the Czar to the idea of a congress; and the last step that had been taken in the matter was the overture by Colonel Kleist in February containing Napoleon's alternative offers of either separate peace with Prussia or a congress of the powers at war. When the Czar came to join his armies, and overhauled the whole peace question in his discussions with the Prussian king, when, also, the English reply to the proposals of Krüsemarck had arrived, a conference came to the decision that this negotiation should be taken up again. It was determined that a reply should be made to the proposals which Kleist had brought, and that Napoleon should be asked the bases on which he would consent to treat in a congress. On the 21st of April, before the convention of Bartenstein had been actually signed, the Prussian king, on behalf of Russia, Prussia and England, sent a letter to Napoleon. He declared that the allies desired a general and honourable peace "which should ground the future independence and repose of Europe upon a stable arrangement of things that should be guaranteed by all the contracting parties". The allies stipulated that the settlement should equitably indemnify those victims of the war to whom the courts of

St Petersburg and London were bound by solemn engagements. England, it was assured, was willing to make sacrifices for the sake of peace; and the Prussian king affirmed "with the most complete certainty", that, far from having any designs against the Ottoman Porte, the Czar merely demanded the maintenance of the existing treaties with Turkey. The participation of Turkey in the congress, therefore, was considered to be out of place; but it was asked that Sweden should be admitted and also that Austria should be allowed to join in the negotiation. These being the sentiments of the allied powers, Napoleon was invited to explain frankly the bases upon which he would treat.[1]

Napoleon declared himself very pleased with the suggestion of Copenhagen for a congress; it was the place he had thought of himself. He was disappointed with the proposal to exclude Constantinople from the transaction, but he thought that the king of Prussia had not said the last word or delivered an ultimatum on this subject. He was displeased also with a reference to indemnities in the Prussian king's letter; though even on this point he liked to suppose that Naples, not Sardinia, was the party in mind.

Within a few days he sent his reply. The king of Prussia had asked that the peace should be general, honourable, and solid.

But would it be general if several of the principal powers at war were not comprised in it, not summoned to guard their interests for themselves? Would it be honourable if it conflicted with the most sacred engagements, by separating those who have made common cause in the present war, while it admitted all the allies of one of the belligerent parties?... The participation of Spain, Turkey, and other powers at war who are allies of France in the present conflict is as necessary as it is just in this work of peace. I raise no difficulty about allowing England and Russia to make common cause, although France has always regarded this as contrary to the first principles of her policy. Why do you refuse me the same thing with respect to Turkey?[2]

Napoleon declared this to be the one obstacle to the opening of the proposed negotiations; and he kept his word. He made

---

[1] Frederick William III to Napoleon, 21 Ap. 1807; printed in M. F. von Bassewitz, *Die Kurmark Brandenburg*, I, 386–7.

[2] *Corresp. de Nap. Ier*, t. xv, No. 12,487; see also No. 12,464.

no mention of an armistice on this occasion; he thought that his enemies would demand this in order to save Danzig, and he was not disposed to grant it until he had secured his object. When, on the 10th of May, the king of Prussia submitted to his arguments and acquiesced in his demands,[1] he replied:

There remains now no objection for me to make. My plenipotentiaries and those of the powers which are making common cause with me in this war, will be at Copenhagen on the day Your Majesty cares to appoint. As to basis. . . everything is contained in these two words: equality and reciprocity between the two belligerent groups.

England and Russia will do for my allies what I do for theirs. . . . [2]

This correspondence seems to have been kept very secret. Talleyrand himself knew nothing until the 24th of April, when Napoleon wrote to him, enclosing the letter just received from Prussia with a copy of those that had passed between himself and the king during the two preceding months. Talleyrand was ordered to say nothing to the Austrian General Vincent. "Since you were not aware of the other letters it is possible that you may be ignorant of this",[3] wrote Napoleon, and it was not until the end of May that he decided to inform Austria of the correspondence. The king of Prussia, whose history told against him, was still distrusted by some people around him, and was suspected of questionable transactions with France; but he had acted with the cognisance of the Emperor Alexander and he informed the British government of the correspondence.

On the 9th of June the Prussian government drew up a communication to be made to the court of London, summarising the situation, and recalling the conditions of the impending negotiation. On the very eve of the congress, and as he was touching his desired object, the king was not too optimistic. Napoleon might be trying to trap him, might use the negotiation to hinder rather than promote the work of peace. His bases were not above suspicion:

---

[1] Frederick William III to Napoleon, 10 May 1807; printed in Bassewitz, *Die Kurmark Brandenburg*, I, 388–9.
[2] *Corresp. de Nap. I*^{er}, t. xv, No. 12,594.
[3] *Ibid.* t. xv, No. 12,464.

It cannot be disguised that a principle so vaguely enunciated, and susceptible of so many interpretations, only gives a very little hope of our reaching the proposed goal, and that it will only be by the most vigorous pursuit of the war, the prompt and effective aid of Austria, and the help furnished by England to the Continental Powers that we can succeed. The consequences which Napoleon will perhaps draw from the proposed basis may be such as, far from facilitating the general peace, only make it more and more distant, especially if he regards himself as master of the part of Continental Europe which he happens to occupy at present and thinks to establish a system of compensation upon this state of occupation....

But, to refuse the opening of the Congress would be to play into the hands of Napoleon....We must therefore lend ourselves to the opening of the Congress and even hasten it as much as possible. The King...will send his plenipotentiaries to Copenhagen as soon as those of the King of England are ordered to go....But the King thinks that this determination of the powers at war with France ought not to excuse any of them from vigorously pursuing operations against the common enemy.

A similar statement was drawn up for the court of Stockholm; and also one in the same sense to be communicated to Austria along with the whole correspondence. It is immaterial whether these documents were actually despatched and reached their destination; the fact that they were drawn up is a register of the situation.[1]

On the very eve of Friedland, therefore, Europe is on the point of seeing the assembly of a congress that is to comprise Austria and all the powers at war. The offer of Napoleon to meet Russia, Prussia and England in a negotiation has been widened by the English insistence upon the interests of monarchs like the kings of Naples and Sardinia, by the Prussian desire to see Sweden and Austria enter the discussions, and by the French counter-claim on behalf of Spain and Turkey and "other belligerent powers who are allies of France". A situation of things has been produced in which both parties are willing at least to make a pretence of negotiating and both are anxious to do it without any preliminary armistice. Both sides, also, welcome the inter-

---

[1] *Projet de l'office à remettre par le comte de Finckenstein au cabinet de Vienne*, 9 June 1807; Ranke, *Hardenberg*, v, 495. *Office à remettre mut. mut. aux cours de Londres et de Stockholm*, 9 June 1807; *ibid.* v, 498.

vention of Austria in the congress though they combined to ensure the failure of the Austrian attempt to mediate peace. They do not refuse to see the court of Vienna take a part in the establishment of peace in Europe but they reject the peculiar implications of the particular movement which that court desires to promote, and, above all, they object to the mediation as the attempt of Austria to evade the real issue and postpone any energetic decision.

This congress, however, which is being promoted by direct correspondence between the belligerent groups, does not promise great hopes. It is a victory in that it fastens Napoleon down to a general negotiation at last, but it is not the finish of fighting. It still leaves Napoleon the opportunity to resort to his usual practices in negotiation, and the French basis for the discussions provides no check, no guarantee against this. In one point at least it promises trouble. Napoleon says, "England and Russia will do for my allies what I shall do for theirs. I shall do for the allies of England and Russia what they will do for mine". It is not a case of Prussia doing anything for her allies; she is a passenger in the affair. Napoleon evidently regards her still as possessing nothing with which to negotiate. She is part of the system of compensation. France accepts a congress on the condition that the existing occupation of Prussia by her armies shall constitute a value in negotiation and shall be the basis of a scheme of compensation. England however has declared her intention of refusing to surrender her conquests merely for a restoration of Prussia, and she demands a positive value in return, a barrier against the power and aggressions of France. Therefore the Prussian king is not hopeful about the impending congress. He declares the inadmissibility of Napoleon's basis of negotiation if that basis is made to imply that he regards "himself as master of that part of Continental Europe which he happens to occupy at present and thinks to establish a system of compensation upon it". Each side, therefore, places everything on the issue of the warfare; each is perfectly determined to prosecute military operations with vigour. The congress, even if it had met, would not have prevented Friedland.

BOOK THREE

TILSIT

CHAPTER I

THE COALITION ON THE EVE OF FRIEDLAND

THE last sands of the hour-glass were now slowly trailing out, and the strange tangle of fate was coming to its unravelling. The men of the coalition were watching the sky and observing the signs and portents. In the last days of April the Czar and the Prussian king were still at Bartenstein, exchanging their pleasant courtesies, giving decorations and dinners, and talking deep schemes with Hardenberg—still floating on their optimism. The glowing mood at the allied headquarters rose superior to crude facts, even flew in the face of facts, and men were walking upon air. One would have said that the Russian troops were strangely inactive, and that the generals gave no promise of energy or capacity; but they found easy excuse for themselves and said that they were only collecting their strength. One would have inferred that the situation was serious, with Napoleon pressing tightly upon Danzig; but they were not crushed with this thought. Danzig, they said, was "garrisoned by sixteen thousand men,...and its magazines plentifully supplied...with every means for carrying on the war for some months". They congratulated themselves that the besiegers were chiefly Germans, who deserted at every opportunity. It pleased them to think with Budberg, the Russian chancellor, that "All accounts agree about the enemy's not yet having siege-artillery in front of this town. The general, Count Kalckreuth, who is in command there, has no apprehensions".[1] Moreover, a Russian force was preparing to move to the relief of the beleaguered city; and this was a hopeful sign, though indeed one might have seen that its numbers were inadequate for the task, and that it was tempting providence with its insufferable delays. Sickness in the Russian armies, and difficulties with the provisioning of

---

[1] Budberg to Soltykov, 14/26 Ap. 1807, in *Sbornik*, LXXXVIII, 39–41.

the troops, might have caused discomfort and discontent at headquarters; but even here the allies could retort that the French were in a predicament far worse; for Polish, German, and Italian soldiers were continually deserting from the ranks of Napoleon, bringing tales of bitter privation, of shortage of food and horses, of troops unwilling to fight, of officers pressing for retreat, and of grave indiscipline. "Several prisoners", wrote Budberg, "have related that the soldiers are reduced to eating horseflesh."[1]

Among the Prussians there was a strong party feeling on the question of peace or war. Zastrow headed the advocates of surrender and enlarged on the hopelessness of the situation. Hardenberg led the war party, and for ever urged a display of vigour. But Zastrow had had his day, and now was out of fashion, and was soon to leave the scene amid some unpleasantness; while the partisans of energy had recently received new support and encouragement by the arrival of Blücher. Blücher had done clanging deeds, had shot defiance at the Corsican; and was returning from captivity like a hero caught from the clutches of the oppressor; he had tales to tell of discontent in Germany—men wriggling under the heel of Napoleon and only awaiting the signal to rise; had one very reassuring story of how at Finckenstein he had seen the Emperor himself and found him impatient for peace. Like the clatter of spurs, or the singing of a martial tune or the telling of old tales of gods and heroes, the coming of Blücher would fire imagination, and give a nervous thrill, and make men feel themselves brave.

The rugged, petulant Swedish king was for once in affable mood; it seemed that he might prove useful at last; he appeared disposed to join in a combined action that should threaten Napoleon's rear. More strange still, there was a general conviction that the Austrians were on the point of a declaration of war. It was imagined that the convention of Bartenstein would precipitate a decision; active steps were being taken to press the occasion; and wise men, winking knowingly, said "There is reason to expect...". Bennigsen claimed that he had good news from Vienna. Hardenberg thought he had cause for believing

[1] Budberg to Soltykov, 14/26 Ap. 1807, in *Sbornik*, LXXXVIII, 39–41.

that the hour had come. The Empress of Austria had recently died and it was pleasant for some people to assume that she had stood in the way and had been responsible for much of the hesitation. Wilson claimed that the official news from Vienna was favourable, and that the public talk "under very high sanction" was "charged with good omens as to Austria's co-operation".[1] These expectations might have come out of the blue—stray thoughts that a wind carries, hopes born of some fond mood—for all the basis that can be found for them. The Prussian minister in Vienna denied that he had encouraged any such anticipations. Robert Adair, British representative there, suspected that some "enemies of the public cause" had been at work, maliciously raising the hopes of the Prussians in order to take advantage of the moment of disappointment when the king should find out his mistake.[2]

Flimsy and unsubstantial the optimisms might seem—poor basis for self-congratulation. Yet something contrived to make the allies very sanguine at headquarters. One man described them as "snug".

From England, no news since the middle of March; no money, no diversion, no message of reassurance.[3] Lord Hutchinson neglected to write to his government, and English ministers seemed "to know nothing but from chance reports and the accounts of merchant captains". Hutchinson would grumble and moan, and dilate upon the strong position of Napoleon.

"He spends nearly all of the day in looking over the map and consulting with Bennigsen", wrote George Jackson. "Consultation

---

[1] E.g. G. Jackson, *Diaries*, II, 106: "Hardenberg told me to-day that they have the best grounds for believing that Austria would soon declare herself". Cf. Hutchinson to Adair, 1 Ap. 1807, in Adair, *Historical Memoir*, Appendix, p. 381: "They have got it into their heads here...that the Austrians are at length determined to take a part in the war, and to act with the allies.... I satisfy myself with saying that they may be better informed than you are".

[2] Adair to Lord Hutchinson, 13 Ap. 1807, in Adair, *op. cit.* Appendix, pp. 394–7.

[3] On the 19th of March 1807 we find Douglas reporting from St Petersburg: "There is reason to suppose that it has...forcibly been put to the Emperor by some people here...that Russia is abandoned by her friends...and that even her intimate ally Great Britain neglects to support her at a crisis when any reverse of fortune might endanger the Empire itself". Douglas to Howick, No. 13, *F.O. Russia* 65/68.

follows consultation, but nothing is done. I confess I should be sorry to see an English army again under Lord Hutchinson's command, for a spirit of procrastination such as one can scarcely conceive or understand, rules him on all occasions....

His lordship is still in 'the Slough of Despond', and as loud as ever in depreciating our resources, and magnifying those of Bonaparte.

Ld H. keeps up the same offensive strain of mingled despair and contempt. He is, of course, treated by both the Emperor and King with invariable attention, but with their ministers he is not on very cordial terms....

Colonel Hougo...has got himself into a scrape...by one day taking Lord H. seriously to task, and exposing to him, pretty unreservedly, what people say of him, and of his manner of viewing and talking of the present state of affairs...."

The Englishman who chanced to be with the armies in Poland would hear murmurings and complaints concerning the apathy of his own country, and would wait with sullen impatience. He would catch a whisper that the British government "have too great an interest in the protraction of the war".[1] He would find Hardenberg surmising that the resignation of "All the Talents" was due to popular dissatisfaction with the ministers for their indifference to the continental cause. He would discover not only Hardenberg, but the Prussian king and queen, and many others, repeatedly declaring the hope that the new ministry would replace Lord Hutchinson and send a more acceptable representative to headquarters.

"This truth Lord Hutchinson and all of us will ever declare", wrote the impetuous Wilson, "that there never was a sovereign, an army, ministers, or a nation, more disposed to carry on a war and to remain faithful to alliances, than the Russian. If that country now adopts a policy which her own interests justify, England, and England alone, is the real friend of Bonaparte and of France."

Feeling relaxed when it became known that the British government was sending a new minister to treat with the Czar, that an expedition of English troops might shortly be expected in Europe, and that Lord Hutchinson was to depart for Stralsund to discuss a military diversion. There was a suspension of

[1] Wilson, *Diaries*, II, 170.

judgment at Bartenstein, a stifling of natural resentment, until the new English minister should arrive and report what his government was doing. But if his coming should be long deferred, if he should bring a mere handful of promises or shifty evasions, if, in the meantime, disaster should come upon the armies and enterprises in Poland—then would the latent store of bitterness be released, and a hideous accusing finger be levelled in the direction of England.

For the present, the chancellor Budberg was writing to St Petersburg:

> The army is in the best possible condition. The cavalry horses are ready for the campaign. The demeanour of the soldier is superb; he is animated with the best of spirits, and thinks only of adding new victories to those which he has already won.[1]

The queen of Prussia wrote to her father on the 15th of May, looking back to the days of misfortune and despair, as to a far half-forgotten world.

> The Battle of Eylau had very important results....Now, with the return of spring and the revival of nature, patriotism also seems to be awakening in every Prussian heart. The activity manifest on all hands, the sending of our excellent Blücher to Pomerania, the number of new battalions which have been formed during recent months, are things which inspire me with hope....Yes, dearest father, I am convinced that all will yet go well, and that a happy meeting is in store for us. The siege of Danzig proceeds most satisfactorily.[2]

Until the middle of May the "snugness" continued at' headquarters. There was a mood for minimising difficulties, and slurring over mistakes, and gazing gladly into the future. It needed but a pinprick to burst the bubble. On the 19th of May the news was abroad that the Russians had failed to relieve Danzig. It ought to have caused no surprise, but somehow the allies were not in readiness for the misfortune, and had prepared no shock absorbers for their minds. The event found them floundering, and cut the cord that kept them buoyant, and very

---

[1] *Sbornik*, LXXXVIII, 39.
[2] Translated in Moffat, *Queen Louisa of Prussia* pp. 166–7.

soon hopes and optimisms were cut away, to go sailing the sky like a bunch of gaudy toy balloons that a gust of wind has taken. "The news from Danzig causes the greatest depression", wrote Jackson, "both here and at headquarters. Surrender is inevitable. When the Emperor read the despatches he was quite overcome by his feelings." Six days later the French were in the city. Day broke upon the dreamers. Men winced at the sudden smell of danger. Soon were unloosed all the things that were the shadow of doom to coalitions—reproaches of betrayal, accusations of lethargy, suspicions and complaints between allies, the torments of irresolution, the awful sense of opportunities gone. A new psychological atmosphere supervened. We are on the high road to Tilsit.

"This misfortune", wrote Wilson, after the fall of Danzig, "has depressed all our spirits, and rendered our situation here very uncomfortable; for the English are accused as the cause of the disaster by their supineness, and our best friends painfully express their regret at such disloyal conduct."

Hardenberg, self-appointed keeper of the conscience of the coalition, played the schoolmaster to England as he had done to the Czar and the Prussian king. On the 24th of May he wrote to the Duke of York, urging the dismissal of all distrust, the hastening of perfect concert, the abandonment of hesitations and lethargy, for "the last act of the great drama" had begun. There is something ironical—something indicative, too, of the new rôle that Prussia is seeking to adopt—in the way Hardenberg makes use against England of the very language which had so long been used against the cabinet of Berlin. "Distrust, slowness, irresolution, disunion, pusillanimity—these", he wrote to the Prussian minister in London, "have been the cause of all our misfortunes." Lord Hutchinson, he declared, whatever his private virtues might be, was a disagreeable, suspicious and dismal diplomat, and a minister was needed who would be "more active, more zealous for the common cause, more versed in affairs".[1] Like beleaguered troops gazing out to sea for a gleam

[1] Hardenberg to the Duke of York and to Jacobi-Kloest in Ranke, *Hardenberg*, III, 362–3.

of the sails that should bring relief, these allies waited for England until they were tired of waiting; and Englishmen on the spot, perhaps too unaware of the difficulties at home, had exhausted their patience and used up their arguments in defence of their country and government. It was useless to go on saying, "Wait until Leveson-Gower arrives". June came in, it was long since there had been news from England, and no Leveson-Gower appeared—"a fact which caused much suspicion". "People here begin to think that our promises are *vox et praeterea nihil*; and at the army they are flung continually into the teeth of our countrymen who are there."

No peace, now, for Alexander. Bennigsen, his chief commander, fell ill in the midst of the depression. The hope that had been placed in Austria gradually dwindled away; it was clear that the loss of Danzig would only confirm the cabinet of Vienna in its timid neutral course. The Czar decided to leave the army, and though some people were not sorry to see him hand over the conduct of the campaign to his generals, the gesture of departure at this particular moment heightened the discontent. The army itself was in difficulties.

Unfortunately there is a great scarcity of provisions, and the Russian army is so distressed that the men actually pass whole days without a morsel of bread. Just now, as an amazing effort, the contractors have promised provisions for three days.

A crisis had been threatening for a long time. Bennigsen said, "I have been preaching for two months". He had preached, but he had not brought remedies. Hungry Russian troops plundered the land still left to the Prussian king. Annoyance and bickering were bound to follow. Hardenberg complained to the Czar:

Everybody is asking how it is that the soldiers of a prince who is a model of humanity and magnanimity, can be allowed to commit excesses without number—which, besides ruining the country of his ally and best friend, compromise the existence and honour of the army itself.[1]

[1] Hardenberg to the Czar Alexander, 17 May 1807, in Ranke, *Hardenberg*, v, 506–14.

Amid it all there came an astonishing bitterness, as of sudden disillusionment. The passions that had leaped to brave music seemed turned into something devastating. We can judge the intensity of the disappointment from the eagerness with which men pounced upon a scapegoat. Queen Louisa, who recently had hailed the spring with warm hope and high anticipation, was like one possessed with a demon, and wrote in a strain like this:

> Danzig, Danzig is lost to us....It is maddening. The place might have been saved if Bennigsen had made a slight diversion to draw off the attention of the besiegers....His apathy is simply indescribable. ...He talks of fighting a pitched battle between to-day and the day after to-morrow. I do not believe him. What I do believe is that some evilly disposed individual has got the upper hand with him. He has won two battles and thereby secured all the orders of the Russian Empire. His huge pension has been augmented by twelve thousand roubles. That is probably enough for a man, so called because he is going about on two legs....I am beside myself, I admit it.[1]

Hardenberg helped the queen to draw up a renewed attack upon Bennigsen[2]—addressed this time to the Czar himself:

> Since my last letter, events have quite changed colour, and the loss of Danzig has plunged all the world into very deep grief. I cannot deny, my dear Cousin, that what tears my heart, is to see the lack of zeal that there is in the execution of your benevolent intentions, and how General Bennigsen does everything to make the whole world believe that it is *we* who do not keep our word and who are the cause of his incomprehensible apathy. Pardon me, my dear Cousin, if I make bold to tell you that I am beginning to doubt his good intentions, for all this week he has been changing the reasons which he alleges in excuse for his inaction. So long as you were at head-quarters he said it was your presence that paralysed his operations. Now that you have made a sacrifice to the good cause by withdrawing from the army...it is *we* who are the victims of his ill-humour. Your glorious army would gather *new laurels* everywhere, if only it were *well led*.[3]

Bennigsen was in league with the peace party, said some—with the Grand Duke Constantine and the apostles of timidity. He

---

[1] Translated in Moffat, *Queen Louisa of Prussia*, pp. 168–9.
[2] Ranke, *Hardenberg*, iii, 441–2.
[3] Bailleu, *Briefwechsel*, pp. 466–7.

was denounced as a traitor, declared worthy of the knout. And Bennigsen, pressed by his master to move forward and make some display of energy, began to give colour to the accusations, and shake his head and augur ill from any continuation of hostilities. In the first week of June he announced some successes, but pleaded sickness and talked of retiring.[1] The Czar replied to him curtly: "I expect you to do what your duty and the honour and glory of Russia demand of you".[2]

It was true that there was a peace party among the Prussians, causing anxious ferment even at the army headquarters. Czartoryski, who in former days had walked arm-in-arm with Alexander, talking over with him the dreams of generous youth, and airing an expansive liberalism, was a spokesman of this group. Having much in common with the Czar, sharing largely of his sympathies, his flying schemes, his mutability, he had yet an essential divergence; for his successive plans revolved around a different constant—in all his bold imaginative recastings of policy he would find his centre in the idea of a new Poland, that should arise under the wing of the Czars. So while Alexander was burning to rescue Europe from the hands of Napoleon, he himself had a different pre-occupation. He had no affection for the Prussians; he had urged the Czar to attack them before Austerlitz; and, reasserting his distrust in the face of the secret Russo-Prussian alliance of 1806, he had surrendered office and made way for the pro-German Budberg.[3] He had promoted Oubril's negotiation and for some time after Jena had been pressing the government to make peace. Novossiltzov, the Charles James Fox among Alexander's early companions, man of reckless habits and wild living, with impressive talents and liberal tendencies and an admiration for the British constitution, was another member of the peace party; also Strogonov, the third of the group of Alexander's youthful friends, who had fought bitterly against Oubril's treaty. So the men who had been

[1] Bennigsen to Alexander, 28 May/9 June 1807, in *Sbornik*, LXXXIX, 3.

[2] Czar Alexander to Bennigsen, 29 May/10 June 1807, in *Sbornik*, LXXXIX, 4.

[3] Czartoryski's attitude towards Prussia is well illustrated in his Memorandum; cf. *Sbornik*, LXXXII, 292–310.

not only the servants and instruments but the close intimates of the Czar in the first phase of his reign, had become out of sympathy with his policy and lent their weight to the opposition; and Alexander, who could not open out his romantic heart to a "realist" politician like Budberg—who indeed was said to be at this moment on somewhat cool terms with the minister— stood out rather aloof, curled in upon himself; perhaps expanding at times at the warmer touch of Hardenberg.

A more sinister atmosphere hangs around opposition that comes in mutterings from the army itself. There is something frightening in the isolation in which an autocrat must live— something terrible for him in the significance of his army, which in a moment can make him impotent. Russia had had a century of palace revolutions, and lightning military conspiracies, and mysterious overthrows; they would seem to have been the recognised way of "tempering" the autocracy. Alexander had been raised to the throne in the track of murder done by night, and he seems to have gone through life like a man haunted as a result—seems to have been at times dogged and overfaced by a relentless second self. The thought of a military uprising could raise a sort of primeval fear in him, opening an uncanny psycho-analytical room in his mind. It is true that we find no hint of revolution on the eve of Friedland; but it is important, in setting the stage for Tilsit, to remember, as a possible element in the situation, that there existed this tract of primitive unredeemed territory in the mind of the Czar. Not only did this nightmare lie hidden beneath the mind and moods of Alexander—not only did he actually imagine sometimes that in the darkness he heard the muffled footfall which had announced to his father his tragic fate—but, as we shall see, there were people prepared to evoke the fear, and conjure up the nightmare and play upon its terrors.

The opposition in the army found its centre and its voice in the Grand Duke Constantine; but Constantine was no traitor, and it is better to regard him rather as the intractable younger brother. Ugly, uncouth, impetuous and untamed, this man was fitted to be the favourite of his father, the wild and shaggy

Emperor Paul, whom he resembled in his backward mentality, in a certain coarseness of fibre, in his fierce tempestuous disposition and his wild and fantastic humours, as well as in his passion for soldiers and for military parade. Yet certain human qualities which seemed once to show themselves in Paul but had been withered by cruel treatment and a relentlessly hostile environment—a kindliness of heart, a generous childlike impulsiveness and a stubborn sort of loyalty—remained to make Constantine lovable and won him the affection of his soldiers. He had a strange liking for his brother, and showed him the strongest devotion, but he did not in the least understand Alexander's mystical fervour, and did not think that such exaltations should be encouraged. He who called himself "the donkey Constantine"—who, when he entered Paris with the victorious army in 1814, rushed to visit not the Louvre but the stables— who had the roughest contempt for everything that looked like dandyism—had a summary way of judging the vagaries of his brother's romanticism. Also, like his father, he had come to admire Napoleon and to have a high estimate of his prowess. During the negotiations at Tilsit he hurried to receive instruction from French officers, and when the alliance with France had been concluded he caused French prisoners to produce a miniature of Napoleon's camp of Boulogne in the gardens of his palace. It is useless to explore for deep and subtle reasons behind the judgments of this erratic haphazard mind; with an eye only for the realistic, with an intelligence that would seize upon the immediate, and with no power to follow his brother's remoter kind of thinking, he would grasp at the tangible elements of the situation; and, stationed with an underfed army amid incapable and quarrelsome generals, in the face of an enemy whom he admired and felt to be superior in war, he would easily find reasons for jumping to an impulsive desire for peace.

So one day we find Hardenberg talking to the Czar of the untrustworthiness of his officers, and the dangerous conduct of the peace party, and the intrigues of men like Constantine. Alexander brushes the talk aside and makes some defence of his brother. Then without warning there appears the impetuous

Constantine himself, raving of peace and declaring that no time must be lost. It is a startling confirmation of all the suspicions that are abroad; we hear that the Czar is much impressed. He apologises to Hardenberg for his unbelief and orders his brother back to the army. It would even seem that he takes more seriously the accusations that have been levelled against Bennigsen; for this same day he sends a general to enquire into the conduct of the commander-in-chief, even orders this man to remove Bennigsen from the post if it should seem a necessary step.[1]

These were the commotions that were stirring around the gentle figure of Alexander—miserable, tantalising bickerings for a man who bore upon his shoulders all the burden of "all the Russias". An iron man would have brushed them away with a sweep of his mighty arm—would have stamped his foot to shake a mountain. But Alexander was not terrible. No monarch was more susceptible to immediate influences and suggestions from the external world. All his mysticisms and philanthropic moods were at the mercy of the crude play of events or of environment. Let him go on soothing himself with his dreams of chivalry, of liberation, and he would sit and smile though the thunders were rumbling destruction—he would sit and feel himself a hero and sense the grand tragedy of the situation. Let him be conscious of the halo that was round him, keep him in his dream of being the centre of an epic, play delicately upon his vanity—and he would float on the poetry of it, nodding benignantly. But set such a man in the midst of petty vexations, under the insistent torment of minor bickerings, amid quibbles and quarrels and sorenesses—treat him as a little man, pester him with annoyances, forget that he is a poet—and, though for a long time he may seem still to swim serenely on his romanticisms, though he may not bully you or brutally thrust you aside as an enraged giant would—yet these things will sink deep and slowly simmer, and gradually he will feel the halo fade away, and he will come himself to fall to the littleness of things—till

[1] Ranke, *Hardenberg*, III, 448–9; see S. Tatistcheff (1891), *Alexandre Ier et Napoléon*, pp. 115–16.

some day, at the beckoning of some other voice, he will turn from you altogether, will find his romanticisms, his poetry, his halo elsewhere, will discover some other rôle in which he can again feel himself the hero of an epic, still nod his head and smile like a benignant god—and then he will turn back upon you all your own pettinesses and squabblings and vexations, to show that they have not gone unremembered.

History gives us only grudging fragments of herself, and it is not possible to tell how the deepest mind of Alexander was working on the eve of Friedland. We know he still averred that he would persist in the war against Napoleon; we do not know with what changed voice he might have come to assert this, or what deep heart's misgivings he stifled or repressed when he spoke. It is impossible not to believe that something in him resented the irritation of these days when the Austrians appeared distrusting, the English seemed bent on rushing off at a tangent in selfish adventures of conquest, the Prussians—no allies, anyhow, rather an added responsibility—were annoying him with complaints about the failure to relieve Danzig, the conduct of his troops, and the incompetence of his generals; while, all the time, there were two parties in his own camp, each tugging at his coat and trying in turn to gain his ear, and Bennigsen himself was becoming a half-hearted, unwilling leader. The surface Alexander might not yet register the change; the external system of his overt ideas and conscious purposes quite possibly remained the same; he may have still *felt* determined; but all these annoyances and disappointments were tapping on the walls of his brain, and if they did not yet seem to touch the surface-thinking, they found the back door into that hidden room of the mind where buried thoughts rankle. Some day a shock would shake them out, and find them festered and sore through having been underground. Already Alexander was accustomed to saying that he "had no ally"; he allowed the idea to eat into his mind, and even when he seemed most defiant, the thought was still his misgiving. And when he said that he had no ally, it was not merely the grumbling of a man of affairs who resents a lack of co-operation, it was something like the cry of a forlorn poet, unappreciated in the world, and lonely under the stars.

In the middle of June we catch sight of the disillusioned Alexander giving expression to his complaints. His bitterness comes to the surface and we are allowed to see a stage in the process by which the Saviour of Europe forgot his rôle and lost his inspiration and gave himself into the hands of the enemy.

Full in the sparkle of gaiety and fashion in the London life of these years—making wise heads shake by his prowess at cards, causing no end of a rustle among the petticoats, and giving rise to much chatter that sent a ripple round the tea-cups —was the handsome, spoiled, and rather moody younger son of a man who had once declined to be prime minister of England. From his infancy he had been petted and idolised by the ladies, and now, at thirty-four, he was still a kind of darling of society. He was the Lord Granville Leveson-Gower, whose correspondence with Lady Bessborough gives such a bright and intimate disclosure of the gossip and social life and petty preoccupations of the Napoleonic times. He was reputed the best whist-player of his day, though indeed the luck persistently went against him, and he was said to have lost as much as £23,000 at a sitting. Also he had a weakness for the fair sex, and drifted into many adventures and indiscretions, about which Lady Bessborough —and the other gossipers—had much to say. When in the year 1804 he was appointed to succeed an unsuccessful minister at St Petersburg, the Russian ambassador in London bewailed the British government's choice, and had unpleasant forebodings— for no one, he said, could succeed with the Russian ministers who had any inclination to gamble. While he was in St Petersburg he disliked his residence there, was wearied with the society of the place, and found diversion in close friendship with the Russian Princess Galitzin; and Lady Bessborough, hearing ominous whispers in London, felt it her duty to warn her friend against the feminine wiles that might lure him to an unwary betrayal of the secrets of his mission. He belonged to that brilliant aristocratic world that was the fine flower of the eighteenth century—where the grave and the gay rubbed shoulders, and the card table was not far from the politician's desk, and a statesman would play all night without forsaking his office next morning. Leveson-Gower, lightly as he trips over the pages of the social history of the day, was not without ability. He carried out the work of his mission; he did much to bring about that third coalition which was the last heart-breaking achievement of Pitt; then he returned to England, determined to marry that Princess Galitzin—his "Little Barbarian" as he called her—if she could contrive to obtain a divorce from her husband. At the end of March 1807 Canning, looking for a man to re-establish the reputation of England with the Czar, after the painful comedies of Lord Douglas's mission, turned to his friend Leveson-Gower, urged upon him the call of "publick duty", said that it was in his hands to rescue the European situation, and that it was in his power to be "useful beyond any other man".[1] Others seconded Canning's persuasions, and Leveson-Gower agreed to serve; but he confessed that his "real motive" for accepting was that he might see his "Little Barbarian" once again. He did not set out straightway; home politics delayed his departure; there were many murmurs because he had to stay so long, waiting for the parliamentary elections; it was not until past the middle of May that he managed to leave England. He was sent, really, to prevent the tragedy that was threatening the coalition—he was sent, though he did not yet know it, to forestall the disaster of Tilsit. And no one quite realised that it might be a race against time.

On the 10th of June he reached Memel. He was not to blame for the last delays; he had left England two-and-a-half weeks earlier; but he had been kept five days in Copenhagen, waiting for a breeze, and after this he had been teased with contrary winds and had needed another week before his final landing.[2] His instructions were hardly calculated to meet the urgency of the situation as it had developed during his renewed delays.

---

[1] Canning to G. Leveson-Gower, 1 Ap. 1807, in *Private Correspondence of Lord G. Leveson-Gower*, II, 245–6.

[2] *Private Correspondence of Lord G. Leveson-Gower*, II, 257–8.

England desired to unite closely with Russia in the conduct of the war, and was anxious to follow the decision of the Czar in regard to the Austrian mediation; but in the shadow of these fine protestations she had many issues to make with Russian policy. There was a distracting campaign which the Czar was conducting in the east against the Ottoman Empire; it seemed important that he should be induced to make peace, and calm the awakened anxieties of Austria, and concentrate on the war in Poland. Leveson-Gower was instructed to press this question, and to show that if he made separate peace with the Porte, the Czar might forestall any inconvenient claim on the part of the Turks to take part in a future congress of the powers at war. Secondly, the time had come for the announcement of the pecuniary aid which England could give to the continent. The limited nature of this demanded excuse and explanation. The Russians had to be reminded that if the Austrians should enter the war and become entitled to financial assistance, then even this limited grant would have to be still further subdivided. The Czar had to be soothed for the disappointment he would have at the refusal of the British government to grant his request for a loan. Again, a Russian minister in Sicily had failed to give adequate support to the English representative there; this compared badly with the sincere attempts that were being made to second the policy of Russia at Constantinople; it was reason for grave complaint. There was a long-standing controversy about the commercial relations of England and Russia; the Czar had been unwilling to renew the former facilities given to British merchants, and Canning expressed a fear that this might mean some "abatement of friendship"; yet Canning realised that it had been unreasonable to ask for a continuance of all the former privileges and concessions; what he desired was a reasonable treaty. He showed his more trenchant, unyielding side in his demand for a guarantee from the Czar against alleged aggressive designs on the part of the Prussians; he threatened to refuse accession to the Convention of Bartenstein unless such a safeguard should be provided; he would not join hands with the Czar in a war for the aggrandisement of Prussia. Many fine controversies underlay these instructions of Leveson-Gower, and if time had permitted all the questions to be pursued there would have been much high argument.[1]

Soon after reaching Tilsit the minister had audience of Alexander. Perhaps he did not quite appreciate a change that had taken place in the Czar; perhaps he made the mistake of still speaking to the exalted monarch of Bartenstein days. He soon had a severe rebuff. He began by offering congratulations on the "brilliant advantages" obtained by the Russian troops —but these had been forgotten by now. He expressed the earnest desire of his government for "the most intimate Union" with Russia. It was a kind of poetry that satisfied the Czar in some of his mystical moods; one wonders if it would not be provoking at a moment when England was being held responsible for the adverse turn of affairs. Leveson-Gower was soon interrupted, he had something of a surprise, and the whole interview turned out to be a chain of unpleasantnesses for him. Summing up the conversation in his report to London he wrote: "The language and tone of His Imperial Majesty were to me perfectly unexpected".

I was interrupted by the Emperor, who expressed his determination not to change his present system of politics and flattered himself that he had given sufficient proofs of his steady perseverance in it. He said he was persuaded of the good intentions of the English Government and relied with perfect confidence on the known firmness of His Majesty's character; but that he had to complain of the whole burden of the war having fallen upon his armies, that he had repeatedly in his audiences to Lord Douglas and in conversations with Lord Hutchinson at Memel, urged the absolute necessity of a diversion upon the Continent being made by England, that hopes had been held out that a British force would be sent to the North of Germany —month after month however had passed, and no troops were even embarked,—that the Russian army had by its bravery hitherto maintained the contest and in every battle which had been fought had gained an advantage of which however he was sorry to say his general had not sufficiently availed himself... but that it ought not to be forgotten that the chances of war were uncertain, and that this

[1] Canning's instructions to G. Leveson-Gower, Nos. 1–7 and 12, 16 May 1807, *F.O. Russia* 65/69.

was the last act of the great drama which had occupied the attention of the world for the last fifteen years. The enemy had the superiority in number as well as military talents, nothing but the unparalleled valour of his troops could have enabled them to maintain the contest against these advantages. The importance of relieving his army from so severe a pressure was incalculable, for nothing less than the last hope of salvation of Europe was now in question.

When Leveson-Gower gave assurance of the preparations that were being made for an English expedition, and described the difficulties that caused delay, and called attention to the limited nature of the land forces which England could raise, the Czar continued:

"Why not send your militia?" I replied that neither the laws nor the feelings of the country would admit of their being employed on Foreign Service. His Imperial Majesty answered, with some degree of haste, "Will your laws be better preserved by a French army laying waste your country? for be assured", he added, "that if the Russian Army experiences any reverse of fortune, the whole mass of the French Force will be turned against Great Britain, and that the defeat of this army would be as calamitous to England as to Russia".

Once again the Czar said: "'Why not draft your militia into your Regulars?' I answered that such a measure could only be resorted to upon some great and very peculiar emergency".

There was question as to the point where the soldiers should disembark. The British government thought of a landing on the Elbe. The Czar reminded Leveson-Gower that there had been a promise to send troops to Stralsund. The king of Sweden was expecting this, would take it as a personal affront if the plan should be changed. It was dangerous to wound the susceptibilities of a monarch who was so much the slave of his personal emotions—especially when he was carrying on the war in defiance of the wishes of his nation. Could the troops be sent in two bodies—one to make landing by the Elbe, the other to disembark at Stralsund? Leveson-Gower had to shake his head; England was in no position to send an expedition big enough to be divided. "The Emperor then ended this subject by saying, Act where you please, provided you act at all. '

Having taken the offensive the Czar did not allow himself to be dislodged. He traversed the situation and kept up a running attack upon the conduct and disposition of England. He complained of the inactivity of the British forces stationed in Sicily; these troops, he said, might have prevented Napoleon from releasing men in Italy and bringing them to bear against Russia in Poland.

The Emperor then turned to another subject upon which he expressed himself with some warmth, and said that having asked the British Government to facilitate the means of raising a loan in England, no attention whatever had been paid to this request. He asked me whether His Majesty's Ministers doubted of his honour, or of the punctuality with which he should fulfil his engagements. He had requested that, which had been done for former sovereigns of Russia by the Republics of Holland and Genoa. The loans made to the Empress Catherine had been faithfully discharged, both interest and capital, and he felt extremely hurt that suspicions were cast upon his honour by the little attention given to the representations that had been made upon this subject.[1]

Leveson-Gower was no stranger to Alexander; he had served at St Petersburg before; but he had not expected to meet *this* Alexander, disillusioned and critical, and of injured petulant mood. This was a far cry from the "snugness" of Bartenstein and that hint of "driving the French beyond the Rhine". There are signs that the Czar was becoming weary, if not of the turmoil, at least of the disillusionments of the campaign. He ceases to speak in ecstatic tones, other voices are drowning in him the voice of divine invocation, he finds himself coming to earth, finds earth becoming cruelly objective. The Czar who explains that the French are superior in numbers and in military talents, and insists upon the uncertain chances of war, and talks of the need of relieving his army from "so severe a pressure", is no longer mere visionary and dreamer peering through mists of romance. He is feeling the cold touch of earth, and precisely because he has been a dreamer he does not like the touch.

[1] G. Leveson-Gower to Canning, No. 1, 17 June 1807, *F.O. Russia* 65/69.

Leveson-Gower reporting to his government feels that he has
not been able to meet the unexpected situation:

> I cannot say that the Emperor appeared perfectly satisfied with the
> answers made by me to the various complaints urged by him against
> the conduct of His Majesty's Government. He begged me to repeat
> to you word for word what I had just heard from him, and ended
> my audience by many expressions of civility to myself....
> I thought it my duty to state respectfully such reasons as occurred
> to me in justification of my Court, but at the same time avoided as
> much as possible any kind of disputatious argument.

It was a duel still more heated and unrestrained when the
British minister had his first interview with the Russian chancellor. The mention of the matter of finance brought Budberg
flashing out with an angry phrase; more than once he would
spring off at a tangent with some blazing irrelevancy; you might
meet his argument about subsidies, you might offer a placating,
disarming thought—then he would wrench himself free, would
tell you that it was not the money that mattered anyway, would
insist that what was needed was actual soldiers on the spot.

> I told General Budberg that such had been the anxiety of His
> Majesty's Government to be prepared to assist his allies upon the
> occasion of any pressing emergency that means had been taken for
> forwarding to Russia a certain quantity of Bullion for such purpose,
> which remained at my disposal. The General replied in rather an angry
> tone that he hoped he was to understand me as making the offer of
> a loan and not a subsidy, that if I meant the latter the acceptance of
> it was out of the question, that if I meant the former he could return
> no answer till he had taken the orders of the Emperor. I answered
> that as I had made no proposal I expected no answer.... He answered
> it is not money, it is men we want, we have to contend against not
> only France, but Italy, Spain, Germany and a great part of Poland,
> and the troops of all these countries are now fighting against us.
> He then preferred against His Majesty's Government complaints
> similar to those I had heard from the mouth of His Imperial Majesty
> upon our not having undertaken any diversion on the Continent,
> which I answered by the same arguments I had used in my audience
> of the Emperor, but which I urged with less reserve than when
> replying to His Imperial Majesty.[1]

[1] G. Leveson-Gower to G. Canning, No. 2, 18 June 1807, *F.O. Russia* 65/69.

There was no time for renewed discussions. On the 15th of June alarming news was flying around. The Grand Duke Constantine was back again urging truce without delay. Alexander was not then at Tilsit, and Budberg "who alone persisted in the opinion that it was necessary to continue the war to the bitter end, objected that the Russian army had not yet been beaten, that it could fall back on numerous reserves, that the Polish provinces were to be trusted, and that the Emperor could count on the backing of his nation". But Czartoryski, who was supposed to know all about the Poles, said that no hope could be based upon this people, they desired only to regain their independence, they would rise up as Napoleon advanced. Constantine ridiculed the idea of attaching weight to the reserves, for these were neither numerous nor equipped. Novossiltzov was there, speaking in favour of peace.[1] Budberg hurried to consult the man whose views he could most count upon; he held a conference with Hardenberg, and the two put heads together. There was no escape from the situation, and they sent their verdict to the Czar. "We could not disguise from ourselves the possibility that as a result of all that is taking place, the army may be obliged to fall back upon our frontier."[2] Then everything was in an uproar, and panic flooded the scene, and the blind world wheeled into the night. On the morning of the 16th of June the Czar, at Olitta, received Bennigsen's confession of defeat. "I should think it necessary and prudent", wrote the general, "to begin some negotiations for peace, if only to gain time and repair our losses. This, Sire, you will decide."[3] Very soon there went dinning through the world the terrible name of Friedland.

[1] Tatistcheff, *Alexandre Ier et Napoléon*, pp. 116–17.
[2] Budberg to Alexander, 3/15 June 1807, in *Sbornik*, LXXXIX, 13.
[3] Bennigsen to Alexander, 3/15 June 1807, in *Sbornik*, LXXXIX, 9–10.

CHAPTER II

AUSTRIA AND PRUSSIA AFTER THE BATTLE OF FRIEDLAND

FRIEDLAND would not have been prevented by the calling of a congress such as had been still contemplated in the early days of June; for there had been no intention of suspending military operations and handing everything over to the diplomats. But if the machinery had been there, ready to undertake the work of peace-making—if there had been plenipotentiaries already at their tables in an atmosphere of discussion and debate and with pacific transactions pending, you might have prevented Tilsit and kept the Czar from pursuing that solitary road that led to the French alliance. For Tilsit was by no means the logical conclusion of Friedland, or the natural corollary. The thing which would have been inherently expected from the result of that battle was not the hearty embrace of victor and vanquished and a proud partition of world empire into realms of East and West. This was a later development, coming out of a tangled web of events and interactions. A strange and tricky path stood between, a path not easily to be traced; for much of it lay along the psychology of a Czar who might have had a swarm of Budbergs and Hardenbergs pressing around him, but yet was in reality a lonely man, sitting high and dry above the mere practitioners of politics and mooning with a mind unbalanced and strange—that worked all the more strangely at the moment because it was beaten and misunderstood.

All the world would not have agreed that even peace must necessarily follow the disaster of Friedland. Almost a month after the battle a lady could write from London, "There are rumours of a flag of truce, but not believed",[1] and later than this Count Vorontsov in London "still offers bets that there will not be peace with Russia—at least not before Christmas".[2]

[1] *Private Correspondence of Lord G. Leveson-Gower*, II, 260.
[2] *Ibid.* II, 265.

Razoumovski, Russian ambassador at Vienna, wrote to the Austrian chancellor, "I am persuaded that never will peace be made, except after a victory". Bennigsen had said that the Czar might find it prudent to negotiate "if only to gain time and repair our losses". It was Bennigsen who asserted that "the way to defeat the French is to increase the distance which separates them from the Rhine, and draw them on to the Dneister".

"What is it that may induce the Emperor to wish for peace"? wrote Vorontsov. "Is it the fear of Napoleon's invading Russia? That would be precisely the thing to be desired. Bonaparte would find himself in the predicament of Charles the XII....Without fortresses, without points of support, with a cloud of our light troops on his flanks and in his rear, he and his army would die of hunger and be compelled to surrender...."[1]

The windy spaces and desert darkness and untried distances of the north were yawning for Napoleon, if the Russians would only give him the gateway. Talleyrand was afraid that they would. Robert Adair at Vienna observed to the Austrian chancellor

that these fresh successes would lead probably to fresh pretensions on the part of France, and that Bonaparte, to whom no project seemed preposterous or impossible, might adopt that of carrying his army into the heart of Russia and attempt to dictate the law even at St Petersburg.[2]

Count Stadion agreed that "this would give us one chance more"; but he thought that Napoleon would rather offer peace. The idea of allowing Napoleon to lose himself in the depths of Russia and go plodding to his own destruction was already in the air. Eylau and the torments of the winter campaign in Poland had made it clear that Napoleon was no match for Nature. In some moods Alexander would have opened his country to the oppressor, and felt it all a solemn tragedy, set under lurid skies. In one mood Alexander actually came to do

---

[1] *Vorontsov Archives*, XVII (1880), No. 91, 14 July 1807, pp. 157 *et seq*. See Sorel, *L'Europe et la Révolution Française*, VII, 169.

[2] Adair to Canning, 27 June 1807, in Adair, *Historical Memoir*, pp. 252–5.

it, and let Napoleon wear himself against the terrors of the north. But Alexander would not do it now—when Czartoryski was muttering that the Poles would rise in his rear, when there was too much reason to believe that the Russian people could not be counted upon, when somebody even breathed that the Czar was in danger of assassination. Alexander was not at this time tuned for the music of 1812; the tragic rôle was not so compelling. For he had not merely lost a battle; it was due to his friends as much as to his foes that he had lost a mood. His heroism fed upon the mood; and the mood was played out.

But even if the world were ready to hear of peace between France and Russia, it was much less prepared for "Tilsit", and the magnificent gesture of reconciliation. One is tempted to smile at the inadequacy of the first conjectures people hazarded concerning the consequences of Friedland. To guard against the illusion that after Friedland "Tilsit" was the only thing that could have happened, perhaps it would be interesting to examine the steps taken by the respective powers of Europe after they had heard of the battle. These will be an index to the fears and expectations and desires of contemporaries; a key, perhaps, to possible alternative courses which were open even after the disaster.

There was great alarm at Vienna when the news arrived. With some people there was a gasp of horror at the tragedy in which they themselves had so nearly become involved; and a heart stood still as though it had just missed death by a hair's-breadth. Perhaps there was some relief that neutrality had been able to spin out long enough. But the Austrians, who have been nervous, and feverish for self-preservation during the whole of this story, found at bottom little reassurance to have the noise of Friedland whistling in their ears. A report from Adair at Vienna shows that they trembled more than ever for their provinces, feared the continuance of war lest they should become embroiled in the struggle, dreaded that the Czar with or without Prussia might conclude a peace that would be damaging to Hapsburg interests, and were jealous even of the assembly of a congress, for fear it should neglect or over-ride their own desires and ambitions. Now there came home to these people all the things that Canning had thundered and threatened; and they knew it would matter little that all Europe should be arranged and pacified, if they themselves were left in isolation, to make what efforts they could for their own welfare.[1]

A General Stutterheim had been instructed, before the news of Friedland reached Vienna, to make his way to the allied headquarters. The Austrians claimed that the intention of his mission was "to express the attachment of Austria" to the Czar and the Prussian king and "to explain to them the degree of activity that Austria was in a position to give to her policy, and the nature and extent of the means she might employ".[2] This assertion was afterwards taken to mean that on the very eve of the battle of Friedland the cabinet of Vienna had decided upon war; but from the instructions that were drawn up for this mission we can now see how unconverted and unrepentant were the Austrians still—persistently clinging to their neutrality.[3]

The cabinet of Vienna confessed that it was unable to join the allies, or accede to the convention of Bartenstein. For its decision it found various pretexts. Russia was at war with Turkey, and this raised complications and embarrassing side issues. The coalition gave no sign of activity, no promise of success. England, to all appearances, was indifferent to the fate of Europe. Stutterheim was ordered to make capital out of the shortcomings of the allies; all of which might have been straightforward for him if it had not been coupled with a further, more delicate commission, based upon "the interest which the Cabinet of

[1] Adair to Canning, 27 June 1807, in Adair, *op. cit.* pp. 252–5.

[2] Stadion to Starhemberg, No. 2, 11 July 1807, *W.S.A. Weisungen nach London.*

[3] The Russian minister in Vienna, Razoumovski, gave a sketch of the situation of Austria in June 1807, and showed why the court of Vienna was likely to maintain its neutrality in the war. According to him the "pacific party is composed of the most powerful families without exception", the death of the empress had placed the emperor more completely under the influence of the Archduke Charles, and "le mot de paix est devenu le cri de ralliement". He did not blame England but he thought that English subsidies and an English diversion on the continent would have altered this situation of affairs. (Razoumovski to Alopeus, 14/26 June 1807, *F.O. Russia* 65/73.)

Vienna must have in seeing that the present struggle does not end in a way entirely contrary to its views by private and isolated arrangements with France, of which Austria would always be more or less the victim". Stutterheim was to rescue Austrian interests from the perils that any future negotiation might promise—was to do this at the very moment when he was giving the last denial to the hopes of the allied powers. It was becoming more difficult for the Austrians to expect that they could discover a back door into a peace congress when they had refused to take part in the war. It would need slanting eyes and subtle sleight-of-hand to find the ends of the tangle with which Stutterheim was faced. His government confessed that it could not show him the way—left him to his own cunning, asked him to spin his threads out of nothing. The Austrian chancellor admitted that

General Stutterheim, being able to do nothing but raise hopes, having to refuse everything which might be interpreted as a precise or positive engagement, lacking any authority to take measures that would bind the Court of Vienna for the future, or compromise its political action, will have few means at his disposal.

Having decided to maintain their neutrality, the Austrians did not intend to remain passive, or quietly await the inevitable approach of a disastrous peace. For them diplomacy should take the place of war; they would weave their subtleties covertly, and gamble on events, like sharp men on the Stock Exchange.[1]

It was while these very instructions were being written that the expected contingency arose, and the news of Friedland arrived. If Stutterheim were to proceed on his mission he would need fresh orders from his court, directed to the precise event.

His instructions had to be modified on the assumption that when he arrived at the armies he would find an armistice concluded and negotiations set on foot.... It would not in that event be a question

---

[1] Lettow-Vorbeck, *Der Krieg von 1806 und 1807* (1893), IV, Anlage VI, pp. 469 and 474, Instruktionen an den österreichischen General von Stutterheim und Antworten des Kaisers von Oesterreich an die Monarchen von Russland und Preussen.

of operations of war; the only thing that would matter would be to make the pacification as little injurious to Europe as was possible in such a disastrous conjuncture.[1]

Stutterheim's new instructions assumed that on his arrival at the allied headquarters he would find "negotiations for peace already set on foot, and perhaps far advanced, between France and the two Allied Sovereigns".

The presence of M. de Stutterheim at the side of the Emperor Alexander may still however be very useful for the interests of the Court of Vienna, if he arrives in time to prevent too great a precipitancy in such an arrangement and to induce the allies to treat... with our amicable intervention.

"It is the fate of the one-time Poland", wrote Stadion, "which is of the greatest moment... in the stipulations of a future peace."[2]

It was feared that Napoleon might keep his promise to the Poles, might even demand that Austria give up her own Polish provinces to form a new kingdom for one of his vassals. And even if he left their possessions intact the Austrians knew that the formation of this new state would be a danger to them, creating disruption and discontent among their own Polish subjects whose national aspirations would be left unrealised. There was another contingency to be apprehended. If France should give concessions to Russia in Moldavia and Wallachia, this would be a new menace in the east. To prevent such an issue it was important to manipulate for Austrian intervention; Stutterheim was ordered to point out to the allies the disadvantages under which they would labour if they treated separately with Napoleon and found themselves with nothing to support them against the overwhelming preponderance of France. Austria offered her mediation.

It was a bold thing to expect that on the morrow of Friedland Napoleon would accept the congress which, in the midst of all his difficulties, it had been his persistent policy to evade. "Without a doubt", wrote the Austrian chancellor, "Napoleon

[1] Stadion to Starhemberg, No. 2, 11 July 1807, *W.S.A. Weisungen nach London.*
[2] Lettow-Vorbeck, *op. cit.* IV, 471.

in his present situation will be less willing than ever to depart from his principle of a separate negotiation."[1] But behind all Austria's plans of pacification there was one idea that was the magnet of her policy. It was reasoned that if Napoleon could see a hope of regaining his lost colonies, if the restitution of maritime conquests could be dangled as a bribe, if you could play upon this—as the Austrians seem to have thought—the master-motive of his policies, then he might be brought to allow the establishment of a general negotiation. The idea of a congress was impossible—it was admitted at Vienna—"unless England declared herself in favour of it, and, so to speak, took or shared with us the initiative".[2]

So while the French and Russian monarchs were at Tilsit making their summary disposal of Empire, an Austrian courier was trailing to England, with instructions for the ambassador in London.

> Napoleon must be interested in putting an end to the maritime war which so far has brought him neither laurels nor advantages. It seems to us therefore that if the Minister of Great Britain declared himself ready to renew negotiations for peace, but at the same time declared his firm resolution to bind them closely with the negotiations for a Continental Peace...there would be in this the strongest motive for France to consent to a Congress....[3]

The motives that led the Austrians to take this interest in the establishment of peace came out in the despatch. "As to the restoration of the King of Prussia to his estates, it can only be regarded as conformable to our views, and it could only be a too considerable aggrandisement of this power, that would be contrary to our political interests...." It was hoped that there would be no question of a re-establishment of Poland, "which, even if it did not touch the two Galicias, would always be an event dangerous and disastrous to Austria".

> ...the integrity of the Austrian Monarchy is of too general an interest for Europe and for England herself to allow us to doubt the

---

[1] Stadion to Starhemberg, No. 2, 11 July 1807, *W.S.A. Weisungen nach London.*
[2] *Ibid.*   [3] *Ibid.*

importance which the Cabinet of St James will place upon refusing any consent to an arrangement which would change our present state of possession.[1]

Napoleon might win his Friedlands, or lose; Austria might be a party in the war, or might remain a spectator; but the ministers of Vienna would have a hand in the peace-making, and would be ready with arguments for the promotion of their own interests. " I have not wished to repeat in so many words the offer of the intervention of Austria ", wrote Stadion, "because the essential thing is that we take part in the pacification in whatever way possible." Austria, renewing her offer of mediation, avoided the explicit use of the unwelcome word; but Stadion saw that there was no rôle for his government save that of mediator, "since we are to be considered as a neutral power and it is only thus that we can intervene in any Congress for peace".[2]

The situation was changing while the Austrians were preparing their despatches. Before the instructions were completed for the Austrian minister in London, it was heard that "the two Emperors pass whole days together, and deal with political affairs in a way that seems to exclude any foreign intervention whatever". The terror of the thought made Stadion more importunate for his scheme. The minister Starhemberg was instructed to press England, "if she places any importance on the amelioration of the situation of Europe, to offer means of compensation by the restitution of the conquests she has made in the maritime war".[3]

Alexander, in coming to his arrangements with France at Tilsit, completely outpaced this Austrian move. By the time Stutterheim reached his destination, everything had been settled; he did not even see the Czar. Napoleon interviewed him, and talked for two hours, saying that he was well pleased with the behaviour of Austria during the war in Poland.

[1] *Ibid.*
[2] Stadion to Starhemberg, No. 3, 11 July 1807, *W.S.A. Weisungen nach London.*
[3] Stadion to Starhemberg, Nos. 3 and 4, 11 July 1807, *W.S.A. Weisungen nach London.*

George Canning, on hearing the news of Friedland, had written to the allied headquarters in Poland to say that he would be willing to join in a general negotiation for peace. Further than this he did not go. He immediately recognised the real meaning of the overture from Austria, and took off its stage costume. To the British minister in Vienna he wrote that Austria had

recommended the British Government immediately to declare willingness to treat for General Peace, and demand the Assembly of a Congress to which His Majesty should insist upon Austria being admitted as a mediating party; and that in the progress of the negotiation Great Britain should hold herself ready to make sacrifices out of her conquests for the purpose of...augmenting the territory and influence of Austria.[1]

When Stadion saw his communication stripped of its philanthropic embellishments, he was shocked, and detected a miscarriage. He sent a severe reprimand to Starhemberg for having exceeded his instructions. "My instructions...did not mention an aggrandisement of the Monarchy", he explained, "but spoke of the general interest which demands...that there shall be no change for the worse in its state of possession."[2] He declared to the English minister in Vienna that the

recommendation was made with the view of effecting a general peace, during the negotiations for which this Government hoped indeed that a guarantee of the present territories of the House of Austria, if not a restoration of some of those which she has lost would be offered as favourable to the re-establishment of an equilibrium which might ensure the future tranquillity of Europe.[3]

Canning, in replying to the overture, did not cease to repeat his former assurances, and declare his willingness to use the colonial conquests for the amelioration of Europe. He still kept them up his sleeve; he would refuse to make sacrifices "for illusory objects"; but he seemed "quite convinced that only by

[1] G. Canning to Lord Pembroke, No. 16, 7 Aug. 1807, *F.O. Austria* 7/85.
[2] Stadion to Starhemberg, No. 1, 6 Sept. 1807, *W.S.A. Weisungen nach London.*
[3] Pembroke to Canning, No. 6, 3 Sept. 1807, *F.O. Austria* 7/85.

putting Austria in the most respectable condition, augmenting her internal and external power, could there be the most distant possibility of repose for Europe". Starhemberg even thought that the recent events might work to the advantage of his own country; for if the Czar had abandoned the cause of the king of Naples, then the sacrifices which would have been devoted to the benefit of this monarch might be apportioned for the promotion of Austrian interests.[1]

There was an apparent desire in England "to see the large interests of the moment discussed in a Congress"; but the Austrian ambassador found Canning too proud to make the first move. Starhemberg offered to go to Paris

to inform the Cabinet of the Tuileries through our Ambassador there of the wish of the Cabinet of London to work along with Austria in a Congress of all the Powers for the purpose of concluding a general peace on bases that would promise security and lasting repose.

The news of the treaty of Tilsit, however, and the receipt of an offer of mediation from the Czar—"the demi-overture of Russia", as Starhemberg called it—cancelled these Austrian efforts.[2]

There was something pleasingly coy about the Austrian overture to Canning. Its assertiveness was deliciously veiled, and in it all there was a hint of tentativeness and doubt. Stadion evidently had an uneasy shyness in putting out some of his suggestions. But there was another state that saw its opportunity in the catastrophe that overwhelmed Europe, and was prepared to rise to valiant schemes of aggression over the ruins of the continent. It did not tamely submit to the platitude that in war the winner must gain and the losers stand the loss; it soared to the sky with the paradox that winner and losers should all make handsome profit, should all come to aggrandisement and power, should all of them be richer than ever they had been before. You would arrange this happy consummation by turning your attention to an innocent third party and making a market

---

[1] Starhemberg to Stadion, No. 63, 8 Aug. 1807, *W.S.A. Berichte aus London*.
[2] *Ibid.*

of the territory of monarchs unable to take care of themselves. It was a scheme worthy of Napoleon; but only a Napoleon could carry it out. It was a glorification of the kind of politics that had produced the partition of Poland. It was put forward with no bashful hesitation or squirm of delicate conscience, but with an impudence and a callousness that would have been more pardonable in a conqueror like Napoleon. The proposal was the last resort of a government that was like a cat in a corner, tormented into ingenuity by the very desperation of its position. Prussia was the sponsor of the scheme; and its creator was Hardenberg.

While the Prussians at Memel at the beginning of the second week of June were still moping over the continued inactivity of the Russian forces, news came to them of Bennigsen's forward movement and his success against the French at Heilsberg. At last the decisive hour was come, and the day seemed promising. The brain throbbed violently to feel the climax so near. "The Queen was quite beside herself with joy. The King writes hopefully about this victory." There was a moment of tension and strain as the world waited for the issue. We are dealing now with people whose nerves were set on edge. The mood of eager hope soon passed. On the 13th there were unpleasant misgivings. It was remembered how Bennigsen had cried "Victory!" after Pultusk, after Eylau—and the old agonies of doubt returned.

"My beloved Queen is so happy!", writes the Countess Voss; but "Bennigsen has retreated....Is he afraid of a second battle? He never follows up a victory and he never follows up the defeated enemy or any advantage he may have acquired; or have we been deceived and this was no victory, only a new catastrophe?"

On the next day: "The Queen came to me early, in great trouble and uneasiness. The King writes that he is very much displeased with Bennigsen, who has lost every advantage from these so-called victories, by his retreat". On the 15th, before anything was heard of Friedland, people were beginning to say, "God alone can help us now", and the Prussian king was "very sad and downcast, believing that everything was lost".

Then the moment of tension broke, and broke in bitterness

and despair. The news of the battle reached Memel on the 16th and found men feverishly angry. The king mooned and mumbled that this was just as he had foretold; that was how he would console himself when calamity overwhelmed him. His unpleasantness turned against Hardenberg. "I defended the man", wrote Countess Voss, "but this only irritated the King more than ever." The queen eased the strain on her mind by giving vent to all her complaints and suspicions against the Russian generals. She made herself ill with weeping. Hardenberg seemed more calm, but it was the calmness of despair; "he seemed incapable of giving the King advice". One person is reported as having taken the news with more of unconcern; for Princess Radziwill remarks that "the ironical expression on General Kalckreuth's face struck me disagreeably. Alone among that sorrowful crowd he seemed indifferent to the calamity that had befallen us". There may be prejudice in this; but Kalckreuth is worthy of notice; he had defended Danzig, was reputed to be the friend of peace, and a man not unacceptable to Bonaparte; and he was to be the minister to negotiate for Prussia in the transactions of Tilsit.

The Prussians received the defeat of Friedland in an ungenerous mood, and there was a commotion in Memel as preparations were made for further flight. It was expected that the royal family would leave Prussian territory and take refuge at Mittau or Riga. But one interesting alternative plan was put forward, and came from a strange quarter. Cabinet councillor Beyme had been one of the enemies of the party of vigour and reform at Berlin, had been the incarnation of those obnoxious principles of government that had estranged men like Stein from the royal service; for no matter who was minister, Beyme always had the ear of the king. But since Hardenberg's return to power, to a virtual dictatorship in Prussia, the man—we have it on Hardenberg's authority—had had a change of heart; he had "behaved very well and constantly followed good principles".[1] We are told that after the news of the final Russian disaster Beyme "appeared to have some heart and hope left". It is pleasant to find him

---

[1] Hardenberg to Stein, 10 July 1807, in Ranke, *Hardenberg*, v, 535.

putting forward a proposal which might have failed completely but which was at least a glorious gesture, a thing to make a Napoleon envious—and which, if it had not saved the Prussian state, would have sent it down in the colour and glow of twilight, and all hung round with the romance that clings to a valiant lost cause.

Beyme was alone in maintaining that, supposing Königsberg occupied by Napoleon, the King had still a nobler alternative left than quitting his country; this was to take advantage of the transports lying at Libau to go with what was left of the Prussian army, and land in Pomerania, where troops, fortresses, Blücher and Gneisenau were at the King's disposal, and when all North Germany, Denmark and Sweden would unite with him; the Queen and the Royal Family could embark for Copenhagen where a very friendly welcome awaited us, and where we should be nearer than at Memel to the seat of war....[1]

Hardenberg seems at a later date to claim credit for having urged such a policy; for in declaring what he would have done if he had been king, he outlines precisely this scheme—putting the blame for its rejection on the shoulders of Frederick William, of whom he writes with some disrespect: "But it is impossible to change a man's character, and it is unwise to try. If it could have been done we should not have been where we are now".[2] Princess Radziwill, however, who describes Beyme as being alone in urging the step, goes on to say, "So much opposition was shown and so many difficulties raised that nothing was done except that we were ordered to get our travelling baggage ready and hold ourselves prepared to start at the first word of the King". So history was cheated of a dramatic moment, an episode magnificently defiant, a fine futile adventure.

On hearing the result of Friedland the Czar, on the 16th of June, wrote a letter to the Prussian king:

It is with a sore heart, Sire, that I fulfil my duty and communicate the tragic news that I have just received from General Bennigsen.

[1] Princess Anton Radziwill, *Forty-five years of my life* (Eng. trans. 1912), pp. 266–7.
[2] Hardenberg to Jacobi-Kloest, 12 July 1807, in Ranke, *Hardenberg*, p. 542.

It is cruel for me to have to give up even the hope of being as useful to you as my heart had wished and as the means which I had employed seemed to justify our expecting....I am resuming my journey to-night to go to Taurrogen; perhaps Your Majesty will think fit to go there yourself; it will be necessary for us to be together and to come to a common decision.[1]

A later messenger advised the king that the Czar would await him at the village of Sczawel. Frederick William was still in unpleasant mood; it made him bitter and indignant to learn that he was to confer with Alexander not on Prussian but on Russian territory;[2] but on the 20th of June he journeyed to Sczawel, and ordered Kalckreuth to follow, Hardenberg having set out the previous night. The meeting with the Czar was a mournful one; Alexander was evidently in great anguish.

"It will be easy for you to imagine the agitation of his soul since the sad events that we have heard of", wrote the king to Queen Louisa. "An armistice is being negotiated...and it appears that closer discussions are to follow. Their results?—we shall have to wait and see. As soon as the business of the Armistice is settled the Emperor intends to go with me to Taurrogen to be nearer to the seat of negotiations and—if necessary—to see the Friend of Mankind [Napoleon]. What an attractive prospect! I shudder to think of it, and yet I see it clearly coming, and, what is more, you will remember I always told you it must come to this."[3]

Perpetual pathetic refrain—"I always told you so".

The Prussian king and his ministers indeed had a number of shocks and surprises before they had been many hours at Sczawel. Hardenberg goes so far as to say that already the Czar was not the same man.[4] There was an unexpected haste on the part of the Russians to conclude their armistice with the French; Alexander was even beginning to familiarise himself with the

---

[1] Alexander I to Frederick William III, 4/16 June 1807, in Bailleu, *Briefwechsel* (vol. LXXV of the *Publicationen aus den K. Preussischen Staatsarchiven*), p. 157.

[2] Countess Voss, *Recollections*, under the date 19 June 1807.

[3] King Frederick William III to Queen Louisa, 21 June 1807, in *Deutsche Rundschau*, CX, 32.

Ranke, *Hardenberg*, v, 539.

idea of having an interview with Napoleon.[1] Napoleon was making the amazing demand for the surrender of the three Prussian fortresses of Graudenz, Pillau and Colberg—was requiring these as a condition of his armistice with Russia, and seemed determined to insist upon the point.[2] If the Russians could evade the concession, he would transfer the demand to Frederick William and make it a stipulation in his armistice with Prussia; and if this could be taken as an index of what he intended doing in actual negotiations for peace, the outlook was more gloomy than ever. It seemed that Napoleon had a predisposition to deal harshly with these Prussians whom he had courted and cajoled since the close of 1806.

The unfortunate Frederick William once again felt the oppressiveness of his station and shook to see the handwriting on the wall. He had unwillingly put everything to hazard and the chances had turned against him; now it had come to the last throw, and there seemed nothing to count upon save a purely personal factor, an utterly incalculable element in the mind of Alexander. There was something unaccountable—defying rationalisation—something like a streak of quixotism which had kept the Czar faithful to Prussia even when she had seemed most unworthy, and had made him uncritical and unseeing even when she most looked like a sponging friend. It was an arbitrary, in a way a capricious side of his purposes, independent of reasons of state; at times it would seem to have cut across the true logic of Russian policy; it was separable from the interests of the Empire. But Alexander was now defeated and might be compelled to look to his own salvation. Everything hung on the secret workings of the mind of a man who was no longer the master of events. And Alexander, mysterious being, mixture of strange impulses, with something baffling in his purposes and unpredictable in his actions, was wearing a haggard look, pursuing a lonely course—his real ideas and intentions a matter for dark whispering or breathless conjecture. He was discussing

---

[1] King Frederick William III to Queen Louisa, 21 and 22 June 1807, in *Deutsche Rundschau*, cx, 33 and 36.

[2] Bennigsen to Alexander, 7/19 June 1807, in *Sbornik*, lxxxix, 23.

very little with Budberg, and Budberg was the man who watched most carefully over the interests of Prussia, over the pro-German side of the imperial policy. Frederick William, who was always feeling the clammy hand of fate upon him, must surely have felt it now.

A Prussian officer named Schladen had been sent to the headquarters of Bennigsen, and had talked to Russian generals. His reports of the 21st of June were received at Sczawel. They disclosed the intensity of the crisis to which Russian policy had come. Widespread conspiracies for peace were on foot; Russian officers were fraternising with the French and holding conferences; the Grand Duke Constantine was active and intriguing.

"I will not stop to speak here", ran the second report, "of the excesses of all kinds committed by the army, or of the imperturbable coolness with which the commander-in-chief listens to the complaints of the poor wretches who are despoiled under his very eyes, so to speak,... but what has surprised me is to perceive that the desire for peace manifests itself almost everywhere; that without the least restraint the officers at the table of General Bennigsen speak of the necessity of concluding it with greatest haste; that no one even seems to think that the Emperor might have a different opinion; and that in general all these gentlemen think they have so managed the affair that they can be sure of succeeding and carrying it out even against the intentions of the Emperor.... It seems certain that the ramifications of this intrigue are very deep; and if the presence and energy of Your Excellency do not save Prussia, I am in great fear of the consequences.... If the armistice is accepted and if the Russians remain in their present position Prussia is ruined."[1]

It would seem to have been expected of Hardenberg that he should think out a way of escape. He was certainly not the man to sit and watch the procession of events and commend his country to the high stars. This was the really desperate moment for Prussia, the time of crucial strain. Hardenberg met it with a flourish. One might almost think that he exulted. Desperation seemed to give drive to his thinking, whipping it to astonishing

[1] Second report of Schladen to Hardenberg, 21 June 1807, in Ranke, *Hardenberg*, v, 522.

rapidity and range. On the 22nd of June, the day after his arrival at Sczawel, Frederick William was writing to the queen:

Unless Napoleon is quite intractable there is no doubt, from the disposition of men around the Emperor, and from the Emperor's own disposition, that there will be an immediate accommodation with France. In what manner? That is the great point under discussion; it is being worked upon continuously. To-day Hardenberg and Budberg have given their joint opinion in a conference we have had with the Czar. *Gigantic* plans are afoot, to try to avoid the blow which threatens us, and it is hoped that, if we humour Bonaparte on different matters which he has very much at heart, we shall succeed more easily in rescuing our common interests. But these are as yet only general ideas, though they have been communicated to Kalckreuth so that he may be able to make tactful use of them in such a way as to learn something of the *benevolent intentions of the Friend of Mankind*....Heaven knows what result we are to expect.[1]

The "gigantic plans" were embodied in a memoir, written on the 22nd of June, and beginning:

Must we make an armistice, or press on to the conclusion of peace? It would be a thousand times better to do the latter promptly than to subscribe to an armistice which would compel us to cede the three fortresses of Graudenz, Colberg and Pillau—for this is a stipulation that can only inspire distrust of the intentions of Napoleon.

Peace will not be difficult to make, if he wishes it sincerely. Prussia is bound to England by no treaty, and has no obligation towards Austria. Russia is in the same position in regard to the latter; she can regard herself as released from her engagements with the court of London, since this court has done nothing since the beginning of the war to fulfil its own obligations....Russia finds herself for the moment unable to continue the war alone, with what remains of the forces of Prussia. It is only with Sweden, therefore, that the two allied courts have an engagement not to cease the war except by joint action; but Sweden has made an armistice, its King thought it superfluous to accede to the Convention of Bartenstein; and, while it would be necessary to act as much as possible in concert with him, still, necessity knows no law.

...We must accept the armistice, if it can be obtained without the cession of the fortresses...but if we cannot achieve this, there is

---

[1] King Frederick William III to Queen Louisa, 22 June 1807, in *Deutsche Rundschau*, cx, 35.

nothing to do but to bring up the question of peace itself without delay, for the cession of the fortresses would make continuation of the war almost impossible, and would certainly deprive us of the assistance of England and Austria, even if they were determined to help us in any real manner.

It appears that in negotiating peace under such circumstances, it is only by a new political system that we shall be able to reach a state of things favorable to Russia and Prussia, and to put an end to the wars that desolate Europe. We are in the condition foreseen in Article 14 of the Convention of Bartenstein, when we must come together to discuss the measures to be taken for our own safety. It is necessary to arrange something which shall be agreeable to Napoleon and at the same time shall establish a strong and firm state of possession guaranteed by an alliance between Russia, Prussia, and France. It is the system which Napoleon has ardently desired in past days. Founded upon bases equally profitable to all three powers, it will impose its settlement on all the rest of Europe, and will force even England to make an equitable peace and to establish less burdensome principles in regard to the freedom of the seas. If this system is adopted Napoleon cannot wish to weaken Prussia; on the contrary he must seek to make her strong.[1]

It reads like the *Arabian Nights*. The ogre turns into a mouse. Europe dwindles to a chequer-board, kingdoms and empires are transformed into pieces for a complicated game of chess, and the inhabitants are as grasshoppers. It is a kind of plan to give its maker the artist's creative thrill. Necessity knows no law, says Hardenberg; reasons can be found to excuse the desertion of allies; Russia and Prussia must abandon the war with France, join hands in an alliance directed chiefly against England, and help Napoleon to impose his system upon the continent. But the point is, Napoleon will have to be bribed; this is the crux of the matter, the master-stroke of the whole scheme; you will inaugurate the new system by a grand *coup*, which shall lure the contracting powers away from their own mutual jealousies and controversies. The triumvirate must find a victim to despoil. Turkey shall be divided between the allies, as Poland once had been—this is Hardenberg's great conspiracy. Russia may have the eastern part of the Balkan peninsula,

[1] Ranke, *Hardenberg*, III, 458–62.

Moldavia, Wallachia, Bessarabia, Roumania, Bulgaria. Napoleon shall take Greece and the adjacent islands. Prussia herself, indeed, will have nothing to do with the spoils of Turkey, will have none of the odium attaching to such usurpations; she will take Saxony, gaining it by a neat kind of exchange, transferring the king of Saxony to Poland. Russia in return for benefits received shall give up her Polish provinces; Austria shall do the same, and shall be given places like Dalmatia, Bosnia, and Serbia; while Prussia shall surrender part of her Polish territory, reserving to herself such important places as Danzig, Posen and Thorn. So shall be formed the new kingdom of Poland which shall be given to the king of Saxony. It was a very profitable scheme for Prussia, and one which would spare her much of the unpleasantness of actually sharing in the partition of Turkey; it included, moreover, a plan by which she would gain those towns of Lübeck and Hamburg, which had brought her into difficulties with Napoleon in the year 1806. England might be allowed to conquer Egypt, to keep Malta and to regain Hanover, if she would consent to adopt more liberal maritime principles; but if she refused this, and failed to come to an arrangement before the forthcoming spring, the Baltic should be closed against her shipping. So all parties would be humoured in some of their favourite ambitions and pet preoccupations, and all problems would find their solution in the removal of "the sick man of Europe".

It was a brilliant improvisation, containing many things calculated to soothe Napoleon and entice some of his cherished ambitions. It flattered his desire to curb the maritime pretensions of England; it humoured the vague plans that he held for predominance in the Mediterranean; it accorded with various thoughts which he had had and which he had never dismissed from his mind concerning the impending destruction of the Ottoman Empire. But it was a monstrous piece of pretentiousness on the part of a power which had done so little to justify its existence as Prussia in this last year. And, addressed to Napoleon when he was almost at the farthest edge of the Prussian dominions, with Europe prostrate behind him and a

Czar suing for peace, it was a sublime exhibition of impudence. It was an offer to outdo Napoleon in all his crimes of conquest, if he would only allow his former enemies to range themselves at his side. It was a proposal to put the Napoleonic system into the hands of a syndicate. It is not an unfair specimen of what may be called Hardenberg's grand manner.

These "gigantic plans" were discussed by Hardenberg and Budberg in conferences held on the 21st and 22nd of June. They were communicated to the Russian Czar and the Prussian king.[1] Both monarchs accepted the scheme, and, although Alexander had some misgivings concerning the reception it would have at the hands of Napoleon,[2] it is certain that while he was holding his early interviews at Tilsit he was promising the king of Prussia that he would use the opportunities of conversation to promote this very proposal. The plan was not merely entertained, but steps were taken to secure its execution; though at first the initiative remained with Prussia. At this time, when actual negotiations for peace between France and Russia were not yet opened, the Prussians still imagined themselves in the position which they had held for the previous half-year—they dreamed that they would be the channel for the discussion of peace between the powers, and they pictured themselves as the principals in the negotiation that should take place.

General Kalckreuth, who was about to make his way to Tilsit to negotiate an armistice for Prussia, was informed of the whole design and was instructed to sound Napoleon on the subject of a partition of Turkey.[3] He was made the bearer of a letter to the Emperor himself, in which Frederick William, speaking for Russia as well as for Prussia, wrote:

I am persuaded that Your Imperial Majesty desires to put an end to the war; I am not less ardent in my wish to see the end of its evils, and I can promise you that my ally, the Emperor of All the Russias, shares my sentiments in this regard. It will therefore be easy for us to come to an understanding.[4]

---

[1] King Frederick William III to Queen Louisa, 22 June 1807, in *Deutsche Rundschau*, cx, 35.   [2] See below, pp. 256–7.
[3] Ranke, *Hardenberg*, III, 463–4.   [4] *Ibid*. III, 464–5.

The letter went on to state that Hardenberg himself would be the principal agent in putting forward the proposals Prussia had to offer; and Kalckreuth would join him as an auxiliary in the negotiation.

Here Hardenberg saw a snare. He remembered the animosity Napoleon had had against him since the close of 1805; he recalled how in 1806 this had led to his estrangement from power. It was a serious obstacle to his proposed mission, and he took steps for its removal. He who had become the incarnation of all that was anti-French in the policy of Prussia—he who had been the symbol and the hope of the Prussian enemies of Napoleon, wrote a cringing letter to Duroc, the secretary of the French Emperor.

"Great men", the letter began, "are the soonest to escape from the prejudices which they may have been led to adopt. Your August Sovereign,...had one against me, I did not merit it, and I hope it will be easy to destroy it. It has not been my fault that at the period when I had the honour of negotiating with Your Excellency, Prussia did not become the ally of France on a plan that was liberal and fine, and conformable to the interests of both States. I would have liked the policy of Prussia to have had character, to have been worthy of a great power....I had no part in the disastrous war which leaves us desolate, never did my policy consist in the art of deceiving. I have been accused of being now English, now Russian. I am neither, but I am a good and zealous Prussian....The stipulations which I shall have to transmit will be religiously observed, and a system of friendship between France and Prussia which we have sincerely in view will be established on a solid and lasting basis."[1]

All this was on the 23rd of June, two days after Frederick William had met the Czar at Sczawel. But as late as the 29th of June Hardenberg was still urging his grand design, recapitulating his proposals in a memoir intended for the eyes of the Czar. There had been news of a revolution in Constantinople —pleasant news for Hardenberg, since it gave reinforced argument and additional excuse and a good opportunity for his destruction and partition of Turkey. Once more the Prussian

---

[1] Ranke, *Hardenberg*, III, 465–6.

minister doled out the fragments of this Empire and juggled with the map of Europe; and in his last sentence he added a fine new touch, a glorious parting thought: "May not Switzerland be erected into a Kingdom for Jerome Napoleon?".[1] It was not that the Swiss had given offence; but there had been a whisper that Napoleon wished to have Silesia for Jerome. To Prussia it was of momentous importance that Jerome should be given a prize elsewhere.

Napoleon in the flush of victory had no patience for the fawnings and caresses of the Prussians. The demeanour of Hardenberg repelled him; he was in no mood to be soothed and stroked. He resented the glib way in which Prussia now came over to claim friendship and to tell him how easily everything could be arranged. In the letter he received from Frederick William he detected an offer of alliance; according to the Czar Alexander the proposal was offensive to him; though Hardenberg, quibbling over the phraseology of that particular letter, retorted that the word "alliance" was not mentioned.[2] Napoleon showed himself irritated, and came down with a malicious swoop upon the one definite proposal that was put before him. He refused to accept Hardenberg as the spokesman of the Prussian peace project, refused to treat with him at all, and further declared that his existing official position in Prussia was unacceptable altogether. No peace would in fact be concluded so long as Hardenberg was in power. Napoleon would prefer to make war for forty years.[3]

The demand for the dismissal of Prussia's patriot minister was a rude rebuff to the Hardenberg proposals of peace, and came as a shock to the Prussians. It meant the removal of the most trusted servant that the king had at hand, and this at a time when Prussia, frantic with desperation, was placing all her remaining hope upon the dexterity with which she could manœuvre the negotiation with France. It was the ruin of the rôle Prussia had imagined for herself in the organisation of peace,

[1] Ranke, *Hardenberg*, III, 493–4.
[2] Hardenberg to Alexander, 6 July 1807, in Ranke, *Hardenberg*, III, 506.
[3] Ranke, *Hardenberg*, III, 477–8.

and, coming at this moment, it was a startling index of the manner in which Napoleon intended to deal with his former allies; for if this kind of stipulation preceded the actual discussions for peace men quailed to think of what the terms of the treaty itself would be like. Things might have fared better for these Prussians, since they *were intending to court Napoleon and exorcise the devil that was in him, if they had stepped forward to a gracious concession on what he was pleased to regard as a point of dignity and honour and confidence. Perhaps better than whinings and scrapings this accommodation would have won his kindly smile. At any rate, to us who catch the fall of after-events, it seems foolish that the Prussians used up all their prayers on questions that were essentially preliminary. They were anxious to win the favour of Napoleon, and Napoleon refused his confidence so long as Hardenberg remained in power. The removal of the minister was therefore a pledge of the sincerity of Prussia, and they might have outstripped his desires in their eagerness to prove how genuine was their reconciliation. They preferred to stand and make issue—yet not to show a resolute face and meet Napoleon's demands with a clear, abrupt refusal; but to pester him with their arguments and weary him with their importunities and nauseate him with their prayers, all the time leaving him to understand that if he was immovable they would not dare to oppose him. So on a question of confidence they made it plain that they would give way only if they were forced.

The queen of Prussia was anxious to make a firm resistance to the attacks upon Hardenberg; but she worked from premises different from those of the king and the minister. She knew that Hardenberg had "gigantic plans" afoot, but she was not admitted to the secret of these—she was not informed that they contemplated alliance with France and a complete reversal of policy. So her arguments were wrong from their first principles. She, amid all the catastrophes, had clung to her indignations and animosities and had not ceased to cry out in bitterness against France. She was prepared to see Prussia punished, she expected serious loss of territory, but she would have no return to the old system of vassalage, she would have her husband truly sovereign in whatever lands he might retain.

A thing which I adjure you to take well to heart is to use all the energy of which you are capable in the whole course of this affair, and do not give way an inch on any point which might destroy your independence.... The sacrifice of territory must be counted as nothing in comparison with the sacrifice of liberty. Let Napoleon rob you of half of what you once possessed, provided that what is granted to you is yours in full possession so that you have the power to do good and give happiness to the subjects God has allowed you to keep, and make your political connections in the place where honour calls you and your inclinations lead. Hardenberg must not be sacrificed— certainly not—if you do not wish to take the first step towards slavery and draw upon yourself the contempt of the whole world. You have two means of keeping him; and they must not be neglected; the first is the Emperor Alexander,...then there is yourself, my beloved, you are a good speaker when once you are prepared. If I were in your place I should tell Napoleon that he would easily see how little you could condescend to his demand, how this would deprive you of your best servant; that it would be as though you demanded him to dismiss Talleyrand who *was serving him well* but whom you had reason to complain of, and distrust; in this way he would see for himself that this is a game that two can play.[1]

Over and over again the indignant and embittered queen reiterated her advice. "If Napoleon says he is *vindictive,* say that you are *stubborn* as a mule. Then we shall see what happens."[2] It was all very well; but the masters of policy had decided to find safety in humouring Napoleon. The queen could afford to regard the dismissal of Hardenberg as an act of servility towards a foreign conqueror; but the government was contemplating Prussia as an ally and coadjutor of France. Frederick William had to disillusion his queen and inform her of the new projects of policy.

Without doubt the arguments of your two letters...are very just, but the execution of their purpose has become all the more difficult, and in part impossible, since it seems to have been decided to embrace

[1] Queen Louisa to King Frederick William III, 27 June 1807, in *Deutsche Rundschau*, cx, 42–3.
[2] Queen Louisa to King Frederick William III, 29 June 1807, in *Deutsche Rundschau*, cx, 201.

a new system of politics *entirely* opposed to the old....Up to the present I have not given way on the question of Hardenberg, but he himself feels, as he did in 1805, that if this point is insisted upon any further, his services will become useless and even harmful to the State and it will be necessary for him to retire.[1]

Every attempt was made to wear out the determination of Napoleon by argument and importunity. A hundred facts were adduced to calm a passion; protestations and reasonings were accumulated—little levers to remove a mountain of a prejudice; with all the weariness of commercial travellers the Prussians would demonstrate the innocence of Hardenberg, would persist in bearding this Napoleon who if he stamped his foot could make them tremble. On the 26th of June Frederick William had his first interview at Tilsit, and it was decided to take the opportunity to dismiss from the mind of Napoleon the misapprehensions that were making for the ruin of Hardenberg. It was arranged that the king should bring up the topic "at the close of the conference", so that the delicate matter should not wreck the other objects of discussion. Hardenberg drew up a series of notes to guide the conversation.

The King makes himself the pledge of the loyalty and impartiality of Baron Hardenberg;...it is absolutely false to say that the Baron has the least connection with England, or has even a partiality for that power; it is twenty-five years since he left the service of Hanover and broke with the Prince of Wales in a way which did honour to him; for seventeen years he has been in the service of Prussia; his conduct... must have been presented in a very unjust way to the Emperor;... the King has few servants at hand to whom he could give the portfolio of foreign affairs; M. Zastrow failed him in many respects; if Napoleon insists upon another negotiator he will appoint one; but the King appeals to the sentiment of the Emperor to appreciate what would result from his making it a preliminary condition that the King should remove from affairs a minister whom he thinks worthy of both his own and the Emperor's confidence.[2]

The king recited his part; he would make poor show with his reasonings; his sense of his own inferiority, his fear of a great

---

[1] King Frederick William III to Queen Louisa, 29 June 1807, in *Deutsche Rundschau*, cx, 203.
[2] Ranke, *Hardenberg*, III, 479–80.

mind, made him more than usually undignified when he came into argument with Napoleon; in any case Napoleon met him with the response which above all others is disconcerting; he granted the king's statements, agreed that Hardenberg might be "a respectable man", confessed that he himself was "vindictive"; and so left the king without weapons.[1]

On the 28th of June Hardenberg wrote to the Czar; he had come to doubt the prudence of remaining any longer in office. His letter is of interest as showing the way his gigantic peace plan still filled his mind. He was willing to resign his place— but if he did this, it would be for the sake of his scheme.

"The whole system of policy is going to be changed", he writes, "and connections are going to be formed with France. Would it not be more conformable to the interests of the King for me to remove myself from his counsels and his service as early as possible, if Napoleon persists in showing implacable hatred against me?...I shall hinder the firm establishment of the new system which, *once adopted*, must be followed with consistency and energy—for God keep us from all palliatives and half-measures."[2]

Still, on the 28th of June, and in face of his own personal down‑fall, Hardenberg was repeating his old phrases about the new system of politics. Perhaps he was beginning to doubt of its realisation—to wonder if the Russians were putting all their energy into its promotion. Writing to Budberg on this day, communicating the armistice of Prussia, he says that the king "puts all his hope in the certainty that his August Ally will not separate his cause from that of Prussia, and that there will be insistence on the negotiations for peace being conducted conjointly and with common accord".[3] He enquires when the discussions are to begin, and who the Russian plenipotentiaries will be, and how the Prussian ministers shall take part, but there is a note of rising fear. On the following day, the 29th, he recapitulates his whole scheme once more, and gives his

---

[1] King Frederick William III to Queen Louisa, 26 June 1807, in *Deutsche Rundschau*, cx, 41.
[2] Ranke, *Hardenberg*, iii, 484–8.
[3] *Ibid.* iii, 488–9.

suggestion as to the way the Czar may put it to Napoleon.[1] It is the final effort of a man who sees the receding of his dreams.

The arguments of the Czar did not overcome the objections of Napoleon. It was obvious that Hardenberg's continuance in office was destroying his own plans for the negotiation. The minister did not dare to sign the armistice that was arranged between France and Russia. Kalckreuth declared that if he came to Tilsit the whole negotiation would suffer. His presence at the head of the government became an actual hindrance to the transaction of affairs as well as a grievance to the French. On the 6th of July he gave in his resignation, and Goltz, who had been ambassador at St Petersburg and had already been joined to Kalckreuth as a plenipotentiary in the negotiations for peace, took charge of the foreign department. Stein was called out of retirement to conduct the internal affairs of Prussia. And Hardenberg, who always has a somewhat malignant streak somewhere in his thinking, declared that he was very pleased to think that his signature would not have to appear on such a treaty as Prussia would be made to accept.

Napoleon once before had driven Hardenberg out of office. It was on the morrow of Austerlitz, and for a long period after this event we find the man whining that he was not consulted by the king, sulking because he was left on one side, gloating over the discomfiture of Haugwitz, and expressing a peevish kind of pleasure in the fact that he had no part in the disasters of his country. There is something distasteful in the attempt which he made to gain the favour of the French Emperor after Friedland. When he argued that it was not his fault if Prussia was not the sincere ally of France, one feels again that he had a kind of mean second self to fall back upon at times. He is a more proud statesman, he is in some ways a more plausible personality when success is near and he can feel the wind at his back, and he is able to look down upon the world from a pedestal. At Bartenstein he lifts his head, becomes director of the coalition, acts as schoolmaster to England and takes custody of the conscience of the Czar; but even here, in that moment of artificial

[1] See below, pp. 257–8.

optimism, he is quick to over-reach himself and, mapping out the aggrandisement of Prussia, he shows a disregard for established rights, a contempt for the interests of the small and weak. After Tilsit he once more displays ability to sweep over the continent with a comprehensive scheme, and ease in handling large masses, and fertility in colossal design; yet it is apparent that he is more callous, more cynically conscienceless, more avowedly selfish than before. Tortured by the desperate moment, he would seem to have fallen to pieces, like some men who can be unscrupulous and Machiavellian all their lives, covering up their crookedness by plausible and diplomatic arts, but come in old age to a kind of disintegration, and lose the convincing mask that was over them, and reveal themselves to the world as crafty and cynical and dotingly dishonest.

In the situation of Prussia during the years 1806 and 1807 there is perhaps some extenuation for Hardenberg and the other ministers. These were men exiled from their capital and clinging fearfully to the last corner of their kingdom; they had received a shock of startling suddenness at Jena. It would appear that the alternate moods of unaccountable optimism and morbid despair among the Prussians, the quick changes from high-handed aggressiveness to abject fright, were the result of something like a psychological collapse. The lack of continuous policy and purpose, the rift within the soul, the general unerectness of bearing and all the fitful starts of energy, together with that perpetual tired way of sinking into an injured tone, signified a sort of nervous prostration. Prussia's egotism, now self-pity, now unscrupulous ambition, is like the infantile kind of selfishness, the lack of consideration for others, the certain absence of scruple, the faulty contact with the outside world, that one finds in a man of distracted or deranged mental condition. Prussia is a pathological case. She has a look of drawn tenseness and cannot relax her mind from the strain of living in one perpetual burning moment of crisis. Even in Hardenberg's voluminous memoirs and proposals, where thought showed itself so disproportionate to ensuing action, there is a wasteful exercise of ingenuity, a frantic turning of wheels that refuse quite to grip the rails, which makes the documents seem like the excessive introspections and endless revolvings of a mind that is racing with fever.

The wildness of Hardenberg's proposals after the battle of Friedland, and the fervour with which he believed in them, and the cleverness with which he urged them, as well as their utter lack of relation to the real condition of Prussia at this period, are typical of the monstrous things that result when a tired mind is whipped to momentary frenzy by sheer desperation.

Prussia, indeed, during the whole Napoleonic period, was impelled by a kind of determinism to the pursuit of a selfish aggressive policy. She was in a tantalising state of unstable equilibrium in which she could feel herself on the brink of being a power in Europe. The career of Frederick the Great had given her a foretaste of this; her geographical position asked for extension and greater security. The Napoleonic wars did not themselves provide a clear call and invitation. It was not at first apparent that the Corsican would be the enemy of every established kingdom and every royal house in Europe. It was not at first assumed that he would be dishonest with even an ally. A kingdom situated between France and Russia would not, like these powers, find immediately the unmistakable direction of its interests; once the two empires were at war it would not be irresistibly attracted to either side; no matter which side she chose, Prussia was bound to take it with some misgiving. As surely as the situation of England demanded an unceasing struggle against Napoleon, the interests of Prussia seemed to dictate an exploitation of more casual chances. Thus, Haugwitz, a short time before he led the country into war with France, explained to the king that if his foremost desire was to be assured of his possession of Hanover, his advantage would lie in the strengthening of the alliance with Napoleon.

Prussia could not be, like Austria, urbane and subtle in her self-seeking. She was in the position of a parvenu, who is straining to better himself. She was anxious to take short cuts to a prize that had become tormentingly near. She would make undignified bids for power. And if in 1806 she fell a victim to Napoleon it was not that she was a martyr of the cause of Europe, but that her selfishness still was not sufficiently far-sighted. The time had come when her own interests demanded that she should generously co-operate with the enemies of Napoleon. It was important for her own sake that she should cease her policy of snatching the immediate moment, and selfishly lying in wait for the local opportunity. But Haugwitz, over-excited by the thought that he had been cheated, did not learn the truth in time. Prussia shouted like a swashbuckler, and rushed into war with Napoleon like some petulant and troublesome Balkan state, that cannot refine its purposes or work for a postponed advantage.

The anger of Napoleon against this power after Friedland seemed to take the character of an unremitting pursuit. He did not bury his animosity in the formulas of diplomatic discourse or cloak it in official terms; Talleyrand described him truly— he was "badly brought up"; having no reason to save appearances he confessed his vindictiveness, aired his hatred, and made no show of moderation. He had not forgiven the Prussians for their double dealing in 1806, when they had followed a dual foreign policy and made secret engagements with the Czar. He had not forgotten how they had resisted all his attempts to win them over during the winter campaign in Poland. He knew that they had taken courage out of his difficulties and embarrassments, that they had exulted at Bartenstein. And even on the 20th of June, after the battle of Friedland, he had learned that it was they who had given the refusal to the Austrian mediation. When, within a few days, they were rushing once more to his side, hankering after their former alliance, it was natural that he should put no faith in them and that he should believe them more dishonest than they really were. We find him wondering why the Czar can show them so much fidelity, reminding his new friend that they will very quickly play their tricks upon him. Napoleon knew them false as allies, futile as foes; they had ended by making their friendship unnecessary to him; he could afford to give way to his passions.

There is something in the history of diplomacy which inclines to be cold and forbidding, and lacks the full-blooded leap of the larger story of human lives. Like the history of institutions it will tend to concern itself with the development of a system, abstracted from its human context; it will aspire to the mathematical theorem. There is a balancing of forces, and adjustment of interests; there is much that proceeds out of the logic of a situation, there is much that seems to come by a kind of automatic interaction. Sometimes, in rationalisation, one can almost forget that human beings are at work, with play of mind and mood and impulse; acts will not seem to cry out for an explanation in personality, but will be referred to some logic of policy. And history will fall to her greatest temptation—hearing the tick of the clock, but forgetting to feel the pulse.

At Tilsit one can make no mistake. Here is the play of personalities, palpable and direct. It is not "Russia" that takes a course of action, like a piece of mechanical readjustment. It is not ministers of departments who balance an impersonal policy. It is not government that evolves an official logic. Here "Russia", the government, is a Czar, bundle of emotions and prejudices, an accident in human nature, "and if you prick him he will bleed". An angry outburst is not mediated by couriers riding across Europe, or tempered by the lapse of time, or cushioned in the circumlocutions of diplomatic jargon. The whole drama is played out on the spot. A revolution is telescoped into a few days. Everything is determined by personalities that act upon one another immediately.

In all these personal contacts, the Prussians were doomed to be unfortunate. They had a scheme that was brilliant and brutal and bold; and it was their one hope of salvation; Hardenberg desperately clung to it as though no alternative could be imagined. But it needed infinite tact in the proposing; only a genius could make it attractive to a Napoleon who was in the mood to be repelled by it; it was a preposterous piece of pretentiousness if it could not be backed by the "grand manner". Yet Hardenberg, who was the one man of personality in the Prussian cause, and was desperately anxious to be the spokesman of his own scheme, was excluded from the discussions by the animosity of Napoleon.

The two Prussian negotiators were badly received at Tilsit, and were not well treated by the French. They did not work successfully together. Kalckreuth wrote in vain to Talleyrand, and for a time could not elicit a reply. When Goltz, his colleague, stepped in, and, after some difficulty, secured an answer, his report to Hardenberg declared:

I hope that Count Kalckreuth will not find a new cause for jealousy in all this. I am determined to make every effort to gain his confidence and establish that degree of harmony between us which alone can make our negotiation prosper....Up to this moment his conduct towards me has been exceedingly ungracious—I can forgive him for it with all my heart, for my personal feelings count for nothing in all this; but I do not forgive him for having done nothing for the service and the interests of the king. It was for him to have been long ago on the most confidential footing with the minister Talleyrand —it surely was not for me to make the way for him—but the king does not seem to credit all this; it has appeared to me that His Majesty justifies his conduct, and it seems that in order to give no displeasure I had better not touch on this point any more.[1]

The Prussian king, himself, was not the man to charm away an antipathy. He was in an unpleasant mood at Tilsit and groaned under the oppressiveness of his burdens. The presence of a mind more masterful than his own always stunted and repressed him, and put an obstruction across his thinking; and Napoleon, more than anyone, paralysed him and froze him up. Pitiful passenger, still, in this history, Frederick William flits ineffectually across the days, one party urging him to be cordial and free with Napoleon, the queen all the time pressing him to share her defiance and indignation, he himself divided in spirit, cursed with an internal smouldering, but outwardly gloomy and cold. He could not drive a weak cause to success by the effectiveness of personality. Napoleon seems to have set out to torment him in the interviews, and entertain him with trivial irrelevancies. "Are you still studying tactics?", he asked

---

[1] Goltz to Hardenberg, 2 July 1807, in Bailleu, *Preussen und Frankreich*, II, 590–1.

on one occasion; and the king answered, "Yes sir".[1] At another
time he enquired if the king did not wish to see Berlin again,
after so long an absence. The Prussian queen knew her Frederick
William. "What was your reply?" she wrote,... "I beg you to
tell me." Napoleon would wonder how the man fastened his
innumerable buttons. Describing one day a review of troops,
Frederick William wrote: "Do you think he addressed a word
to me! Not once. I, for my part, tried to do so whenever there
was an opportunity—Then he replied politely and briefly, but
all that he said to me was to ask if Tilsit was an old town". It
is apparent that Napoleon merely amused himself.

Frederick William confessed that during the first interview
that he had at Tilsit, it was Alexander who did most of the talking.
We may take it that he himself attended in no genial or pleasant
mood; for we find him writing the same day:

> I have seen him, I have spoken to that monster, choked out of
> hell, formed by Beelzebub to be the scourge of the earth—It is
> impossible for me to describe to you the sensation I had at the first
> sight of him. Never yet have I passed through a more rude trial;
> all my faculties were in revolt during that terrible interview.[2]

On the second occasion he felt Napoleon "infinitely better
disposed", and said, "I confess that I was not in any way
embarrassed in his presence"; but Frederick William would not
know how to be cordial. His negotiator, Kalckreuth, wrote to
him on June the 30th:

> Your Majesty will succeed... if you will bow to inevitable necessity,
> and treat Bonaparte with friendship and cordiality. This is all he
> expects and asks for, and it is easy. There is much distress at the
> dangerous coldness of Your Majesty towards him; it is imagined that
> Your Majesty sulks with him, and openly despises him. There is a
> pretence of feeling uneasy, which is not genuine, and no explanation
> can be found except by assuming that Your Majesty was ill. Your
> faithful subjects, even the Emperor of Russia, are distressed at this.
> If it costs Your Majesty so much to speak with frankness and

[1] A story that De Maistre reports, *Mémoires et Correspondance*, p. 276:
'Le roi, en portant le doigt à son chapeau comme un grenadier qui salue,
répondit 'Oui, Sire'".

[2] King Frederick William III to Queen Louisa, 26 June 1807, in *Deutsche Rundschau*, cx, 40–1.

cordiality to Napoleon, I offer myself for anything you will deign to command; I might ask an audience. The Emperor of Russia is on the best of terms with Napoleon; Your Majesty might very easily be on the same footing....Napoleon only asks the glory of receiving your confidence....[1]

On the 1st of July Frederick William, after another interview, writes:

All parties united in pressing me to open myself to Bonaparte and to appeal to his heart—in general to pay court to him more assiduously—although I had thought until then that I had left nothing undone to this end....But [Napoleon] seemed to have a more preoccupied air than before and to be out of temper. So it was in vain that I appealed to his heart and his magnanimity, and trooped out all the fine phrases and promises that my feeble eloquence could prompt.[2]

A little later we are allowed to have a glimpse of an actual outburst between the two monarchs. It comes from the pen of Princess Radziwill:

When I again saw the Tsar of Russia, a year later, he told me he had been terrified to see the discussions between the king and Napoleon taking a disquieting turn. Both began to speak vehemently and with bitterness, and Alexander never remembered having felt a more poignant anxiety.

The question was that of the restitution of Silesia. "I must have that province", declared Napoleon, "for the king of Saxony, who needs a free line of communication between Saxony and the Duchy of Warsaw...." The king was cut to the heart and cried: "You do that, to reward him for having abandoned me, for an act of desertion that accelerated my ruin!"—"Desertion! What do you mean by desertion?", retorted Napoleon angrily, "he only did his duty to me and his country."

The Tsar did not remember the rest of the discussion; at the time his only thought was how it would end....At the sight of the king's red excited face and Napoleon's pale and angry countenance, he resolved to cut short the interview....[3]

[1] Kalckreuth to Frederick William III, 30 June 1807, in Bailleu, *Preussen und Frankreich*, II, 590.

[2] King Frederick William III to Queen Louisa, 1 July 1807, in *Deutsche Rundschau*, CX, 209–10.

[3] Princess Anton Radziwill, *Forty-five years of my life* (Eng. trans. 1912), p. 271.

It was natural that Frederick William's subjects should have a regret when they looked upon the happy ease of the Czar, and saw Alexander and Napoleon fraternising like kindred spirits. It is not surprising that Kalckreuth should write to his master: "The Emperor of Russia is on the best of terms with Napoleon; Your Majesty might very easily be on the same footing". The Prussians seem to have been conscious that their king had a manner which irritated the French Emperor, and that their cause was lacking in the personality which might have made it attractive. They had not an Alexander, so they decided to exploit a woman's charm and meet Napoleon with a queen. It was Kalckreuth who wrote from Tilsit to ask that Queen Louisa should come to the seat of negotiation.[1] She who had been the most passionate in her hatred, and had rejoiced that she was not compelled to see Napoleon, was called upon to intervene, and was expected to be charming. If the king had not desired it, she would not have consented to go to Tilsit, and for any torture that she suffered he, more than Napoleon, must be held responsible.[2] She spoke to Napoleon as a mother and implored him to consider her children, and perhaps this kind of dynastic argument, this way of considering Prussian territory as the family property of the house of Brandenburg, was not calculated to induce Napoleon to alter his political plans; though it was not an unsound instinct that made the queen appeal to Napoleon's feeling for family. He, for his part, steeled himself against expected charms, and at one moment attempted to talk about the queen's dress materials. The whole incident only adds to the impression that in these Tilsit days the Prussians consistently took the wrong turn, and did the forbidden thing.

It has been seen what was the conduct of the various powers after the battle of Friedland. England declared herself ready to join in a general congress if the Russians should decide that they

[1] King Frederick William III to Queen Louisa, 29 June 1807, in *Deutsche Rundschau*, cx, 205. Kalckreuth claimed that the suggestion came from Murat, *ibid.* p. 207. Kalckreuth's letter to Frederick William, 28 June 1807, is printed in Bailleu, *Preussen und Frankreich*, ii, 589.

[2] *Deutsche Rundschau*, cx, 207 and 213.

could not continue the war. The court of Vienna came forward again with a not disinterested mediation. And the Prussians placed all their hope upon a reversal of policy that involved alliance with France and the partition of Turkey. The Czar, during all this time, was coming to an arrangement with Napoleon, and it is the course of this transaction that now remains to be followed. But it is interesting to note that while these events were keeping men breathless and expectant, news came through that the Swedish king had just denounced an armistice and attacked the French. His own allies begged him to desist. Fate seems to have played strange tricks with him. His fantastic deeds are a red streak in this grey story of balanced, calculated actions.

CHAPTER III

RUSSIA AND THE ALLIANCE OF TILSIT

On the 16th of June, the Czar Alexander, as we have seen, received Bennigsen's letter confessing defeat at Friedland and urging the commencement of negotiations, "if only to gain time". The news was soon confirmed by a report which the Russian chancellor received from Zismer, a diplomat at the army headquarters.

...I take up my pen to inform Your Excellency of the great disaster which has come upon us. General Bennigsen did not reveal it in full to the Emperor straight away, for fear of giving him a shock. ...Disorder came upon our army, and the soldiers disbanded themselves in a moment. It was a complete rout, no order, no leadership. ...If an eye-witness of the whole campaign may be permitted to speak unreservedly to his chief, Your Excellency will perhaps forgive my zeal for the service and my attachment to my country when I dare to give you my advice in the present circumstances. It seems to me that there is nothing to be done except to demand an armistice as soon as possible, or further, to set on foot negotiations for peace until the rest of the army and the reinforcements behind the Pregel are in a position to give us once more the means of obtaining honorable conditions. It is impossible for me at the moment to determine the losses we have just had; but they must be immense....The picture that General Bennigsen gives to the Emperor...is infinitely less black; but I am bold enough to assure Your Excellency that I have exaggerated nothing, persuaded as I am that you ought to be informed of the truth, even if you do not wish to make use of it.[1]

Evidently there was a panic at the Russian headquarters; the blinding whirl of events carried men off their feet; though in a very few days we find that there was some recovery. The troops, for the moment at least, were completely disorganised; no one knew where to look for food; no one knew how far this wreck of an army could collect itself again or could hope for effective reinforcements from Russia. The country-side was

[1] Zismer to Budberg, 3/15 June 1807, in *Sbornik*, LXXXIX, 10.

filled with stragglers and pillagers, and showed all the desolation that comes in the track of a lost battle. The generals were more than ever discredited, many were sick or wounded; it seemed useless to trust an army any further to blunderers such as these. Sir Robert Wilson remarked: " If Bennigsen retains the command the Emperor will finally lose his throne";[1] soldiers would not consent to be sacrificed continually to such incapacity and mis-direction. Those officers who had mumbled that peace ought to be made, found in disaster their own corroboration; it was said against them that they secretly rejoiced; henceforward they were louder in their insistence that the war should come to an end. There was talk of cabals in the army, of the dangers of a Polish insurrection in the wake of the retreating troops, of the possibility of a peasant rising in Russia if the contest should proceed. We are told that of the generals only Barclay de Tolly was in favour of fighting still. And all the time, to complete the maddening psychological state of things, Prussians reproached the Russians with their failure to achieve the promised success, and Russians reviled the Prussians for their helplessness as allies.

Alexander was not at St Petersburg, viewing events from afar, and taking his decisions in the cool of a council chamber. He could not quietly sit down to a problem which lay beyond far horizons and which he merely visualised by moving pins on a military map. Not in wide perspectives and through the sobering distances, but in its present maddening immediacy, the situation faced him; and he had to think out his conduct in an atmosphere that was strained. For he had kept within calling distance, the noises were humming in his ears, the catastrophe stared at him all day long, and he himself was in the whirlpool of the events that he had to consider. Quite recently he had had to move, to take precautions for his own safety.

Yet his first measures when the news of the battle overwhelmed him are astonishing in their cautiousness. After all that he had heard he ordered his aide-de-camp Popov to make his way to the army headquarters and confirm the verdict of Bennigsen. It

---

[1] Wilson, *Diaries*, 18 June 1807, vol. II.

was as though Alexander was determined not to have his hands forced by his commander—he might have half-suspected the pacific advices of headquarters. If Popov found the situation as critical as had been reported, and if the Russian generals had "no other means of extricating" themselves, then Bennigsen might ask for an armistice, only—here an added touch of cautiousness—he must ask in his own name.[1] Bennigsen was not to enter into the actual discussions for the armistice for which he was to apply "in his own name". Alexander left no loophole for his commander. Prince Lobanov—a noble of old standing, a man of the great days of Catherine—was entrusted with the mission, receiving the verbal commands of his master, together with the following instructions:

Work for the conclusion of an armistice of one month, during which the respective troops shall keep their present positions; do not propose negotiations for peace, but if the French should express a desire to put an end to the war, reply that the Emperor Alexander also wishes for a pacification....[2]

Alexander takes every precaution against committing himself, or surrendering to the peace party at headquarters. At the same time he writes to the king of Prussia, and decides to concert measures with him.[3] There is no hint of an intention to take a separate isolated course; there is no dream, as yet, of Tilsit.

Already, after this short space, men seem to have recovered their heads a little at headquarters, and can take stock of their defeat. Zismer corrects his former pitiful narration. "I am very happy to be able to announce... that our loss is not so prodigious as the rout that I saw seemed to forebode."[4] Bennigsen also reports:

I am happy to be able to announce that affairs are righting themselves and are going better and better.... The continual return of

---

[1] Alexander to Bennigsen, 4/16 June 1807, in *Sbornik*, LXXXIX, 16.

[2] Alexander to Lobanov, 4/16 June 1807, in Tatistcheff, *Alexandre Ier et Napoléon*, p. 121; see Appendix A.

[3] Alexander to Frederick William III, 4/16 June 1807, in *Sbornik*, LXXXIX, 16–17.

[4] Zismer to Budberg, 4/16 June 1807, in *Sbornik*, LXXXIX, 14.

stragglers proves to me that our loss was not so considerable, and that there is nothing to regret except the capture of the town of Königsberg. The enemy did not dare to pursue me and has not done so yet; my soldiers are animated with the same courage.[1]

When the Czar's instructions reached headquarters the generals decided to ask for an armistice; Popov, who had been sent to examine the condition of affairs, agreed that it was necessary; and on the 18th of June Bennigsen ordered one of his generals to "inform the chiefs of the French army" of the step that was to be taken. "The issue may perhaps be all the more salutary", he wrote in a letter that was intended for French eyes, "in that there is already question of a general congress."[2] Murat, who received the communications from the Russian generals, at first seems to have suspected a ruse; but Napoleon was immediately informed of the overture, and very soon an aide-de-camp of Marshal Berthier brought a favourable reply. This man, a nephew of Talleyrand, reported that the French "were equally desirous of putting an end to the existing war".[3] So Lobanov passed over to Tilsit to begin his negotiation and enter upon discussions for an armistice with Marshal Berthier.

The French had evidently decided to court and coax the Russians, and enchant them with studied politeness, and flatter them with their attentions. Lobanov found his path strewn with flowers; he received an enthusiastic welcome, was addressed in terms highly complimentary to himself, and was treated with affability. At first he stood on his guard, declaring that "in spite of the desire of Russia to put an end to the effusion of blood, she could not accept a peace which would be humiliating for her dignity, nor could she tolerate any modification whatever of her existing frontier".[4] He was reassured in the strongest terms; Napoleon meditated no humiliation for Russia; the supposition of such a thing would be an insult. Whereupon, the terms of the

---

[1] Bennigsen to Alexander, 5/17 June 1807, in *Sbornik*, LXXXIX, 17.

[2] Bennigsen to Bagration, 6/18 June 1807, in *Sbornik*, LXXXIX, 22. For the congress in question see above, p. 177.

[3] Bennigsen to Alexander, 7/19 June 1807, in *Sbornik*, LXXXIX, 23–4.

[4] Lobanov to Alexander, 19 June 1807, in Tatistcheff, *Alexandre Ier et Napoléon*, pp. 125–6.

armistice were discussed and Lobanov, to his intense surprise, found himself coolly asked to sign away three places that were not in Russian hands at all—the Prussian fortresses of Pillau, Graudenz and Colberg. He did not hesitate in his reply; he refused to assent to such terms, declared that Bennigsen himself had no powers to make these concessions, and returned to the Russian army to await the further orders of his Emperor.[1]

Very soon came Marshal Duroc to the headquarters of Bennigsen, to report Napoleon's renewed decision. He conferred with Bennigsen and the Grand Duke Constantine, while Lobanov and Popov stayed up all night expecting to be called to the discussion. Duroc announced that Napoleon would not be contented with an armistice, but would desire the conclusion of peace; and this time it would seem to be Bennigsen who was not quite genial, for he declared that his instructions merely had reference to a suspension of arms; and when Duroc reported Napoleon's persistence in his demand for the Prussian fortresses, Bennigsen replied, if we are to trust his accounts: "...then there is no further question, and we go on with the war. You told me that your master was desirous of treating not only for an armistice, but for peace. Very well. Let us negotiate for peace, and fight in the meantime".[2] Bennigsen, whom all the world was reviling as a traitor, made bold to remind Duroc that the Czar had formidable resources at his disposal, and could call on reinforcements—could even make the war a national one and resort to a *levée en masse*. These words may seem remarkable in Bennigsen, but they are quite in line with the rôle that he was beginning to adopt, and they reveal the direction of his thoughts. Duroc expressed Napoleon's wish for a closer connection with Russia, and even dropped words to show the desirability of an interview between the two Emperors. Some of these scraps of conversation leaked out in Baubeln, where the Russian headquarters were fixed, and they are confirmed in the reports of the Prussian representative there. This man, Schladen, heard, among other things, that the Russians had replied to Duroc's advances by

[1] Lobanov to Alexander, 19 June 1807, in Tatistcheff, *Alexandre Ier et Napoléon*, pp. 125–6.   [2] Tatistcheff, *Alexandre Ier et Napoléon*, p. 127.

saying that they thought Alexander would not be averse to peace, provided that no demand should be made for him to abandon the interests of Prussia.[1] Finally accounts were sent to the Czar, relating what had taken place. Popov complained that Bennigsen had excluded Lobanov and himself from the interview with Duroc; in spite of imperial orders the commander-in-chief had presumed to take things into his own hands; Popov seems to have had suspicions, as well he might, for this was the second time that he had been sent on a mission to supervise and check the movements of Bennigsen; but he concurred in the opinion that an armistice ought to be concluded.[2]

To the Czar Alexander two questions now come for consideration, representing the second stage in the course that leads to Tilsit. Firstly, there is the fact to be faced that Napoleon seems determined to secure the cession of the Prussian fortresses. Secondly, it becomes apparent that the Czar must definitely decide whether the armistice shall be followed up by regular negotiations for peace. All this emerges from the reports of what has happened in the recent discussions between the armies; and perhaps it is significant that the man who travels to the Emperor with the despatches from the Russian headquarters, and so has an opportunity to reinforce their tenour in actual verbal conference, is none other than the head of the peace party, the Grand Duke Constantine.

Undoubtedly this is an opportune moment for the Grand Duke, who knows what he wants; excellent chance to push a thought home in the mind of a Czar who is still floundering in mists and indecisions.[3] Sufficient is known to make it clear that Constantine did not merely offer a report to his brother, but made a vigorous effort to direct his deliberations, if not actually to force his hand. This is the occasion when he reminds Alexander of the fate of his father and raises fears of assassination. He says that if battle is offered again and the gates of the empire opened

---

[1] Schladen's first Report, 21 June 1807, in Ranke, *Hardenberg*, v, 520.
[2] Tatistcheff, *Alexandre Ier et Napoléon*, p. 128.
[3] *Deutsche Rundschau*, cx, 35, 37. Schladen's second Report, 21 June 1807, in Ranke, *Hardenberg*, v, 522.

to the ever-victorious French, the Czar might just as well give every soldier a pistol and order him to blow out his own brains. It is significant that at this time of strain and crisis there were men around Alexander who were anxious not merely to offer him the benefit of their counsels but also to play upon his nerves. Constantine had already begun fraternising with the French, had taken pains to address Murat as "Your Highness", had done everything to promote the negotiation; he would not be the man to minimise the activity of the peace party at headquarters when he made his reports to the Czar. We learn from the despatches of the Prussian General Schladen that the officers were calling loudly for peace, and seemed determined to have it, whether Alexander wished it or no.

"It is incredible", wrote Schladen, "how little these people guard their expressions, and to what extent the officers of all grades forget the language which befits their uniform. They roundly curse this war, declare themselves completely beaten...and say to any one who will listen that *cost what it may*, peace must be made....Every minute I am more assured that the generous intentions of the Emperor Alexander will fail against the force of the intrigue that is carried on here—of which the Grand Duke is the servile instrument."[1]

Constantine would make good use of the support which he could claim to have among the Russian officers; we have good reason to believe that he would not moderate his language.

Even if he himself could have forgotten, there were people who were interested in reminding the Czar of that long agony of waiting when all eyes had looked for messages from England, and of the bitter story of an ever-promised diversion that never came to realisation. These people would recall to him that policy which the *Edinburgh Review* called "our love of sugar islands", by which England, forgetting her allies, had scattered her forces in overseas expeditions; they would remember how, instead of providing generously for the coalition, England had kept tight hold of her own purse strings. It would be impossible for the Czar to forget how eagerly all eyes had looked to Austria, how even on the eve of Friedland men had set anxious gaze

[1] Schladen's third Report, 23 June 1807, in Ranke, *Hardenberg*, v, 525.

towards Vienna till hope had dwindled away. Perhaps the Czar
would remember the advice he had received in the days of
optimism after the convention of Bartenstein. Gentz, the true
European of these days, the fervent devotee of coalitions, had
shown that there was no choice but to make peace, since it was
useless to try to fight without the aid of Austria. It was Gentz's
perpetual creed that you could not defeat the French without
Austrian assistance,[1] and already in April this arch-enemy of
Napoleon had given up all hope in the existing struggle. He
had suggested that it might be useful to threaten the government
at Vienna; the Czar might declare his intention of joining hands
with Napoleon; but the Russians had refused to adopt an attitude
that would throw the Austrians into the arms of France.[2] All
these things must have returned to the mind of the Czar as he
struggled to a decision, with a Grand Duke roaring at his side.
And, as Prussia was a helpless burden to the coalition, an
encumbrance and a responsibility, there must have come back
to the Czar that old complaint: "I have no ally". The generals,
the Czartoryski's, the Novossiltzovs, were all anxious to see the
end of the war, each for his own reasons. Popov, who had been
specially sent to the army to give an account of the situation,
was writing: "Every moment is costly, time is flying and circumstances demand the conclusion of peace or else an armistice
as early as possible". Bennigsen had discredited himself, as a
general, and even now was under suspicion because of his conduct
in regard to the negotiation; there was little hope of finding
salvation by confiding another army to his leadership. Moreover,
Napoleon had made demand of Prussian fortresses and had
declared that he would not be content with an armistice but would
require the conclusion of peace. It would have been very bold to
offend him in both these matters, it would have been a determination tantamount to a willingness to renew the war. So the

[1] For Gentz's theory that without the union of Austria and Prussia no
plan for the curbing of France can be of any effect, see e.g. Gentz to Jackson,
25 Sept. 1805, in M. H. Weil, *D'Ulm à Jena* (1921), pp. 65 *et seq.* In a letter
to Jackson on 5 Dec. 1805 (*ibid.* p. 140) Gentz points out the mistake that
had been made in the late war of "making Russia the principal actor" in the
struggle against France.   [2] F. de Martens, *Recueil*, VI, 419.

Czar made a definite decision and sent new instructions to his
officers; and Lobanov received powers to enter into negotiations
for peace.[1]

In finally reconciling himself to the idea that he must enter
upon such discussions, and even in agreeing to the conclusion
of a separate armistice by Russia, the Czar by no means allowed
it to be implied that he had any thought of deserting Prussia.
He wrote: "I am sure that the King of Prussia will not delay
sending a person of confidence to represent him".[2] His instruction to Bennigsen ran as follows:

> Neither Graudenz, nor Pillau, nor Colberg belongs to me. I have
> not even any of my troops in these fortresses, therefore I cannot give
> consent to their cession. In general this demand seems to me inad-
> missible. Order Prince Lobanov to give a reply on these lines to
> Marshal Berthier and tell him to say that I sincerely share their desire
> to put an end to the effusion of blood and make peace; that the said
> Prince Lobanov was authorised by me to enter into discussions of peace
> as soon as an armistice of one month's duration should be concluded
> allowing our troops to keep their present position. Prince Lobanov
> has received my instructions and I desire, General, that he be con-
> stantly employed on all the missions that there may have to be sent
> to the French army and that he participate in the discussions which
> you may have with those who may be sent to you on the part of the
> French Government.[3]

So Grand Duke Constantine returned to headquarters; with
what high spirits, we are left to infer; but soon after his arrival
we discover disconcerting rumours abroad at Baubeln; it would
seem that he had divulged some hints of the possibility of an
interview between Alexander and Napoleon.

The Prussian king arrived at the side of the Czar, reaching
Sczawel soon after Constantine had left. Hardenberg says that
he was surprised to discover the state to which things had
developed, and relates that he found Alexander already a changed
man.[4] Alexander, moreover, wore the harassed look of a person

[1] Lobanov's full powers, dated 8/20 June 1807, are given in *Sbornik*,
LXXXIX, 26. The accompanying *Instruction* (p. 25) is translated in Tatistcheff,
Alexandre Ier et Napoléon, p. 130.
[2] Alexander to Bennigsen, 8/20 June 1807, in *Sbornik*, LXXXIX, 25.
[3] *Ibid.*   [4] Ranke, *Hardenberg*, v, 539.

torn within himself, and it was disquieting to find him talking
of having an interview with Napoleon. Hardenberg felt that he
had arrived just too late—that Constantine had forestalled him.
It would seem that the Grand Duke had done something more
than give an impulse to the Czar's wavering mind or add the
final arguments that brought him definitely over to the side of
peace; perhaps Constantine's real achievement was not that he
induced his brother to break away from the alliance with
England and Austria, but that he succeeded in winning his
acquiescence to the idea of meeting Napoleon in person.

It seems ironical that while all this is taking place, Bennigsen
should be writing to Alexander a letter like the following:

Your Imperial Majesty may be assured that I am not exaggerating
when I say that it was only a part of the infantry which was for a
moment put to rout by the last charge of the enemy after the battle
of Friedland...this rout of a part of our infantry only lasted a
moment....

...I am not sufficiently informed to be able to say if it can be done,
but the best thing for the army of Your Imperial Majesty would be
to fill up the regiments and to use the...officers of the militia to
replace those who are killed or grievously wounded; then, with the
addition of the division of Prince Lobanov, which is on the point of
arrival, the army will be more formidable than it was when we
resumed the offensive, and it will be in a state to begin action again
as soon as circumstances should demand. I regard it as my duty to
give you this assurance, Sir, in case the pretensions of Bonaparte are
such as we cannot admit.

...For the rest I make bold to assure Your Imperial Majesty that
the check received in this battle has not at all lessened the courage of
the troops...and if circumstances should demand it the army would
fight to-morrow with the same courage as though the battle of
Friedland had never occurred....I must add that...the enemy has
suffered infinitely greater losses than ours in these different combats,
and cannot repair them so soon, while our reinforcements come in
daily and will very shortly put us in a position to be more formidable
than ever to Bonaparte.[1]

This quite agrees with the conversation the Russian general had

---

[1] Bennigsen to Alexander, 9/21 June 1807, in *Sbornik*, LXXXIX, 27–8.

with Schladen, the Prussian representative, two days later, when
he said that

the present situation was anything but embarrassing...that there
was really no danger except that of becoming discouraged;...that
[Napoleon's] recent combats had cost him an immense number of
men...that it was necessary therefore that no one should lose his
head or in any way consent to the evacuation of the [Prussian]
fortresses...that it would be better to break the armistice on the
spot; that he, Bennigsen, with the means that he had actually at his
disposal, did not at all fear the recommencement of hostilities...and
that if by negotiations with Napoleon one could gain a little time
without conceding anything, one would be in a position to collect
one's resources and await a definite categorical reply from Austria
and England.[1]

All this is confirmed by a report of Mackenzie, the British agent,
who visited the Russian headquarters on the 22nd of June:
"The General [Bennigsen] declared...he would undertake to
beat the enemy again and again with 60,000 men; but no one
replied ".[2] In this way, as the negotiation advances, we find
Bennigsen protesting violently; perhaps he protests too much.
It might have been a sudden surge of self-assertiveness in a man
who felt that he had been weak—Bennigsen taking hold of
himself and determined to be strong. It might have been—as
appears from the interview with Duroc—that the commander,
hearing of Napoleon's extravagant demands, was provoked to
a real ardour which before he had been unable to feel, was given
an inner impulsion which had been lacking in his previous
conduct of the war. We hear of him urging a plan to retreat into
the heart of Russia and lure the French into the northern wilds
far from their own country. It would seem impossible to
resolve into a unity the successive phases in the mind of such
a person; moods seem to succeed one another like capricious

[1] Schladen's Report of 23 June 1807 in Ranke, *Hardenberg*, iii, 469.
Cf. Schladen's second Report of 21 June 1807, where he writes: "Bennigsen
looks as though he had beaten the French and triumphed over his enemies".
Ranke, *Hardenberg*, v, 522.

[2] Mackenzie's Report of 23 June 1807 enclosed in G. Leveson-Gower to
G. Canning. Separate 26 June 1807. Printed in J. H. Rose, *Napoleonic
Studies*, p. 157.

changes of the weather; the men who led the Russians had a kind of startling discontinuity in their souls, and one must be prepared for self-contradiction and sudden rifts within a single personality. There is a temptation to find a too-facile continuity in history, and see after the battle of Friedland a simple ascending ladder to Tilsit; in reality the issue is the result of a conflict of forces, and a collision of wills. There is an interplay of personalities who themselves are not always unities, but, repeating the conflict within their own spirits, are torn with irreconcilable moods and purposes, divided against themselves. The decision of Alexander to become the ally and friend of Napoleon is like the gradual emergence of a green shining film on the surface of a boiling cauldron in which a score of ingredients have been in perplexing effervescence. An account of that decision would be over-simplified if it were not written with a sort of counterpoint, to show the under-currents that sometimes ran against it. It would be untrue if it did not allow for the fluidity of events, the certain element of the capricious that is in people. Perhaps if one night the stars had only shone a little more brightly to awaken a more sentimental mood—perhaps if one night Queen Louisa had only been near to give Alexander a reminder, then in that mysterious borderland of the mind where such winds have play and subtle influence, there might have arisen a mad desire; the divine mission might have become once more compelling; Bennigsen might have had his way. It is easy to take a short cut with history and see things move evenly towards some great event; in reality life is more complex. In the Russian mind above all there seem to be mysterious fervours and subtle workings and strange broodings; and in Alexander himself there was a curious interweaving of German transcendentalism with all this, making character and motive more difficult to analyse. The question why at this moment Alexander and Bennigsen reversed their former rôles, Bennigsen being now the optimist, the enthusiast for war, is a problem of psychology, a study in moods. Any puff of wind might have altered history.

Prince Lobanov resumed his negotiation and the French once more took up their policy of flattery and smiling affability. The question of the Prussian fortresses was dropped and an armistice was signed on the 21st of June;[1] the Russian negotiator was admitted to the presence of Napoleon, who, we are told, was in high spirits and covered him with kindness, talking with him for two hours and bestowing compliments enough to turn his head. Napoleon drank the health of Alexander, declared that he had ever had a fondness for him, insisted that an alliance between Russia and France was a thing that the mutual interests of the two powers demanded, and swore that he had never entertained aggressive designs against Russia. He made some suggestion that the Czar ought to have some accession of territory to give his empire its true and natural frontier on the Vistula. There is even mention of his taking the map of Europe and denoting, with a sweep of his arm, what might be the limits of Russian and French dominion in two majestic empires of East and West.[2] The tale Lobanov had to tell when he returned to his master was like the opening of a dream. Coming to men who had felt dejected and desperate and beaten, it must have seemed magnificent release; for it meant that instead of cringing miserably and creeping disgracefully out of the war, Russia might make her peace treaty the very source of unbounded prestige and might find glories greater than that of victory in sharing dominion with Napoleon. Alexander grasped the splendid moment, and caused Napoleon to be informed that everything could be easily arranged provided that the two Emperors should treat without intermediaries. Marshal Duroc was sent from the French headquarters to propose an interview; and on the 25th of June the two Emperors met at Tilsit and embraced one another on a raft that had been built in the middle of the river Niemen.

The idea of making an alliance with France would not surprise Alexander as a fantastic unheard-of thing. Napoleon had thrown out a vague hint through Marshal Duroc on the first day of the negotiation, though this might have been taken as

---

[1] The armistice is printed in *Sbornik*, LXXXIX, 29–30.
[2] Lobanov to Alexander, 21 June 1807, in Tatistcheff, *Alexandre Ier et Napoléon*, pp. 135–6.

only a disarming phrase. The Czar had recently been induced to
think seriously about a complete reversal of policy, and had
accommodated his mind to the idea and had actually given
some sort of adhesion to a scheme that was based upon this,
before Lobanov had brought his report of Napoleon's proposals.
The impulse had come from a different quarter. It was Hardenberg who had painted glowing pictures of the glory that
would spring from a desertion of the coalition and an arrangement
of alliance with France; he had been formulating a reconstruction
of Europe, based upon a dismemberment of Turkey. He was
still elaborating his plans on the day Lobanov brought the
French offer of alliance—was pursuing his policy in the assurance
that he had won over the Czar to the scheme.

It is apparent that in the early days before events had come
to precision, Alexander, accepting the proffered alliance of
France, conceived himself as adhering to the main principle
of Hardenberg's scheme; he did not in any way imagine that he
was separating himself from the Prussians. We are dealing now
with very subtle thoughts that lie behind man's surface conduct;
and Alexander, following his solitary way, an autocrat responsible to no man, under no necessity of explaining himself to a
superior, gives but few clues for the elucidation of his secret
purposes. Yet there are some chinks in the wall that shuts him
away from the enquirer, and if we look carefully into these we
shall see him with the Hardenberg proposals still hanging in his
mind, after he has had more than one interview with Napoleon.
We shall see him even inclined to take it as an opening, as
"something to work upon" in this matter, when Napoleon makes
an allusion to Turkey. We shall gather that when the Czar goes
to Tilsit he has by no means thrown aside the stagey cardboard
policies of Hardenberg.

Here we are brought back to the letter of the 22nd of June
in which the Prussian king, writing to Queen Louisa, makes
reference to "gigantic" plans that are afoot—attempts to
rescue the defeated states from their desperate position. Hardenberg and Budberg, according to this letter, declare their
joint opinion in a conference with their monarchs, and we are

given the unmistakable suggestion that their plans are approved and being adopted as the common policy of the two powers, and are under process of further elaboration. "These are as yet only general ideas", the king adds, "but they have been communicated to Kalckreuth so that he may be able to make tactful use of them in such a way as to learn something of the benevolent intentions of [Napoleon]."[1] There is nothing to show that on the following day, the 23rd, the Prussians feel their plan losing ground. The instructions addressed to their negotiator on this date prove Hardenberg to be full of hope. Kalckreuth is not ordered to make definite proposals to the French or to spring Hardenberg's scheme full-grown upon Napoleon; rather it is "trusted to the ingenuity of the Marshal" so to manage the affair that the actual suggestions shall come from France; but Kalckreuth is instructed to sound Napoleon, to put out feelers particularly in regard to the partition of Turkey; he is to convey the hint that "it will be easy for us to come to an understanding", he is to make it clear that Hardenberg has some proposals to offer and that these will be welcome to Napoleon. Everything is contrived, in fact, to create the impression that Prussia has a plan up her sleeve such as will surprise the French with its agreeableness if only they will consent to listen to it. It is assumed that the Czar is moving in step; the papers make reference to the fact that he shares the feelings of his ally; it is Alexander as well as Frederick William, it is "their Majesties", who think that "in half-disclosing their ideas on the subject of peace and in listening to those of Napoleon, the Marshal will easily succeed in preparing the way for a negotiation".[2] Hardenberg is evidently acting upon a policy in which he feels sure of the co-operation of the Czar.

On this 23rd of June we find Alexander in receipt of Napoleon's offer of friendship and alliance. He is faced with the difficulty of drawing up instructions for Lobanov, the man who is to treat for peace. It will be seen later that Alexander, while accepting Hardenberg's plan of turning defeat into glorious victory by

[1] See above, p. 218.
[2] Ranke, *Hardenberg*, III, 463.

sleight of hand, is more sensitive than the Prussian in recognising the delicacy of the proposal. He seems to be anxious as to how much he shall disclose to the French, and how soon. More than one project of instructions had been drawn up for Lobanov, only to be laid aside; and from these preliminary drafts it is certain that Alexander had no intention of making sudden parade of Hardenberg's programme. But though these drafts do not dare to base themselves upon the presumptuous principles which the Prussians were advancing, though they have in their totality little in common with Hardenberg's suggestions, yet they contain one or two points that are remarkable and that seem indeed eccentric —points that, after Friedland, seem to belong to some bold imaginative policy. We see in one of the papers that Russia is greatly concerned to secure Hamburg and Lübeck for Prussia.[1] Hardenberg had specified these in his remapping of Europe; possibly he had been even more insistent in his discussions with the Czar than actually appears in his writings; but it is a bold thing to mention the Hanseatic towns after Friedland, for in 1806 Napoleon, even though it had been a question of peace or war, had refused to concede them to Prussia. There is another curious suggestion among the Russian projects at this period; we find the idea that Prussia might have Bohemia; the excuse being, "the duplicity with which Austria has conducted herself towards Russia as well as towards Prussia".[2] There is a slashing boldness, as of Hardenberg, in this summary disposal of neutral territory; one might hazard the thought that this looks like an interesting variant of the Hardenberg proposals—a stray spark struck off at a heat in the hammering-out of the Prussian scheme. It is difficult through all the mist of unreported conferences to trace such ideas to their source; one can only detect a reminiscence of Bartenstein, a cadence that fits all Hardenberg's tunes, a sample of the things which the Prussians were perpetually putting into the mind of Alexander but which we

[1] "Quelques idées qui pourront trouver place dans les instructions du négociateur russe qui sera chargé de traiter de la paix." *Sbornik*, LXXXIX, 33–7. See Appendix B on the Institutions of Lobanov.

[2] Memorandum in *Sbornik*, LXXXIX, 37–8. This is in the handwriting of Budberg; see Tatistcheff, *Alexandre Ier et Napoléon*, footnote to p. 144.

must hope he did not originate himself. These sketches for an instruction to Lobanov show that the Russians had a strong sense of the importance of their alliance to the French; they seemed determined to sell it for value; they even talked of drawing out Napoleon on the subject of the Ottoman Porte.[1] This is of some importance, for as the days go by the Czar weakens, and forgets to remain so on his guard. Above all, the Czar was certainly true to Prussia; was playing no double-handed game; was determined to be strong against Napoleon when the interests of his ally were concerned. He would have no increase of territory for himself, no extended frontier on the Vistula, unless Prussia should be provided with compensation.[2] These are the experimental ideas for the instructions of the negotiator Lobanov. On the 23rd of June they were cast aside in favour of a bolder proposal of alliance. It would almost seem that the flattering message which Lobanov had brought from Napoleon had determined Alexander to enter more fully into the policy of Hardenberg. Lobanov's instruction ran:

You will explain to the Emperor Napoleon how deeply I appreciate all that he has said to me through you, and how much I wish to see a close union between our two nations make up for the past evils. You will tell him that this union between France and Russia has constantly been the object of my desires, and that I hold the conviction that it alone can secure happiness and peace for the world. An entirely new system must replace that which has existed up to the present and I flatter myself that we shall easily arrive at an understanding with the Emperor Napoleon, provided that we treat without intermediaries. A lasting peace may be concluded between us in a few days.[3]

Alexander does not face the necessity of having to put down his plans in black and white; does not even entrust this delicate transaction to a minister who may bungle or misunderstand. Like Hardenberg in his instructions to Kalckreuth he merely hints that he has a plan in his pocket and that it will be easy to settle everything with France; and he sees the solution of his whole problem in treating with Napoleon "without inter-

[1] *Sbornik*, LXXXIX, 38. [2] *Ibid.*
[3] Tatistcheff, *Alexandre Ier et Napoléon*, pp. 148–9.

mediaries". When he says that "an entirely new system must replace that which has existed up to the present", and that "we shall easily arrive at an understanding with the Emperor Napoleon", and that "a lasting peace may be concluded in a few days", he is not merely voicing the same thrill of expectation, he is using the same kind of language that appears in the Prussian documents, he is repeating what might be called Hardenberg's "stock phrases", he is making the identical kind of insinuation and euphemism with which Hardenberg cloaked his scheme, and he is trying to give the same impression that all will be simple and there will be no controversy, because he has a plan up his sleeve and it is one which Napoleon cannot but accept. It is certain that Alexander for some time continued to give the Prussians the assurance that he was hoping to promote their plan of pacification; it is difficult, in the face of all the facts that can be recovered, to believe that he was deceiving them in this. At the back of his mind—with what vagueness it would be hazardous to say—he held the idea of joining Prussia in an alliance with Napoleon, and sharing with her its benefits, and sealing the happy transaction with a partition of the Ottoman Porte.

The matter which requires elucidation in the mysterious transactions of Tilsit, is not Alexander's determination to withdraw his connection with the coalition; for Constantine, in the early days of the negotiations, had already induced this decision. Neither is it the Czar's acceptance of alliance with France even to the point of joining in the campaign against the maritime pretensions of England. Hardenberg had secured this change of system before the Czar saw Napoleon at all. There are no signs that during the interviews at Tilsit Alexander was troubled in mind or tormented in conscience or at all involved in a struggle with himself on any of these matters. The thing which asks for explanation and gives evidence of having tried his soul was a much more subtle transition in his attitude towards Prussia. He who on the eve of Tilsit had declared that he would have nothing to do with Napoleon's offer of territory and an extended frontier on the Vistula, unless compensation should be found for

his ally, finally accepted the increase of territory, acquiesced in
the humiliation of Frederick William, and became a party to
the mutilation of Prussia.[1] Adopting the main features of
Hardenberg's scheme—desertion of allies, friendship with
France, co-operation against England, and the dismemberment
of Turkey—he abandoned the idea of comprising Prussia in a
grand "triumvirate", abandoned it without making any overt
struggle for it. He made in fact a more complete surrender to
Napoleon than he had intended or imagined on the eve of the
meeting. This was the real achievement of Napoleon in the
conversations that took place. It was the proud consummation
of Tilsit. For it left the two Emperors alone, arm-in-arm on a
mountain of their own, in close mysterious intimacy and
picturesque alliance; it enabled them to strike the imagination
of the world with the vision of magnificent empire dividing the
east and the west.

Alexander told Frederick William, after his first interview with
Napoleon, that he had found the Emperor, "reserved, cold, but
polite".[2] We can gather that this would not seem a favourable
time for plunging into the discussion of Hardenberg's scheme.
Yet Alexander talked about Prussia—enough to invite the
remark of Napoleon, who asked him why he was so interested
in this country—and he secured that the surrender of the three
Prussian fortresses should not be insisted upon during the
armistice. He also returned with an invitation for Frederick
William to meet Napoleon on the morrow.[3] It would seem that
he began well; but undoubtedly he found himself face to face
with Napoleon's astonishing antipathy to Prussia, and probably
the result of the interview would be to increase his hesitation
concerning the proposed Hardenberg policy; for, however sincerely he might accept the idea of a joint alliance—of a "triumvirate", however much he may have assented to the plan of
partitioning Turkey, he certainly felt bashful when it came to the
point of putting the idea to Napoleon, and he must have been

[1] On Alexander's desertion of Prussia see also Appendix C.
[2] King Frederick William III to Queen Louisa, 25 June 1807, in *Deutsche
Rundschau*, cx, 38–9.   [3] *Ibid.*

doubtful especially concerning some of the ramifications of the scheme. He could not show Hardenberg's brazen face in such a contingency as this, and so, even while he made it understood that he was keeping the plan in view, he confessed that he did not know how to meet Napoleon with it, he dallied, waited for an opportunity to arise, and talked of the need of circumspection. It was unfortunate that Hardenberg had misread the mood of Napoleon and had failed to advance his own proposals with the delicacy they demanded; Napoleon, when he received the letter from the Prussian king, detected an offer of alliance, and was repelled by the coolness of the suggestion. It was to Alexander himself that he expressed his discontent, and the result must have been to make the Czar more guarded, more hesitant than ever. On the 27th of June we find him writing to the Prussian king:

I think I must report to Your Majesty that after a long three hours' conversation with Napoleon after dinner yesterday I have hopes that things will turn out well, for he himself brought up the subject of the dissolution and partition of the Ottoman Empire. This gives us something to work from, but, Sire, we must move with the greatest precaution and prudence. Your Majesty must have confidence in me, and I hope to be able to serve you with that zeal and attachment which you know I have for you.[1]

The Prussian king replies with a most gracious expression of trust and gratitude,[2] but Hardenberg begins to feel that his policy is not being pressed with sufficient vigour, he seeks to overcome the Czar's reserve and hesitation, and takes the opportunity to urge his proposals more strongly. He recapitulates his suggestions in a memorandum which he desires the Czar to communicate to Napoleon:

and in case His Imperial Majesty should hesitate to speak in his own name of what relates to Turkey (even after what Napoleon has said on the subject) it seems to me that he would not be in any way

[1] Alexander I to Frederick William III, 15/27 June 1807, in Bailleu, *Briefwechsel* (vol. LXXV of the *Publicationen aus den K. Preussischen Staatsarchiven*), p. 158.
[2] *Ibid.* p. 159.

compromised if he communicated the Memorandum as my idea. This would perhaps at the same time have the effect of destroying Napoleon's prejudices against me.[1]

The paper is dated the 29th of June, and proves that even four days after the Czar had met Napoleon at Tilsit, Hardenberg was still fondling his grand design and hoping by the spoliation of Turkey to turn Napoleon's anger away from Prussia; but he was beginning to be impatient and to see how his desires were slipping away from him. Queen Louisa seemed to understand the situation: "I think that Russia has made a false step in being too easy—in trying to flatter, where she ought to have shown the utmost pride and strength".[2] Frederick William wrote early in July:

It would be vain to hope that the Emperor Alexander will ever speak to Napoleon with energy. All that he can do for me by way of conversation he will do,...but nothing more....In this sense all semblance of energy on the part of Russia has disappeared. They seem to resign themselves to necessity, as they say, and they are trying to come to business over Turkey.[3]

So the Czar weakened, and every minute that he faltered and delayed must have made him fall still more completely to the glamour of Tilsit, till Hardenberg and his conspiracies faded away from his mind, and the voice of the Prussians ceased to be compelling, and the trend of affairs so fixed itself that the last opportunity was gone.

The Prussians, on their side, did not make things easy for Alexander. The injured tone they perpetually adopted, their alternations of abjectness and bitter anger, their repeated wranglings concerning the preliminaries in negotiation, were sufficient to discount anything an ally could do for them. It must have become ludicrous to ask Napoleon to believe that they were anxious to bring cordiality into their relations with France. Besides hardening Napoleon's heart still more, the un-

[1] Ranke, *Hardenberg*, III, 493.
[2] Queen Louisa to King Frederick William III, 1 July 1807, in *Deutsche Rundschau*, CX, 208.
[3] King Frederick William III to Queen Louisa, 4 July 1807, in *Deutsche Rundschau*, CX, 216.

fortunate tone and gesture of the Prussians was calculated to estrange something in Alexander. Nothing could have made more glaring contrast than the demeanour of these people in the contingencies of the moment, set alongside their pretensions for the future. Hardenberg's plan was doomed, perhaps, to stumble and break upon Napoleon's irreconcilable soreness against Prussia, but on the eve of Tilsit Alexander had shown himself ready to be strong for the sake of his ally, had recognised that, since his friendship was important to Napoleon, he could afford to be exacting in return. He might have boldly demanded the inclusion of Frederick William in the benefits of the new system of policy; he might have regarded his connection with Prussia as more binding than the invitations of France; he might have put a pistol to the head of Napoleon. If he did not do this the Prussians were perhaps partly responsible; for they contrived to render themselves and their cause the most unattractive in the world, and they conducted themselves in a way that could only make their ambitions seem ridiculous.

Not that the Czar ever ceased to feel himself the friend of these unfortunate people, or ever consciously set out to deceive the man whom he had so long overwhelmed with kindness. It is difficult to believe that he would have continued raising the hopes of the Prussians if he had actually abandoned their design. It would be unjust to say that he was out to make alliance with France whatever might happen to his ally. He certainly would not be able to prophesy the harshness with which Napoleon would treat Prussia after the peace treaties were signed, or guess how the settlement of Tilsit was to be twisted into something which he did not mean. He would begin at Tilsit as the secret friend of the Prussian project, having the private intention of bringing Frederick William into his system, hoping to insinuate the ideas of Hardenberg by gradual steps into the negotiation. As the days went by it must have dawned upon him that he was leaving the Prussians on one side, but there would seem to have been a period when he refused actually to face the fact. Before the clear determination of Bonaparte and under the spell of this man's personality, he would allow himself to slide away from his first intentions by a quiet, almost unconscious transition. It would be easy for him to slip into a position in which he still felt kindly towards the Prussians, still interceded to secure an amelioration of their lot, but became accustomed to regarding them as poor victimised creatures instead of potential partners in the glory of Tilsit, and so allowed Hardenberg's scheme to drop entirely out of sight. We do not know how much Alexander over-estimated his influence with Napoleon, or how soon he hoped that his efforts would bring the Prussians back to favour. We cannot estimate what mood of dejection, what fever of exaltation made him finally surrender in a way that he had not intended, to the personality of Napoleon. But one thing we know—and this we have good reason to be sure of—that at some point during the interviews at Tilsit, he lost his grip on externalities, some mist over his eyes blurred his vision of the objective world, and before he knew it he was back in the sky, carried on the wings of a dream, so that flimsiest promises seemed to him for the moment like actualities and his faith fixed itself on things unsubstantial as a cloud. In this state of mind he was contented to lull himself with the unpledged words of the French Emperor, and to be fed with dainty allusions to schemes of empire in the east. It is little wonder that he allowed himself to lose concrete grasp and the critical eye in the matters that concerned his relations with the Prussians. So the astounding scheme flickered out, Alexander cannot greatly be blamed.[1] And in any case it was Hardenberg who had enunciated the principle that "necessity knows no law"—it was he who had provided the reasons to justify desertion of allies—it was he who had dangled before the eyes of the Czar the dream of a partition of Turkey.

[1] The Prussian king wrote to his minister in London of Alexander's efforts on his behalf: "Quelqu'eût été son désir de m'être utile et de me donner dans cette occasion décisive de nouvelles preuves réelles de son amitié, il y perdit ses peines. Les négociations restèrent isolées". Der König an Jacobi-Kloest, 19 Juli 1807, in Hassell, *Geschichte der Preussischen Politik* 1807 *bis* 1815, I, 339. This would confirm the view that the real diplomatic issue at Tilsit was the question of the joint negotiation of Russia and Prussia with France, such as Hardenberg hoped to see set on foot; and that Alexander hoped to secure this in his interviews with Napoleon.

In the volume of documents relating to this period, published by the Russian Historical Society, there are three letters in which the Chancellor Budberg explains the reasons for the change in Russian policy that came at Tilsit.[1] One is intended for Austria and is dated the 16/28th of June; the second is for the minister in Sweden and is presumably of the same date, for Budberg in a previous letter mentions these as though they were sent simultaneously; the third, which we can gather was sent later, was to Lord Granville Leveson-Gower, who in his own despatches gives the date as the 30th of June. The despatches for London and Vienna are a summary of the grievances of Russia, and excuse the defection of the Czar by blaming the apathy of other powers. But the one that is to inform the Swedes of the change of policy stands apart from these. It speaks of "the nobility, the loyalty, and the energy displayed by the King of Sweden", and adds that "whatever turn events may take, His Swedish Majesty may always count upon the sentiments of friendship and attachment which our August Sovereign has always entertained". This, written on the 28th or 29th of June, was communicated as late as the 3rd of July to the acting foreign minister in St Petersburg, as a statement of the policy of the Czar.[2] But the 5th article of the treaty of alliance concluded between France and Russia on the 7th of July, stipulates that if England refuses to make peace with Napoleon, under the mediation of the Czar, and if Sweden refuses to answer this by closing her ports against English shipping, recalling her ambassador from London and declaring war against Great Britain, then Sweden shall be "treated as an enemy" and even Denmark shall be compelled to declare against her.[3] Now it would have been easy for the Czar in the first place, if he had ever dreamed of this contingency, to fore-arm himself against the criticism that he was turning against an ally, whom he had so recently called "noble, loyal and energetic", and to whom he had so recently given renewed promises of undiminished attachment. The discrepancy between the Czar's intention and the actual commit-

[1] *Sbornik*, LXXXIX, 41–5.   [2] *Ibid.* LXXXIX, 40.
[3] *Ibid.* LXXXIX, 61–2.

ment at Tilsit, the contradiction between the impulsive generosity
of the former and the sinister cold cruelty of the latter, show the
kind of duality that was in the soul of Alexander. Also they seem
to confirm the idea that Alexander, after some days at Tilsit,
allowed himself to be drawn farther than he originally intended.
They corroborate the thesis of this essay: that at the very end of
June, or even later still, the Czar reached a new stage in his
discussions with Napoleon—reached it perhaps by an unconscious transition—and came to allow his new alliance to cut him
away from Prussia and Sweden to an extent which he had not
previously envisaged. He learned to accustom himself to a line
of thought which would have shocked him a little earlier. This
means that for a few days he kept his ground even at Tilsit;
either holding out against the enticements of Napoleon, or
refusing to face the full implications of what he was doing;
unless, during this time, Napoleon himself was waiting, holding
his hand until the propitious moment should come and only
disclosing his intentions as the Czar fell more completely before
the novel delights of Tilsit.

Alexander after Friedland did not leap to the great system of
Tilsit, by one sudden flash of thought, but as he came to feel at
home in one sort of thinking that would have revolted and
shocked him before, he allowed the idea of reconciliation with
Napoleon to pierce a little deeper into his mind and he pushed
his reasoning to a further stage. Napoleon had set out to win
him and had spared no effort to be charming. At every stage of
the negotiations he had played generous victor to the Russians
and had smiled beckoningly. One thing only was needed to
complete the spell, and this was an actual interview. First, a
desire to soften the victor's heart and facilitate an honourable
peace, would make Alexander desire the meeting; perhaps also
an eager curiosity to see this wonder of the world; perhaps, later,
an intention of creating an impression upon Napoleon and
securing a personal triumph. Long before the actual interview
the Czar had been moving towards Tilsit in order to be at hand.
The two Emperors met amid pomp and parade, and for some
days they had lengthy conversations. This was the forbidden

step that brought Alexander into the magic circle, for he was putting himself into the hands of a man who was conqueror above all in the personal interview, and who had a certain magnetism in himself that captivated the most hostile. If Napoleon set out to be charming Alexander was not the one to resist. He, the most impressionable of men, the most amenable to all immediate influences, simply asked to be won, to be charmed. Napoleon would play on his romanticisms, would please him with his generous gestures, and would exhaust the whole realm of plausibilities and illusions to capture the loyalty of this loyal soul. It is plain to see who was the dominant partner in the interviews. It is clear that Alexander did not meet Napoleon as an equal, as a prospective ally with whom he was transacting business—did not know how to be peremptory or rattle his sword or thunder out an ultimatum. His gullibility while in the actual presence of his old enemy, can scarcely be doubted. On the 3rd of July Frederick William writes:

Napoleon was very busy yesterday and worked above all with Talleyrand....The Emperor of Russia thinks he has information that this work chiefly concerned the projected partition of the Ottoman Porte, which seems to have become a favourite idea of Napoleon's....[1]

It is not the Prussians now who whisper their gigantic schemes in the ear of a receptive Czar. Alexander has found a new Hardenberg, and has rediscovered his Bartenstein.

The tragedy of Tilsit was that at a certain point in the discussions Alexander became sincere. If, for the sake of the interests of Russia he had been content to forgo his feelings and agree to a policy of co-operation with France—if he had conceded this with heart ever unreconciled—there came a time when he forgot all play-acting, forgot to be on his guard, and became inwardly reconciled, like a man who has found his true home. Alexander's was not a psychology that could content itself with compromise, however successful the compromise might be. He would not have been happy at the side of Napoleon if he had

---

[1] King Frederick William III to Queen Louisa, 3 July 1807, in *Deutsche Rundschau*, cx, 214–15.

remained there merely because it was profitable. Hardenberg had constantly urged that if there should be a reversal of policy, this should be carried out whole-heartedly, without mental reservations or attempts at half-measures. It is difficult to imagine the Prussians themselves, especially Queen Louisa, achieving the state of mind that would be necessary for this; but it is almost impossible to think of the Czar doing anything other than this. And so it came to pass that at times Alexander in his new alliance with Napoleon gave the appearance of a man who had been converted in religion rather than a ruler who had merely changed a policy. He seemed repelled by everything that reminded him of his former ways, and fell out of love with his old associates. It annoyed him to hear mention of some of his recent ministers who had thought they were furthering his interests by being fervent for the coalition. He did not seem to like to remember Razoumovski, Vorontsov, Alopeus.[1] They were men who had sacrificed Russia to a cause, and that cause a wrong and wretched one; they had beckoned and lured their Czar on a path which had proved disastrous and had never promised profit to the Empire; and they had made their own country a pawn in a game that was played for the benefit of others. Alexander gave vent to an indignation against England and Austria that was by no means a sham indignation. It was the recoil of a man who had come to feel that hitherto he had been blind. Like a converted sinner he looked regretfully back on the years that he had lost. He was grateful to Napoleon for winning him from the error of his ways. Now he had seen his salvation and the light had broken upon him. We find him writing to his sister, as one sure of corroboration and applause: "What do you think?...I! passing my days with Bonaparte, remaining for whole hours alone with him".[2] But his sister could not move so

---

[1] See e.g. Caulaincourt to Napoleon, No. 14, 31 Dec. 1807, in Grand-Duke Nicholas Mikhaïlovitch, *Relations diplomatiques de la Russie et de la France*, I, 41. See also Introduction to the same work, p. lxxi. Savary to Napoleon, 21 Oct. 1807, in *Sbornik*, LXXXIII, 148.

[2] Alexander to Grand-Duchess Catherine, 17 June 1807, in Grand-Duke Nicholas Mikhaïlovitch, *Correspondance d'Alexandre Ier avec la Grande-Duchesse Cathérine*.

quickly, she was still in the days before Tilsit, she could walk—
she could not fly. She took the liberty of saying "what she
thought"—

> I will not make my peace with this peace...unless we secure great
> acquisitions, the Vistula...the Danube. For without these we shall
> have nothing but shame for fraternising with a man against whom
> we have rightly raised our voices in condemnation, and there will not
> be the smallest real gain or honour for Russia in return.[1]

A Hardenberg could bring out a reversal of policy, a new
diplomatic scheme, if a crisis confronted him, and could do it
impersonally, as one would solve a mathematical problem. With
him it was a direct adjustment to a situation or a necessity, a
conscious and deliberate reorganisation of practical issues, a
manipulation with things outside himself; and the whole process,
in one sense, left his personality untouched, went on so to speak
above his head. Alexander could not rest here. Having put
himself under such a system of policy and purposes he had to
project himself into these, till he and they became interfused.
He did not patch the new policy mechanically on to his political
system, he grafted it upon himself and took it into his blood.
What in others would have been a mere question of diplomacy,
in him developed into a mighty issue of the soul. He did not
merely become the calculating ally of Napoleon; he added to the
relationship a new dimension, an extension in personality; he
came away from Tilsit more than an impersonal ally—an enthusiastic and adoring friend, priding himself peculiarly in the
human side of his contacts with Napoleon, betraying towards
the man that expansiveness of heart which he had once shown to
Czartoryski and which he seems to have yearned to show to
somebody. In the same way he had shown a friendship for
Frederick William of Prussia which was not commensurable
with the actual political alliance of the two governments.
Tilsit did not remain for him merely the seat of a negotiation,
a place of practical transactions; he fondled it in his memory,
to him it was more like a sacred lover's rendezvous; he would

[1] Grand-Duchess Catherine to Alexander, 25 June 1807, in Grand-Duke
Nicholas Mikhaïlovitch, *Correspondance*.

refer to it as to some epoch in the life of his spirit, a day of his soul's renewing; he would think of it essentially as a portentous human moment. He did not merely find excuses for breaking with England, did not with misgivings and reluctance declare war against his former ally; he became bitter and indignant and hostile as the French, and himself urged Napoleon to conclude no peace with the court of London.

So the mere outlines of events at Tilsit, considered as a diplomatic transaction, are nothing as compared with the richness of the moments as spiritual experience to Alexander. There was something in the man that is not commensurable with the map that we can make of the outward acts and happenings of his life. The whole of him did not externalise itself in actual deeds, in concrete facts and forms; much was wasted in spiritual anxieties and secret introspection and terrible searchings of soul —much was lost by a desolating process that was a sort of internal combustion. The truth is that he lived in an imperfect relationship with the world of actuality, and never quite found that world adequate to his inner mind. And, as his inner experience far outran his concrete life, overflowing the mould in which it could find overt forms for itself, there is more in his history than can actually register itself in tangible measurable facts. History must take account of this, and look upon events with an inward eye, if it is to keep pace with the movement of things at Tilsit; the narrative must break into an essay. The effort to understand the Czar is more like the effort to understand a literary mind; the days count for little, and happenings are not the important matter, and it is essential to value events in their relation to an inner experience. A trivial incident may snarl into terrible importance and leap at us like a gargoyle because of its mysterious interrelation with an individual's state of mind. We find ourselves in a world where causes seem hopelessly inadequate to effects. Time itself will seem violated in the way the mind of the man becomes reorganised to make something like a change of personality, all the process telescoped into one day that shows no sign of outward events adequate to the change. With Alexander, more even than with most personalities, it is necessary

not to infer the man from the deed, from the outward form, but
to bring his whole lifetime to the elucidation of any particular
moment, and to use the psychology of the individual as we know
him, for the illumination of any specific act. Above all things it
is necessary to bring the story out of the plane of mere incident
and event.

That Alexander intended to make personal profit out of the
transactions with Napoleon is a fact beyond all doubt; for
Alexander, even when he flew away with the most far-fetched
visionary schemes could hold one eye narrowly fixed upon the
most definite mundane self-interests. This characteristic was like
a black streak across his soul. When in the year 1804 he put
forward schemes that have no comparison save with those of
President Wilson, urging the formation of a league of nations,
pressing the governments to join him in a crusade to end war,
and even enunciating a principle of national "self-determination",
he had a dark under-current of ambition and was planning to
secure a partition of Turkey which should give Russia Moldavia,
the Dardanelles, Constantinople, Corfu and the important
stronghold of Cattaro on the Adriatic Sea. And if at Tilsit he
overlooked the necessity of securing definite guarantees from
Napoleon, still the very thing which intoxicated his mind was
the grand prospect, the large perspective of a scheme to give
him dominion in Turkey; and when he returned to St Petersburg
we soon find that the more earthly, the more calculating side of
his mind, has gained the fuller possession; he urges Napoleon
to hasten the partition of the Porte, and shows himself energetic
and resourceful and importunate; he is clever enough to declare
that the Russians are more "realist" than he himself, that they
will not be reconciled to the new alliance unless they see concrete
advantages. Even though the French secured the tactical gain
in the treaties, the emergence of this side of the Czar's character
proved that even Napoleon perhaps had illusions at Tilsit; and
in this matter, history itself is liable to be cheated. It was not
without reason that after 1815 the very allies of Russia began
to fear this Alexander, as formerly they had feared Napoleon—
suspecting that his dreams and mysticisms and apocalyptic air

were but the cloak for unscrupulous self-seeking. It was wrong to think for a moment that he was a black deceiver, a clever hypocrite; the higher side of his nature did not cloak or merely disguise the lower; each existed concurrently and in each he was simultaneously sincere; and the elusiveness of the man, both to contemporaries and to later historians, lay in the fact that he could change without conscious transition or evil intent from the most quixotic of idealists to the most bold and determined of self-seekers. The dreamer had a queer under-side to himself; just as his signature would vary from one day to another, his conduct, his moods, his total attitude to things would alter in such a way that it is misleading to look for a unifying principle in his life and it is an over-simplification to call him an imposter. Now we find him working for eighteen hours a day; now he will neglect even the most urgent business for months. At one time he is a liberal, planning to reverse the course of Russian history; at another he is a dark reactionary, trembling for law and order. Here we find him leading a crusade against Napoleon; there he is adoring the man, rejoicing to call him friend. At Bartenstein he will forget all else in his rôle of deliverer of Europe; at Vienna he will be willing to wreck a congress for the sake of his ambitions in Poland. In all these things he is equally sincere, equally himself, over and over again he will be heartily repentant of his former self; very often the two natures of the man will be confounded, and it will be on the wing of some concrete self-seeking that we shall find him rising to vague visions which cloud his perception of his interests. He is unbalanced, unstable, impressionable, like a person who has never grown up. He is a Russian to delight the heart of Dostoevsky—"the man of acute sensibility, the man who hails not from Nature's womb but from a chemical retort"—with a strong element of German mysticism, but still with the background of Russia behind that, and something in him of the contradictions of "a chaotic, split, irrational tragic race".

CHAPTER IV

NAPOLEON AND THE SYSTEM OF TILSIT

TALLEYRAND, writing to congratulate the victor of Friedland, ventured to season his compliments with a warning:

"But it is not that I picture this victory", he said, "merely as a matter for glory. I like to consider it as a forerunner, a pledge of peace....I like to think of it as the last which Your Majesty will be obliged to win; that is why I value it so much; for, fine as it is, I must confess that it would lose more in my estimation than I can say, if Your Majesty had to go forward to new battles, and expose yourself to fresh perils."[1]

Talleyrand had no desire to see the success pursued across the Niemen; and his was no outcast voice, wilfully perversely protesting. The war had out-spent the impulse; victory had come, but it had come late in the day; behind the broken armies of the Czar unrolled the unenticing north, and no one knew what Russia could fall back upon, in hidden reserve of power. A homesickness came over the troops; "from Napoleon, or at least from the marshals, to the drummer-boys, all the army without exception clamoured to return to France"; according to Mackenzie, a British agent at the allied headquarters, there was a report that when a Russian negotiator reached the French lines he was saluted with loud cries of "vive la paix"; and it was observed by a French officer who accompanied Duroc on a mission to the Russian generals, "that all hands must now be tired by the length and obstinacy of the campaign. If the rival Emperors wished for another, let them fight together".[2]

It may be true that Napoleon himself was not given to such nostalgia. Perhaps he was not the man to loiter dreaming of the return of peace that summer-time in Europe. Yet we may take

---

[1] P. Bertrand, *Lettres inédites de Talleyrand à Napoléon Ier*, No. cccxix.

[2] Letter of Mackenzie enclosed in G. Leveson-Gower's "separate" despatch to Canning, 26 June 1807, in J. H. Rose, *Napoleonic Studies*, p. 157.

it that he would wish a truce to the kind of warfare he had lately been pursuing, that even with victory at the end of it he had found the campaign bleak and wasteful, and that he had fought his Friedland with an air of finality. When we have made all allowance for words of politeness and flattery that were part of the vocabulary, the ritual of Tilsit, we may say that he had a genuine respect for his Russian enemy; his self-assurance had not risen to the point of bigotry that it reached in 1812. He was not confident of the Austrians, could not hope to hold them neutral for ever, could not dare, perhaps, to offer them temptation in his rear. Even if we admit that a thought may come into a mind like a new star out of the emptiness, we may say that these elements of the political situation conditioned if they did not determine, at this point, Napoleon's desire for peace; they were the constituent factors of the problem which evoked the new decision. He could not hope to dictate terms as though his armies were at St Petersburg. He had not, this time, struck the crowning blow which could enable him to dispose the situation at will, like an ordaining god. He had merely beaten an army in the field and so had produced rather the position that existed after Austerlitz—had creased and crumpled the wings of the Czar's crusading passion, had disorganised and discredited one more coalition that had threatened him, and by this had won a certain field in which he had no further need to fear that Russia would intervene to thwart his imperial designs.

Yet it may be presumed that there was to be no question of another Oubril. The old dilemma might arise—Napoleon to forgo some of his pretensions in Europe, or to drive his armies further into Russia. Napoleon had no intention of beating against these alternatives any more. No one could equal him in making virtue of necessity. No mind could be so flexible in the face of new contingencies. He would recast his map of Europe, reshuffle his policies, and achieve a new synthesis to sweep the whole range of his problems. The power he could not conquer he would turn into an ally. The government which had jealously worked to guard Europe against his ambitions, he would win over as accomplice. In 1806 he had suggested to the

British cabinet something like a division of empire; England to hold the seas, but to leave France her supremacy on the continent. The system of 1807 has a different line of demarkation: Russia shall have the east, empire of mosque and minaret; France shall be left to work her will in western Europe. This is the idea of Tilsit, and this is the way we are compelled to rationalise it for ourselves, and to relate it to the purposes of Napoleon; though it is impossible to find out how the new inspiration, the lightning fusion of ideas and motives, the crowning imaginative resolve, flashes into the mind of a genius. Whoever was responsible for small elements of the settlement at Tilsit, the wide sweep of the arc, the culminating, all-embracing thought, was Napoleon's; and his was the directing mind. It was he who from the outset made every effort to be gracious to the Czar. It was he who so fixed the large lines of the peace treaties that they left him master of the continent. It was he who secured the present advantages, the immediate, palpable gains; pushing his chief concessions into the vagueness and remoteness of the future.

History must stand baffled when a personal conversation is to be recovered, and even in diplomatic transactions where the issues are more precise than in larger human affairs, a vagueness must always hang around the story when the event turns on direct verbal discussions. At such times we strain our eyes to find precision where a twilight dimness, which at once teases and enchants, gives us blurred contours, gives us colour but not line, gives us the vagueness of half-remembered things. Occasional scraps of the conversations at Tilsit come to us on a puff of wind; but lost from their larger context they may lure us on a false trail. So we can merely see Alexander moving mysteriously as the men around him saw him; we can merely have a Rembrandt picture with little gleams of light against a dark background. Perhaps there will always be people to argue that at Tilsit it was Napoleon who was the dupe, and Alexander the grand deceiver; and in discussing such a matter, it is a mistake to dogmatise too heavily. We know that before the Emperors met they had each independently decided to seek the alliance of the other; they had each by separate routes found the climax of their thinking in a project of partition of the Ottoman Porte. If Napoleon at Tilsit imagined that he had secured a perpetual ally and accomplice in a Czar who would complacently forgo all his own interests in Poland and Turkey, then indeed Napoleon was the dupe at Tilsit. But from the vagueness and remoteness of his promises of Turkish partition; from the way in which, when he returned to Paris, he turned round and said "that he saw no advantage for France in the dismemberment of the Ottoman Empire, that he asked for nothing more than to guarantee its integrity";[1] from the absence of any sign on his part that he had the least intention of carrying out his promises; from the fact that it was the Czar who was the persistent futile beseecher in this matter, after the conclusion of the treaties—we can infer that Napoleon was luring the Czar with visions which he never for a moment intended to convert into actualities, that he was quite well aware of how some time he would be found out and would come into collision with Russian policy; we might safely say that he conceived of the arrangement as an interim one, destined to secure him the maritime peace which he desired and to enable him to consolidate his empire in the west, also perhaps to postpone the renewal of the more decisive conflict with Russia. If he dreamed that the alliance with the Czar would solve his western problems, once again he was mistaken; but the check which he received in Spain, and behind that the grim persistence of the British government, caused his failure here, rather than any half-heartedness of Russia. And when he drove his army to Moscow in 1812 with Prussians and Austrians at his side, he had found a more favourable political period for the pursuit of his further struggles with the Czar than the summer of 1807 would have been, when the Prussians were ranged against him and the Austrians were prepared to growl sullenly in his rear. If there was a dupe, this must rather have been the Czar. It was he who thought that the partition of Turkey was "a favourite idea of Napoleon's". It was he who wrote joyfully to his sister: "What do you think?...I! passing my days with Bonaparte...". The man who, after the treaties had been

---

[1] Tolstoy to Romantsov, 26 Oct./7 Nov. 1807, in *Sbornik*, LXXXIX, 178.

concluded, showed himself the more embarrassed in diplomacy by the documents he had signed was not Napoleon but Alexander. The alliance must be regarded as essentially a master-move of Napoleon himself.

If Napoleon had long advertised the fact that he must find an ally somewhere in Europe, he had given it to be understood that only in the last resort would the ally be Russia. Experimenting with various moves and combinations, he had not seriously entertained the idea of making a connection with the Czar. He had even dismissed the notion as fanciful, and if he talked of it at all, it was merely to raise apprehension in Prussia and Austria. His attempts to secure a separate peace with the Prussians had been measures of undisguised hostility against Russia. At Tilsit, when both Alexander and Frederick William were in his presence, he insisted that he had never dreamed of fighting Prussia but that he had promised himself to have the government of Berlin at his side in a war against the Czar.[1] If he tried to win over the Austrians or to entice a Sultan or to patronise a Shah of Persia, this was always part of a large scheme to make Russia the grand enemy. And for a long time he had laid great importance in all negotiations, whether with friend or with foe, upon the securing of a guarantee against the designs which Russia might have in respect to the Ottoman Porte.

At Tilsit, whatever the points at issue had been, Napoleon abandoned his quarrel with Russia, or at least thrust it for the moment into the background. He shelved the designs or postponed the jealousies that he had had on the whole subject of the Ottoman Porte. Perhaps some dream of dominion in the west, and enterprises in Spain, had come uppermost in his mind. Perhaps everything else had become subordinate to his desire to see the isolation of England. We may even picture the diplomacy of Napoleon as moving with a certain rhythm, Russia and England standing as two arch-enemies whom he could never quite reach and overthrow in the way in which he dismissed Prussia and Austria; so that alternately one or the other had to

---

[1] Frederick William III to Queen Louisa, 26 June 1807, in *Deutsche Rundschau*, CX, 41.

become the prime object of his hostility, only to leave him frustrate. On this interpretation the problem of England might be said to have come into the forefront of Napoleon's mind in June 1807, driving him to make terms with the Czar. It was to be Russia's turn again in 1812. But perhaps it is most true to say that one straightforward purpose is not sufficient to account for any of his great strokes of policy. In his mind everything was astonishingly interwoven. A number of expedients dove-tailed into one another, a number of plans worked into one great design, a mosaic of problems solved by one sweep of thought—that is how one is compelled to envisage a Napoleonic master-move. We are guilty of a kind of Hegelian fallacy, we are imputing to Napoleon too much of the mind of a philosopher intent on unifying his thought, we are forgetting how much he made his decisions with the mind of a strategist, if we assume that his policy had one central running purpose, to which all his actions can ultimately find reference. He had no fixed star in his sky, no definite plan for the day after to-morrow to be an obsession to his mind, and if he had a vision of the future he purposely kept it vague and fluid and essentially contingent. At a crisis like that of Tilsit such an opportunist does not merely reorganise his policy in the light of one all-consuming purpose; he changes his actual purposes and we must make a new map of his mind. Napoleon merely saw in an alliance with Russia a solution to more of his immediate problems and an opening to larger schemes of aggrandisement than he could discover in any alternative method of dealing with the Czar at that moment. In the most literal meaning of the words he changed one bag of tricks for another, with his eye upon the contingencies of the passing day.

Sweeping many things out of sight for the time being, one may concentrate upon the significance of the Russian alliance in respect to Napoleon's peace policy. It is a question that narrows down still further, to the single problem of peace with England, since the conclusion of the Polish campaign brought the collapse of the continental resistance. To trace out one set of implications in a complex Napoleonic decision, to disentangle one element and examine it in isolation, is an artificial way of splitting up the facts of history: and though it may be a necessary step to a fuller and more final reintegration of the past, it is only valid if we accompany it with a mental reservation. By our very act of concentrating upon it the question of peace with England will assume a factitious importance. We shall be compelled to check ourselves from saying that it is the key to the mystery of Tilsit. We shall be in danger of making the whole history of this time swing around the one principle that we have taken as the central object of attention.

In the revolutions that occur in characters, in policies, in institutions and in thought, some threads can always be tracked down to vindicate the continuity of history and the persistence of vital principles; and if Napoleon in the summer of 1807 broke off one line of policy completely, he succeeded at the same time not merely in maintaining the continuity of a line of thought, and persistence in one process of action, but in carrying what had hitherto taken place to a climax, and in raising it to a higher power. Tilsit, which is in some way a shifting of centre in Napoleonic policy, and which in regard to some questions seems to come as a bomb from the sky, is at the same time in one matter merely the next step of an argument, the rational working-out of a principle already in operation, the logical conclusion of what has gone before. It is a further development of what, in the fullest meaning of the words, may be called the Continental System.

Having assured himself of the mastery of the continent by his alliance with the Czar Alexander, Napoleon proceeded to turn his system of Tilsit into a stupendous instrument for war. He set the angle to which all the governments of Europe had to swerve in their contacts with Great Britain, and he made them give due leverage to his policy towards that power. He would punish the continent for England's refusal to come to terms with him, and keep his army sprawled across Europe until there should be a settlement. No peace in St Petersburg or Vienna, no rest from Hamburg to Naples so long as the war continued. This was an ideal state of affairs to induce the governments to desire a maritime peace. The system of Tilsit left room for no more neutrality; all the powers were to combine in a grand boycott of Great Britain; "drive the English diplomatic establishments out of Europe", was to be the imperial command. But these things soon wriggled themselves into more arguments for peace. You might compel the powers to shut out British merchandise from their coasts; but compulsion was answered only by unwilling ineffective compliance. You might order the governments that called themselves neutral to break with the government of England; but the command merely produced declarations of war that were little more than a kind of legal fiction. The powers feared the retaliation of Great Britain. Some of them hoped to see their strength restored by England's influence in negotiation. They were unwilling to show even the semblance of hostility towards the cabinet of London. There was only one course left open to them. It was not any superadded compulsion, it was the mere implications of the system of Tilsit, that urged the European states to work for the conclusion of peace; and, moved by an inner impulsion, they were often more earnest, more pressing, and more resourceful, than if they had started into action at a mere word of command.

BOOK FOUR

ENGLAND AND THE SYSTEM OF TILSIT

CHAPTER I

PRUSSIAN ATTEMPTS TO INDUCE ENGLAND TO MAKE PEACE

THE king of Prussia had lost more than he had actually signed away in the clauses of his treaty of Tilsit; for the terms to which he had submitted were not a peace and a forgetting. There was nothing to prevent Napoleon from still further exploiting his downfall; there was nothing to make it certain that Napoleon would keep the stipulations of the treaty which he had himself dictated. If the Czar still stood as the advocate of his unfortunate friend, he had changed his ground in that he had ceased to make the welfare of Prussia the first charge upon his efforts; and at best he was in a position to do little more than come forward with an appealing gesture. He could not prevent the continued military occupation of Prussian territory. He could not induce Napoleon to treat Prussia as a power with which he had made peace. Frederick William could not hope to see Berlin until he had paid impossible indemnities. It seemed that the Prussians were not to breathe freely again until all Europe should be at peace, and the last pretext for Napoleon's vindictiveness be altogether removed.

When a new English minister took up his residence at the Prussian court, Count Goltz, the successor of Hardenberg, gave expression to the belief that it would be "a leading object in a negotiation for peace that Great Britain should provide for the strengthening of the Prussian monarchy".[1] At a time when the French were draining money from the country, making every possible exaction, the Prussians flattered themselves with the hope that England would come forward with a loan to relieve the difficulties of the monarchy; though such a loan would merely have placed more money in the pockets of the French.[2] The Russian minister at Memel declared that

the Queen and her Court and all who wish to please her, have gone to the point of the ridiculous in their Anglomania. To listen to them,

[1] G. Garlike to G. Canning, No. 15, 15 Sept. 1807, *F.O. Prussia* 64/76.
[2] G. Garlike to G. Canning, No. 2, 26 Aug. 1807 and No. 5, 27 Aug. 1807, *F.O. Prussia* 64/76.

there is no doubt that England, when she makes peace with France, will have the interests of Prussia in view above everything else.[1]

Setting their hopes in this way upon England and upon a revision of the settlement of Tilsit, the Prussians might have been tempted to applaud the persistence of England in carrying on the war. They had reason to rejoice in the successes that British enterprises might obtain; they were able still to pray that Napoleon might come to his undoing. So we find that with some lack of tact they betray their joy in the expedition to Copenhagen, in Canning's summary treatment of Denmark. At the risk of intensifying the anger of the French they show great favour and welcome to Englishmen in their country.[2] They cause displeasure even in Russia by allowing a British minister to continue at their court. The only excuse they can offer is that the man has not delivered his credentials and so is no more than a private citizen.[3] The Prussians, who for so long have been on no happy terms with Great Britain, are of a sudden all friendliness and creep hazardously close. They are eager to stand well with the one remaining government that has the power to extort from Napoleon a revision of the treaties of Tilsit. It is inevitable that they will not desire to alienate the English ministers and at the same time incur new dangers and obligations for themselves by declaring war against the power to which they trust for their own restoring. They have not forgotten the inconvenience they suffered from the blockade of a year ago; they have no desire to invite the retaliation of England to the closing of their ports. So if they are compelled to join Napoleon in the great war of land against sea, they will delay the moment as long as possible, and in the meantime they will give every indication of friendship to Great Britain so that their complicity with France will be seen to be purely involuntary.[4] They dread the

[1] Krüdener to Romantsov, 30 Sept./12 Oct. 1807, in *Sbornik*, LXXXIX, 93 (see also p. 238).

[2] *Sbornik*, LXXXIX, 94.

[3] *Ibid.* 239. See also Der König an Jacobi, 27 Aug. 1807; Hassell, *Geschichte der Preussischen Politik* 1807 *bis* 1815, I, 346.

[4] G. Jackson to G. Canning, No. 4, 24 July 1807 and *Private*, 24 July 1807, *F.O. Jackson Papers*, 353/55. See also despatches between Jacobi-Kloest and the Prussian government in Hassell, *op. cit.* I, 340 *et seq.*

inevitable moment. They hate the dilemma they are in. They suffer from the prolongation of the war. Beneath everything they desire the end of hostilities and upheaval, and they look to the conclusion of a final general peace in which their own interests shall not be passed over.[1] Finally by a curious inversion they come to be impatient with the British government for obstinately continuing the war and cheating them of their hopes.

"There is nothing but the return of general peace that can save the existence of Prussia and prevent a final overthrow of the whole Continent", wrote Goltz to Jacobi, the Prussian Minister in London. "This truth is too obvious to escape the eyes of the British Ministry, but all the same you will do well to put it forward in all its strength, and try the ground and see if in the counsels of His Britannic Majesty there is still cherished a serious intention of re-entering into pourparlers with France, and putting an end to the evils of war."[2]

The Prussian king was of the opinion that this was "the wisest thing that the Cabinet of St James's could do", and that it was "the only means of raising Prussia again, and of saving the rest of the Continent".[3] He complained that the British government did not show sufficient moderation. And when the Prussian minister in London was compelled to ask for his passports, he expressed the renewed desire of his court to see "a prompt and happy general peace restored soon".

The Prussian king ordered his minister, in parting from the English foreign secretary, to say

that as soon as matters begin to disentangle themselves a little and I have an idea that the question of a general peace is being raised, I shall send a trusted man to London. He will come as an ordinary traveller, and will be charged to renew our relations secretly, and he will be able to act as intermediary between the two Cabinets.[4]

Canning's reply was that "Nobody in this country could fail to recognise how much England ought to take to heart the question

[1] See e.g. G. Garlike to G. Canning, No. 42, 21 Dec. 1807, *F.O. Prussia* 64/76.
[2] Der König an Jacobi, 6 Nov. 1807, in Hassell, *op. cit.* p. 352.
[3] Der König an Jacobi, 12 Nov. 1807, in Hassell, *op. cit.* I, 353. The king goes on to criticise the English proposals made to the Czar by Sir Robert Wilson (see below, p. 298 *et seq.*) as far from moderate.
[4] Der König an Jacobi, 29 Nov. 1807, in Hassell, *op. cit.* I, 354.

of ameliorating the lot of Prussia in general, and promoting his
independence in particular"; but he did not hint that these
problems would find an early or easy solution. "He greatly
feared that serious negotiations for peace with France were far
distant; he did not at this moment see a glimmer of hope." Yet,
if discussions should be opened and the Prussian king cared to
dispatch a person of confidence to London, "under any guise
whatever", the man would probably receive a welcome.[1]

The Prussians imagined the settlement of Tilsit to be for them
an interim one. They contemplated a future pacification in
which their interests should not be overlooked; they hoped that
they themselves should have a voice in its arrangement, and that
their situation should come under revision. This hope made them
eager to hasten the moment of final settlement. They, like other
continental powers, hankered to see the British government
bring its overseas conquests out of storage, and dangle them
before Napoleon, and barter them for the welfare of Europe.
Canning was willing to accept the principle and "take to heart
the question of ameliorating the lot of Prussia"; but Frederick
William and his ministers would seem to have lost sight of an
important element in the problem. Napoleon after Tilsit had
greatly raised his pretensions; now, less than ever, would he
be willing to admit English interference on the continent; the
maritime peace, for him, was to be a private transaction between
England and France; it was to adjust the legitimate interests
of the two contracting powers; he would not allow it to roam
over the whole field of continental relations; he had no intention
of making it a revised edition of the treaties of Tilsit.

[1] Jacobi an den König, 10 Feb. 1808, in Hassell, *op. cit.* I, 360. It seems
that the king's speech at the opening of the English Parliament gave
Napoleon reason to suspect the existence of some intimacy and secret
understanding between Prussia and England, and the French minister of
foreign affairs gave a hint to the Prussian minister in Paris that this had
done harm to the Prussian cause. Report of Brockhausen, 22 Feb. 1808,
in Hassell, *op. cit.* I, 495.

CHAPTER II

THE RUSSIAN MEDIATION

By article 14 of the treaty of peace concluded at Tilsit, Napoleon accepted the mediation of the Czar for the establishment of peace between France and England, on the condition "that this mediation be also accepted by England within one month after the ratifications of the present treaty have been exchanged".

Article 4 of the secret treaty of alliance at Tilsit ran:

If England does not accept the mediation of Russia, or if, having accepted it, she has not by the 1st of November consented to conclude peace, recognising that the flags of all the powers are to enjoy equality and independence on the seas, and restoring the conquests secured from France and the allies of France since 1805, a note shall be communicated to the Cabinet of St James by the Ambassador of [Russia] at some time during the said month of November. This Note...shall contain the positive and explicit declaration, that, on the refusal of England to conclude peace under the above-named conditions...the Ambassador of Russia will receive by December the first, the eventual order to ask for his passports on the said date, and to leave England immediately.

Article 7 of the same treaty stated that if England made peace on the above terms, Hanover should be restored to the king in return for French, Spanish and Dutch colonies. The rest of the document provided for the extension of the continental system, and the ranging of all Europe on the side of France, in the event of the Russian mediation proving unsuccessful. Napoleon explained to the Czar that, if the war should have to continue, the date the 1st of December would fall conveniently for Russia.[1] This was the beginning of winter and would give an interval of five months before action could be taken, while in the meantime the British government might reconsider its decision. A little later Napoleon sketched out a note which would serve for the official announcement of the treaties of Tilsit and of the proposed

[1] *Corresp. de Nap. Ier*, t. xv, No. 12865.

mediation.[1] A note substantially the same was presented to the English foreign secretary on the 1st of August by Maximilian Alopeus, Russian minister in London.[2]

Russia in these early years of the nineteenth century was unfortunate in the way her affairs were handled by her ministers abroad. Perhaps her fate was that of a nationality not yet realised; the same drawbacks are to be discovered in American diplomacy for a long period. In Russia there seems to have been difficulty in finding sufficient talent at home to work the machinery of state; from the time of Peter I, offices high and low had very often fallen to foreigners. So under Alexander we find Czartoryski, a Pole, and Pozzo di Borgo, a Corsican; the physician who attended the Emperor and was present at Tilsit was a British subject; and if Budberg belonged to the Empire he was a Teuton from the Baltic provinces. At the same time there was something lacking in the way foreign affairs were managed from the centre. Men who are sent for service to capitals abroad must tend to form attachments in the place where they have their stay, and err by excess of sympathy for the point of view of the country in which they reside. But with Russian ministers at this period the tendency was more distinct than is even usual.[3] These envoys, like the Americans in the nineteenth century, seemed to surrender to the glamour of the courts and capitals of western Europe, compared with which their own St Petersburg was perhaps a little uncouth. Razoumovski became one of the Viennese, and, even when superseded at his official post, did not care to return to Russia. Similarly Vorontsov made his home in England. Having imperfect contacts with a distant and defective centre these ministers

---

[1] *Corresp. de Nap. Ier*, t. xv, No. 12884.

[2] Alopeus to Canning, 1 Aug. 1807, in *Parliamentary Debates*, x, cols. 113–14 (No. 4).

[3] De Maistre in his *Mémoires et Correspondance*, p. 201, describes the suspiciousness of the Russian court in regard to foreign ministers resident in St Petersburg ("Elle décachette toutes nos lettres"), but he proceeds: "Et cette même cour souffre que ses ministres vieillissent près des cours étrangères, qu'ils y deviennent propriétaires, s'y marient, et que leurs dettes (ceci est curieux) y soient complètement payés par le souverain du lieu, enfin qu'ils y soient naturalisés par le fait".

tended to fall all the more readily to the influences that were immediate; and this affected their transaction of business, until occasionally it seemed to amount to a transference of loyalty. We find in the twentieth century that President Wilson, sending a minister to London, will say: "Now, be an American! Our men only last six months in England; then they become anglicised". In the same way we discover Alexander, with eyes newly opened at Tilsit, turning away from men who have served him for years, denouncing them for their apostasy and reproaching them with having neglected the interests of the Empire.

This is how the imperial displeasure had come to fall upon Maximilian Alopeus. This man, who was almost sixty years of age when he was transferred to London in 1807, had served for many years as Russian minister at Berlin. There the French ambassador described him as "consummate in intrigues". At the time of the second partition of Poland he was accused of acting in connivance with the Prussians, and there were grounds for controversy as to whether he had been in the pay of the ministers in Berlin, even concocting his despatches with their assistance.[1] An English minister once mentioned him as one of those foreign representatives who were "much more like *agents* of [the Prussian] Court than like men of rank sent to attend to the interests of their own".[2] At the time of the third partition of Poland, Alopeus was again suspected of sacrificing the advantage of Russia to that of the government at Berlin. In the year 1800 he was relieved of his functions in the diplomatic service at St Petersburg because Rostoptchin considered him "Prussian in body and soul". And five years later, when he was once more resident minister in the Prussian capital, an envoy despatched on a special mission to that place was instructed to keep watch over him, and examine his actions and discover why the intimacy and obvious good relations which he enjoyed in Berlin had resulted in so little that was of any advantage to

---

[1] Lord, *Second Partition of Poland* (1915), p. 111 (note 3). Lord in this controversy takes the view that, although undoubtedly pro-Prussian, Alopeus was not actually in the pay of Prussia.

[2] *Dropmore*, II, 493 (Lord Malmesbury to Lord Grenville. Private. 9 Jan. 1794).

Russia. The agent was ordered to send a special report to St Petersburg, so that the Czar might decide how much confidence he could place in his representative.[1] In those days the electric telegraph had not yet given governments quick control over their ministers. A man like Alopeus enjoyed a peculiar kind of autonomy at his foreign post. Perhaps it must be charged to the inadequacy of the Russian diplomatic service that, living in such an atmosphere of suspicion, Alopeus was employed until his sixtieth year.

In 1807 he came to England with a reputation for industry and intrigue. He was known as a strong pro-Prussian and life-long friend of Hardenberg. The appointment was not popular. Englishmen distrusted everything that found breath in Berlin; there was an idea that Alopeus had been sent to London chiefly out of consideration for Prussia; he had come to exorcise that devil that was in Englishmen; it was even said that he had been appointed because the queen of Prussia implored it of the Czar. We soon hear that the Alopeus family have buried themselves in Richmond; they see little of society, and "do not get along very famously". The minister himself "has no confidences for anybody except Jacobi", the Prussian representative; he "conceals everything from other people and employs nobody but his confidential secretary Benckendorff, who was with him at Berlin".[2] He ignores even Vorontsov, who might bring him into touch with English sentiment. Canning himself makes the assertion that he believes the man to be watched by an agent who secretly informs against him direct to St Petersburg.[3] This seems to be the reason for something unaccountably acrimonious in the representations of Alopeus to the British government.

After the peace of Tilsit the Russian government did not pay any serious attention to Alopeus in England. This minister, if he had had no other failings, was too much a man of the coalition. No attempt was made to inform him of the inner purposes of his

[1] F. de Martens, *Recueil*, VI, 358 (Instructions to Baron Winzingerode, 16 Jan. 1805).

[2] *Vorontsov Archives*, XVII, 156.

[3] Canning to G. Leveson-Gower, No. 17, 20 June 1807, *F.O. Russia* 65/69.

court, or to put him into touch with the intimate sentiments of
the Czar. A note was despatched to him announcing the conclusion of the treaties and the offer of mediation, and he was
merely instructed to present this to the British government.[1]
For the rest he was more in the dark than even Canning himself;
was left at the mercy of garbled reports in English newspapers;
and was at a loss when he had to decide how the Russian reversal
of policy was to be construed and acted upon.

The position was serious and disquieting for Englishmen,
because Leveson-Gower, who had been sent to the Czar in
Poland, was equally left in perplexity. The Russian chancellor
merely evaded him while the negotiations were proceeding, and
finally, in a letter of the 30th of June, informed him that there
had been a change of policy. "The conduct which has been
pursued by your government of late", wrote Budberg, "is
calculated completely to justify the determination which the
Czar has just taken."[2] The air of mystery that hung around the
proceedings at Tilsit, and the silence and secrecy of the Russians,
filled Englishmen with apprehension.[3] Everything that happened
seemed to reinforce the growing suspicions. In a private letter
of the middle of July the English minister wrote from St
Petersburg:

Whilst in England Politicians are occupying themselves in squabbles
in Parliament, and the People in following Sir F. Burdett's Chair,
the most deadly blows are aiming at the very existence of the country;

[1] Alopeus informed Jacobi-Kloest, the Prussian minister in London, that
he had not received a copy of the Treaty of Tilsit (Jacobi an den König,
3 Aug. 1807, in Hassell, *Geschichte der Preussischen Politik 1807 bis 1815*,
I, 342). See also p. 348.

[2] *Sbornik*, LXXXIX, 44.

[3] "Lord Hutchinson, le général Wilson essayaient d'employer leur crédit
auprès de Strogonov, par l'intermédiaire du jeune Voronzov, sinon pour
contre-carrer les projets politiques du moins pour savoir ce qui se passait
au grand quartier." Leveson-Gower attempted at least to induce the
Russians to refuse their assent to any peace that should not be general,
and, having failed to see Alexander or to learn anything definite from
Budberg, attempted to enlist the influence of Czartoryski; but this prince,
though of the same opinion as Leveson-Gower, was helpless against the
increasing ascendancy of the Grand Duke Constantine. M. Handelsman,
"La 'Question Czartoryski' à Tilsit (1807)", *Revue des Etudes Napoléoniennes*,
Sept./Oct. 1923, pp. 142–5.

for be assured that the dangers which threaten England at this moment infinitely exceed what we ever before apprehended.[1]

It became a matter of the utmost importance to discover how far the Czar's new connections and commitments implied or foreshadowed his complete estrangement from his former allies. The whole policy of Canning was directed to the solution of this problem. An idea was entertained that the Russians might be lured into a course of action which would announce a continued friendliness towards England, notwithstanding any engagements that might have been made at Tilsit. Canning looked to the Czar for some act that should be a "token". The secret articles of Tilsit might be communicated to the court of London. Perhaps negotiations could be resumed for the arrangement of a treaty of commerce. On the very eve of Friedland Budberg had shown himself willing to concede privileges to British traders,[2] and if the threads of the discussion could be picked up again, this indulgence might be of service, said the English minister, "in giving to the offer of Mediation a character of amicable inter- ference, and perhaps in deciding His Majesty as to the expediency of availing himself of such an offer".[3] It was known that the Prussians were in dread of the retaliation that was to be expected from England in the event of the closing of their ports. They were imploring the British government to show leniency. Canning proved himself subtle in answering them, and put forward an idea that the Prussian minister could only call "extraordinary". If Russia could be persuaded to "make a few insinuations to the English ministry concerning her desire to see Prussia spared", then England "might be able to treat Prussia more leniently in the event of her closing her ports".[4] It was an attempt to

---

[1] *Private Correspondence of Lord G. Leveson-Gower*, II, 272.

[2] G. Leveson-Gower to G. Canning, No. 4, 19 June 1807, *F.O. Russia* 65/69.

[3] Canning to G. Leveson-Gower, No. 29, 4 Aug. 1807 and No. 32, 12 Aug. 1807, *F.O. Russia* 65/70.

[4] *Add. MSS*. 32,273. Jacobi-Kloest to the Prussian king, 18 Aug. 1807. On the 21st of August Jacobi reported that the same proposal had been made by Canning to Alopeus. On the 24th of September the Prussian king gave an outline of the appeal he had made to the Czar as a consequence of the English offer. This last letter, only, is printed in Hassell, *op. cit.* I, 350.

test the attitude of Russia towards her two former allies. The Czar's refusal to intercede for the Prussians would, said Canning, "only be additional proof of his total reversal of policy".

But Canning would not accept a mediation that could not show itself friendly, would not allow Russia to intervene in the French war purely as the ally of Napoleon. On the 5th of August he gave his answer to the peace proposals of the Czar. He showed that England had not been reluctant to enter into negotiation with France. He referred to his acceptance of the recent Austrian mediation. He recalled the promise he had given to accede to the convention of Bartenstein. He mentioned the readiness he had shown, after the battle of Friedland, to join in any negotiation which the Czar should think expedient for the establishment of a general peace. These facts, he said, were proofs of the pacific intentions of his government.

His Majesty trusts that the character of the Treaty of Tilsit and of the principles upon which France is represented as being ready to negotiate, may be found to be such as to afford to His Majesty a just hope of the attainment of a secure and honourable peace.

In that case His Majesty will readily avail himself of the Emperor of Russia's mediation.

But until His Majesty shall have received these important and necessary communications it is obviously impossible that the undersigned should be authorised to return a more specific answer to the note presented by M. d'Alopeus.[1]

As August advances we discover a growing doubt in the mind of the Czar, something which looks like a misgiving. On the 2nd of this month Leveson-Gower, in an official report from St Petersburg, declares:

It is with pain I inform you that everything I have heard and observed since I came here strongly confirms the apprehension... that the Emperor Alexander has completely thrown himself into the hands of Bonaparte...but, whatever may be the ultimate intentions of this government, it appears that they are desirous of avoiding a quarrel with the Court of London, for the present, at least till the return of their fleet from the Mediterranean.[2]

[1] Canning to Alopeus, 5 Aug. 1807, in *Parliamentary Debates*, x, cols. 114–15.
[2] G. Leveson-Gower to Canning, No. 2, 2 Aug. 1807, *F.O. Russia* 65/69.

We find Alexander defending his change of policy in a conversation with the Swedish ambassador. He says that his armies were in a deplorable condition after Friedland and that Napoleon refused to conclude an armistice unless this should be followed by the negotiation of peace; that therefore there was no opportunity for Russia to consult with her allies. He hopes that the king of Sweden will not persevere in the war against Napoleon, especially as public opinion in his country is unfavourable to this. The Swedish minister replies that the trading community will not tolerate any war with England; he goes on to say that this reasoning would apply equally to Russia where the language of the merchants in fact always constitutes public opinion. The Czar looks "extremely grave", and answers, "It may be so!" It appears that the Czar has some vague dread of the hostility of the court of London. The Swedish minister comes away with an impression that tallies with that of Leveson-Gower.[1] Alexander might have felt secure in promising to declare war against England by December; it would have been war under the cover of winter; but now it is August and winter seems far away, and the tone of the British ministers is alarming. The Russian fleet has not yet returned from the Mediterranean. There is reason to be anxious concerning the fortifications at Cronstadt. And all the time the city of St Petersburg is voicing disapproval of the politics of Tilsit.

And, if the Czar in the month of August was striving to make delay, the English government for its own part was not anxious to hasten a crisis. It was determined to give the Russians no pretext for any change of system. Although there was a certainty that designs hostile to Great Britain were in contemplation, Leveson-Gower was ordered "to feign ignorance of what he only knew too well".[2] An expedition was sent to Copenhagen to give a drastic check to the maritime policy that had been decided upon at Tilsit; but the ambassador at St Petersburg was ordered

[1] G. Leveson-Gower to Canning, No. 16, Separate, Secret and Confidential, 17 Aug. 1807, *F.O. Russia* 65/70.

[2] Canning to G. Leveson-Gower, No. 30 (Most Secret), 5 Aug. 1807, and Separate and Most Secret, 27 Sept. 1807, *F.O. Russia* 65/70.

to let no hint fall that the British government knew of the connivance of Russia in Napoleon's maritime league.[1] The minister was to announce that the Danish expedition was directed against Napoleon—not intended as a threat to the Czar. He received powers to call upon Admiral Gambier's fleet for "an effective demonstration" against Cronstadt, in case the Russians took some step of a hostile character; but

in the other, and it is hoped more probable alternative of the Russian Government being disposed to defer and if possible to elude stipulations hostile to this country...it is by no means the wish of His Majesty to press matters to any extremity on the mere fact of the existence of such stipulations, however clearly ascertained.[2]

There was a possibility that the Russians would construe their treaty-engagements in the way that would be most generous towards England. It might even have been argued that their alliance with France was but a ruse and a temporary extrication. At the very least there was room for the hope that the passage of time would bring a reaction at St Petersburg. Leveson-Gower imagined that the "intemperance" of Bonaparte would soon afford disillusionment to the Czar.[3] And since Alexander's subservience at Tilsit might be attributed to the personal ascendancy of Napoleon, Canning could not think that the infatuation would endure for a long period after the return to St Petersburg had broken the direct contact. Englishmen therefore still looked with confidence "for some token of the Emperor's remaining friendship, some proof of the Equality at least with which His Imperial Majesty is prepared to consider the interests of both parties in the course of the negotiation".[4] They were soon rewarded by the receipt of a token more pleasing than they could have anticipated.

Here struts upon the scene, irresistible but half-comic, a cheerful, bustling Britisher, who had caught madness from

[1] G. Canning to G. Leveson-Gower, No. 30, 5 Aug. 1807, *F.O. Russia* 65/70.
[2] G. Canning to G. Leveson-Gower, No. 33, 13 Aug. 1807, *F.O. Russia* 65/70.
[3] G. Leveson-Gower to G. Canning, No. 22, 19 Sept. 1807, *F.O. Russia* 65/70.
[4] Canning to G. Leveson-Gower, No. 32, 12 Aug. 1807, *F.O. Russia* 65/70.

melodrama. One of the most popular and animated figures among the Englishmen in St Petersburg at this period was Sir Robert Wilson, a knight-errant born out of due time; a soldier and a rover, who relished a dangerous game. Man of many battles and charming friendships, he seems never to have grown out of the recklessness and erratic enthusiasms of a school-boy; and it would appear that he was honoured by every country but his own. Moving in that society of the Russian capital which was by no means reconciled with the Czar's recent reversal of policy—moving under the jealous eye of the French minister who could not share his popularity—he received everywhere signs of regard and high esteem, and heard conversation that was friendly towards England. The Czar had always covered him with kindness, and, even after Tilsit, showed him unbroken affection. "During the whole of the dinner", wrote Wilson, when he had seen Alexander in the middle of August, "we talked in as lively and unceremonious a manner as at Bartenstein." And these experiences in St Petersburg prepared Wilson for the drama in which he was to be the central figure.

On the 7th of September he made the following entry in his diary:

On the 2nd instant I went by appointment to the Emperor who received me alone, and for nearly an hour talked on important political subjects: a conversation very interesting to England.... From him I went to General Budberg.... He conversed confidentially for an hour, and the conversation was also of a most important character. I then went to Gower; he was much pleased at what I was enabled to tell him, which rendered my personal appearance in England more interesting to ministers.[1]

In these conversations there was given to Wilson a glimpse of the inner purposes and unavowed intentions that underlay that new Russian policy, concerning which the Czar had always been so reticent. It was revealed that the Russian government had been seized with apprehensions and had feared the evils that would come to pass if Napoleon should gain a foothold in the north of Europe. For this reason it had made an alliance with

[1] Wilson, *Diaries*, II, 365 (*et seq.*).

France, though it did not contemplate a permanent connection. Wilson even gained the impression that the Czar was not displeased by the expedition which had been sent against Denmark —that the Czar would actually welcome the continued occupation of Zealand by the English troops.

Wilson's was a happy, picturesque, vivid mind, which magnified simple suggestions and small half-betrayals of confidence into matters of mighty import, and high secrets of state; throughout this period he is found perpetually flattering himself that the business he has in hand for the moment is the key to the whole situation. If he receives the slightest hint, he puts all his imagination into the enlarging of it, and jumps to some grand conclusion, till he feels the wide world rock with the crisis that he has discovered. In a quixotic way he will scent an adventure, and ride off with a flourish. Soon after his important interviews in St Petersburg he was sailing proudly towards England. "My despatches admit of no delay", he said; "England and Russia are deeply concerned in them." The winds could not carry him too quickly. He was the bearer of the secret of Tilsit.

But it was not merely that Wilson was informed in this unconventional way of the altered disposition of the Czar. The ambassador in a more official interview was given a similar impression, though he did not report it in the same glowing colours. He, too, saw the "change in tone and temper of General Budberg's conversation", and was told that "the Continental Peace cannot be of long duration".[1] Budberg, writing to his master, had even gone further in this new direction than the English ministry ever realised. He had advised his master to disclose the secret articles of the treaty of Tilsit to the cabinet of London.

Since the secret articles have already been communicated to Prussia it is more than probable that England will get to know of them sooner or later, and we shall have gratuitously thrown away an opportunity of showing confidence to an old ally who may still be useful to us in the future. I am therefore of opinion that we ought

[1] G. Leveson-Gower to Canning, No. 19, 2 Sept. 1807, in *Parliamentary Debates*, x, cols. 197–8 (No. 2).

not to refuse this request, but make the best that we can out of the confidential communication of the articles to England. As to the renewal of the Treaty of Commerce, I do not see any harm in granting this also. The great point which England makes of it would cause the mere willingness to follow up the negotiation, to have the best effect immediately.... Your Majesty could always drag out the discussions as long as you pleased, and time would bring developments which would regulate our subsequent conduct.[1]

This was a change of tone, for Budberg had been a good servant of the Tilsit cause during this recent period, and the French minister Savary had reported exactly a week before that "M. de Budberg...has entirely come over to our system".[2] It was remarkable that Budberg should give his master advice of this character; this is no case of a document that is to be used as a form of propaganda or as a means of creating illusion; the idea of regarding England at all as "an old ally who may still be useful to us", carries an ominous suggestion, and it is strange that it could be presented to Alexander at this moment. It is difficult to speak of Budberg as a good "Tilsit" man in connection with all this, and it is not correct to imagine that in the change of tactics at the beginning of September the Czar was merely taking advantage of the radiant gullibility of Wilson.

When Wilson arrived in London his messages were accepted only with mental reservations. Ross, the secretary of Canning, expressed the official attitude when he wrote concerning the changed conduct of Russia:

We attribute a great deal of this mild spirit to our [Danish] expedition...it has created a great deal of apprehension at St Petersburg. At Cronstadt they practise firing with red-hot shot every day. This change of tone may not perhaps be followed up by any permanent change of conduct; it may be merely for the purpose of gaining time and from the dread of some immediate hostility on our part; but at all events it will give us the winter to look about us and the chapter of accidents for some bickering to arise between the two Courts of the Tuileries and St Petersburg.... The sum of all this seems to be either that His Imperial Majesty is already weary of his new ally

---

[1] *Sbornik*, LXXXVIII, 155–6.
[2] Savary to Talleyrand, 23 Aug. 1807, in *Sbornik*, LXXXIII, 34.

and that the recollection of the Tilsit dinners is wearing away, or
else (to use his own words on a former occasion) "il faut ménager
l'Angleterre pour le moment".[1]

But, said Ross,

we have only to cultivate this change of sentiment to derive from it
in time, and that perhaps not very distant, the best possible effects.
Budberg, I believe, had not strict justice done to him on the subject
of the Treaty; he was on the spot, in office, and the Emperor made
him the cat's paw, to put his fingers in the fire. He was not much
consulted, and disliked the peace. He insinuated to Sir R. Wilson
that the *secret articles* might not be withheld from a person sent from
here. I believe Sir R. Wilson will return in a few days. Russia is
anxious, since the deed is done, that we should retain the possession
of Zealand, not merely for the sake of the King of Sweden, but also
as a security to her own frontier. She is quite aware that when we
quit it the French will occupy it.[2]

Concerning the response which the British government was to
make to the advances of the Czar, Ross further explains:

It is good policy, I think, to send Sir R. Wilson back; he is a
military man, has served with the Russians, has been spoken to
confidentially by the Emperor, and may do better than a better man.
Nothing important is however to be left to his sole discretion. If
Russia is sincere, it is worth while to keep her up to it by showing
a disposition to cultivate and strengthen our former good understanding; if she is not sincere or if she has only acted in this instance
on the spur of the occasion, and even should she have relapsed into
French politics before Sir R. Wilson returns, there will be no harm
done; we shall be but where we were.[3]

So Wilson was sent back to St Petersburg and was made the
bearer of new instructions to Leveson-Gower. These demanded,
as the condition of England's acceptance of the Russian mediation, first the frank communication of the articles of the treaty of
Tilsit, secret as well as avowed; secondly the distinct explanation
of the bases upon which the negotiation would be conducted;
and thirdly the disclosure of the Czar's general views of policy,
and of any engagements into which he might have entered,

---

[1] Malmesbury, *Diaries*, II, 48–9.   [2] *Ibid.* II, 50.   [3] *Ibid.* II, 51.

together with a plain and decisive proof of his continued friendship towards England. As a test of the feelings of the Czar, Leveson-Gower was instructed to invite his mediation in the quarrel between the courts of London and Copenhagen.[1] These stipulations represented the official policy of the British government, and were meant to measure the sincerity of the recent assurances of the Czar. A more pretentious reply to the communications from St Petersburg was confided to Wilson himself, to be transmitted direct to Alexander.

There was a Russian minister in London—the mysterious Maxilian Alopeus. He had long been floundering in the incomprehensible tangle of Tilsit, and had been himself waiting for the illumination that was to come from Russia. True to his former habits, the old pro-Russian had caught the atmosphere of his locality, was now notoriously pro-English, and was irredeemably out of favour in Russia. Taking things at their face value he had determined to press the Russian mediation upon England, had wished to make it acceptable, had earnestly worked for peace. Now, though he had received no intimation from his own government, he opened his arms to the wildest madcap in Europe who came brimming with the confidences of the Czar. He joined Canning in rejoicing in the messages of Wilson and the new complexion of affairs; and it is interesting, in the light of subsequent events, to find him writing: "No unprejudiced person could help being struck by the justice of the views of His Majesty the Emperor, as they are expounded by Sir Robert Wilson".[2]

The English troops in Denmark were already pledged to evacuate Zealand within a stated period; but when it was learned that the Czar was willing to connive at their further stay, it became important that the occupation should continue. Canning decided that the Prince Royal of Denmark should be induced to work in collusion with the British government, to

---

[1] G. Canning to G. Leveson-Gower, No. 34, 27 Sept. 1807, printed in *Parliamentary Debates*, x, col. 200 *et seq.* and No. 35, 28 Sept. 1807, *ibid.* col. 203 *et seq.*

[2] Alopeus to Lisakewitch, 13/25 Sept. 1807, in *Sbornik*, LXXXIX, 207–8.

accept the protracted stay of the English troops while all the time pretending to protest; and for the persuasion of the Prince Royal it was agreed that Lisakewitch, the Russian minister at Copenhagen, should inform him of the secret sentiments of the Czar, and secure his assent to the stratagem. There was no time for writing to St Petersburg to ask for imperial instructions to be sent direct to Lisakewitch, so Alopeus provided a more short and summary way. He himself wrote to Denmark to inform the Russian minister of the real aims and intentions of the Czar and to point out the appropriate line of action.[1] On the authority of Englishmen he took it upon himself to declare the policy of his government and instruct a fellow-minister. The bearer of the communication was to be Sir Robert Wilson himself; who, having called at Copenhagen, was to make his way to the Russian capital.

Before Wilson had arrived at St Petersburg, before he had even reached England on his outward journey, the Czar had revealed his true disposition. On the 10th of September, Leveson-Gower was informed that the secret articles of Tilsit were not to be divulged, though it was asserted that they contained nothing of a hostile character which might make it necessary to conceal them from England.[2] A few days later the British minister was writing:

> The continuance of peace with this country I am inclined to attribute rather to the means which we possess of injuring and distressing Russia, and the extreme unpopularity here which would attach to measures of hostility against England, than to any remaining sentiments of friendship on the part of His Imperial Majesty towards Great Britain. General Savary continues to be received by the Emperor with every mark of favour and distinction.[3]

The expedition to Copenhagen provoked mutual reproaches and an exchange of angry notes between Leveson-Gower and the

---

[1] *Sbornik*, LXXXIX, 207 (see also, Copie d'une dépêche secrète de M. d'Alopéus en date de Londres, 13/25 Sept. 1807, *ibid*. 205).

[2] *Sbornik*, LXXXVIII, 177–9.

[3] G. Leveson-Gower to G. Canning, No. 23, 19 Sept. 1807, *F.O. Russia* 65/70.

Russian chancellor.[1] Alexander had been deluding the Englishmen; it would seem that he had been playing with Budberg;
Budberg at any rate conveniently disappeared from the scene,
resigning on the ground of failing health, at the moment when
the situation was becoming clear.

At the close of August and the beginning of September the
news of the English attack upon Copenhagen and the proximity
of the English fleet created real apprehensions in the mind of
the Czar. From his conversations with the French minister it
is apparent that he feared the very thing which Leveson-Gower
had been empowered to evoke—an English demonstration
against his shores. His one anxiety at the moment was to prepare
the fortifications of Cronstadt, and he set to work with energy
upon them. He made no change of tone towards Savary, but
showed himself even reconciled to the thought that hostilities
were being prepared against him; and he put himself into the
arms of France. This, then, was the cause of his momentary
change of conduct towards England; he seems to have been
satisfied when he had had an interval for the work of fortifica-
tion; his deception was a palpable "ruse de guerre".

Wilson, when he reached St Petersburg on the 17th of October,
found in official circles "an unpleasant aspect of affairs".[2] He
communicated with the Czar,[3] but his letter was returned un-
opened; so he was compelled to address himself to the new
chancellor. Undespairing still, he could write at the end of
October:

I went to Count Romantsov, and had with him an important
interview; it lasted an hour and a half. I say *important* as the *essential*
interests of the two great nations depended upon its issue....The
attention of every person in the city has been attracted to my mission,
and good or ill success will in some degree be attributed to my personal
ability or incapacity.

Talking to Romantsov, he began with an apology for the recent
conduct of England; the government had been apprehensive;

[1] *Sbornik*, LXXXIX, 146–8.
[2] Wilson to Canning, 18 Oct. 1807, in *Diaries*, II, 432.
[3] Wilson to the Czar Alexander, 18 Oct. 1807, in *Diaries*, II, 432.

it had long waited for a friendly sign from the Czar; it had feared that Russia would not or could not preserve her neutrality; yet all the time its policy of alliance with Russia had never been abandoned. What was desired now was that Russia should prove herself an independent nation. England did not seek to lure her back into the coalition, or to bring her into hostility with France; she would not break into the Franco-Russian connection. She did not ask for preferential treatment from the Czar, would not even insist on a commercial treaty, would not, said Wilson, require Russia to make any formal engagement at all. For her own part she was ready to continue the war and was prepared for a lengthy struggle with France, but she would fight alone or make alliances elsewhere. What she did ask of the Czar was that he should stand erect, and treat his former ally on the same terms as the new one. There was one way in which he could do this, and at the same time assert his independence. He could intervene in Denmark to ensure the neutrality of that power, and check the encroachments of Napoleon. He could enable the British troops that were in occupation there to remain for an extended period. In doing this, the Czar would be stepping no further than his interests demanded, for if the French were to occupy Zealand the actual safety of Russia would be menaced.

In return for this "impartiality" which was expected from the government at St Petersburg, England would be willing to make great sacrifices. She had always opposed any plan for the dismemberment of Turkey, and indeed she could not suggest such a scheme at the moment,

but nevertheless if any arrangement could be made between Austria and Russia on the basis of occupying or exchanging Moldavia and Wallachia, which arrangement would secure the sincere alliance of both countries, England never would make that a cause of quarrel which proved the bond of a union she desired so much to establish.

Wilson demonstrated that France did not at heart desire the aggrandisement of Russia; he offered the Czar a better guarantee of the possession of the Turkish provinces than the one Napoleon had given; but he made the offer conditional upon the arrangement of an alliance between the courts of St Petersburg and

Vienna. The alliance would be unobjectionable to Napoleon, since the Austrians were already neutral; but it would enable the Czar, even while the partner of Napoleon, to retain some of the connections that were the legacy of his former policy. It had the flavour of the old coalition. For this reason Canning pressed it upon the Russians, and, with different arguments, urged it upon the court of Vienna.

Talking of peace, Wilson informed the Russian chancellor

...that if ever England consents to make cessions of some of her conquests, she must have an equivalent that would augment the barriers still remaining against the universal dominion of France— that indeed a general peace was not likely to be obtained until the powers of the Continent, and particularly Russia, had assumed the attitude of independent nations who would form no other than salutary connections and who would not suffer aggression with impunity.

There is the clear, clean ring of an infant heart in the offer, that Wilson made in this interview, "to extricate Russia from the embarrassments which the treaty of Tilsit had occasioned". The language has a flavour and a fine felicity, by reason of all the questions that it begs. One can see that Wilson's soul was generously moved by the benevolent proposals of which he was the bearer, and it is plain that he communicated to the overture something of his own fond philanthropic mood. He insisted

that England sought no recompense, no preference, her reward was the restoration of confidence...that it was, however, necessary for Russia to act with impartiality and prove to France that she is an independent power...that England never could think of making peace with France whilst there was no prospect of diminishing her continental preponderance.

Dupe of two governments, Wilson could not see to what an extent his whole discourse was inapplicable to the existing situation, and to what a degree his proposals were calculated to hasten and intensify the rupture between Russia and England.

"I cannot promise success", he wrote to Canning, "but certainly the conference which I had this day seemed to interest the Count

much, and I would flatter myself that every hope of a private understanding being formed is not unwarrantable....I shall endeavour to
obtain indisputable assurances of the friendly intentions of Russia
and then return to England."[1]

The whole incident showed England unrepentant. Combined
with the rash conduct which Wilson permitted himself in St
Petersburg at this time, it brought the anger of the Czar to a
head.[2] A government burning with indignation against the
injury which had been inflicted upon the Danes did not welcome
a proposal that asked for its connivance or participation in the
outrage. The Russian minister communicated the overture to
the French, and declared that the opportunity had arrived for
the demonstration of fidelity to Napoleon.[3] The English minister
began to find difficulty in securing an interview with the chancellor.[4] The notes that he transmitted were merely ignored.[5]
Alopeus, who had leaped to welcome the thing which he was
anxious to believe—who had sublimely congratulated the Czar
upon the wisdom of the sentiments which Wilson had attributed
to him—had missed his step completely. His share in Canning's
conspiracy for the extension of the occupation of Zealand was
roundly condemned. Lisakewitch alone came out of the transaction with advantage, for he had refused all complicity in the
scheme. Within a few days the Czar, as "one of the guarantors
of the tranquillity of the Baltic, which is a closed sea", declared
war against England and took up the cause of the Danes, demanding complete satisfaction for the injury done by British
vessels to the mercantile interests of his subjects, and announcing
his refusal to renew relations with the court of London until
England should have given satisfaction to Denmark and made
peace with the French government.[6]

[1] Wilson to G. Canning, 29 Oct. 1807, in Wilson, *Diaries*, II, 434–9.
[2] *Sbornik*, LXXXIII, 147, 174–5; Appendix, p. 31. See also Vandal,
Napoléon et Alexandre Ier, I, 164–7.
[3] Savary to Napoleon, 4 Nov. 1807, in *Sbornik*, LXXXIII, 174–91.
Romantsov's account of Wilson's conversation is given on pp. 184–6.
[4] G. Leveson-Gower to G. Canning, No. 34, 4 Nov. 1807, in *Parliamentary
Debates*, X, cols. 215–16.
[5] G. Leveson-Gower to G. Canning, No. 33, 29 Oct. 1807, *ibid.* col. 214.
[6] Declaration of Russia, 20/31 Oct. 1807, in *Parliamentary Debates*, X,
cols. 218–21.

The dark implications of Tilsit were beginning to come out into the daylight, and the mystery was moving to its own elucidation. It was remarked in St Petersburg that the person in England who would receive the greatest shock on hearing the news of the declaration of war would be none other than Alopeus, the Russian minister himself.[1] But if it was expected that Alopeus should have misread the import of the treaties of Tilsit, it was more strange that Count Tolstoy, the new Russian minister in Paris, should discover that he had misconstrued the intentions of his government. Tolstoy had been specially appointed by the Czar to represent and to promote the new system of alliance. He was half-unreconciled to the new policy; he worked unwillingly in Paris.

"The views of Napoleon in regard to us are evident", he wrote in November. "...There is nothing even yet to show that he has ceased to be consistent in his plans. He wishes to turn us into an Asiatic power, to throw us back upon our ancient frontiers and to carry his rule into the heart of our provinces....It is impossible to foresee where his volcanic imagination will drive him."[2]

When he heard of the declaration of war Tolstoy awoke to the fact that he had misunderstood the intentions of his government. In all his dark forebodings he had never expected this, and he announced his disappointment. He thought that a "prompt pacification" between England and France,

apart from the good it would do the whole world, seemed the only means of extricating Russia from the embarrassments into which the Treaty of Tilsit had plunged her. I thought I ought to neglect nothing that might help to modify the dispositions of the Emperor Napoleon against England and to make his pretensions more moderate....The Emperor Napoleon, sure of the help of Russia, will consult nothing but his animosity and renounce all idea of moderation....I could scarcely imagine that you would hurry so with a measure that we had so many reasons for delaying.[3]

[1] Caulaincourt to Champagny, No. 12, 29 Dec. 1807, in Grand-Duke Nicholas Mikhaïlovitch, *Relations diplomatiques de la Russie et de la France*, I, 28.
[2] Tolstoy to Romantsov, Private and Secret, 26 Oct./7 Nov. 1807, in *Sbornik*, LXXXIX, 185 (cf. p. 228).
[3] Tolstoy to Romantsov, 3/15 Dec. 1807, in *Sbornik*, LXXXIX, 284–5.

Ten days later he returned to the subject:

> To evade entirely this stipulation of the Treaty of Tilsit would certainly have been impossible; but it seems to me that we might have adjourned it still, and abstained from fulfilling it until we had seen a more decided intention of fulfilling the conditions of the Treaty on the part of the French Government. This was the very intention which Your Excellency expressed to me verbally at St Petersburg, and confirmed by a note addressed to me when I was on the point of departure. In this way we might have offered our rupture with England as the price of the evacuation of the Prussian States, which it will be very difficult to obtain now.[1]

Tolstoy, Alopeus, Budberg—even while they worked for the "system of Tilsit", felt the true interests of the Empire to lie in the speedy establishment of peace and the avoidance of any rupture with England. They carried into their appreciation of the new policy of the Czar some of the prejudices of the old. They did not, like their master, ratify the new system with their hearts. Though they consented to work within the limiting terms of the new treaties—though they did not make issue over the actual letter of those engagements, as Czartoryski and Novossiltzov had done—they quarrelled with the implications of the new system as these gradually unfolded; they reached a point at which they found that they had put a wrong construction upon the French alliance.

It was the spirit in which Alexander accepted the system of Tilsit and opened himself to the alliance with France that disqualified him from the rôle of peace-maker. It was this spirit that Canning was persistently trying to test when he sought from the Russian government some act that should be a "token". Canning did not cry out against the desertion of the coalition by Alexander, did not seek to re-kindle the continental war; if there had been stipulations in the treaty of Tilsit directed in a hostile way against Great Britain, still he specifically declined to make the mere signature of these the occasion of a break; and even in the final overture which he sent by Wilson to St Petersburg he did not ask for any repudiation of the alliance with

---

[1] Tolstoy to Romantsov, 15/27 Dec. 1807, in *Sbornik*, LXXXIX, 313.

France. He was quite prepared to acquiesce in the position to which the Czar had committed himself, if the Czar had made his engagements merely under the stress of a desperate military defeat; he seemed even willing to accept the situation if only the Czar would refrain from construing his engagements in the manner most hostile to Great Britain. He would have been happy to see the treaties of Tilsit carried out in the way Alopeus, or Budberg or Tolstoy would have desired. But he did insist that the mediation of Alexander should at least be an impartial one, not a veiled act of hostility or a prelude to the declaration of war. When we consider that at this period Napoleon was making a similar intervention in the war between Russia and Turkey, and, in the negotiation, was not proving at all indulgent to Russia—was, for example, inexorable in his demand for the evacuation of Moldavia and Wallachia—we might be tempted to say that the Czar was unnecessarily hostile to England, and that if he had interpreted the system of Tilsit as cleverly as Napoleon—if he had taken his stand on a merely literal fulfil-ment of his engagements—he would still have been able to give the satisfaction that was demanded by the British government.

Because he had started from a disposition to be unfriendly to Great Britain, Alexander was fully prepared to put the most hostile construction on any doubtful point in her policy. His anger existed already, hankering after an object; it sprang from something deeper than logic, but it was crouched and lying in wait for a fact around which it could explain and rationalise itself. For this reason the expedition to Copenhagen was the most unfortunate thing that could have happened. It enabled him to work up his mind into burning indignation on an issue that was entirely to his heart. He was annoyed that the enter-prise should have been undertaken and Russia not warned of the intention; as the ally of France he would be jolted and shocked by the challenge which was thrown down to his "system of Tilsit"; but as the guardian of the Baltic and the north he was indignant that such an outrage could have been committed at all. The actual threat to his own coasts—the danger in which the fortifications of Cronstadt in particular seemed to stand—would heighten his feeling of horror. And when Sir Robert Wilson came to ask him to sanction and support the crime, everything in him that was chivalrous, all that was spiritually proud, seems to have been revolted at the impudence of the proposal. If he had had the slightest misgivings concerning his treatment of an old ally, and if there had been anything uncharitable concerning England that he had wanted to believe, the expedition to Copenhagen gave him full release; it was the very thing needed to make all the Alexanders that were in him beat as one. Declaring against England, he had now no need to resort to shifty evasions, to flinch at his own inconsistencies, or to make a treaty with his conscience; he was the champion of a small neighbour, he was raised to a pedestal of moral indignation, and, once more on the side of the moralities, he could feel that his deed was good.

But even if Alexander had stood impartial, and had offered a mediation that could be pleasing to the English and had become the father of a negotiation, it is difficult to believe that the result would have been different. The British government refused to undertake any negotiation with France unless the terms of the settlement were to comprise the larger affairs of Europe. As in the year 1806 it declined to be regarded as a merely maritime power, and it considered the security of the continent as a matter which closely concerned itself. If England consented to negotiate she would look upon the transaction as one which should convert the partial arrangements of Tilsit into a final " general pacification ". Napoleon, on the other hand, was willing only to discuss the matters that directly concerned the interests of the negotiating parties; and on this view England was excluded from continental affairs with the exception of those relating to Hanover. It irritated the cabinet of London to hear Napoleon reiterating his willingness to concede this German electorate, and implying that, this matter being settled, there was nothing more to arrange in Europe. When the Russian chancellor took up the cry, and reminded Sir Robert Wilson that " You have Hanover to reclaim ", the Englishman with grandiose patriotism could reply: " Your Excellency must be well aware that Hanover does not comprise the views of England with regard to the Continent. Her policy is more enlarged, more general, and more enlightened ".[1]

Napoleon, master of the land, declared his intention of interfering in maritime affairs—of checking the extravagant claims of England and the various abuses of power. Canning had heard whispers of "maritime rights", and the faintest hint of these was always sufficient to put an Englishman on the alert; he would submit to no tampering here. England and Russia, even when they had been allies, had not always felt at ease in this matter. The subject was one which could not fail to be raised if the Czar broke with England and if Russia and France came to put heads together to find common ground at Tilsit.

So we have land-power and sea-power unreconciled, each claiming to interfere in the realm of the supremacy of the other. Ruling over two mutually exclusive worlds their conflict is like the clash of two different planes of existence or like some mythic tale of Ulysses deriding Polyphemus. The greatest army in the world can only stand on a giant cliff-head and shudder with rage and mutter ineffectual threats against the world's greatest navy where the Atlantic booms below. Each power can only tease the other in a tantalising shadow-fight, and make lunges at abstractions and pursue its foe vicariously. Edicts of Milan will grapple with "Orders in Council". England will pounce upon an island at the end of the world, and Napoleon will revenge himself upon Portugal. The treaties of Tilsit have not won this warfare from futility and frustration. Neither power is yet able to force a settlement upon the other by inflicting a direct and palpable defeat.

The treaties of Tilsit were themselves sufficient to destroy the possibility of maritime peace. They made Napoleon too sure of the support of Russia; they intensified the arrogance of France; they made England haughty and alert, like a man who has received an affront. Canning, as well as Napoleon, had personality, and was streaked with veins of fire. He too could see a dramatic moment and meet it with a gesture—could turn governmental

---

[1] Wilson, *Diaries*, II, 437. See also e.g. G. Leveson-Gower to G. Canning, No. 11, 15 July 1807, *F.O. Russia* 65/69.

action into a kind of poetry. There was an arrogance, there was something proud in his impulses, which was to be chastened and a little tempered when he returned to office fifteen years later, but which at this period, flashing out in some stroke of policy, or becoming incandescent in a diplomatic despatch, enlivened the policy of the British government. All that was challenging in the system of Tilsit only provoked him further; and all the things that might have been arguments for peace merely confirmed his obstinacy.

Canning belonged to the type of leader that is warm and intemperate, a type that was coarsened a little in Palmerston and further vulgarised in Lloyd George. His policy was not to be gnomely wise over the heads of a sleeping people, but occasionally to turn round and take men into his confidence and show them the point to which he was leading them—occasionally to whip up their passions and make them his accomplices. The man who called in the new world to redress the balance of the old was not content with manœuvring in a corner, with a diplomacy of mere technique, with subtle and recondite action. He would seize on the grander elements of policy that could be communicated to the platform, he would strike an attitude that the people could recognise, he would do the dynamic thing. In this respect the expedition to Copenhagen is the clue to the mood of Canning in the period after Tilsit and gives the key to the diplomacy of England in the new state of Europe. It was exactly the kind of action which the Cannings and Palmerstons and Lloyd Georges always will take, to the disturbance of the graver "Balliol" type, the statesmen of the grand manner. It dramatised the moment. It gave a lead to the country. For it was a defiant gesture, a shout of derisive laughter in the face of the Franco-Russian conspiracy; and as such it must be remembered whenever we are discussing Canning's attitude to the question of maritime peace.

Napoleon, for his part, did not carry out his imperious policies and haughty designs without reference to public opinion. Unlike the monarchs of the *ancien régime* he could not trust to a mere inertia in the masses that would allow him to govern at his mere caprice. At the same time he was not the man to listen from a palace window for the popular voices that might come from the market place. He made the people his accomplice. He himself would start the tune for them. In the army and in the state he succeeded by arts of leadership. He would seize upon the propaganda value of events, and catch public opinion at the effective moment, and exploit all the dramatic and passionate elements of a situation. He was not slow to see in the expedition to Copenhagen a signal and an opportunity.

"I think that if the English go on in this way", he wrote to St Petersburg, "we must close all the ports of Europe, even those of Austria, and have all the English ministers driven from the Continent. ...If the Emperor is of this opinion we will join in making a declaration to the Austrians, who will be obliged to conform to it."

It pleased him to regard the Danish expedition as a demonstration of the real intentions of England, as the type of her perpetual policy. The kind of moral revolt which had been raised against his own practices on land he was now able to turn against the tyranny of the maritime power. England had shown herself the Bonaparte of the seas.

From this moment he ceased even to make pretence of any inclination for the conclusion of peace. Russia, he said, might regard this outrage as the answer to her offer of mediation. No further discussion was needed, no ultimatum such as the Czar had intended to give. Napoleon saw the full force of the moment, and blazed its moral across the length and breadth of Europe. For the event had challenged all that was noble and proud in his generous military soul, and it had put into his hands a new weapon against his irrepressible foe.

We learn from Metternich how little the Emperor desired peace after the expedition to Copenhagen had excited his indignation. The French foreign minister disclosed the new attitude of his government in a conversation with the Portuguese ambassador. According to him, Napoleon had decided to make no further attempt to come to an arrangement with Great Britain.

This power was sovereign of the seas. The moment had come when he,
Napoleon, wished to dominate the continent; all that opposed his views,

all that made the least resistance, would be crushed out; with the friendship of Russia, he no longer had fear of anyone; at last the dice had been thrown.[1]

It would seem that after the Danish expedition Napoleon was more immoderate, more arrogant than before. The event had provoked his worst characteristics. His expressions became more wild, his tone more unbalanced, his bravado more loud and extravagant than we have seen it hitherto. He decided to move a step further in the execution of the policy of Tilsit.

Drive the English diplomatic establishments out of Europe. The Viennese Court stands alone; it must be forced to join the common cause.... This expulsion of all English Ministers from the Continent will make a great impression in London, and will especially and strongly affect their trade.[2]

---

[1] Metternich to Stadion, 16 Oct. 1807, in *Mémoires du Prince de Metternich*, II, 129.

[2] Napoleon to Champagny, 7 Sept. 1807, in "Memorandum on the present state of Continental Affairs", *New Letters of Napoleon* (Eng. transl. Lady Mary Lloyd, 1898), pp. 46–7.

CHAPTER III

AUSTRIAN POLICY AND THE AUSTRIAN ATTEMPT TO BRING ABOUT PEACE

ANDRÉOSSY, French minister at Vienna, was a military man and a bitter anti-Austrian—far more bitter than Napoleon who at this time seems to have paid little attention to his outbursts. He took a cruel pleasure in recording and perhaps exaggerating the anguish of the Austrians in the critical weeks of July and August. "The news of the battle of Friedland made very little impression on the Court and Ministry", he wrote. "It was not so with the news of the armistice...this has caused a most disagreeable sensation and inspires the most lively fears."[1] Austria, he reported, was continuing her armaments; she was full of fear and loneliness, and felt that her hour had come. He gloated over her discomfiture. Concerning the intentions of France he kept up a deliberate air of mystery, hoping thereby, as one Englishman said, "to draw the Austrian cabinet into some decisive measure which might furnish Bonaparte with an excuse for turning his arms against them".[2] Andréossy's despatches were written in the following strain:

The silence which is kept towards her is giving her anxiety, and she feels humiliated that she, mediating power, was not warned in any way.... It will be possible, I think, to make any demand of Austria that may suit the arrangements of His Majesty. The more we adopt a high-handed tone befitting the prodigious ascendancy which His Majesty has acquired, the more easily we shall obtain demands which in other circumstances would have been difficult to obtain or would have been passed over in silence.... [Austria] is afraid of her isolation. ...They seem to wish for a rapprochement with France and are disposed to be condescending.[3]

[1] Andréossy to Talleyrand, 13 July 1807, in A[rchives du ministère des] A[ffaires] É[trangères] [Paris], Autriche, t. 380.
[2] G. Jackson to G. Canning, No. 4, 20 July 1807, F.O. Prussia 64/75. See also Alex. Wassiltchikow, Les Razoumovski, II, 3me partie, p. 131.
[3] Andréossy to Talleyrand, 24 Aug. 1807, A.A.E. Autriche, t. 380.

A glance at the Austrian minister in St Petersburg would confirm this impression of the nervousness of the court of Vienna. Merfeldt also was a military man, an unfortunate diplomat to employ. While the treaties of Tilsit were being arranged he had heard rumours that Russia was to have increase of territory at the expense of Prussia and Austria. He had asked the acting foreign minister at St Petersburg to inform him of the tenour of the treaties; this in return for the "unlimited confidence" which the court of Vienna had always given to the Czar. Merfeldt conjectured that Napoleon would have a grievance against his country, which had so often declined a French alliance; he insinuated that, "Whatever desire the House of Austria might have to remain at peace with all its neighbours, it was far from shrinking from the risks of a new war. The Austrian monarchy had perhaps never been in so flourishing a state as at the present moment".[1] Tactlessly at a later date Merfeldt addressed himself to the French minister Savary, and spoke with some indiscretion. According to Savary he was "furious" that peace had been made. He made wearisome demands to learn the terms of the arrangements. He said, "I confess that it is difficult for me to believe that you can have made a lasting peace without us"; and when Savary replied that he did not know of any questions that remained to be settled with Austria, he declared, "We cannot be indifferent to the fate of Wallachia and Moldavia", and even made some wild references to war. "Allow me to say", replied the French minister, "that your imagination sometimes makes phantoms for itself in order to have the pleasure of fighting them. At this moment you are already seeking a motive for war in a treaty that has hardly been signed." The Austrian seemed discontented with the settlement of the Polish campaign at Tilsit. Savary referred to the neutrality of Austria. "Had you an indirect part in this War? Were you interested in seeing it prolonged?"[2] Merfeldt, who had acted unwisely at a time when it had been important to promote good feeling between

[1] Soltikov (acting foreign minister in St Petersburg) to Budberg, 25 June/7 July 1807, in *Sbornik*, LXXXVIII, 74–6.

[2] Savary to Napoleon, 6 Aug. 1807, in *Sbornik*, LXXXIII, 7–10 and *passim*.

Austria and Russia, was now restless and over-anxious, and too good a coalition man. He made himself too ostentatiously a member of the English party at St Petersburg—showed more respect to the British ambassador than to the minister of Napoleon. "If the English ceased to have a legation here", wrote Savary, "M. de Merfeldt would watch over their interests". So Napoleon demanded Merfeldt's recall, and the Austrian chancellor had to complain that "Russia treats us with coldness, or rather with reserve".[1]

Starhemberg in London was also an enemy of France and of the Tilsit system. In the early days of 1807 he had been severely reproved for his excess of zeal in confiding to his official despatches to Vienna sentiments that were of a nature to compromise his government with France. He, also, was nervous for his country after the battle of Friedland, and, stepping beyond his instructions, he had "several friendly but not official conversations with the Secretary of State on the possibility of our being attacked at some time without provocation". Canning took the question seriously, and the result was a situation of some irony; rôles were reversed for the moment, and it was the British minister who urged the Austrians to keep the peace at all costs and avoid any differences with France. Austria could not be considered as having the same incontestable right to the assistance of England as if she had come to the help of Russia. "Only in the case of a war of self-defence in the strictest meaning of the words" would England give any consideration to the idea of helping the court of Vienna. Canning deplored that the Austrians had distrusted Russia more than they had feared Napoleon; he urged them to make a close union with the Czar; this was the system he desired to see established in Europe; the king, he said, recommended this policy, "at a moment when, if the rumours of the Continent are to be credited, he has himself to apprehend at least an unfriendly disposition, if not a hostile determination against him, on the part of Russia".[2]

[1] Stadion to Starhemberg, 6 Sept. 1807 (No. 4), *W.S.A. Weisungen nach London*.

[2] Starhemberg to Stadion, No. 63, 8 Aug. 1807, *W.S.A. Berichte aus London*. G. Canning to Lord Pembroke, No. 16, 17 Aug. 1807, *F.O. Austria* 7/85.

The government at Vienna had felt its fate hang in the balance when the conclusion of the treaties of Tilsit had left Napoleon free to deal with Austria. For a time there had been a breathless suspense, as men waited to learn what Napoleon's decision might be. It was no question, for the moment, of coalitions and conspiracies against France, of measures to check the usurper, of wide ulterior schemes; the Austrians held their minds feverishly centred on thoughts of self-preservation. The duplicity of two years had seemed about to receive its answering stroke; and if anything could be judged from the tone of the French minister, Andréossy, the stroke threatened to be vindictive. Then the silence in which Andréossy had seemed to exult, the cruel suspense, had broken. Napoleon declared to General Vincent that he was pleased with the late conduct of Austria; Duroc wrote to Andréossy in the same friendly spirit; and Talleyrand reported that the Emperor was disposed to enter into explanations with the court of Vienna on all matters that required to be settled.[1] This meant the end of a crisis, but not the end of nervousness, for Austria. She could not immediately readjust her psychology and leap out of the tense atmosphere and lose her cowering dread. Everything that had happened had only confirmed this power in a policy based upon fear. She did not need a Canning to warn her against offending France; the Austrian chancellor quickly retorted to such advice that it was his intention "not to give France any reasons for complaint, but to preserve friendly relations with her".[2] The ministers in Vienna shrank from making any move at all, lest their action should be misconstrued or resented by the French government.

Austria was afraid, said Adair in his memoir, "that any attempt to re-establish, even for the purposes of peace, a good understanding with other powers, would draw down upon her the vengeance of Napoleon". She was prepared not to have any foreign policy at all, save that of seeking favour with France. She was ready to take it as the first rule of her conduct that she must avoid too close an intimacy with England.

[1] Duroc to Andréossy, 18 July 1807, *A.A.E. Autriche*, t. 380. Talleyrand to Andréossy, 3 Aug. 1807, *ibid*.

[2] Stadion to Starhemberg, 6 Sept. 1807 (No. 1), *W.S.A. Weisungen nach London*.

There were reasons why the Austrians could reconcile themselves to the necessity of keeping England at a distance. The
cold reception which Canning had given to their peace proposals
after Friedland, the withering way in which he had resolved
these into their naked selfishness, and the haughty tone of the
comments with which he had surrounded his reply, had created
dissatisfaction in Vienna.[1]

"Judging from extracts from the despatches to Lord Pembroke",
wrote Stadion when the messages arrived, "we cannot expect much
from the opinion and good-will of the present English ministry. The
instructions...consist of bitter reproaches for the past, unpleasant
refusals of demands which we have not made and do not wish to
make, and counsels for the future which seem to me rather uncalled
for."[2]

But even if the British government had adopted an attitude
more warm and sympathetic, Stadion recognised that there had
come into existence a new state of affairs in which it was impossible for England to be useful to Austria in the way that had
once been contemplated. Napoleon had made his arrangements
in Europe and it was vain to hope that he would alter these for
the sake of peace with England. It was not expected that he
would now restore the Austrians to their former power, even
in return for the recovery of his lost colonies.

Although it is none the less desirable that there should be peace
between the Courts of London and Paris to relieve the present
political situation, we can no longer flatter ourselves that the pacification can produce essential changes in what has been agreed upon in
the Treaty of Tilsit.

Under these circumstances it was less necessary to cultivate the
close friendship of Great Britain. Starhemberg, while ordered
to strive to "keep the court of St James's in good feeling towards
us", was instructed to "abstain for the moment from any

---

[1] Adair, *op. cit.* p. 264. Cf. Stadion to Metternich, 3 Aug. 1807, quoted
in Beer, *Zehn Jahre Oesterreichischen Politik*, p. 296.
[2] Stadion to Starhemberg, 6 Sept. 1807 (No. 2), *W.S.A. Weisungen nach
London.*

proposition which would tend to unite us more or less directly with the present policy of the English Cabinet".[1] Starhemberg was to adopt the rôle of observer, to watch carefully over England's relations with her former allies, to note especially the conduct of England in regard to France; but he was to evade any attempt that Canning might make to bring Austria into closer touch with Great Britain. "You will content yourself with giving general declarations of goodwill."[2]

It required some weeks for such instructions to reach London from Vienna. Starhemberg in the meantime, like his Russian colleague Alopeus, had come under the spell of Canning. He had found his way to a deeper sympathy with the efforts of England and a closer understanding of her policy than his home government cared to show. While that government complained against the existing cabinet in England, he, in London, would argue like an Englishman and declare that "every one who desires to see the welfare of England would wish the present ministry to remain in power". Though he admitted that to some people Canning's attack upon Denmark might seem "odious", he himself set out its virtues,[3] and repeatedly noted its "wisdom and foresight", and went beyond many Englishmen in expressing his admiration. To him the Czar's offer of mediation was "vague and ill-worded", but Canning's reply "left nothing to be desired"; he could expect no tolerable peace until the secret articles of Tilsit should be divulged. He felt that the mediation of Austria might be more acceptable to the British government than the intervention of the Czar. He saw reason to hope that France might make some overture direct to London or through the Austrian minister in Paris.[4] But no Englishman could have shown himself at heart more hostile to the idea of maritime peace than Starhemberg. No one could have expressed a clearer conviction of the necessity of continuing the war. His reports

[1] Stadion to Starhemberg, 6 Sept. 1807 (No. 3), *W.S.A. Weisungen nach London*.

[2] *Ibid.*

[3] Starhemberg to Stadion, No. 65, 2 Sept. 1807, *W.S.A. Berichte aus London*.

[4] Starhemberg to Stadion, No. 66, 4 Sept. 1807, *ibid.*

bear strong marks of the influence of the English foreign secretary, and it is evident that in the conversations that took place in London Canning's was the ascendant mind. We may take it as the opinion of the British foreign office, when Starhemberg puts forward the view:

> It is impossible for an impartial observer not to take alarm to some extent at the thought of the harm that may happen to England in the present state of things. It is beyond doubt that the malignity of Napoleon is about to collect its efforts against the country which is the object of his deepest hate; and the most dangerous weapon which he could employ would be the attempt to delude England with the semblance of peace, offered with a disinterested air as coming from a desire for tranquillity.

This, said Starhemberg, would be "complete degradation", would amount to "the last act of submission of the whole of Europe". "It seems to me that so long as the fires of war burn in some corner of the universe there still remains a hope that one day success may be achieved." England, he said, had many ways of causing inconvenience and disturbance to France; she had nothing to fear from the continuance of the war, for the idea of an invasion was a "chimera"; only by making peace and allowing Napoleon to recruit his naval power would she stand in danger of being faced by some future attack.[1] Starhemberg, it is apparent, had surrendered to the whole reasoning of Canning. He, like Alopeus, had given his heart to the coalition. Merfeldt, his fellow countryman at St Petersburg, was in entire agreement with him. He, too, wrote to London to urge the continuance of the war with France.[2]

The Austrian minister in Paris worked more closely to the intentions of his government than either Starhemberg or Merfeldt. After Austerlitz Napoleon, exercising that same felicity of choice as when he proposed Stein to succeed Hardenberg, had fixed upon Metternich for this post. Gentz wrote to this man,

---

[1] Starhemberg to Stadion, No. 65, 2 Sept. 1807, *W.S.A. Berichte aus London.*

[2] Caulaincourt to Napoleon, No. 115, 12 June 1808, in Grand-Duke Nicholas Mikhaïlovitch, *Relations diplomatiques de la Russie et de la France,* II, 186.

for the diversion of historians, "Your nomination to Paris was a blow to me, and I have not yet been able to recover from it. ...A soul so pure and elevated as yours ought never to have come into contact with the seat of so many crimes and horrors". This soul so pure and elevated, picking its way not too disdainfully among the contaminations of the French capital, burned with inner hatred of Napoleon. Metternich handled the policy of Austria with the subtlety and resources of a diplomat born to the technique. It was he who negotiated the treaty of Fontainebleau which settled various questions that had been in controversy between the courts of Paris and Vienna. He did not like the treaty, fought bitterly to secure better terms, and felt that his work needed apology; but whenever he had raised a protest he had been silenced by ugly threats from France. "I have unfortunately been only too well able to see at every moment of the negotiation that not only has Napoleon ceased to know any bounds, but he has completely thrown off his mask."[1]

Napoleon for almost a year had been pressing for a treaty of alliance with Austria; it had taxed the ingenuity of the ministers at Vienna to evade the question and postpone such a commitment until hostilities should have come to an end. It was now Austria's turn to be suitor, and it was the work of Metternich to urge her cause. There were rumours that a partition of Turkey had been discussed in the conversations at Tilsit, and it was a point in the policy of Stadion to see that the Ottoman Porte should not be dismembered; but in case Napoleon chose to carry out such a scheme Austria had no intention of permitting the exclusive partnership of Russia in the affair; she was anxious to have a share of the spoils. If the harshness that had been shown in the negotiation for the treaty of Fontainebleau could be taken as an index of the treatment that was to be expected from Napoleon, the court of Vienna could have little hope that France would welcome its proposal of more intimate friendship. It could congratulate itself that, at last, it had settled all doubtful controversies with Napoleon, and that "no question of

[1] Metternich to Stadion, 12 Oct. 1807, in *Mémoires du Prince de Metternich* (2nd ed. 1880), ii, 125.

any importance was left open". But, once the idea of an alliance had been tentatively put forward in Paris, it was the opinion of Metternich that "it is due to our dignity that we should wait until France makes a move".[1]

Yet behind *arrière-pensée* lurks deeper *arrière-pensée*, and every purpose is lined with mental reservation. In examining the diplomacy of Austria, we can never be sure that we have reached the last filtering, and discovered the final irreducible element. When Tolstoy, the Russian minister, comes to Paris to take charge of the new policy of the Czar, we find that Austria has a still lower stratum of hidden ulterior motive. Metternich fastens himself upon his Russian colleague, assures himself that Tolstoy is at heart a servant of the coalition, and makes the man his confidant. It would seem that there are quiet nudgings and secret whisperings between these two ministers, almost under the very eyes of Napoleon. Metternich will say:

> We all have, and can have, only one end, that of preserving our integrity in the midst of the general overthrow.... The Emperor Napoleon will caress you to-day, only to fall upon you to-morrow; he will do as much with Austria; we shall both of us have to carry on an eternal struggle against his subversive designs....

Tolstoy will reply: "I am entirely of your opinion.... I do not know what these people wish to do with me, but they are fools if they think that I shall be their dupe". Metternich's conclusion will be that: "We have more chances than any other power in Europe of being intact when the great day comes for putting an end to this state of affairs—a state that is essentially precarious, because against nature, and against civilisation".[2] Austria, then, is waiting silently, waiting fearfully, for one culminating moment. She is cursed still with an unreconciled heart, and behind all thoughts of alliance with Napoleon she has a remote hankering after a new coalition.

[1] Metternich to Stadion, 12 Nov. 1807, in *Mémoires du Prince de Metternich*, ii, 128.

[2] Metternich to Stadion, 12 Nov. 1807, in *Mémoires du Prince de Metternich*, ii, 136–9. Cf. *Sbornik*, lxxxix, pp. 252–5. Tolstoy to Romantsov (Particulière et secrète), 27 Nov./9 Dec. 1807.

Merfeldt in St Petersburg may walk in the shadow of a British ambassador, and have undignified controversy with the minister of Napoleon, and, in the face of the Tilsit system, show an air of grievance that is out of season. Starhemberg in London may rigidly persist in avowed hatred of Napoleon, and may take his prejudices from Canning until he seems to become a mouthpiece for English official policy. But the diplomats in Vienna will be cold and formal in their relations with England, eager and friendly towards Napoleon, earnestly working for the alliance of France. They are prepared to cover up their true antipathies, and they will only betray their hatred by some evil glance when Napoleon is not looking. Recondite and impassive, proceeding obliquely and always on tiptoe, trusting to subtlety and pure technique, they are men of the *ancien régime*; one can see the handkerchief and the pinch of snuff. In their high abstract world these diplomats are like the giants of the financial market, using a specialised science and terminology, pursuing thought in dry categories of their own, and utterly forgetful of the farmer with his corn, the worker at his loom, the small shareholder at his desk, over whose heads the abstruse speculation is carried on, like a kind of fatality, remote and sinister. Austrian diplomacy works with a point fine as an etching-needle, and is gloriously conscienceless, and is not tortured by a misgiving. It has subtle nuances and courtly euphemisms and polished artifice to cover and cushion cynical purposes. Metternich in Paris serves its ends better than Merfeldt or Starhemberg. He gives it its true tone and flavour. He will secure state secrets by making love to a sister of Bonaparte. And there is an atmosphere in it all that Englishmen come to associate with the name of Metternich, as something malevolent and jesuitical—the shadow of the Holy Alliance.

This is a game for powdered aristocrats, and it is to be played in full dress. One has pictures of dazzling nights, curtained rooms. One seems to hear, coming from the distance, sounds of music by Mozart. The whole is a world entirely over the heads of the mass of people, working out the web of their destiny like the stars. The policy and the procedure cannot be democratised.

There is nothing communicable to the platform in the diplomacy
of the remote *arrière-pensée*. You cannot take the people into
your confidence, you cannot evoke national passion as a power
behind you, if your immediate object of policy is an alliance with
France, and your secret ultimate aim is war. You cannot make
a public cause out of a policy of "mental reservation". So it is
useless to expect from Vienna a significant and revealing gesture
such as Canning would give at times; the last secret of Austrian
policy is rather to be caught in an almost imperceptible flicker
of the eye that conveys something from Metternich to the
Russián Tolstoy, when Napoleon's back is turned. The rulers
of Austria were unwilling to make the people their accomplices.
They knew too well that if they made war itself national and
popular, and called upon their subjects to help them against the
French, they would be raising at their very doors a monster that
would be more terrible to them than Napoleon himself. They
were not yet reconciled to this.

Such was the situation, and attitude and character of the
power which Napoleon, after he had heard of the expedition to
Copenhagen, decided to call out of its persistent neutrality into
the war against England.

In October 1807 Napoleon was in violent mood. Portugal had
dared to show defiance; England had made the surprise attack
on Denmark. Man of giant angers, the Emperor did not know
how to meet a thwarting, and made an undignified outburst in
public. Lord Whitworth had seen such a display in 1803, had
found Napoleon "evidently under very considerable agitation",
speaking "loud enough to be overheard by the two hundred
people who were present", and conducting himself "with the
most extreme impropriety...the total lack of dignity as well
as of decency".[1] Kleist had had a similar experience during the
recent campaign; Napoleon "really had the appearance of being
greatly disturbed; and it made him distracted and caused him

---

[1] Lord Whitworth's despatch of 14 Mar. 1803, in O. Browning, *England
and Napoleon in* 1803, pp. 115–17.

to keep on repeating the same thing".[1] Metternich was to be confronted with the same violence at Dresden in 1813—dramatic boasts, explosive threats, wild ejaculations of a man who "allowed his anger to carry him away".[2] Napoleon found it useful to make his name terrible to Europe, and had a policy of intimidating diplomats; but it is a mistake to regard such demonstrations as always consciously contrived; they belong to an unreclaimed tract in the personality of the Corsican, the something ungovernable in his nature, a wildness at the seat of his mind. These noisy and petulant outbursts would recur at times to shock a well-bred Talleyrand, and ruin the impressiveness and the fine finish that had been upon the courts of more royal days. They betrayed a weakness or distress of Napoleon himself in the contingencies of the hour.

On the 16th of October 1807 Metternich in a despatch from Paris describes such a dramatic moment. Napoleon at an audience exploded into "one of the most violent outbursts that he has ever made in a diplomatic circle". The minister of Portugal received the first shock. "If Portugal does not do what I want," said the Emperor, "the house of Braganza will have ceased to reign in Europe within two months from now."

I will not allow a single British envoy in Europe; I will declare war against any power which has one two months from now. I have three hundred thousand Russians at my disposal and with a powerful ally like this I can do anything. Since the English have declared that they will not respect neutrals on the water any longer, I will not recognise them on land.

He passed on to the ambassador of Etruria. "Your Queen is in secret connection with England—but I have settled with that." To a deputy from Bremen he asked, "How are things going with you?" The deputy said, "Badly sir". "Very well," was the retort, "they will go worse even yet. Bremen and Hamburg are English towns; I shall know how to treat them for this." Metternich did not attempt to describe the impression

---

[1] Bericht von Kleist, 2 Mar. 1807, in Bailleu, *Preussen und Frankreich, 1795–1807*, II, 586–9.
[2] *Mémoires du Prince de Metternich*, I, 146–54; II, 461–3.

these exclamations made on all the people present, or the violent manner in which they were uttered.[1] For this episode was merely the prelude to an incident that more nearly concerned Austria.

An hour after this disconcerting experience Metternich had an interview with the French foreign minister. Champagny had unpleasant revelations to make. The Emperor, said he, would be satisfied with half-measures no longer. England had refused the mediation of Russia—she must be compelled to make peace.

Only three powers are left in Europe; France, Russia and Austria. It is for you to contribute directly to the salutary work which the Emperor is undertaking. You have had reason to see for a long time that your flag is not respected any more than the others; the King [of England] has just declared that he will recognise no neutrality. ...Russia is going to make common cause with us. All Italy obeys the impulse from France. There remains only you to close all access to the Continent.... You, more than any other power, are interested in seeing peace and tranquillity restored, but this is impossible without the maritime settlement.... The Emperor wishes you to say that if England does not give up the Danish fleet and revoke the principles enunciated in her latest declaration, you will recall your minister from London and at the same time—say the first of December —dismiss the English minister from Vienna.

Metternich protested against this demand. The Austrian ports were already closed to English vessels; no good would be achieved by making a definite declaration of war; and much harm would result to Austria. Metternich asked how it could happen that Napoleon could make this demand and yet when the Austrians had proposed that their "relations of friendship and good understanding should be grounded in the same way upon more decided bases", he had given no answer, as though he did not desire a more intimate alliance.

Metternich, though he protested against the demand, could not recommend his government to resist, but wrote:

Every reflection on the communication which the present report puts forward, seems to me to be rendered superfluous by the positive

[1] Metternich to Stadion, 16 Oct. 1807, in *Mémoires du Prince de Metter-nich*, t. II, pp. 129–30.

fact that Napoleon, scorning all moderation and even policy, *has made it understood that he would* accompany the *official demand...with a declaration of war, in the event of our refusal.* I can vouch for this assertion.... *There has recently been a total change in the methods of Napoleon; he seems to think that he has reached a point where moderation is a useless obstacle.* The peace of Tilsit and the extreme weakness of the Emperor Alexander, could not but bring him to this point.... Of all the continental powers we are the one most directly and immediately menaced.... On this occasion more than on any other the fury of Napoleon will have no limits; and his thirst for universal dominion could not be better served than by our coming short of satisfying his desires.[1]

The court of Vienna which had already resolved to make no hesitation in answering to the wishes of Napoleon, and indeed had no intention of braving the fury of France, did not remain indifferent to the force of Metternich's words.

In the last week of November Starhemberg in London received an angry despatch from Vienna. It was dated the 27th of October and had been sent to England via Paris so that it might come under the eyes of the French government. It began by enumerating the successive attempts which Austria had made to promote the peace of Europe; it deplored the failure of the mediation that had been offered before the battle of Friedland and complained of the unfavourable welcome which Canning had given to the further overtures that had followed the battle. By rejecting the good offices of Russia, and by making the attack on Denmark—an outrage which indeed had never been satisfactorily accounted for—England, said Stadion,

seems to have announced far and wide, her intention of removing all possibility of a pacification, and of refusing to do anything to restore tranquillity to Europe...and if the British court has not once and for all renounced any thought of uniting and identifying her interests with the cause of Europe, it ought to be convinced on its own account of the disastrous consequences of this conduct.

It was impossible to calculate the evils which would result from the policy of Great Britain, the despatch went on to say; but

[1] Metternich to Stadion, 16 Oct. 1807, in *Mémoires du Prince de Metternich*, t. II, pp. 128–36.

things had reached the point at which the court of Vienna felt itself compelled "to insist more peremptorily than ever on learning the real intentions of the Cabinet of St James's in this matter, and on impelling it if possible to sentiments more just and more conformable to the situation". Starhemberg therefore was to address himself "for the last time, and officially", with a "formal proposition" to the English ministry. He was to secure a sincere declaration of England's willingness to negotiate for peace; and "as a preliminary guarantee of its intentions", the British government was to renounce completely the hostile measures recently taken against Denmark and to cancel the declarations that accompanied these.

"You will feel the importance of the commission which has been entrusted to you", wrote Stadion. "There is no reasoning which you ought not to employ, no argument which should be left unused to make the English Ministry appreciate the only point of view in which this proposition can be envisaged. If on one side the welfare of Europe depends to a great degree on the decision which the British Cabinet will choose to take in these circumstances, its own position equally demands that it should at last put an end to a struggle... which will inevitably involve the destruction of England herself."

If the British government should refuse to give satisfaction on these questions or should provoke deliberate delays, then Starhemberg was to ask for his passports and Austria would break off relations with England.[1]

An accompanying despatch of the same date recounted the private grievances of the court of Vienna against the British government. It referred to the injuries done to Austrian shipping in defiance of neutral rights. It complained of the ineffectiveness of Austrian protests that had been made periodically against the injuries. "The Court of London has for nearly a year treated us in this matter as though we were veritable enemies." If the British government showed itself reasonable on the question of peace, Starhemberg was still to press this maritime issue, and was to demand satisfaction.[2]

[1] Stadion to Starhemberg, 27 Oct. 1807 (No. 1), *W.S.A. Weisungen nach London.*
[2] Stadion to Starhemberg, 27 Oct. 1807 (No. 2), *W.S.A. Weisungen nach London.*

All this was in the language of unmistakable hostility, and was calculated to provoke rather than to persuade. Nothing in it bore the mark of a sincerely mediating power, and everywhere there seemed a disposition to raise points of dispute rather than to smooth them over. But a secret and cyphered despatch was drawn up for Starhemberg at the same time, and was not sent via Paris at all, but was transmitted by a more direct route. This revealed the true situation of affairs.

We have had to choose between instant war and the measure we have just taken. The cabinet of London might have spared us a step which costs as much to the heart as to the judgment of His Imperial Majesty, if it had chosen to enter with more friendship and more consideration for the well-being of Europe, into the repeated representations which we have been making for six months. As things are at present we have had to give way to the necessity of the moment. If I have gathered the real meaning of the last advice which M. Canning charged Lord Pembroke to give us I am assured that that Minister foresaw in some manner the extremity in which we were soon to find ourselves, that he felt that we ought in such an event to make this last submission and that he saw it was important to Europe and to England that our existence should be preserved intact in the midst of this universal political overthrow.[1]

Stadion at the same time explained to the English minister Adair "that no concession which His Imperial Majesty had been called upon to make during the whole course of his reign, affected him more deeply than the measures which had been extorted from him upon this occasion".[2]

Starhemberg was alarmed when he received the commands from Vienna. He had approved of the reply which England had given to the Russian mediation; he had applauded the "wisdom and forethought" of the Danish expedition; he had declared that it would be disastrous for Europe if Canning should make peace with France. He sought counsel of his Russian colleague

[1] Stadion to Starhemberg, 27 Oct. 1807 (No. 3), *W.S.A. Weisungen nach London.*
[2] R. Adair to G. Canning, Separate, 25 Nov. 1807, *F.O. Austria* 7/84. Printed in Adair, *op. cit.* p. 291.

Alopeus,[1] and the two put heads together. They decided that the Austrian overture, presented in the hostile terms in which Count Stadion had drawn it up, would only defeat its own ends.

"I know too well", wrote Starhemberg, "the sort of pride and even of violence which always characterises the English Ministers of whatever party, and I could not fail to see how necessary it was not to give them a direct affront.... The faintest show of menace would have destroyed all hope at the very start."

Starhemberg's official overture to Canning therefore was embodied in a note that omitted any point likely to cause offence.[2] In particular, it made no mention of Denmark.

I did not hide from [Mr Canning] at the same time in my conversations, that we were making the demand of reparations to Denmark an essential point.... The verbal reply of the Secretary of State "that if negotiations were commenced they would bring up the question of Denmark, which would enter into the general settlement", seemed to me too definite and too sincere for me to lay stress in my Note upon an object which at the present moment would have given the signal for an immediate rupture. It would have been considered that we wished to dictate terms in an imperious manner.[3]

Canning in reply to the vague note of Starhemberg merely renewed his previous protestations of a desire for peace. He affected to regard the overture as a repetition of Austria's previous proposals.[4] But the court of Vienna had distinctly declared that the kind of pious assertions, which Canning had hitherto given, would by no means satisfy its demands; and since its minister in London had already taken the liberty of diluting the sense of his instructions and softening the peremptory nature of the commission that was entrusted to him, it was not to be expected that that court should feel contented if Canning on his

---

[1] "As I know for certain", wrote the Prussian minister in London. Jacobi an den König, 29 Dec. 1807, in Hassell, *Geschichte der Preussischen Politik 1807 bis 1815*, p. 356.

[2] Starhemberg to Canning, 20 Nov. 1807, in *Parliamentary Debates*, x, col. 104, No. III.

[3] Starhemberg to Stadion, 27 Nov. 1807, *W.S.A. Berichte aus London*.

[4] Canning to Starhemberg, 23 Nov. 1807, in *Parliamentary Debates*, x, cols. 104–5, No. IV. Cf. G. Canning to R. Adair, 19 Jan. 1808, *F.O. Austria* 7/84.

side failed to respond to the friendly action and produced the very reply that had been declared insufficient. The proper thing, the expected thing, at this point, therefore, was that Starhemberg should at least follow out the remainder of his instructions and meet Canning's evasiveness by breaking off relations with England.

Instead of this Starhemberg acted again on his own responsibility. He declared that Canning's reply

while not coming near to what I would desire, seems to me more satisfactory than I had dared to hope....It seems to me that it is possible to perceive in these expressions, if one looks for them, a real opening and a disposition to listen to peace proposals....

The British government was insisting that before negotiations should be opened, the French should make an announcement of the principles upon which they would consent to treat. This was a point which the Czar himself had consistently demanded until the battle of Friedland had made him rush into the arms of Napoleon. It represented no new concession on the part of England, no departure from previous policy. Starhemberg feigned to see in it a ray of hope, and nothing more than this was needed to make him once more disobey the commands of his government. He deferred the breaking off of diplomatic relations, and took no steps to withdraw his mission from London. He decided first to communicate with Metternich in Paris and discover whether Napoleon would meet the English demands. He asked the French to make an avowal of the principles upon which they would consent to negotiate. To his government he sent his excuses:

It is below the dignity of a great court to bring the affair to a standstill on a mere matter of *punctilio*—a question of who shall make the first overtures. The interests involved are too great for us not to make every attempt to attain our object....I take the liberty of observing to Your Excellency that if France should now make just and reasonable offers to Great Britain, and this power reject them with contempt, all Europe would see the real designs of England, and the present ministry would be absolutely unmasked.[1]

[1] Starhemberg to Stadion, 27 Nov. 1807, *W.S.A. Berichte aus London*.

Starhemberg sent a duplicate of this despatch to Metternich in Paris, and Metternich, after making careful modifications,[1] posted a copy, together with Canning's note, to the French foreign minister who was with Napoleon at Milan.

"His Majesty the Emperor Napoleon", wrote Metternich, "will in his great wisdom decide if he thinks he can discover in the British Cabinet's reply, any motives for following up this opening. Nothing but the hope of being useful to the cause of peace has made our envoy put off the declaration of a rupture in the official form, such as he was instructed to give. He awaits precise directions from me. I in my turn ask for those of His Majesty the Emperor of the French, and am convinced that by this new mark of confidence I am entirely fulfilling the views of my court."[2]

It becomes evident at this point that, like Starhemberg in London, Metternich himself is anxious to see the conclusion of peace between England and France, in order that his country may be liberated from the dilemma in which it is placed—in order that it may avoid the declaration of war which Napoleon has ordered to be made against England. But the government of Austria, like that of Russia, is ready to move more quickly than its servants abroad, is more anxious to prevent anything that might give the faintest shadow of offence to France, and is more disposed to hasten the quarrel with England. This is illustrated by the reproof which Starhemberg receives from Vienna, when it is learned that he has taken it upon himself to disregard the extreme tenour of his instructions. The Emperor of Austria is so severe that Tolstoy, the Russian minister in Paris, is soon found declaring: "it is a thing certainly not out of keeping with all the queer antics of fate in this century to see France checking Austria in her resentment against England".[3]

The Austrian government was greatly perturbed by the conduct which its minister Starhemberg had taken upon himself to follow. It did not imagine that Napoleon was anxious to make

---

[1] The despatch is printed (with marginal notes of the alterations which Metternich made) in *Sbornik*, LXXXIX, 287–9.

[2] Metternich to Champagny, 4 Dec. 1807, in *Sbornik*, LXXXIX, 286–7.

[3] Tolstoy to Romantsov, 29 Dec. 1807/10 Jan. 1808, in *Sbornik*, LXXXIX, 324.

peace or to have the question of a negotiation so pressingly pursued at London. It had had from Metternich the report of the warlike and intemperate language which the French Emperor was using in regard to England. It had been anxious to show Napoleon its readiness to join his continental policy and break off relations with the court of London—had ordered Starhemberg, in case England gave satisfaction on the prime question of a negotiation, to pick a further quarrel on the private maritime grievances of Austria. Much as Austrian interests might require the conclusion of a final peace, Starhemberg, by taking his pacific rôle too seriously, had compromised his government, had made it appear that his country was a slow and unwilling partner in the confederacy against England. He had put the court of Vienna in the danger of receiving a swift rebuff from France.

"Once it was determined to transmit an official Note on this subject, this diplomatic document ought of necessity to have comprised the whole of the demands which you were instructed to give", wrote the Austrian chancellor.

"Mr Canning had a right to say in his reply that what Your Excellency is insisting upon in your Note is nothing but a repetition of our former overtures on the same subject, and that he therefore could only repeat...the same declaration he made to you at that time....And you, Prince, must recognise for yourself that a note from that Cabinet, merely a duplicate of those which England has already addressed to us and to Russia, could not be in any way satisfactory."

Unless Napoleon should be willing to follow up the overture, unless England should make a more explicit declaration, and unless the French court should signify through Metternich its desire to see Starhemberg prolong his stay in London, the minister was to open the question straight away, and in an official manner, to Canning, and follow literally the instructions which had been sent to him at the end of October. "His Majesty also desires you to mention about the demand of passports in the official Note...or simultaneously with it, at least; and he wishes you to allow no delay in replying, beyond two or three days."[1]

---

[1] Stadion to Starhemberg, 22 Dec. 1807 (No. 1), *W.S.A. Weisungen nach London.*

An accompanying despatch ordered Starhemberg to follow the counsels of Metternich in future; Vienna was too far distant to allow for communication. If the improbable thing happened and France really wished to renew the discussions with England, then Prince Starhemberg "must use all possible zeal" to promote the negotiation, following all the time the directions of Metternich.

We have too keen an interest in seeing the re-establishment of general tranquillity not to desire such an event. The Emperor commands...that you make a point of fastening with zeal and activity upon everything which might provide a nucleus for a real rapprochement between the two belligerent Powers.[1]

This reproof was sent to Starhemberg via Paris, under a flying seal. Metternich showed it to the French government. The Russian minister in Paris saw the meaning of the severe language of Austria; Stadion had taken this course "probably with the intention of making capital out of it here".[2]

"Napoleon", said the French minister, "applauded the wise and strong conduct that the Court of Vienna had followed on this occasion; it did the greatest honour to the Emperor of Austria; the Prince of Starhemberg, having dared to forgo the execution of the orders of his Court, deserved the reprimand....But it might be detrimental to the success of the affair for Starhemberg to be turned from the course he had followed; and the Emperor believed it would be more useful to avoid upsetting his point of view in the matter, by preventing despatches which might throw him into doubt, from reaching him."[3]

The French minister, writing to Metternich from Milan, had already disclosed the intentions of Napoleon. Comparing the reply which England had made to the latest Austrian overture with the answer recently given to the Czar's offer of mediation, he found the "same method of evasion", he saw "the desire to gain time and to postpone an Austrian measure that is calculated to cause a sensation in England by no means favourable to the present ministry". Canning had said that His Britannic Majesty

---

[1] Stadion to Starhemberg, 22 Dec. 1807 (No. 2), *W.S.A. Weisungen nach London.*

[2] *Sbornik,* LXXXIX, 324.

[3] Tolstoy to Romantsov, 30 Dec. 1807/11 Jan. 1808, in *Sbornik,* LXXXIX, 331.

was as willing to negotiate with France as he had always been, that a fresh declaration on this matter was unnecessary, but that he was quite willing to give it.

"But did England desire peace when she rejected the mediation of Russia?" wrote Champagny. "...The English ministry does not say it wishes for peace. It makes its willingness to enter into negotiations depend on a thousand conditions; it desires a peace which will establish on equal bases the respective interests of the powers taking part in the war, a peace conformable to the fidelity which England owes to her allies (has England an ally in Europe now?)—a peace which will provide for the security and tranquillity of Europe....When England expresses her desire for peace we are therefore entitled to ask for proofs. In the present situation, let her prove her sincerity by naming plenipotentiaries to treat for peace with France and Russia. Prince Starhemberg might in that case remain in London, and he will be authorised to deliver passports to these ministers, so that they may cross over to the continent."

The whole French declaration was drawn up in a manner hostile, provoking and proud. Napoleon did not break off the discussion; he allowed everything to depend upon the next movement of the British government; he was determined to put England in the wrong; that is why he threw upon Canning the burden of declining to send plenipotentiaries to Paris. The note stated that if Austria would join hands with those powers which had declared against England, this step, "taken in the same month as that of the emperor of Russia, would be the very thing to scatter perfidious hopes and open the eyes of the English people to its true situation".[1] The edict of Milan, dated the 17th of December and containing a renewed attack on English trade and on the remnant of neutrality that still existed in Europe, confirms the idea that at heart Napoleon had no desire for peace, no intention of making concessions that would conciliate the court of London. Metternich spoke truly, in transmitting the French note to England, when he said that Canning would have to be very careful in his choice of plenipotentiaries.

Metternich was anxious to make it plain to Napoleon that Austria was completely entering into the views of France. When

---

[1] Champagny to Metternich, 15 Dec. 1807, in *Sbornik*, LXXXIX, 300–3.

he despatched the French note to London, he sent to Starhemberg a statement of his own views, taking care to catch the mood of the French government, and writing in an unfriendly strain.

"It seems to me essential", he declared, "that when you acquit yourself of the honourable commission with which you are charged you should at the same time declare positively that the refusal to send negotiators furnished with full powers sufficient for treating, will be the signal for the immediate demand for your passports."[1]

But he accompanied this ostensible and official instruction with a private and secret letter that was not allowed to come under the eyes of the French. "Your Highness will see at first reading", it began, "that my despatch of the 23rd December is drawn up in an offensive manner. It was in fact intended to be shown to M. de Champagny."[2] In this more intimate letter we are justified in finding the real sentiments of Metternich on the subject of maritime peace; for his arguments are earnest and cogent, and they dovetail into the whole system of his views at this period. Metternich was anxious to see peace in Europe for the moment, in order that Napoleon might have no pretext for further exploitations of his military supremacy. His desire was to see the powers acquiesce in the settlement of Tilsit, and end the universal chaos by making an interval in the contest; but it was only a case of stooping to conquer, the enemies of Napoleon would be quietly gathering power, and some future contingency would call out a coalition once more. It was in conformity with this design, this last lurking *arrière-pensée* of the Austrians, that Metternich, writing privately to Starhemberg at this moment, should press England to make peace—a peace riddled, it is true, with mental reservations, and resting on secret hostility—and should use every argument to prove that this policy was for the enemies of France the highest opportunism. The fact that after the expedition to Copenhagen, Napoleon showed himself little disposed for a settlement, seemed only to confirm Metternich in his fundamental idea that the event most disadvantageous to France in the contingencies of the moment would be the conclusion of

[1] Metternich to Starhemberg, 23 Dec. 1807, in *Sbornik*, LXXXIX, 306–7.
[2] Metternich to Starhemberg, 26 Dec. 1807, in *Sbornik*, LXXXIX, 308–10.

a maritime peace which should rescue England from her dangerous isolation, and should disarm Napoleon at a time when his power seemed irresistible and so should relieve the burdens of the European states. Thus we find Metternich writing:

Let the British ministry think seriously about the step it is taking; the bows are drawn as tightly as possible; few of the states of the old Europe have escaped the prolonged scourge of the maritime war; two of them, only, remain strong, powerful, intact. Let England not wait for new complications and evils which are too easily to be foreseen and which will weaken the last supports of the old order of things. Let her make peace or at least negotiate. Months gained now are worth years at any other time or under other circumstances.

Many things, thought Metternich, made the moment opportune. The Russians "by every motive of commerce and existence" were interested in seeing the establishment of peace. England would find in Austria an intermediary whose sole desire was for the immediate establishment of a tolerable if not a stable condition of things.

When will a negotiation with France be renewed under such auspices if the present opportunity is allowed to slip?...

Let the English ministry above all things not bring the affair to a halt on preliminary questions, such as the announcement of bases prior to the assembly of negotiators. It will be impossible to defend your position in London, Prince, if in place of the sending or the positive announcement of the arrival of negotiators, there is a mere desire to continue pourparlers.[1]

At a later date Metternich added in a further private and secret despatch: "The British ministry will be very foolish if it does not lend itself to a negotiation".[2] Starhemberg, in the meantime, had been working in London to prepare the way for further measures. He was pleased to think that at least his conduct had not met with impetuous reproof from Napoleon. "The courier's delay gives hope that he will bring overtures from France, and I am bold enough to flatter myself that these will not be rejected if they are at all reasonable." Canning, indeed, had said "that

---

[1] Metternich to Starhemberg, 26 Dec. 1807, in *Sbornik*, LXXXIX, 308–10.

[2] Metternich to Starhemberg, 10 Jan. 1808, in *Sbornik*, LXXXIX, 335.

a counter-proposal would certainly be sent from England if the French proposals gave any sign of there being a real desire for peace".[1] It now became the business of Starhemberg to be the apologist of the French proposals, to point out how acceptable they were, and to make a pathetic fight for a cause against which he had recently written with so much eloquence and conviction.

Between this man and the English foreign secretary there ensued a wearisome argument on the question of a negotiation with France. It quickly developed into an unpleasant kind of duel with futile fencing and evasiveness on both sides. Before it was finally abandoned it had produced irritation between the two ministers, and even something that seems like an estrangement.

Metternich's recondite policy of peace with mental reservations, and Austria's cool cautiousness, were not the course that would appeal to Canning, hasty emotional man, "all nervous and a-quiver". The treaties of Tilsit had found him masterly and unrelenting; in the mediation of Russia he had detected veiled hostility and even direct deception; he was not thereafter disposed to put faith in vague peace moves engineered from Paris. He complained, as he had always done, that France persisted in refusing to avow the basis upon which she would negotiate. It did not placate his fiery heart when Starhemberg argued that this was a proof of Napoleon's good faith, that France was merely unwilling to raise preliminary discussions which might wreck the negotiation before the plenipotentiaries had come together. The Austrian minister described Napoleon's eagerness for peace, declared himself ready to provide passports for English plenipotentiaries and communicated with members of the opposition, in order to reinforce his case.

"I cannot omit to say", he reported, "that the secretary of state has appeared to me to be struck at times with the force of my arguments, and even embarrassed for a reply to my redoubled objections ...and I have noticed him resorting to the most weak of pretexts to account for his refusal."

[1] Starhemberg to Stadion, 22 Dec. 1807, *W.S.A. Berichte aus London.*

But impatience and unpleasantness resulted from this argumentation. It became dangerous for Starhemberg to remain in London, if he could have nothing with which to justify the course he was pursuing. On the 1st of January he made official communication of the proposals he had been authorised to make; drawing up the note, as he informed his government, in the most moderate terms that were possible, "in order not to ruin everything by too much energy or hastiness", and "to put the English ministry completely in the wrong before Parliament".[1]

On the 8th of January Canning wrote a reply which the irritated Austrian called "very long, very diffuse, and very ungracious, as well as badly drawn up".[2] He declined to avail himself of the opening that France had given. Napoleon had refused to declare the principles upon which he intended to negotiate. A hostile capital, like Paris, was an unsuitable place for the meeting of plenipotentiaries. England would not make any arrangement with France unless her allies should be comprised in it. Finally, the overture was defective in form.

"The overture of Prince Starhemberg...", wrote Canning to Adair, "...was made by him without the knowledge or sanction of his court, and simply on a suggestion of one of the French ministers, which is believed to have been conveyed in a rather unofficial form to Count Metternich at Paris."[3]

The Austrian minister, having received the English reply, immediately wrote to ask for an interview with the foreign secretary. Canning, at this time in a bad state of health, was away in the country when the letter arrived; but the under-secretary Hammond had been instructed to open his correspondence, and he replied to the Austrian. "Mr Canning", he wrote, "...considers the subject which he has been discussing with you to be of so delicate and important a nature as to render it desirable that all communications respecting it should be made

---

[1] Starhemberg to Stadion, 5 Jan. 1808, *W.S.A. Berichte aus London.* Starhemberg's note to Canning (1 Jan. 1808) is printed in *Parliamentary Debates*, x, cols. 105–6, No. v.
[2] Starhemberg to Stadion, 10 Jan. 1808, *W.S.A. Berichte aus London.* Canning's note is printed in *Parliamentary Debates*, x, cols. 106–8, No. vi.
[3] G. Canning to R. Adair, 19 Jan. 1808, *F.O. Austria* 7/84.

solely in writing."[1] Starhemberg gave the appearance of becoming more and more irritated. He decided to make it known verbally and unofficially to the British government that he proposed very soon to ask for his passports. Before doing this he played his last card, and wrote to Metternich:

If at the present moment you could send me propositions and a basis of peace to offer to England, together with an authorisation for my conduct such as would silence all objections, the ministry, already embarrassed for excuses for its present conduct, could not go on refusing to enter into negotiations. It would be worthy of the generosity of Napoleon for him to make this last offer for the general good of Europe.[2]

But Metternich was now as peremptory as his government, requiring the instant departure of the Austrian mission from London, if England did not accept the clear alternative of sending plenipotentiaries to Paris. On the 16th of January he made it known that Napoleon expected the final break with England to take place by the 21st. Before this announcement arrived, Starhemberg had abandoned his efforts and had decided to leave England.[3]

He was not convinced, even yet, that the possibilities of the situation had been exhausted. He was still obsessed with the idea that peace was the superlative object, and that his business was to promote a negotiation. But perhaps he was conscious of having lost favour with Napoleon, and desired to restore his credit; for his arguments took more and more a turn hostile to the British ministers. He asserted that "if France had seriously desired it" she could have induced the English ministry to negotiate, and "might still do so to-day".[4] He cited Canning's own words as his justification:

As soon as the Basis of negotiation shall have been satisfactorily ascertained and an unexceptionable Place of Negotiation agreed upon, His Majesty will be prepared to name Plenipotentiaries to meet those of the other Powers engaged in the War; but his Majesty will not again consent to send his plenipotentiaries to a hostile Capital.

[1] Hammond to Starhemberg, 9 Jan. 1808, *F.O. Austria* 7/87.
[2] Starhemberg to Metternich, 10 Jan. 1808, *W.S.A. Berichte aus London*.
[3] Starhemberg to Stadion, 21 Jan. 1808, *W.S.A. Berichte aus London*.
[4] Starhemberg to Stadion, 4 Feb. 1808, *W.S.A. Berichte aus London*.

But even if Canning should prove still intractable, Starhemberg continually played with the idea of "forcing the ministry to treat". He had been careful to communicate his overtures to members of the opposition in England—to Grenville, Holland, Grey and Sheridan. He had noted the embarrassment of Canning at times, and had talked of "having the ministers completely unmasked". He declared: "The opening of parliament provides the means of destroying the only obstacle, and annihilating the prejudice that the present ministry has inculcated throughout the country, that Napoleon does not seriously wish to see the end of the war".[1] He announced his intention of pointing out all this to the French Emperor, if he could secure an interview as he passed through Paris: Metternich in the same way had talked of "calling the English ministry before the tribunal of public opinion". The Austrians and the French at this period were paying watchful attention to the stability and strength of the existing cabinet in London. In the French foreign office archives there is mention of a scheme to offer England a treaty of commerce in order to seduce the British traders and place them in opposition to the warlike policy of their government.[2] Napoleon had good reason to work for the overthrow of Canning.

Starhemberg sent a long justification of his conduct to his government at Vienna, explaining how little he had departed from the intentions of his government.[3] It is interesting to see that he called Alopeus—of all people—to bear witness to his good policy. Certainly his decision to depart from the original tenour of his instructions was made after consultation with this man. "I thought it best to give him every confidence", wrote Starhemberg; and the old intriguer did not cease to assist with his "advice and good offices", even after the Russian government had ordered him to break off diplomatic relations with England. He declared that he would have disobeyed the positive instructions of the Czar and would have withheld the declaration of

[1] Starhemberg to Stadion, 26 Jan. 1808, *W.S.A. Berichte aus London.*
[2] Réflexions sur la Paix avec l'Angleterre, *A.A.E. Angleterre*, t. 604.
[3] Starhemberg to Stadion, 4 Feb. 1808, *W.S.A. Berichte aus London.*

war, in order to be able to lend official support to the Austrian overture, but that he was prevented from taking this course, since the British government had already learned of the rupture. It was Alopeus who counselled moderation and patience; advised Starhemberg, even at the end of the negotiation, to postpone the demand for his passports; and even recommended him to make some delay before using them, when they had actually been obtained. "Perhaps he would have preferred me not to leave London so promptly as I did." When the harassed Austrian at a perplexing moment writes to his government that he "does not know how to be thankful enough" for Alopeus, we who know the wily Russian can conjecture what had taken place; and we can see it as all the more significant in the light of one final episode which remains to be examined—and in which Alopeus is the central figure.

CHAPTER IV

ALOPEUS MAKES A FINAL EFFORT
ON BEHALF OF PEACE

Vienna declared war, and the Austrian minister left England
—and Alopeus still stayed on. He alleged the sickness of his
wife, but the Czar smelt more intrigue and flew into a passion
and told him to quit England, bag and baggage, without delay.[1]
Tolstoy in Paris took the side of Alopeus and wrote to say that
the Czar was more severe than Napoleon himself—that Napoleon
indeed was quite content for Alopeus to stay in London, that it
would be useful to find out what happened at the opening of the
English parliament.

Before he left the country the Russian minister had several
conversations with the English secretary of state. At the request
of Canning he reported these directly to the Czar and begged
that Romantsov, the chancellor, should not be informed of them.
Canning, making his declaration of policy, began by saying that
France, and not Russia, was the real enemy of England.

"It has been constantly our system to contribute to the greatness
of Russia...", he said. "This system will be invariable if she [Russia]
will return to her former principles; in the contrary event I do not
conceal from you that we shall adopt a system diametrically opposed
to the old one. It will then be to our interest to limit the power of
Russia and to work as much against her interests as we have been
concerned till now to advance them. If we really have to renounce
the continental system we shall make peace with France, abandoning
the Continent to Bonaparte...in that case he will no longer contest
our Empire of the seas."[2]

[1] For the Czar's dissatisfaction with Alopeus, see e.g. despatches of
Caulaincourt printed in Grand-Duke Nicholas Mikhaïlovitch, *Relations
diplomatiques de la Russie et de la France*, I, 28, 161, etc.

[2] Alopeus to the Czar Alexander, 14/26 Feb. 1808, outlined and quoted
in F. de Martens, *Recueil [des Traités et Conventions conclus par la Russie]*,
XI, 147–9. The conclusions of Martens in regard to these despatches of
Alopeus cannot be maintained; but his actual citations of documents may
be trusted, as they are confirmed by the rest of the evidence concerning
this episode.

Napoleon should have the land; England should have the ocean. And then where would the Russians be? Canning put this forward as a threat, and the fact is of some importance; it was a piece of menace that he had persistently used since his very first days at the foreign office. England would make peace if pressed, but she would leave the continental nations to deal with Napoleon as best they could.

Then, on the eve of the departure of Alopeus, one would have said that Canning was keeping his threat. Under the seal of the greatest secrecy, he made a declaration, protesting that this embodied the most intimate sentiments of the British government on the subject of a maritime peace. He would prefer, he said, to continue the war, rather than make a peace that could not be lasting, but he was willing to admit "the uti possidetis and perfect reciprocity" as the basis of a negotiation, and he gave Alopeus to understand that he would enter into immediate and direct discussions with France on this understanding, without the intervention of any other power. The Russian minister was enchanted. "This, Sire," he wrote to the Czar, "is the secret of the Cabinet of St James's. Mr Canning in confiding it to me demanded that on my word of honour I should communicate it to no one but Your Majesty."[1]

Napoleon in Paris awaited the arrival of Alopeus with some interest, for it was known that the man would have something to disclose concerning an English peace. Before his arrival, in fact before the Austrian negotiation had quite come to an end, the French government had, for some reason, made a more plausible pretence of a desire to enter into negotiation. When Napoleon returned to Paris at the new year the representatives of foreign powers found him "penetrated with a desire for peace".[2] He seemed alarmed to learn that his hostile and provoking note to Metternich on the subject of the Austrian overtures, had been forwarded to England.[3] On the 7th of January an article in the *Moniteur* expressed the French govern-

[1] Martens, *Recueil*, p. 149.
[2] Tolstoy to Romantsov, 29 Dec. 1807/10 Jan. 1808, in *Sbornik*, LXXXIX, 324.
[3] *Sbornik*, LXXXIX, 324–5.

ment's desire to achieve a maritime settlement, a willingness to remove some obstacles to an understanding, and a conciliatory disposition on the vexed subject of maritime rights.[1] If Napoleon had adopted a provocative attitude in his statements to Metternich, turning the negotiation into such a course that England was bound to reject his proposals and Austria was bound to declare war against her, he seemed now to have some reason for pretending to hold a more serious desire for peace. When Alopeus reached the French capital he had long interviews with both the Emperor and the minister for foreign affairs; and he "was treated with a distinction rarely accorded to foreign ministers".[2] Napoleon was astonished with the information that he brought and did not conceal his pleasure. It seemed that he was anxious to take advantage of the situation. He gave it to be understood that on the conditions outlined by Canning, on the principle of "uti possidetis and perfect reciprocity", peace could be signed immediately.

"But why stop at this Latin phrase", he said to Alopeus. "Let us say this: that if England desires peace and does not intend to procrastinate—I hate delays—I shall not refuse it. It must be of importance to them that Portugal be re-established—very good. That is no sacrifice. Pondicherry—very well! A mere island, a village! Malta, the cape of Good Hope; granted! Hanover—if the King of England clings to it—readily! Swedish Pomerania—let it return to the Swedish King; but Finland," said Napoleon to the Russian Alopeus, "Your Master needs it; it is too near to St Petersburg."[3]

Napoleon insisted, it would seem, that there should be no delay in communicating with the ministers of London. Smirnov, who had belonged to the mission of Alopeus, prepared himself for a return to England, ostensibly to discuss the situation of Russian prisoners, really to bear a letter which would convey the views

---

[1] See *Sbornik*, LXXXIX, 332–4 for references to Napoleon's desire to have copies of the *Moniteur* sent to England.

[2] Champagny to Caulaincourt, No. 7, 9 Mar. 1808, in Grand-Duke Nicholas Mikhaïlovitch, *Relations diplomatiques de la Russie et de la France*, VII, 27.

[3] Martens, *Recueil*, XI, 150. It seems that Alopeus gave the Prussian minister in Paris to understand that Napoleon had a pronounced desire for peace but that the British government was determined to continue the war, in Hassell, *Geschichte der Preussischen Politik 1807–1815*, I, 498.

of France on the subject of peace.[1] For a fortnight the matter was gravely discussed. On the 29th of February the Russian minister in Paris had written to his government to explain how important it was that Russia should not be excluded from the negotiation.[2] On the 18th of March he returned to the theme.

M. d'Alopeus cherishes the highest hopes and thinks that the propositions of the Emperor Napoleon will determine the British Government to set negotiations on foot. I only ask you now to draw up the instructions and full-powers necessary for our participation in the affair, and it is of the utmost importance to send them from St Petersburg as promptly as possible. As it cannot be foreseen just now whether the seat of the negotiation will be London or Paris it seems to me essential that you should send at the same time similar full-powers for a plenipotentiary who may have to go to London.

Tolstoy, in fact, could not resist another opening for the expression of his political views. "It is only in a rapprochement between France and England that I can as yet see any possible chance of dragging Russia out of the situation she is in."[3]

In the archives of the French ministry of foreign affairs there is a curious letter that reveals the mind of Napoleon at this period.[4] It is the missive that Smirnov was to have carried to London in March 1808, in reply to the opening made by Canning. It was written by the French foreign minister, and carefully corrected by Napoleon; it exists in three drafts; it was a letter

[1] Alopeus to the Czar Alexander, 6/18 Mar. 1808, in Martens, *Recueil*, XI, 151.

[2] *Sbornik*, LXXXIX, 445.

[3] *Ibid.* 452.

[4] "Projet de lettre de M. d'Alopeus à Lord * * * à Londres, rédigé par M. de Champagny." The letter is printed in P. Coquelle, *Napoleon and England* (Eng. transl.), 1904, in a chapter headed, "A curious document (September 1808)", p. 183. M. Coquelle, however, seems unaware of the movements that were taking place around Alopeus in March 1808, and so he has no context for the letter. He places it rather as a "preamble" to the proposals of Erfurt, and so puts it six months too late. There is a reference in the letter to Smirnov, as the bearer. There is a remark to the effect that England is "in a position to save the King of Sweden who will otherwise lose his whole country this summer". Further, Alopeus himself left Paris early in April. The letter can only be dated March 1808. It is to this letter that Napoleon refers in his note to Champagny, "ce mars 1808", printed in Fournier's *Life of Napoleon* (Eng. transl.), II, 520, No. 17.

which Alopeus was to sign and transmit as his own message. It was addressed to an English lord, though the name of the lord is not inserted; but it was evidently really intended for the eyes of Canning himself.

After some enquiries about the health of "My Lord", the letter attacks the problem of peace:

> After all I have seen and heard in England I feel compelled to break my silence.
>
> My first idea was to communicate with Mr Canning in person, but I fear he might think that in view of the actual state of affairs I should not be justified in addressing him directly.
>
> The financial position and resources of this country are far more prosperous than is believed in England, and everything prompts one to think that the prolongation of the war is not only a misfortune for the Continent, but, in addition, most disadvantageous to your country. Peace will have to be made some day, and each delay will be to your disadvantage.

From this opening we can gather that Alopeus is being made to say something which would have no force if it came from a Frenchman. He had been under a cloud of late, because of his notorious anglophile tendencies, so the message, coming from him, would be likely to have more weight in London. The last time he had seen Canning they had been whispering secrets together; now, in this letter, he is to resume the touch of intimacy, and return the confidences of Canning, keeping up that anglophile air. So he is to pass a stealthy tip to the British, and say that peace is a more urgent necessity for them than they thought. The letter is simply a way of exploiting the credit which Alopeus was thought to have in England. "I have had the privilege of an hour's interview with the Emperor", the document continued, "and told him that the basis which I thought would be acceptable in England would be that of the Uti possidetis and the admission of the allies to a Congress." Then the letter described how Napoleon accepted the uti possidetis, or perfect reciprocity, each power giving compensation, "pound for pound, ounce for ounce", for every piece of territory it abandoned. Napoleon for his part would give up Hanover, Portugal, and

Swedish Pomerania, in return for colonies captured by England.

Consequently in my opinion, you are in a position to save the King of Sweden, who will otherwise certainly lose his whole country this summer.... The Emperor's attitude has appeared to me to be sincere, for he expresses no desire for any elaborate negotiations, notes, or discussions. I believe that if you are at one with him, he is determined to bring matters to a speedy conclusion, or, if no understanding can be arrived at, to continue the war by every means in his power.... Before bringing my letter to a conclusion, my Lord, I am to notify you of a circumstance which is, in my opinion, of the utmost importance. This country will make no difficulty in sending a confidential agent to London to treat there, unless you prefer to send a representative to Paris yourselves.

Probably Alopeus never saw this letter, or discovered how he was to be used by the French government. Certainly the letter was never sent. Napoleon suddenly became silent. On the 2nd of April Alopeus interviewed the foreign minister.[1]

"He has got nothing out of the man", wrote Tolstoy, "except the certainty that all hope of a peace with England is at an end, M. de Champagny has said to him that he imagined [Napoleon] would not for the moment follow up the idea he had had of renewing a negotiation with the British Government. In consequence M. d'Alopeus proposes to leave Paris shortly."[2]

And if that was all Alopeus could learn of the failure of the peace effort and the reasons for the reversal of policy, history cannot hope to know very much more.

It is a strange episode, and one would like to understand it. Canning, in putting forward his views to Alopeus at all would seem to have made a considerable retreat from his former position. Even Napoleon was surprised. The English minister affirmed that he would conclude peace on terms which Napoleon had been seeking to force upon the country ever since the battle of Trafalgar. This compromise, this principle by which England was to have the sea, Napoleon the land, each negotiating on the basis of actual possession, was in fact much more acceptable to

---

[1] Report of Alopeus, 19/31 Mar. 1808, in Martens, *Recueil*, XI, 151.
[2] Tolstoy to Romantsov, 22 Mar./3 Ap. 1808, in *Sbornik*, LXXXIX, 490.

France than the idea of dividing empire with the Czar, Russia to have the east and France the west. It is strange that Canning should feel himself reduced to the acceptance of such a basis. One is tempted to pause a moment. Perhaps he did not feel himself so reduced. Nothing goes to show that he had really weakened. One is struck by the fact that all this was an excellent thing with which to frighten the Czar, that it was the precise thing with which Canning had threatened Alopeus shortly before, and that all which passed in the interview in question was really meant for the Czar's private ear. Perhaps it was not so much Napoleon who was subtle and clever at this period, making a cat's paw of Alopeus. Perhaps the whole transaction was a ruse on the part of the English minister, a trick to frighten the Russians. If so, it is interesting to see how it succeeded.

The Czar, when he knew that Napoleon had an idea of making peace with England, was overcome with panic. The Russian chancellor mooned and fretted like a discarded lover, and showed himself peeved and petulant. They quite granted the fact that Napoleon intended to take account of Russian interests in the arrangement, but this did not calm them in the least. They adopted an injured tone, they pestered the French ambassador for news, and they had no rest until they knew that the whole matter was at an end. Altogether they stood out in defence of the system of Tilsit, as though Napoleon had made attack on it. They set forth the praises of the alliance, as though they felt that France was deserting them. They took up Napoleon's recent sayings, and his Tilsit vocabulary, and condemned him out of his own mouth. "It seemed possible that France would come to terms with England," said Romantsov, "but if Russia had to continue the struggle alone she was prepared for it and would prove that she could sustain it more easily than England."[1]

The French made excuse that Alopeus was at the bottom of this transaction. The Czar need have no fear since everything was to be worked through a Russian minister.[1] But it was insisted at St Petersburg that the minister was dishonest. The

[1] Champagny to Caulaincourt, No. 14, 13 May 1808, in Grand-Duke Nicholas, *Relations diplomatiques*, VII, 38.

favourable reception that was given to Alopeus in Paris was unwelcome; the Russians declared the man unworthy. The Czar roundly stated, "Alopeus is a liar".[1]

"As to peace with England," said the chancellor to the French ambassador, "the Emperor Napoleon has a genius so far above everybody else's, that I must not criticise his intentions; but I think all the same that I must recall what I have already said to you; the English do not wish for peace; it is not in their interests to make peace at this moment; the ministry has a profound desire for war, and the Emperor Napoleon is wrong if he thinks he can draw this Cabinet into a pacific disposition. Perhaps some arrangement will result from the propositions that have been put forward, but it would only be an armistice....To force England to a durable peace needs large measures, as the Emperor said some time ago. It will be the sway of circumstances, not the rule of reason that will make her consent to it...."[2]

"We must move perfectly together", said the Russian chancellor. And Caulaincourt said that the Russian minister showed himself at heart more disturbed, more distracted than he actually expressed in direct terms. He was moderate in his definite utterances, but a lurking feeling of deeper dissatisfaction pierced through at times.[3]

The English government did not guess the existence of a real hostility like this, on the part of Russia; and though it did not welcome the ambitious designs which the Czar might have against the Ottoman Empire, it did not wish to make these an obstacle to friendship. Hence Canning's persistent attempts to prove to Russia that England was more anxious than France to promote the extension of Russian power. The idea that the Czar's declaration of war was a "legal fiction", a merely "ostensible" act of hostility, an unwilling fulfilment of a promise exacted at Tilsit, persisted in a strange fashion in England. At a time when Austria and Prussia, though breaking off relations with the

[1] Despatches of Caulaincourt, in Grand-Duke Nicholas, *Relations diplomatiques*, e.g. II, 22, 31, 44, 103.

[2] Caulaincourt to Champagny, No. 92, 26 Ap. 1808, in Grand-Duke Nicholas, *Relations diplomatiques*, II, 95.

[3] Caulaincourt to Champagny, No. 92, 26 Ap. 1808, in Grand-Duke Nicholas, *Relations diplomatiques*, II, 95.

court of London made avowals of secret friendship; at a time, moreover, when the representative of Russia in London was "English" in his real sympathies and no lover of the "Tilsit" system, and so was likely to read his own sentiments into the intentions of his government, it was perhaps natural that Canning should divine "mental reservation" behind the dramatic declarations of hostility that were issued from St Petersburg. But when in 1809 Austria found herself at war with France and renewed her connection with England it is curious to see Starhemberg, returning to London again, instructed to say that the British cabinet was treating this question in a mistaken fashion —that if it wished to win over the Russians, it must send an English fleet to the Black Sea or the Baltic;[1] it is curious to see Starhemberg replying a few months later that the English cabinet seemed decided at last to abandon its former attitude to Russia, and it is significant that we find him adding:

I have had much trouble before I have been able to induce the British Ministry to take vigorous measures, for in spite of the incontestable proof it has had daily for some time of the hostility of the Court of St Petersburg it could not persuade itself that Russia was sincere in her alliance with Napoleon and has for a long time nursed the hope of leading her back to a system more conformable to her real interests.[2]

Russia was incensed against England; but at the same time, this was not the full explanation of the fear which came upon her in March 1808 when she heard that France was flirting with peace negotiations. The French ambassador saw the larger reason for her attitude, and reported it to his government. Russia, he said, was half afraid that "the eagerness which [Napoleon] displayed for this negotiation was motived by a desire to elude in that way the arrangements that had been made concerning Turkey".[3] It was the Czar himself who said: "When we have settled things in Turkey and India, this will force

---

[1] Instructions to Starhemberg, 15 Ap. 1809, *W.S.A. Weisungen nach London.*

[2] Starhemberg to Stadion, No. 27, 20 July 1809, *W.S.A. Berichte aus London.*

[3] Caulaincourt to Champagny, No. 92, 26 Ap. 1808, in Grand-Duke Nicholas, *Relations diplomatiques*, ii, 95.

England to make peace".[1] Alexander was as eager as Napoleon for the Franco-Russian alliance, and the policy it implied. He was still exulting in the phrases of Tilsit. But he was not blind-folded any longer. He was not willing to be a dupe. He had come to earth and was objective and critical. In a moment he was prepared to believe that his ally was planning to evade him. He was a partner less docile, less amenable, than Napoleon had once imagined. And his eyes were fixed upon the one tangible piece of advantage that the alliance with France had promised him.

The Czar had carried away from Tilsit the happy anticipation of extended empire, the vague prospect of acquisitions in Turkey. But he had pledged himself in a solemn treaty to accept the mediation of France in his war with the Ottoman Porte, and to withdraw his troops from the Principalities of Moldavia and Wallachia. It is apparent that Napoleon had not fettered himself by any grave commitments. There was indeed a clause in the treaties, which declared that if the Turks refused to accept Napoleon's mediation or to conclude a satisfactory peace, France and Russia should make common cause against them, and deprive them of provinces in Europe; but Napoleon knew that the Turks would submit to his dictation, in order to prevent the French from joining hands with the Russians against their empire. Having convinced the Czar that he was ready to take part in the dismemberment of Turkey he was in a strong position; for nothing could have more successfully calmed the jealousy which the Russians had persistently shown in regard to his activities in the Near East. He was now able to move his troops in those regions, without fear of hostility and suspicion at St Petersburg. He was able to explain to the Czar that the possession of Corfu had never been important to the interests of Russia, save for the purpose of checking French designs in that part of the Mediterranean; that, now, when the two Empires had come into partnership, "the motives which Russia had for retaining this distant possession, existed no longer";[2] that

---

[1] Caulaincourt to Champagny, No. 93, 27 Ap. 1808, in Grand-Duke Nicholas, *Relations diplomatiques*, II, 103.

[2] *Sbornik*, LXXXVIII, 58–61. See also *Corresp. de Nap. Ier*, t. xv, No. 12846.

indeed it would be salutary and useful if the place were in French hands. In this way, by the illusions which Napoleon fostered at Tilsit, the Czar was to a certain extent disarmed.

Russian policy in the hands of Romantsov, the new chancellor, became, however, more realistic. Romantsov had always set his eyes upon the Turkish provinces. The Czar, removed from the enchantments of Tilsit, began to show a tenaciously self-seeking under-side to his character, which Napoleon had not discerned. He generously fulfilled his treaty engagements and eagerly declared war against England, but, in his relations with Turkey, he proved an intractable ally. He denounced an armistice that had been concluded, he persisted in the occupation of Moldavia and Wallachia, and he neglected to provide his minister in Paris with the necessary powers for the negotiation of peace. The Turks could not fail to see the hostility of this course of conduct, and if they should become convinced that Napoleon was an accomplice in these actions, they would quickly hold out their arms to the English. In November 1807 the alliance was already becoming strained; Napoleon himself was astonishing the Czar by his harsh treatment of the Prussians, and was inviting re-proaches from St Petersburg by his continued occupation of Prussian territory. He made use of the letter of the treaties of Tilsit, to confound his ally. He declared "that he, for his part, saw no advantage to France in the dismemberment of the Ottoman Porte, that he asked for nothing better than to guarantee its integrity";[1] but if the Russians should persist in their refusal to evacuate the Principalities, he offered to admit this breach of the treaties on the condition that he should receive compensation in Prussia, and hold Silesia and its fort-resses.[2] The proposal was calculated to alarm the Russians, for the French army in Silesia would be dangerously near their frontiers. It was a proposal which the Czar refused to entertain, and it gave him an opportunity to make a display of fidelity towards Prussia. He announced that he would lose hope that he had placed in his secret treaty with Napoleon, if the future

[1] Tolstoy to Romantsov, 26 Oct./7 Nov. 1807, in *Sbornik*, LXXXIX, 178.
[2] *Sbornik*, LXXXIX, 178–9.

of the Turkish provinces were made to depend upon the fate of the Prussian monarchy.

The French attitude to the Turkish question was disclosed on the 12th of November in the instructions that were drawn up for Caulaincourt, the newly-appointed ambassador to St Petersburg. The fall of the Ottoman Empire might be inevitable, the letter admitted; but it was important that it should not be accelerated; it was necessary, in fact, to postpone the event until the conclusion of the war with England, lest the English should seize Egypt and secure the richest spoils of the partition. "The true desire of the Emperor at this moment is that the Ottoman Empire should remain in its present integrity and should live at peace with Russia and France." Caulaincourt, the instruction continued, would find it imprudent to alarm the Russians by roundly refusing their desires; such a course would only induce the Czar to seek an agreement with Austria. The question was rather to be postponed. Alexander would remember the agreement which had been reached at Tilsit, that the Turkish enterprise should only be undertaken after the two Emperors had come together in a further interview. "This ancient project of Russian ambition is a bond which may hold Russia to France, and from this point of view it is necessary to guard against the danger of destroying her hopes."[1] Napoleon thought for the moment to lure the Czar from his preoccupations—attempted to turn Russia's ambition towards Finland. He would have found it useful to conclude peace with the English, in order to relieve himself of a certain dependence which he was compelled to place upon the Russian alliance. We find him beginning to make vague advances to the Austrians. "You must seek to gain time," he instructed his minister at St Petersburg, "but you must do this with sufficient art to prevent the delay from having a disagreeable effect upon the court of Russia."

Alexander, the dreamer, had become a man obsessed. In high places at St Petersburg there were still members of the English faction, to whisper that he was a tool. In Paris there was a

[1] Instruction for Caulaincourt, 12 Nov. 1807, in *Sbornik*, LXXXVIII, 292–302.

minister, Tolstoy, keeping malevolent eye upon the movements of Napoleon. It seemed that Alexander was apprehensive lest he should be compelled to stand before his subjects and confess that he had been duped by the French. Russian society had learned with a shock of the war with England, the blockade promised to be detrimental, merchants saw the prospect of ruined trade, producers feared the loss of foreign markets for their goods, prices were rising, the exchange was adverse. It was necessary that the Czar should offer some tangible advantage that would bring his new policy into favour, and present his subjects with compensation for the evils of this unpopular war. Savary wrote: "The Emperor and his minister, Count Romantsov, are the only true friends of France in Russia.... The nation would be quite ready to take up arms again and make new sacrifices for a war against us".[1] Alexander became nervous, irritable—would storm against the French minister one day, feebly caress him the next. It was necessary, he said, to show that the French had not a monopoly of the advantages that resulted from the system of Tilsit; France herself was interested in seeing that the alliance should become popularised in Russia. The French minister remembered the frequency of palace revolutions in this dark autocratic empire, recalled the summary treatment that an obstinate Czar might expect. When spring should come and clear the frosts away and Russia should lose her immunity in the war with England, discontent would become still louder. Alexander was already beginning to show some reluctance in the fulfilment of his engagements and Savary and Caulaincourt had both taken alarm at the situation. The Russians would give way, said Caulaincourt, if Napoleon should insist upon the evacuation of Moldavia and Wallachia, "but that would be the end of confidence, though not the end of the alliance. We should no longer find, however, that enthusiasm and good feeling which makes the Czar try to anticipate the wishes of the Emperor [Napoleon]".[2] It seemed that Napoleon would be compelled to give way for the sake of the alliance, and would be driven into acquiescence in the Russian designs upon the

[1] *Sbornik*, LXXXVIII, 327.   [2] *Ibid.* LXXXVIII, 386–90.

Principalities. Yet this was a concession which implied a betrayal of the Turks; it might throw the Porte into the arms of the English.

Napoleon evaded the dilemma by his famous letter to Alexander of the 2nd of February 1808, and by his mysterious instruction to Caulaincourt, which was afterwards destroyed. The letter was conceived in the spirit of Tilsit, and expressed in the language that the Czar most loved to hear. It is a letter not to be read before sunset:

"If an army of 50,000 men," it said, "with Russians, Frenchmen, and perhaps a few Austrians, were to make its way into Asia, through Constantinople, it would not reach the Euphrates without making England tremble....I am ready in Dalmatia; Your Majesty is ready on the Danube. One month after we have made our arrangements the army might be on the Bosphorus."[1]

Alexander's eyes travelled down new vistas, and widened to larger perspectives. Having read this letter he was content to forgo immediate designs in Moldavia and Wallachia, and forget his previous importunity; he was content to pass the days in a discussion of hypothetical plans and partitions, and the building of castles in the air, with Caulaincourt; he was willing to surrender once more to the complacent moods and exaltations of Tilsit —even though Caulaincourt insisted that he had no powers to treat for anything, even though Napoleon had avoided all commitments, even though it was agreed that nothing could be resolved until the two Emperors should have met again in personal interview. The letter was intended to evoke once more the dreamer in Alexander, to perform the same magical feat that Napoleon had achieved by actual contact with the Czar; it was a dynamic appeal to the non-rational side of the Russian. Caulaincourt lent himself to the discussion, made wearisome argument on the subject of Constantinople, but took care always to assert that the projects should remain purely hypothetical. Napoleon himself made advances to Austria, succeeded in arousing resentment against any plan for the dismemberment of the Ottoman Porte, and prepared to conjure the demon of

[1] *Sbornik*, LXXXVIII, 456–8.

jealousy between the courts of Vienna and St Petersburg. The whole scheme was but a piece of entertainment contrived for the amusement of a fretful Czar. On the 9th of March new orders were drawn up for the minister Caulaincourt, instructing him to avoid any open rejection of plans that the Russians might have for the partition of Turkey, urging him to refrain from the absolute refusal of co-operation, but reminding him that careful examination was to be made of the consequences that would follow the execution of such designs, and ordering him to attach much importance to these ulterior matters.

Since France cannot lend herself to the execution of such designs without the violation of treaties by which she is bound, she must not do this lightly and she is justified in asking for herself such advantages as shall be compensation for those which she allows. This matter, therefore, cannot be the result of a sudden determination, but must be the object of an important negotiation.[1]

Napoleon recalls a previous engagement, remembers a former treaty, finds that he has a conscience. He is already making his withdrawal and stirring up new topics that will bring delay. This is on the 9th of March, and at this moment Alopeus is in Paris, preparing to return to England with proposals for a negotiation. Napoleon is flirting with peace overtures from Canning, and thinking of a back-door escape from the system of Tilsit. This will be the end of victories on the Euphrates and expeditions to India and oriental designs. It is easy to see why the Czar is troubled and tormented by this last indiscretion of Alopeus. It does not matter that Napoleon changes his intentions and refuses to proceed with the question of peace with England. On the 2nd of April, he is on his way to Bayonne, and once more the Turks can breathe freely.

During the whole of this period it is the policy of Napoleon— a policy not fundamentally changed at Tilsit—to preserve the integrity of the Ottoman Empire, to thwart the aggressive designs of Russia and to prevent the assertion of British influence at Constantinople. The most blind and battered power in Europe, the one which most helplessly lay open as the obvious

---

[1] *Sbornik*, LXXXVIII, 525–30.

prey of an adventurer such as Napoleon, the very empire which might have been fixed upon as the first and most likely to crumble and fall in an upheaval like that which opened the nineteenth century, was the one which seemed to remain almost unscathed while Prussias and Austrias were toppling, and its integrity was regarded with a special kind of sanctity by the man who brushed the Holy Roman Empire aside, and made a prisoner of the Pope. The military despotism that emerged from the French Revolution and did so much to sweep the remnants of feudalism out of Europe, showed singular solicitude for an abuse that was more ramshackle and more crusty than mediaevalism, and solemnly called upon the world to take off its hat to an institution which was more disturbing to the continent —which could less justify its existence—than the petty German potentates who had been so easily written off the map. Certainly it may be said that if Napoleon could not possess Constantinople, it most suited his interests to see the city remain in the hands of the Turks. But if we consider his early expedition to Egypt, his desire to turn the Mediterranean into a French sea, his gradual encroachments in the Balkan regions, his ambition for Constantinople, his oriental dreams and his perpetual concern with plans for the Near East, we may infer with M. Driault that Napoleon desired for himself this Ottoman Empire, which seemed fated to be a prize for European brigandage. His ambition was to possess it, without the inconveniences of a partition, without the necessity of allowing the partnership of Russia and Austria, and perhaps England. Romantic though he might seem, he had something in his imagination that took the classic mould. Under him warfare had the antique ring; he caught inspiration from the Roman eagle; his was the last day when the Arc de Triomphe actually signified something and had a real relevance to the experience of men. Empire for him meant unique dominion, meant Rome, meant the possession of Constantinople. And Russians to him were the barbarians pressing ominously upon the Empire from the north—hordes from the depths of Asia, from inaccessible lands, from unapproachable fastnesses. When he said they were a menace to Europe, he was making the picture that an old Roman might have made if he had felt the roll of those waves of population that broke upon the frontier from the north of the Danube. When Talleyrand, after Austerlitz, proposed that the Austrians should be conciliated and that their attention should be turned to plans of extension on the side of Turkey, he was working in a smaller realm of ideas than his Emperor who was perpetually thundering that the Russians were the enemy of mankind. It was not the Austrians whom it was desirable to shoulder out of the west; it was not they who were to commence the dismemberment of Turkey. The Russian Tolstoy, watching suspiciously in Paris, divined the intentions of Napoleon. "He wishes to turn us into an Asiatic power, to throw us back upon our ancient frontiers and to carry his rule into the heart of our provinces....It is impossible to foresee where his volcanic imagination will drive him."[1] The alliance of Tilsit was not for him, as it was for the Czar, a pleasant haven in which to drop anchor, a state of felicity that had no misgiving save the thought that it might come to an end. It was a temporary combination, and an interlude. It was a condition of momentary poise. It was a weapon which Napoleon chose in June 1807 because it was the most useful thing that lay to hand.

*   *   *   *   *   *

After Tilsit it is difficult to avoid the conclusion that the personality of Napoleon takes a turn for the worse, and that he is spoilt by too much power. The British attack on Copenhagen aroused his most violent moods, and the Czar encouraged his arrogance by showing too great readiness to serve his system. Contemporaries confirm the idea that his manner now became more domineering than ever; there were undignified scenes at diplomatic circles. Napoleon at this time was at the height of his power—feeling himself able to count only too much on the subservience of his ally—and the result of this situation seems to have been that he thought he could live without any diplomacy at all. Since the continent was at his feet it would appear that there was no power which he had need to be diplomatic with. So he bullied everybody alike, rattled his sword, and gave the

[1] Tolstoy to Romantsov, Particulière et Secrète, 26 Oct./7 Nov. 1807, in *Sbornik*, LXXXIX, 185.

direct word of command to all the world, without any delicate
manœuvrings or diplomatic circumlocutions. He attacked Portugal, directed the Czar to make war on Sweden, drove the
British missions out of Europe and invaded the papal states.
One might say that he lacked a Talleyrand to turn all these
things into something more diplomatically inoffensive; one
might also say that Talleyrand was right in smelling danger at
this period. Napoleon afterwards confessed that his mistake in
regard to Spain at this time was precisely in this failure to cover
himself by more plausible diplomatic manœuvre; "the immorality
of it", he acknowledged, "was too patent". After Tilsit we have
the Grand Empire, and everything is done in the heaviest
imperial manner; but by spring 1808 it had become clear that
one power could not be treated in this fashion. This power was
the ally, Russia. It was not that Napoleon consented to surrender his point in regard to the Ottoman Porte; but in connection with this matter he saw the need for finesse; and, in this
sense of the word, he consented to be diplomatic once again.
Russia, at any rate, did not belong to the Confederation of the
Rhine. Perhaps Napoleon, even in this was too late. It would
seem that from this point Alexander begins in some subtle way
to escape. Certainly at Erfurt in September 1808 the Czar is a
different man and no longer consents to be deluded by talk of
a partition of Turkey.

In April 1808 Italy, Germany, Holland, Austria, Portugal,
Spain and Denmark are held in Napoleon's imperial system;
Russia and Turkey are allies; and Sweden is being brought to
surrender. It is the isolation of England;[1] the continental sys-

---

[1] Lord Palmerston, writing from Havre in September 1827 says: "The
Douaniers and some of the civil inhabitants seem to be great Bonapartists.
I was amused with a little boy of about eight years old whom I heard
screaming out a song as he walked along the street and the words of which
I collected to be:

> Bientôt plus de Guerre!
> Tous les Rois sont morts
> Il n'y a que l'Angleterre
> Qui résiste encore.
> Tiggi Riggi Dong Dong La Beauté,
> Tiggi Riggi Dong Dong ah c'est beau!"
>   (Airlee, *Lady Palmerston and her times*, 96.)

tem has gripped the whole of Europe; land and sea are at war; and each side seems unrelenting. It appears that Napoleon has now made the maritime power the object of his concentrated attention, that he is collecting the strength of a continent in order to show what Land can do against Sea. But this very month sees a new thunderbolt hurled upon the scene; the question of Spain comes to the fore. Spain, although nobody realises it as yet, brings a fresh element into the whole problem, commences a new period in the Napoleonic era, and alters the whole meaning of the wars that are being waged against the usurpations of France. Therefore, though history never breaks off and never leaves any threads hanging loose and unconnected, this month of April 1808, when the isolation of England seems achieved and the last efforts of Alopeus have failed, is a convenient place at which to close a chapter of the Napoleonic story.

APPENDIXES

THE CONDUCT OF ALEXANDER ON THE 16TH OF JUNE 1807

M<small>AX</small> L<small>ENZ</small> has put forward the view that Alexander immediately after the battle of Friedland determined upon a betrayal
of Prussia.[1] The thesis is based upon the fact that Lobanov,
on the day after the battle, was instructed not merely to treat
for an armistice but to pursue the following course of conduct:

> Do not propose negotiations for peace, but if the French should
> express a desire to put an end to the war, reply that the Emperor
> Alexander also wishes for a pacification, and in case the French ask
> if he has powers to negotiate, show the full powers signed by the
> Emperor.[2]

Lenz has re-written the history of these days with this preoccupation and he has interpreted Lobanov's instruction so as
to make the 16th of June the real day of decision. He leaves no
room for the crisis of the 20th of June[3] and the struggle which
the Grand-Duke Constantine was supposed to have made on
behalf of peace at this later time. The whole story in this way
becomes so much different from the narrative in the present
work, where it is suggested that the Czar allowed himself rather
to slide into a desertion of his ally, that some examination of it
seems necessary.

Bennigsen, immediately after Friedland, wrote: "I should
think it necessary and prudent to begin some negotiations for
peace, if only to gain time and repair our losses".[4] Zismer wrote
that the situation was worse than Bennigsen had dared to
describe.[5] The Czar, when he received the news, adopted a
cautious policy; he distrusted his commander, and in particular

---

[1] Max Lenz, *Tilsit (Forschungen zur Brandenburgischen und Preussischen
Geschichte*, vol. VI, pp. 181 *et seq.*), especially pp. 195–6.

[2] Alexander to Lobanov, 16 June 1807. This document is printed in
Tatistcheff, *Alexandre Ier et Napoléon* (1891), p. 121, but is not to be found
in *Sbornik*, LXXXIX, in which many of the documents which Tatistcheff
quoted from manuscript have since (i.e. in 1893) been published. See also
above, p. 240.

[3] See especially Lenz, *op. cit.* p. 195, note 1.

[4] Bennigsen to Alexander, 15 June 1807, in *Sbornik*, LXXXIX, 10.

[5] Zismer to Budberg, 15 June 1807, *ibid.* pp. 10–11.

distrusted his inclinations for peace.[1] He allowed nothing to be done until Popov had confirmed Bennigsen's accounts,[2] ordered Bennigsen, if he had "no other means of extricating himself" to conclude an armistice "in his own name", and said: "I have judged it proper to send...Prince Lobanov whom I find in all respects qualified to be charged *by you* with this negotiation".[3] In pursuance of these instructions Bennigsen, writing an "ostensible" letter to Bagration[4]—a letter intended for French eyes— goes out of his way to say of his application for an armistice: "cette intention de ma part". If he refers to peace in this letter it is only to allude to the General Congress which the various powers had agreed to hold. Lobanov, when he arrived at the French headquarters still kept up the principle that he was negotiating on behalf of the commander-in-chief, for when he was asked for the surrender of the Prussian fortresses he said that even Bennigsen himself had no powers to make these concessions.[5] When Duroc was sent to continue the discussions it was to Bennigsen that he came, and it is significant that the commander-in-chief brought upon himself more suspicion and

---

[1] See above, pp. 192 and 239–40. Lenz (*op. cit.* pp. 206–7) further emphasises his position by criticising the conduct of Bennigsen after Friedland. This is partly on the strength of a letter in which Napoleon said: "It is this last clause [i.e. the clause in the armistice relating to the cession of the Prussian fortresses, see above, p. 242] which has prevented the armistice from being signed yesterday, *since we have to wait for the authorisation of the king of Prussia*". *Corresp. de Nap. 1er*, t. xv, no. 12,782 (my italics). I cannot take this as evidence that Bennigsen had shown any weakness on the subject of the fortresses, for, writing to Alexander on the 19th he called Napoleon's demand "as extravagant as it was dishonourable", and he does not seem to have desired the Czar to concede Napoleon's conditions but rather suggested that they might create difficulties with Sweden. *Sbornik*, LXXXIX, 24. The fact that the boldness which Bennigsen attributes to himself in his memoirs (quoted in Tatistcheff, *op. cit.* pp. 126–7) was not entirely a means of exculpating himself before the Prussians or a pure piece of romanticism conceived in retrospect is proved from the letters, growing in boldness, which this commander wrote to the Czar himself between the 17th and the 21st of June. See above, pp. 240–1 and pp. 247–8; cf. Lenz, *op. cit.* p. 203.

[2] Alexander to Popov, 16 June 1807, quoted in Tatistcheff, *op. cit.* p. 120.

[3] Alexander to Bennigsen, 16 June 1807, in *Sbornik*, LXXXIX, 16 (my italics).

[4] Bennigsen in a letter to Alexander, 19 June 1807, describes this as "une lettre ostensible", *ibid.* p. 23. The letter to Bagration, 18 June 1807, is to be found *ibid.* p. 22.

[5] Lobanov to Alexander, 19 June 1807, quoted in Tatistcheff, *op. cit.* p. 126.

a renewed reproof from the Czar by actually excluding Lobanov and Popov from the interview altogether.[1] From these facts I should gather that Bennigsen, and perhaps his generals, were distrusted by the Czar; that Bennigsen was to be responsible for the armistice but that Popov was to be the person to say if the step was necessary and Lobanov was to be the man to do the actual treating. Further, from the "lettre ostensible" which Bennigsen sent to Bagration, as well as from the subsequent interviews, I should infer that if anybody was to be deluded it was the French. This is confirmed by the fact that the Czar described the application for the armistice as an "épineuse négociation".[2]

In regard to Lobanov's full powers it must be said in the first place that the text of them does not seem to have been discovered. It might even be argued that their mention in Lobanov's instructions was in respect to the negotiation for the armistice, and had no reference to the conclusion of peace; particularly as Lobanov himself was interpolated into this affair so that his position was not quite conventional. In any case one is entitled to ask why Lobanov should have to be provided with full powers afresh on the 20th of June—for these do exist[3]—and further why, if these were being given to him for a second time, it should have been found necessary to give him an explanation of their tenour in his accompanying instructions. Lobanov is informed on the 20th that the powers given to him at this date "are similar to the declaration which served as full powers for Oubril"; as though it were necessary to assure him that they are adequate.[4] What is interesting to see is that Oubril's "full powers" authorised him to enter into "pourparlers" with the French government and to sign a treaty *sub spe rati*,[5] but when he concluded his treaty in July 1806 he was declared to have exceeded not only his instructions but his powers.[6] It is stranger still to find that Lobanov's powers of the 20th of June did not even come up to those of Oubril, after all; they were a mere authorisation to "enter into pourparlers," and they were without

[1] Popov to Budberg, 20 June 1807, quoted in Tatistcheff, *op. cit.* p. 128. Alexander to Bennigsen, 20 June 1807, in *Sbornik*, LXXXIX, 24–5.

[2] Alexander to Bennigsen, 16 June 1807, in *Sbornik*, LXXXIX, 16. Bagration betrayed the trick by informing the French that Bennigsen was acting under imperial orders.   [3] Printed in *Sbornik*, LXXXIX, 26.

[4] Alexander to Lobanov, 20 June 1807, in *Sbornik*, LXXXIX, 25–6, translated in Tatistcheff, *op. cit.* pp. 129–30.

[5] *Sbornik*, LXXXII, 364.   [6] *Ibid.* pp. 457 and 460.

any reference to the conclusion of a treaty.[1] One may ask what the "powers" given to Lobanov on the 16th must have been like, for at this date Alexander was showing a far more definite appearance of caution. We know what Alexander said on this subject; and this, which was unknown to Lenz, is the most damaging thing that can be urged against him. Writing to Bennigsen on the 20th he said: "Prince Lobanov *was* authorised by me to enter into pourparlers for peace".[2] Thus, if Lobanov was given any "powers" at all, then, they were similar to the ones given to him on the 20th, and we are left to wonder why they should have to be repeated on that date, and why it was felt necessary to explain without too much accuracy that these latter were similar to those of Oubril. In any event these facts would seem to confirm the thesis that Alexander, even down to the 20th of June, was playing for time, was trying to do something which if necessary could be disavowed. This is further strengthened by the fact that it was the French who were deliberately made to believe that Bennigsen was responsible for the armistice. Considering that Lobanov's "full powers" were never used, and that they were evidently intended for a contingency that did not arise, I can only guess that they were perhaps given to him on the 16th because at a moment when the need of an armistice seemed desperate the Czar was afraid that it might be refused unless it could be shown that Russia was ready to treat for peace.[3] It is all the more difficult to believe that Alexander was making a conscious betrayal of the Prussians on the 16th when it is realised that on this very day he wrote to Frederick William: "It will be necessary for us to meet and to

---

[1] Article five of the armistice concluded between the French and Russian armies on the 21st of June, 1807, provided that the two Emperors should send "Plenipotentiaries furnished with powers necessary for negotiating, concluding and signing a definitive peace". *Sbornik*, LXXXIX, 30.

[2] *Sbornik*, LXXXIX, 24–5 (my italics).

[3] This interpretation is confirmed by Bennigsen's letter (p. 201, above) advising Alexander to negotiate in order to gain time; cf. p. 290, above, where the Czar says that Napoleon refused an armistice unless there should be a negotiation for peace. See also Lobanov's instruction (p. 361). It is true that the instruction to Lobanov was not communicated to the Prussians, and Frederick William was not informed that the Russian negotiator had any orders to enter into pourparlers for peace. Alexander's letter authorising Bennigsen to propose an armistice was sent to the Prussian king with the words "armistice" and "en votre nom" underlined, though there was apparently no underlining in the original (Lenz, *op. cit.* p. 194; Ranke, *Hardenberg*, v, 518; cf. *Sbornik*, LXXXIX, 16). But Alexander wrote at the same time to Frederick William to say: "It is cruel for me to have to give

come to a common determination",[1] and that on the 20th he wrote to Bennigsen: "I am sure that the King of Prussia will not delay sending a person of confidence to represent him".[2]

Above all, it is not possible to reject the traditional view that the Grand-Duke Constantine on the 20th of June made his great effort to persuade Alexander to conclude a definite peace. Lenz's thesis demands that the famous arguments and threats of Constantine should be put back to a time before the news of Friedland had arrived, a time when they were unsuccessful. The Grand-Duke himself placed the date "after Friedland" and "before the interview"; he says "immediately afterwards we concluded the armistice and the peace".[3] This limits the date to the 20th, which Hardenberg's own accounts confirm.[4] And Schladen, upon whom Lenz relies, says that Constantine returned to headquarters on the 21st with the news that Alexander had decided to desert England.[5]

up even the hope of being as useful to you as my heart had wished", and Frederick William was not given a false view of the situation. Alexander called the Prussian king to him, and though he displeased his friend by making the appointment within the Russian frontier (see above, p. 215), I cannot think that he could have had any intention of discouraging Frederick William from meeting him; the news he had received from Friedland is sufficient to account for his decision. It is not possible to believe that Alexander seriously tried to hide anything from the Prussians, for at the earliest moment after Frederick William had reached the appointed place of meeting the Czar revealed to him the whole situation and made it clear that there would be negotiations for peace (Frederick William to Queen Louisa, 21 June 1807, in *Deutsche Rundschau*, cx, pp. 32–3; Ranke, *Hardenberg*, iii, 456).

[1] *Sbornik*, lxxxix, 16–17.

[2] *Ibid.* p. 25.

[3] The conversations of Constantine on this subject are reported by Lesseps in a despatch to Talleyrand of 22 Aug. 1807 (*Sbornik*, lxxxviii, 121) and in a later one of 4 Nov. 1807 (*ibid.* p. 278). Constantine's statement to the Czar to the effect that if he did not make peace he had better tell his soldiers to put their pistols to their own heads, is reported by Lesseps in the latter despatch, not, as is stated by Lenz, *op. cit.* p. 190, note 4, and Vandal, *Napoléon et Alexandre Ier*, i, 50, in the despatch of 22 Aug. 1807.

[4] Lenz, *op. cit.* p. 190, note 4, admits that Constantine did not see Alexander between the 14th and the 20th of June. See also Ranke, *Hardenberg*, iii, 456; v, 539.

[5] Postscript to Schladen's First Report of 21 June 1807 (Ranke, *Hardenberg*, v, 522). It is true that Chlebowsky told Schladen that Constantine already at Tilsit, i.e. on the 13th of June, had warned Alexander of the fate of his father; cf. Lenz, *op. cit.* p. 191, note 1.

Finally, if Alexander had made his resolutions on the 16th, would Popov, who knew his intentions, have written to Budberg on the 20th: "With an astute and enterprising enemy one must take the most decisive measures in the case of peace as well as in war. In God's name lose no time. The proof that Bonaparte desires peace is the sending even of Duroc at midnight"?[1]

[1] Popov to Budberg, 20 June 1807, quoted in Tatistcheff, *op. cit.* p. 128.

THE INSTRUCTIONS TO LOBANOV, JUNE 1807

In *Sbornik*, LXXXIX (Publications of the Imperial Russian Historical Society) are two undated documents which contain suggested instructions to a Russian negotiator after Friedland. Both are apparently in Budberg's hand, but the shorter one, printed as a "Memorandum," consists of brief jottings conjectured by Tatistcheff to be notes of an interview with Alexander, and possibly even written at his dictation[1]; while the longer one is more finished and elaborate so that Tatistcheff has assumed it to be an actual instruction that was drawn up for Lobanov[2]. Tatistcheff even takes the view that this longer paper represents the changes which Budberg was able to make in the Memorandum, the twist he was able to give to the Czar's intentions, in the process of redaction over which he had charge; and he infers from this a divergence of policy between the sovereign and the minister.

The longer document is headed: "A few ideas which might find a place in the instructions of a Russian negotiator"; it is in the form of notes, of separate paragraphs; it has neither address nor signature; it refers to "a Russian negotiator" but neither to Lobanov nor to anybody else by name; and if it is an enclosure to an official instruction the more formal document which might be expected to accompany and explain it has never come to light.

Both of these papers contemplate the difficult negotiation which a defeated power must anticipate when it meets the victor[3], and both of them are concerned almost entirely with

[1] *Sbornik*, LXXXIX, 37–8, *Mémorandum*; cf. Tatistcheff, *Alexandre Ier et Napoléon*, p. 144, footnote.

[2] *Sbornik*, LXXXIX, 33–7; Tatistcheff, *op. cit.* p. 144.

[3] This is apparent e.g. from the fears which are expressed concerning the demands Napoleon might make; from the care which is taken to sum up the advantages Napoleon will gain from the mere fact of being at peace with Russia; and from the intention which is shown of bargaining with France and fixing a price, for example, upon the recognition of Joseph as king of Naples. The Russians are preparing to negotiate with a victorious enemy; they are not contemplating a negotiation in which the idea of alliance is already taken for granted.

the question of a peace-treaty. If they mention the idea of an alliance they say that this is not a matter for the peace-treaty and that it is a question which must be brought up at a later date[1]. They seem to acknowledge the possibility that Napoleon may suggest the conclusion of an alliance; both of them express an apprehension that Russia may be required to close her ports to English shipping; and the longer document shows a serious fear that Napoleon may demand the accession of Prussia to the Confederation of the Rhine. The fact that they speak of the alliance of France in these terms, that is to say, in its aspect as a form of servitude to Napoleon, proves that both documents are drawn up in a spirit that is very reserved if not unfriendly to the idea. In any case the significant matter is that these documents relate only to the problem of peace and definitely set out to limit the negotiation to this problem. In their whole purport they are utterly inconsistent with the actual instruction which we know that Lobanov received on the 23rd of June. Even if that instruction had not rendered them superfluous by basing itself on the principle that the two Emperors should negotiate "without intermediaries," it is clear, as will be shown below, that neither of these drafts has any relation to the state of affairs envisaged in the instruction. The two documents are rejected schemes for a peace-treaty; the very form in which we have them is a confirmation of the fact; they were superseded by the 23rd, and they probably belong to the 21st or 22nd of June when we know that Budberg was discussing the problem of peace with Hardenberg.[2]

The longer document seems to be the earlier. In reference to the integrity of Russia it says: "D'après les dispositions que l'ennemi a manifesté lors des premières propositions d'armistice qui lui furent faites, il ne paraît nullement qu'il veuille contester ce point capital".[3] This is the kind of phrase which shows that a person is not quite assured. The sentence could not have been written after Lobanov's report of his interview with Napoleon had been received; for that report gave the precise assurance

---

[1] *Sbornik*, LXXXIX, 35, 38.

[2] See above, p. 218. This would tend to be confirmed by the fact that the longer paper speaks of "instructions for a Russian negotiator" and does not mention any minister by name. Hardenberg gives the impression that the question of negotiators was discussed at this time and that the Russian choice was still open. He speaks of "the Russian plenipotentiary". Ranke, *Hardenberg*, III, 462.

[3] *Sbornik*, LXXXIX, 33.

that the integrity of the Russian empire would be respected.[1] It arrived on the 22nd of June on which date Kurakin reported its contents to the Empress-Mother and expressed his jubilation in regard to this very question of Russian territorial integrity.[2] The shorter Memorandum omits this point altogether, and would seem to have been compiled after Lobanov's letter had been read. This view is confirmed by the fact that while the longer document contains no mention of the extension of Russia to the Vistula, the Memorandum runs: "Frontière de la Vistule. La Russie ne peut l'accepter qu'en autant que la Prusse serait dédommagée"[3]; as though the Vistula had actually been offered by France. Lobanov in that same report of the 21st of June had announced that Napoleon desired Russia to have the Vistula. The shorter Memorandum, therefore, seems to come after the reception of Lobanov's letter. The longer document seems to represent an earlier stage in the discussions.

The Memorandum contains what seems like an appendix on the subject of an alliance with France. Though it asserts that for the present it would seem sufficient to conclude peace, it mentions the idea of drawing out Napoleon on the subject of Turkey; and though it shrinks from the idea of the closing of Russian ports to English shipping at the moment, it suggests a possible combination with Sweden and Denmark, a league "qui mettrait la Baltique à couvert de toute insulte et qui pourrait même forcer les Anglais à adopter des principes plus libéraux".[4] It is possible to believe that this "appendix" is an afterthought; it is difficult to believe that the idea of an alliance with France, a partition of Turkey and a maritime crusade against England was introduced into this Memorandum as an independent suggestion totally unrelated to the Hardenberg proposals which were being formed on that very 22nd of June. It may be inferred from this "appendix" that the Czar was rather doubtfully flirting with some ideas that the Prussian minister had put forward. The two Russian drafts, indeed, are very favourable to Prussia. Alexander, planning a difficult peace-treaty with France, had not lost his solicitude for his ally. It is remarkable that the longer document suggests that Hamburg and Lübeck should go to Prussia. The idea seems exceedingly

---

[1] Lobanov to Alexander, 21 June 1807, in Tatistcheff, *op. cit.* pp. 135–6.
[2] Kurakin to the Empress-Mother, 22 June 1807, *ibid.* pp. 136–8.
[3] *Sbornik*, LXXXIX, 37.
[4] *Sbornik*, LXXXIX, 38.

bold; it appears as part of the Hardenberg proposals.[1] The shorter document contains the still more extravagant question as to whether Bohemia could not be given to Prussia; and this bold handling of the map of Europe, and the pretext that is put forward for the idea[2], as well as the fact that the scheme once again is in favour of Prussia give colour to the suggestion that Hardenberg may have been making still more of his facile redistributions of territory. We know that on the 21st and 22nd of June the Russian and Prussian ministers were not working entirely in isolation. It seems safe to say that these two Russian drafts are either suggestions or notes of discussions which were made at this period, and that they were compiled before attention had been fully given to the possibilities which an immediate alliance with France might offer.

On the 22nd of June Budberg and Hardenberg placed "combined proposals" before the King and the Emperor, and Frederick William said that "gigantesque" plans were being formed but that these were as yet only general ideas.[3] Some time later on the 22nd—how late we cannot tell—Hardenberg completed his scheme, worked out the whole synthesis and put his ideas into writing.[4] On the evening of the 22nd Alexander moved forward to Taurrogen,[5] where on the following day Lobanov himself appeared and supplemented by word of mouth the report he had given of his interview with Napoleon.[6] On this 23rd of June—perhaps even early on the 24th[7]—Lobanov's actual instruction was drawn up and it is easy to see that this document is out of all relation to the two drafts that have just been examined. Alexander is now no longer reticent on the

---

[1] Ranke, *Hardenberg*, III, 462.

[2] "Duplicité avec laquelle l'Autriche en a agi envers la Russie comme envers la France." *Sbornik*, LXXXIX, 37.

[3] Frederick William III to Queen Louisa, 22 June 1807, in *Deutsche Rundschau*, CX, 35.

[4] Hardenberg dates the document "Sczawel 22 June 1807" (Ranke, *Hardenberg*, III, 461). He prefaces the scheme with the following words: "Den 21 und 22 Junius wurden mehrere Konferenzen theils zwischen dem Herrn von Budberg allein, theils im Beisein der beiden Monarchen gehalten, davon ich das Resultat, wie hier in zwei Stücken folgt, zusammenfasste. Er wurde vorgelesen, nochmals erwogen und dann als die anzunehmende Grundlage der anzugehenden Unterhandlungen festgesetzt". Ranke, *Hardenberg*, III, 458; cf. Frederick William's account quoted above, p. 218.

[5] *Deutsche Rundschau*, CX, 36. Ranke, *Hardenberg*, III, 467.

[6] Tatistcheff, *op. cit.* pp. 139–40.

[7] The document is undated: *Sbornik*, LXXXIX, 31; cf. Lenz, *Tilsit*, p. 225, note 2.

subject of an alliance with France; he talks about nothing else; he speaks of his desire for the cordial union of France and Russia. When he thinks of the alliance he no longer envisages Napoléon as making an unfriendly demand for the closing of Russian ports against English shipping. He declares that Russia is about to adopt "an entirely new system". He speaks as though he himself has a great design. It is obvious that to him the idea of the alliance comes as the solution of the problem of peace; peace under his scheme will be an easy matter, he says, provided the two emperors treat without intermediaries.[1] The whole idea is utterly different from the assumptions upon which the two previous drafts were made; for there it was explicitly stated that a peace-treaty was sufficient for the present, and that an alliance with France, if it came at all, was to be discussed as a separate question afterwards. It is interesting to see that Hardenberg also drew up his instruction for the Prussian negotiator at Taurrogen on the 23rd and wrote: "Leurs Majestés [i.e. both Alexander and Frederick William] pensent qu'en faisant entrevoir leurs idées sur la paix et en entendant celles de Napoléon, le maréchal parviendra aisément à préparer les voies à une négociation dont il resterait chargé de concert avec le baron de Hardenberg".[2] Hardenberg and Alexander both had some scheme to divulge to Napoléon—some scheme which they were not quite satisfied to leave to intermediaries. Both were determined to go to Tilsit to fascinate Napoléon with a grand design. Hardenberg certainly thought that his scheme had been accepted by the Czar[3] and it does not seem possible to believe from Alexander's general conduct at this time that he was practising a conscious deception. It was not until the 25th that it became apparent how relentless was Napoléon's hostility to Prussia, and how hopeless was Hardenberg's desire to take a personal part in the negotiations. It would seem that Alexander had accepted the main idea of the Hardenberg proposals, when these had been finally worked out. Perhaps the verbal reports of Lobanov had convinced him of the possibility of the scheme, and so clinched the matter. Frederick William III and Hardenberg, though they afterwards lamented the Czar's weakness, did not accuse him of treachery in this matter.

[1] Alexander to Lobanov, 23 June 1807. See above, p. 254.
[2] Ranke, *Hardenberg*, III, 463.
[3] See above, pp. 251–2.

ALEXANDER'S DESERTION OF PRUSSIA AT TILSIT

THE Russian army concluded a separate armistice with the French on the 21st of June 1807 and article 3 of this armistice provided that a similar convention should be concluded separately between the French and the Russian troops and that in the four or five days which this would require, no hostilities should be committed against the Prussians.[1] But this does not mean that Alexander left his friends to take care of themselves. Napoleon, negotiating with the Prussian plenipotentiary Kalckreuth "absolutely refused to withdraw his demand for the three fortresses" which he had originally stood out for, but, says the Prussian king, the Czar "had the good fortune after a very keen struggle to secure that the three fortresses in question should not be handed over to the French during the period of the armistice".[2]

The same process was repeated in the case of the negotiations for peace. It might be asserted that Alexander deserted the Prussians and broke the convention of Bartenstein[3]; but at Tilsit "there was no negotiation with Prussia. She was passive, like Poland".[4] The truth was that she had previously placed her fate in the hands of the Czar,[5] and the Czar after Friedland had to make decisions on behalf of both powers. It was Alexander who conducted the negotiation in the interests of Prussia. It was he who secured the concessions Napoleon made.

In regard to this negotiation, particularly in its later stages, a further point of discussion has been raised. It has been asserted that the Czar's earnest intercession for his friend was made with the definite view of securing certain particular Russian ambitions. It is necessary to examine the problem that here arises.

---

[1] *Sbornik*, LXXXIX, 29–30.

[2] Frederick William III to Queen Louisa, 25 June 1807, in *Deutsche Rundschau*, CX, 38–9.

[3] Lenz, *Tilsit*, p. 195 *et passim*.   [4] Driault, *Tilsit*, p. 186.

[5] Hardenberg realised this, and regarded it as the policy of Prussia (see above, p. 77). The fact is apparent also in the language of the Czar, immediately after Friedland (see above, pp. 214–15).

Under Napoleon's first scheme for a partition of Prussia Silesia was to be taken from Frederick William and given to a French prince.[1] It seems also that for some reason Napoleon offered Poland to the Czar, or perhaps proposed to make the Prussian provinces of Poland into a kingdom for Constantine.[2] In these circumstances, however, Prussia was to receive back some of her territory on the left bank of the Elbe, though she surrendered the rest of her possessions in that region.[3] An intense struggle with Napoleon took place as a result of these proposals. Both the Czar and the Prussian king[4] took part in it and it was at this period that Frederick William wrote of his friend: " L'Empereur de Russie qui souffre mort et martyre... ".[5] On receiving the news of this plan Hardenberg made the second version of his famous scheme and suggested that the French prince should be given Switzerland instead of Silesia.[6] It is evident that Alexander refused to agree to this dismemberment of Prussia, and would not accept even Poland at this price.[7] On the 29th of June he informed the Prussian king that he "was making little progress with (Napoleon). In the last resort Bonaparte dropped his demand for Silesia which he had intended giving to Jerome", but, says Frederick William, "he makes a further demand of South Prussia and New East Prussia (i.e. the Polish provinces) for Saxony. Nor has he dropped his

[1] Frederick William to Queen Louisa, 30 June 1807, in *Deutsche Rundschau*, cx, 206. Ranke, *Hardenberg*, III, 492.

[2] On this question see Handelsman, *Napoléon et la Pologne* (1909), pp. 128–30; and Hans Delbrück, *Die Frage der Polnischen Krone und der Vernichtung Preussens in Tilsit* (pp. 315–36 of *Studien und Versuche zur neueren Geschichte,* Max Lenz gewidmet).

[3] Napoleon afterwards wrote in a note to Alexander, that "in proposing to retain Silesia for himself or for a prince of his house he said at the time that he did not see any difficulty in departing from the basis already adopted, namely the cession of the countries on the left of the Elbe". Note of 3 July 1807, in *Sbornik*, LXXXVIII, 58. That Napoleon was not prepared to restore all the Prussian territories in this region at this time is proved by a letter written by Frederick William to Queen Louisa on the 30th of June: "Nor has he [Napoleon] dropped his demand for the Prussian provinces beyond the Elbe" (*Deutsche Rundschau*, cx, 206).

[4] See the account of an interview between Frederick William and Napoleon (as reported by the Czar to Princess Anton Radziwill), p. 235, above.

[5] *Deutsche Rundschau*, cx, 206.

[6] Ranke, *Hardenberg*, III, 492–4; see above, pp. 222–3, 227–8, 257–8.

[7] Handelsman, *op. cit.* p. 128. De Bray reported: "As for Silesia, the Emperor [Napoleon] wished to give it to Jerome and offered in return to recognise the Emperor Alexander as king of Poland" (*ibid.* p. 130).

demand for the Prussian provinces beyond the Elbe, though he will grant the restoration of some 600,000 souls in the different districts there".[1] At this period the discussions were still by word of mouth,[2] but Frederick William in person had secured nothing from Napoleon, and neither of his plenipotentiaries had been allowed even to see Talleyrand.[3]

The negotiation reveals itself to us again on the 3rd of July, in a Note from Napoleon to Alexander, and as this note not only created a further problem for the Czar but is the solution of many of the difficulties of this period, its meaning is important:

It is the policy of all states to work for the acquisition of natural limits.... It is to be desired that the treaty which gives peace to the continent... should assign to [Russia] her natural limits. To the north of the Prussian states the Niemen seems to trace the boundary of Russia. The loss which Prussia would suffer by the cession of what she possesses north of the Niemen would be a small matter and the Emperor Napoleon would consent to leave at the disposition of the Emperor Alexander the equivalent on the left bank of the Elbe for any sacrifice which Prussia would make on the right of the Niemen.

After the battle of Jena the king of Prussia made the surrender of all his possessions on the left bank of the Elbe.[4] This is what the Emperor [Napoleon] has always understood, and when he proposed to keep Silesia for himself or for a prince of his house he said at the time that he saw no difficulty in departing from the basis already adopted, namely the cession of the countries to the left of the Elbe.

In consenting to-day to give the king of Prussia compensation on the left of the Elbe... the Emperor Napoleon desires Russia to receive the limit of the Niemen.[5]

From this letter it appears that when Alexander told the Prussian king that 600,000 souls would be restored to him on

---

[1] Frederick William to Queen Louisa, 30 June 1807, in *Deutsche Rundschau*, cx, 206.   [2] *Ibid.*

[3] Goltz to Hardenberg, 2 July 1807, in Bailleu, *Preussen und Frankreich*, ii, 590–1.

[4] See above, pp. 11, 14, and 75.

[5] Note to Alexander, 3 July 1807, in *Sbornik*, lxxxviii, 57–8. Omitted from *Corresp. de Nap. Ier*, t. xv; see no. 12,846. In connection with this letter it is interesting to remember that Lobanov claimed to have heard Napoleon describe the Vistula to be the true boundary of Russia (see above, p. 250), and that there is the evidence above mentioned (see note 2, p. 373 above) to suggest the offer of the Polish provinces of Prussia by Napoleon to the Czar. If these accounts are all accepted Napoleon would appear to have been very anxious to make Alexander share in the dismemberment of Prussia.

the left of the Elbe, either he was misinforming his friend for some reason or he was under a misapprehension himself. The latter seems to be the truth for this note came to Alexander under a covering letter from Napoleon which opened with the explanation: "I send Your Imperial Majesty two notes...in order to clear up a misunderstanding which appears to have taken place in our conversation".[1] Also it is plain that in the note itself Napoleon is for the first time revealing to Alexander that he had not intended granting anything to Prussia on the left bank of the Elbe, and that he is in a subtle way apologising for this fact.

Further, it appears from the note that it was Napoleon who, after all, desired Alexander at this time to annex Memel and push forward to the Niemen.[2] Napoleon is endeavouring to persuade his friend. He seems to be raising the subject for the first time. He is writing as though the Czar needs some inducement. He is actually ready to give Prussia her desire if Alexander will only take Memel; and unless Alexander will consent to the annexation Prussia shall be kept behind the Elbe. Since Napoleon was vindictive against Prussia, since it was his policy to make an ally commit himself to a piece of aggrandise-

[1] Napoleon to Alexander, 3 July 1807, in *Corresp. de Nap. Ier*, t. xv, no. 12,846, and *Sbornik*, LXXXVIII, 56–7.

[2] Cf. J. Holland Rose, *Life of Napoleon I* (1924), II, 131–2. I cannot agree either with the same writer in footnote 1, p. 132: "Tatistcheff (pp. 146–8 and 163–8) proves from the Russian archives that these schemes were Alexander's and were in the main opposed by Napoleon. This disproves Vandal's assertion (p. 101) that Napoleon pressed Alexander to take the Memel and the Polish districts". The former reference to Tatistcheff alludes to the drafts made for an instruction to a Russian negotiator before Alexander had thought of himself as the ally of Napoleon. These have been dealt with in Appendix B. They prove only that Alexander at that time would have liked Memel and that he must have found the offer of it a temptation, and that he was ready to make an exchange of territory with Prussia in order to acquire it. Alexander, however, at that time did not know how Prussia was going to be treated by Napoleon. The second reference to Tatistcheff (i.e. pp. 163–8) does not bear the construction placed upon it. Tatistcheff provides certain materials but does not come to any conclusion or express any personal opinion on the problem. On pp. 162 and 163 he does give references to Napoleon's note of 3 July "on the extension of the Russian possessions to the mouth of the Niemen". I have tried to show below that the question of the Bialystok region was a separate matter in the negotiations. Vandal, *Napoléon et Alexandre Ier*, I, 101, seems, however, to be incorrect when he asserts that "le Tsar avait dû repousser plusieurs fois ce cadeau presque offensant" (i.e. the Niemen frontier).

ment like his own, and since he was doubtless interested in embroiling the Czar with his Prussian friends, I cannot share the feeling of some other writers that there is even any inherent improbability in all this. Napoleon was quite capable of suggesting aggrandisement to his clients or his friends.

We do not know the precise nature of Alexander's reply on the following day, for it is really embodied in his notes upon a projected treaty.[1] But we can gather something of its character from Alexander's covering letter, which said, "My demands are moderate, they are disinterested, since I only plead the cause of an unfortunate ally".[2] We can gather a little more from the reply which Napoleon made either to the Czar's letter or to the same proposals which the Czar had previously put forward in conversation. At one point he writes: "To call Prince Jerome to the throne of Saxony and Warsaw would in an instant overthrow all our good relations". He was rejecting a suggestion from Alexander about which nothing very satisfactory is known[3]; but from the general idea as it is referred to in this sentence one would infer that the proposal was intended to bribe Napoleon, and to induce some further concessions. It seems also, from this letter, that Alexander had accepted the offer of the Niemen and had specified the compensation to be received by Prussia on the left bank of the Elbe.[4]

But Napoleon in this letter of the 4th of July, is changing his ground again. The whole point of his disquisition is that Prussia must be contained between the Elbe and the Niemen. Alexander has accepted the increase of territory at the expense of his friend; but Prussia is to be compensated partly in Poland and partly by a piece of Saxon territory taken from the *right* bank of the Elbe. Napoleon has withdrawn his previous offer.

Alexander was still dissatisfied, so two days later Napoleon proposed "a mezzo-termine" on all points. Russia at this moment was demanding 200,000 souls to the left of the Elbe

---

[1] Alexander to Napoleon, 4 July 1807, in *Sbornik*, LXXXVIII, 61–2.

[2] *Ibid.*

[3] Handelsman, *op.cit.* p. 131; Waliszewski, *Le règne d'Alexandre Ier* (1923), p. 233, which seems to me very doubtful; Driault, *op. cit.* p. 184, where it is allowed that Napoleon was making a great pretence of moderation to the Czar, that he was giving the appearance of sacrificing the idea of a marriage between Jerome and the heiress of Saxony, and that he was claiming to do this for the sake of the Russian alliance, when in reality he had decided a year before to marry Jerome to Catherine of Würtemberg.

[4] *Corresp. de Nap. Ier*, t. xv, no. 12,849.

for Prussia. Napoleon's compromise is interesting, for it was embodied in the secret articles of Tilsit.[1]

If Hanover, at the conclusion of peace with England, comes to be joined to the kingdom of Westphalia, then lands on the left bank of the Elbe to the extent of three to four hundred thousand souls will be restored to the king of Prussia.[2]

Considering the fact that article 7 of the Treaty of Alliance concluded at Tilsit stipulated that Hanover should be restored to England if the British government accepted Napoleon's terms[3]; considering also that in the period after the treaties were concluded Napoleon always made capital out of the fact that he was offering George III the restoration of his electorate,[4] it is impossible to believe that this "mezzo-termine" was anything but a defeat for Alexander.

Napoleon in the same letter, however, did grant the Czar's desire that Prussia should have an increase in her Polish territory, so that she had a continuity of possession between Berlin and Königsberg. Napoleon also wrote: "As to the exchange of Memel for a portion of Saxony, that does not create any difficulty".[5]

On the important question of the left bank of the Elbe Napoleon had no real concession to make. It would seem that before this final letter reached its destination,[6] the Czar had already written his own letter which is also dated the 6th of July, and in which he makes two proposals that concern the present problem. In the first he asks that Napoleon

in return for the evacuation of Moldavia and Wallachia, the cession of the principality of Jewer, of Cattaro and of the Seven Isles,[7] will

---

[1] *Sbornik*, LXXXIX, 59.   [2] *Corresp. de Nap. Ier*, t. xv, no. 12,862.

[3] *Sbornik*, CXXXIX, 62.   [4] See above, pp. 305–6.

[5] *Corresp. de Nap. Ier*, t. xv, no. 12,862.

[6] Tatistcheff, *op. cit.* p. 168. This is confirmed by a comparison of the two letters.

[7] All these cessions were actually made by Alexander at Tilsit, and are to be found, respectively, in article 23 (p. 57), article 17 (p. 56), secret article 1 (p. 58) and secret article 2 (p. 58, of *Sbornik*, LXXXIX), so that it would appear that these points were conceded by Alexander in any case, and that he was promising Napoleon nothing new. Alexander begins this paragraph of the letter: "I have shown the Emperor Napoleon that I was ready to acquiesce in his plans and cede the principality of Jewer and the Seven Isles, but he will recall at the same time how pronounced was my wish to use these cessions for the amelioration of the lot of an unhappy ally". Alexander, in this way, put himself in a weak position at Tilsit by promising a concession and leaving himself with nothing but the wish for the *quid pro quo*. (See above, p. 258, and below, pp. 379–80, on the weakness of Alexander in negotiation.)

ameliorate the lot of the king of Prussia by a restoration of 200,000 souls on the left of the Elbe, including the old March and the rest of Magdeburg, and Halberstadt, which the Emperor himself admits that he promised to me....

In the second he says:

As to Memel and that region, I am ready to renounce it; and Saxony will therefore retain the equivalent which she was to have ceded to Prussia.[1]

Alexander originally accepted the region of the Niemen at a time when Napoleon had made this annexation the condition of any restitution to Prussia on the left of the Elbe. It would seem a possible and even probable interpretation of his final letter to say that he was willing to abandon the line of the Niemen in the region of Memel, if by this sacrifice he could induce Napoleon to make a concession on the left bank of the Elbe. At any rate he was determined not to have Memel, if Prussia were not given the promised restitution; he declined to admit the Saxon territory as an equivalent. I cannot interpret these facts in the sense that Alexander interceded for Prussia merely in order to obtain Memel.[2]

He did come into controversy with Napoleon on a matter that touched his self-interests, and this was in reference to the acquisition which he made in the district of Bialystok. The territory had formerly belonged to Prussia, but since that time the Grand-Duchy of Warsaw had been agreed upon, and the district of Bialystok was on the eastern frontier of this new state. If Alexander had refused to annex this land, Prussia would not have retained it, for it did not in the least approach her new frontiers. Alexander differed with Napoleon on the question of the "natural limits", but this was a quarrel with the Duchy of Warsaw and Napoleon treated it as such.[3] The debate reveals something of the Czar's tenacity in matters of self-interest; but this makes only more remarkable his refusal to take Memel. It is the confusion of this episode with the more important question of the Elbe and the lower Niemen that has

[1] *Sbornik*, LXXXVIII, 70–2.

[2] Cf. Driault, *Tilsit*, p. 185: "Il est vrai que lorsqu'Alexandre demandait quelque chose pour la Prusse à l'ouest de l'Elbe, il espérait lui-même s'approcher davantage de la Vistule".

[3] According to the Czar's account the dispute began only on the 5th of July (*Sbornik*, LXXXVIII, 71). The Czar states his case in this letter of the 6th and Napoleon provides his "mezzo-termine" in his letter of the same date (*ibid.* p. 68).

caused some historians to misjudge the Czar in respect to his treatment of Prussia at this period.

It does not seem that even in' the peace-treaties Alexander definitely deserted or betrayed his friend. The real betrayal was a more subtle one. He allowed Prussia to be excluded from the benefits of the alliance. He did not dare to make his own alliance with France conditional upon the admission of Prussia to the splendid scheme.[1] Since—apparently through weakness— he failed in this, the rest followed like a remorseless piece of machinery. The Czar was in a weak position for conducting the Prussian negotiation. Napoleon, after all, was the conqueror of this country, he could present the *fait accompli*, he could face Alexander with power. He took his stand upon the principle he had adopted in November 1806, that Prussia was his by right of conquest, that Prussia had no rights, that Prussia had nothing with which to make a bargain in negotiation.[2] If anything at all were restored to Frederick William, this was a gift; it came of Napoleon's grace; it was easy to say that it was conceded as a favour to Alexander.[3] Alexander admitted this point of view which was calculated to flatter his self-importance, and in accepting the favour he conceded Napoleon's first principle: that Prussia had no rights.[4] This was a kind of subtle betrayal— but it was this type of betrayal that the Czar really did make at Tilsit, and not the more deliberate and conscious sort. Further, Alexander seems to have been shocked from the start by Napoleon's astonishing antipathy to Prussia, and he may have been more ready to consent to the terms finally dictated to this country in that these certainly came as a relief after the original drastic proposals. If he took the district of Bialystok into his empire I can only regard this as a further tactical victory for the French; it could not possibly be argued that Prussia lost anything by this rectification of the Russian frontier which was made at the expense of the Grand-Duchy of Warsaw; but Napoleon knew that he would be out-manœuvring Alexander if he could persuade him to take land that had formerly belonged to Frederick William.

[1] See above, pp. 256–60.   [2] See above, pp. 29 and 178.
[3] Article 4 of the Treaty of Tilsit, in *Sbornik*, LXXXIX, 52.
[4] Alexander afterwards said: "I was a witness at Tilsit of the things which [Napoleon] accorded to the King of Prussia at my instance" (Savary to Napoleon, 9 Sept. 1807, in *Sbornik*, LXXXIII, 63), and later still: "It was only out of grace that he did it, since the success of his armies permitted him to do anything" (Savary to Napoleon, 6 Dec. 1807, *ibid.* p. 242).

Finally Napoleon secured perhaps the greatest victory of all. Having conceded certain restitutions of territory to the house of Brandenburg there remained the question as to when the French armies should evacuate the lands now recognised as belonging to Frederick William. Though the Russians bound themselves in the Treaty of Tilsit to evacuate Moldavia and Wallachia, Napoleon, on his own confession persuaded the Czar to leave the evacuation of Prussia to be settled in a subsequent convention. Champagny, giving Napoleon's account, wrote:

> The Emperor Alexander will recall that it was with intention that this term was not fixed for the Prussian provinces as it was for Wallachia and Moldavia; it was with the view of not losing all the chances that the future might offer, and so that we might be ready for any opportunity. We limited ourselves therefore to saying that a convention would determine this period. The convention was not made between France and Russia; therefore Russia has nothing more to require from France.[1]

Napoleon evidently secured Alexander's assent to his scheme by dazzling him with the Oriental Design; and in this way again, perhaps, the Czar made a subtle betrayal of his friend. The convention that was afterwards concluded is interesting, for it fixes the dates for the evacuation of the Prussian places and says that "On the first of October all Prussia will be evacuated up to the Elbe". In article 4, however, everything that was given with the one hand is taken away with the other: "The above disposition will be carried out at the stated times provided that the contributions levied upon the country have been paid".[2] From the negotiation of this convention Russia, as Napoleon said, was excluded. "Russia could not have intervened in the question of the evacuation of the Prussian provinces without intervening also to press the payment of the contributions, and this was an obligation which it did not suit her to take upon herself."[3] So Russia was kept out of this discussion by the threat that it would implicate her in Napoleon's financial exactions, and the French were able to say that even the execution of the convention was a matter in which the Czar had no right to interfere.

---

[1] Champagny to Savary, 8 Nov. 1807, in *Sbornik*, LXXXIII, 212.
[2] *Sbornik*, LXXXIX, 116–17.
[3] Champagny to Savary, 13 Oct. 1807, in *Sbornik*, CXXXVIII, 236–7. Cf. Napoleon's Note to Champagny, 9 Oct. 1807, *ibid.* p. 225, omitted from *Corresp. de Nap. 1er*, t. XVI.

INDEX

Adair, Robert, English minister in Vienna, personality, 117–18; Austrian government and, 118, 123; omissions from *Memoir* of, 123; and the probability of Austrian intervention, 108, 112, 123, 183; and Pozzo di Borgo's mission, 118–19, 123; and Austrian mediation, 120; on Vincent's mission, 124–5; on Friedland, 203; on Austrian policy after Tilsit, 313. *V.* also *Leveson-Gower; Stadion*

Adriatic, Austria and the, 107, 126; Napoleon and the, 15, 20; Russia and the, 15, 34, 107. *V.* also *Dalmatia*

Albania, Russia and, 34

Alexander I, Czar of Russia, personality, 190, 192–3, 216, 249, 251, 262–3, 265–8; his ambitions in 1804, 267; his peace policy in 1806, 33; and renewal of war with France, 25, 36; his friendship for Frederick William, 47, 54, 216, 265; and Krüsemarck's proposal of peace congress, 57–8; reasons for his decision, 58, 59–63; goes to Memel, 99, 138; and the convention of Bartenstein, 147, 161, 366, 372; leaves the army, 187–8; and the peace party, 188–92; his psychological condition on the eve of Friedland, 187–99; his cautious policy after Friedland, 238–41, 361–6; decides to make peace, 246, 365–6; reasons for this decision, 203–4, 244–6, 290; instructs Russian negotiator, 252–5, 367–71; psychology of, at Tilsit, 203–4, 216, 239, 244–6, 258–60, 262–8, 379; his dissatisfaction with his allies, 97, 183 n., 193, 197–200, 244–5, 261; and Prussia in the negotiations after Friedland, 214–17, 240, 245–6; 251–60, 361, 364–5, 370–80; and Hardenberg's scheme, 221, 251–60, 369–

71; desires interview with Napoleon, 216, 246–7, 254–5, 368, 371; interviews Napoleon at Tilsit, 234–5, 256–7, 262–3, 271, 273, 375; talks to Swedish ambassador on Tilsit, 290; spirit in which he followed the system of Tilsit, 263, 303, 345–6, 355; genuineness of his hostility to England, 264, 304–5, 346–7; and Alopeus's peace move, 345–6, 353; the oriental design and the moods of, 347–53; at Erfurt, 356. *V.* also *Alopeus; Bennigsen*, etc.; and *Copenhagen, expedition to*, etc.

For Russian foreign policy *v. Russia*

All the Talents, Ministry of, formation, 38; foreign policy, 93 *et seq.*, 148–9; weakness of its diplomatic representation, 97, 100–1, 150; Starhemberg on, 94; and English diversion, 96, 104; and overseas conquests, 41, 75, 96, 101–4, 145; and policy of isolation, 96–7, 101, 103–4, 132; and subsidies, 42, 96; and peace negotiations of 1806, 37–42; views on future settlement, 101–4; and Austria, 102–4, 145; and Austrian intervention, 110, 118; declares war on Prussia, 95; hostility to Prussia, 45, 49, 62, 71, 75, 91–6, 100, 103, 143, 145, 230; makes peace with Prussia, 151; and Russia, 39–41; and Russian commercial treaty, 95–6; and Russian loan, 96–7, 104; hostilities against Turkey, 49, 134; fall of, 49, 148; Austria and fall of, 148; Hardenberg on fall of, 184. *V.* also *Fox; Grenville; Howick; Whigs*

Alopeus, Maximilian, Russian minister in England, career, 285–6; Czar Alexander and, 264, 285–6, 339, 345–6, 353; as minister in England, 100, 286, 296; and